ARMS GRANTED TO THE COLONY OF NOVA SCOTIA
BY KING CHARLES I

HIS HONOUR THE HONOURABLE
McCALLUM GRANT, LL.D.
Lieut.-Governor of Nova Scotia.

NOVA SCOTIA'S PART IN THE GREAT WAR

COMPILED AND EDITED

BY

M. S. HUNT
(Captain R.O.)

ILLUSTRATED FROM HALF-TONES

The Naval & Military Press Ltd

Published by
The Naval & Military Press Ltd
5 Riverside, Brambleside, Bellbrook
Industrial Estate, Uckfield, East Sussex,
TN22 1QQ England
Tel: +44 (0) 1825 749494
Fax: +44 (0) 1825 765701
www.naval-military-press.com
www.military-genealogy.com
www.militarymaproom.com

In reprinting in facsimile from the original, any imperfections are inevitably reproduced and the quality may fall short of modern type and cartographic standards.

To
The Immortal Memory
of
Our Fallen Comrades

PREFACE

TWO years have passed since the last gun was fired in the Great War on the Western Front and hitherto no attempt has been made to place before the people of Nova Scotia a comprehensive history of the various Military Units and Patriotic Organizations which won for the Province imperishable fame.

Anyone who makes an impartial investigation of Nova Scotia's response to the call of duty will concede that the sturdy little Province by the sea achieved an enviable record. In some respects it surpassed the other Provinces of the Dominion in promoting the successful conclusion of the great conflict—not only by the number of splendid troops it supplied in proportion to its population, both for Overseas and Home Service, but also because it had in its capital city, Halifax, the Naval Base of the British Empire on the Atlantic Coast, and from its spacious harbor sent many hundreds of ships Overseas laden with Canadian and Allied troops and received them after the Armistice when they were employed in returning the victors to their homes. From Nova Scotia ports, chiefly Halifax and Sydney, were also shipped munitions, supplies and equipment required by the Army in the field. The appreciation of the troops and their dependants on their return from Overseas of the welcome given them by the representatives of the citizens of Halifax, and the comforts and kindnesses bestowed upon them, has been attested by many grateful letters received from homes scattered over the North American continent. The patriotic work of the Nova Scotia Branch of the Red Cross Society, with its country auxiliaries, was magnificent. All other patriotic societies and organizations gave equally valuable service. In fact, Nova Scotia played a role in the conduct of the war which will redound to her glory for all time. May the same sense of unity and spirit of self-devotion, which characterized her people during the war, be retained undiminished and be used wisely in time of peace.

In giving a review of each of the Military Units which were mobilized or organized in Nova Scotia for service in the Great War, narrative has been adhered to as far as possible. Official war

PREFACE

records were consulted in so far as they were available, but a great deal of information had to be gathered from personal war diaries and interviews. The book contains as complete a history of Nova Scotia's part in the Great War as could be compressed into a single handy library volume. And it has several unique features. It contains many engraved portraits of Nova Scotian officers who made the supreme sacrifice, of officers commanding Units, leaders of patriotic organizations, and groups of special persons and events, and a reproduction of the authentic Nova Scotia Coat of Arms, granted by Charles I—all of which will be of great interest to readers of this history.

Before closing this preface special recognition should be made of J. D. Logan, M.A. (Dalhousie Univ.), Ph.D. (Harvard Univ.), formerly Sergeant in the 85th Battalion, Nova Scotia Highlanders, for his patient, keen, and thorough reading of the entire manuscript, with important alterations and corrections.

I am also deeply indebted to Major J. G. Johnstone, R.O., for his indefatigable assistance in the compilation of this volume.

For information and assistance my thanks are also due to: Colonel W. E. Thompson, Colonel Thos. Cantley, Lt.-Col. S. G. Robertson, C.B.E., Lt.-Col. H. Flowers, Lt.-Col. Joseph Hayes, D.S.O., Lt.-Col. D. H. Sutherland, Lt.-Col. R. B. Simmons, Lt.-Col. A. W. Duffus, Lt.-Col. T. M. Seeley, Lt.-Col. J. L. McKinnon, Lt.-Col. E. C. Dean, Major C. E. McLaughlin, Major G. B. Cutten, Acadia Univ., Major A. A. Sturley, Univ. of King's College, Major J. F. Taylor, Major M. D. McKeigan, Major W. G. McRae, Major D. A. McKinnon, D.S.O., Major P. O. Soulis, Capt. G. C. McElhinney, M.C., Capt. Angus L. McDonald, Hon. Capt. Clarence McKinnon, Capt. B. M. Beckwith, Capt. F. G. Kingdon, Capt. G. T. Shaw, Lieut. W. H. Whidden, Dr. H. P. McPherson, St. Francis Xavier University, Professor Fraser Harris, Medical School, Dalhousie University, Principal F. H. Sexton, Nova Scotia Technical College, Mr. A. A. Campbell, Mr. F. A. Crowell, Mr. McI. Miller, Mr. Stuart McCawley, Mr. Wilfred Hearn, Mr. J. McL. Fraser, Mr. J. A. Walker.

M. S. HUNT,
Capt. R.O.

HALIFAX, N.S.
ARMISTICE DAY, 1920.

CONTENTS

	PAGE
NOVA SCOTIA'S COAT OF ARMS (Granted by Charles I)	i
PORTRAIT of His Honour the Honourable McCallum Grant, LL.D., Lieutenant-Governor of Nova Scotia	iv
DEDICATION	vii
PREFACE	ix
PORTRAIT of Sir Robert Borden, Premier of Canada, during the War	xiii
PORTRAIT of the Honourable George Henry Murray, Premier of Nova Scotia	xvi

CHAPTER		
I.	Headquarters Military District No. 6	1
II.	6th Canadian Mounted Rifles	9
III.	9th Siege Battery	22
IV.	10th Siege Battery	28
V.	17th Field Battery	31
VI.	23rd and 24th Field Batteries	41
VII.	36th Field Battery	43
VIII.	14th Brigade, C.F.A.	56
IX.	Royal Canadian Regiment	58
X.	17th Battalion	65
XI.	25th Battalion	70
XII.	40th Battalion	92
XIII.	64th Battalion	95
XIV.	85th Battalion and Band	99
XV.	106th Battalion	116
XVI.	112th Battalion	119
XVII.	185th Battalion	122
XVIII.	193rd Battalion	130
XIX.	219th Battalion	133
XX.	246th Battalion	146
XXI.	2nd Construction Battalion	148
XXII.	Forestry Corps	154
XXIII.	No. 6 District Depot	157
XXIV.	Canadian Army Service Corps	161
XXV.	Canadian Ordnance Corps	173
XXVI.	Canadian Army Medical Corps	177

CONTENTS

CHAPTER		PAGE
XXVII.	Canadian Army Dental Corps	226
XXVIII.	Canadian Army Pay Corps	231
XXIX.	Royal Canadian Garrison Artillery	236
XXX.	Canadian Engineers	242
XXXI.	Militia Units on Home Service	243
XXXII.	1st Regiment Canadian Garrison Artillery	245
XXXIII.	11th Brigade, C.F.A., and Composite Artillery Company	250
XXXIV.	63rd Regiment	253
XXXV.	66th Regiment	259
XXXVI.	94th Regiment	263
XXXVII.	Composite Battalion	268
XXXVIII.	Depot Battalion	272
XXXIX.	"B" Unit, M.H.C.C.	275
XL.	University of Acadia College	280
XLI.	University of Dalhousie College	282
XLII.	University of King's College	289
XLIII.	University of St. Francis Xavier's College	294
XLIV.	Presbyterian College, Pine Hill	296
XLV.	Recruiting in Nova Scotia	300
XLVI.	Ocean Transport	305
XLVII.	Munitions	311
XLVIII.	Demobilization	322
XLIX.	Vocational Training	330
L.	Patriotic Fund	345
LI.	Victory Loan	347
LII.	Red Cross Society; and Willing War Workers, Green Feather Society and Catholic Ladies Society	350
LIII.	Knights of Columbus	370
LIV.	Young Men's Christian Association	377
LV.	Halifax Citizens' Reception Committee	381
LVI.	Creche at Pier 2	386
LVII.	St. Matthew's Church	394

SPECIAL SKETCHES, with Portraits 399
"FELT DAWN"—A Literary Appreciation of a phrase in McCrae's poem, "In Flanders Fields" 436

SIR ROBERT LAIRD BORDEN,
Premier of Canada during the Great War.

HON. G. H. MURRAY,
Premier of Nova Scotia during the Great War.

Nova Scotia's Part in the Great War

CHAPTER I

HEADQUARTERS MILITARY DISTRICT No. 6.

UPON the opening of the World War the following were the principal Staff Officers at Halifax, the headquarters of Military District No. 6:—

Col. R. W. Rutherford, G.O.C.; Col. W. W. Humphrey, A.O.C.; Major R. J. Hayter, G.S.O.; Major A. H. W. Powell, D.A.A. & Q.M.G.; Major W. Gibsone, D.A.A. & Q.M.G. Fortress.

Military District No. 6 then embraced the Maritime Provinces, but later in the war, when Compulsory Service came into force, New Brunswick was made into a separate District, No. 7.

The aforementioned Staff bore the brunt of this sudden change from peace to war, and met and overcame the resultant many new problems with great credit to themselves.

The sudden deluge of work included the calling out and recruiting up to strength of the Halifax City Regiments, viz.: 1st Regiment, Canadian Artillery, 63rd Regiment Halifax Rifles, and 66th Regiment Princess Louise Fusiliers, as part of the War Garrison of Halifax; supplementing this Garrison later by a Regiment styled the Composite Regiment, called up by Companies from other Militia Regiments in Nova Scotia and from the 82nd in P. E. Island; calling out the 94th Argyll Highlanders to guard the cable and wireless stations at North Sydney, Marconi, Louisburg, and Canso, and detachments of Artillery from the P.E.I. Heavy Brigade to protect the Harbors of North Sydney and Canso; the provision of guards for the wireless station at Newcastle, N.B., for the International Bridge at St. Leonard's and Vanceboro, and the calling out of the 3rd Regiment Canadian Artillery and the 62nd Regiment Infantry for the defence of St. John, N.B.

This meant that the immediate necessities of war called upon the Maritime Provinces to furnish, equip and train and keep supplied some 3,000 officers and men, of whom almost 2,600 were supplied by the Province of Nova Scotia; and of these more than 1,500 men from the City of Halifax.

This accounts for the fact that in the mobilization of troops for the first contingent at Valcartier there were not so many men reported there for duty from the City of Halifax or from rural Cape Breton as might have been expected. The officers and men, though keen to enter this larger sphere, were compelled to do this guard and garrison work, and were only relieved and permitted to join Overseas Battalions as new men could be found willing to take their places.

In addition to equipping this force the further pressing duty upon the H. Q. Staff was the working out of a system of recruiting to take care of the thousands of young men anxious to get into the Overseas Battalions as they were authorized, and to train these men and officers.

The first change in H.Q. Staff came in December, 1914, when Major W. E. Thompson was called in from his Regiment, the 63rd Halifax Rifles, then doing duty on McNab's Island, to take over the work of Inspector of Outposts and Detachments throughout the District, with the rank of Lieut.-Colonel.

This officer succeeded, upon the retirement of Colonel Humphrey in March, 1915, to the appointment of Assistant Adjutant-General and Officer in charge of Administration. He remained at H.Q. throughout the war and until October 1, 1919, having succeeded to the command of the District in December, 1918, upon the retirement of Major-General Lessard. He was promoted full Colonel in May, 1916, and during the summer of that year he acted as Commandant at Aldershot Camp in addition to doing his work as A.A.G.

Every officer at H.Q. was continually on the watch for an opportunity of proceeding overseas. The chance came first to Major Hayter, who was offered the position of Brigade Major at Valcartier and was permitted to accept in September, 1914. A careful, most painstaking officer, always at work, always thinking about his work, he left his impress; and at Valcartier, in England, and in

HEADQUARTERS MILITARY DISTRICT No. 6

France the same qualities marked his value. His great modesty may have somewhat retarded his promotion, though he won the rank of Brigadier-General before the war closed.

For some time the work of G.S.O. was rather perfunctorily performed by officers awaiting their chance to go overseas and was not again severely faced till it was taken on by Major A. N. Jones on his being invalided home from France after service with the 25th Battalion. He carried on till his health broke down in January, 1917, when Major Soulis acted temporarily till the arrival of Col. W. R. Lang, who arrived in this station with General Lessard, remaining till May, 1918, when he was succeeded by Major W. G. Haggarty.

There was a bit of a struggle between Major Gibsone and Colonel Thompson for the command of the 40th Battalion, the second Overseas Battalion to be raised in this District, but the prize fell to the former, and his place was taken by Major R. B. Willis, who filled the duties of D.A.A. and Q.M.G. Fortress for the balance of the war with great credit.

Early in 1915 Major Powell was promoted to the rank of Lieut.-Colonel. His special work was responsibility for recruiting and the organizing, officering and equipping of Units for Overseas Service. He brought great energy and ability to this work, and when New Brunswick was converted into a separate District he was detailed to that District as A.A.G., February, 1916.

Lieut.-Colonel Powell was succeeded by Lieut.-Colonel B. R. Armstrong, of St. John, N.B., who came out with his Regiment, the 3rd C.A., at St. John upon the outbreak of the war, and who in addition to this command was the representative of the Officer Commanding the District in New Brunswick, and had a special supervision over recruiting in that Province. He carried on the duties of D.A.A. and Q.M.G. for District No. 6 till demobilized in September, 1919.

His work was of a very high order, his grasp of details was unusual, and his knowledge of shipping and business affairs was of great assistance, particularly in connection with the very important work of transporting, embarking and disembarking troops.

This latter work assumed such dimensions that it was found necessary to provide him with an assistant. Major W. D. Tait served in this capacity for a time till he assumed command of McGill Heavy Battery for service Overseas, when, in June, 1916, he was succeeded by Major P. O. Soulis, who came out on the outbreak of war with his Regiment, the 1st C.A.

Major Soulis was given the special department of Statistics and Documents, and the supervision of all embarkations and disembarkations. The combination of these two officers made this most important work proceed so smoothly that hundreds of thousands of men went through this port with the bulk of the citizens not realizing that anything unusual was going on.

It should be mentioned, however, in this connection, that the work of H.Q. could not have met with the success it did, were it not for the very efficient executive work of Major A. P. Lomas, the executive head of the Department of Transport and Supplies during the rush-time of this most important work. Nor could the work of H.Q. have met with success in this matter had it not been for the energy and co-operation which the Clearing Services Command, represented here first by Lieut.-Colonel H. F. Adams and later by Lieut.-Colonel Cram, brought to its work of passing troops going and coming through its depot at Pier 2.

When after Compulsory Service came into operation the necessity became evident for an officer to be detailed to give exclusive attention to the compilation and care of soldiers' documents, the choice most naturally fell upon Major Soulis. He made a close study of the work, and his system met with so much approval that many of his ideas were adopted by Militia Headquarters and were put into general operation. Major Soulis continued to hold the appointment of District Record Officer till demobilized in July, 1919.

Both Colonel Armstrong and Major Soulis were South African Veterans, the former having lost a foot in action there, and the latter having been mentioned in despatches.

In December, 1914, Colonel Rutherford was promoted to the rank of Brigadier-General, and in October, 1915, was given his step to Major-General. He was an officer of much more than ordinary attainments, and filled well the office of General Officer Commanding, always carrying the confidence and respect of his Staff. A noticeable increase in defective hearing shown during a

HEADQUARTERS STAFF, M.D. 6.

conference of General Officers at Ottawa led Militia H.Q. to bring about his retirement, and in November, 1915, he was succeeded by Major-General Thomas Benson.

General Benson brought a long training in military affairs, a broad outlook, an attractive personality, and good judgment to cope with the many questions arising in the District. He gave up his command in February, 1918, to the regret of his Staff and of citizens who had been wont to do business at Military Headquarters. He was given leave till July 1st of that year, and his valuable services were recognized by investment with the order of C.M.G.

General Benson's successor was Major-General T. L. Lessard, who retained command till December 28, 1918, when he was succeeded by Colonel W. E. Thompson.

The work done by the Garrison at Halifax during the war was most arduous, exacting and valuable. From August 7, 1914, when Canada entered the war till final demobilization, the work was kept up continuously, and upon the strictest laws of military discipline.

Only such officers whose places could be filled by volunteers were permitted to proceed Overseas, and no man was relieved for this broader field of action unless there was a man ready to take his place. This being so, it was the exception for an officer once on the Staff or for any well-trained officer of the Units out, particularly of the Artillery, or for good non-commissioned officers and specialists to get a chance for Overseas. They all knew that should the war terminate without their getting over they would for the rest of their lives be compelled to explain that they were not permitted to go and felt keenly how flat such an explanation would fall. They had, however, the consolation that they were doing a necessary and valuable work and were buoyed up with the hope their chance would yet come; and if not, the State would at least recognize their voluntary services as at least equal to the services of those, many of whom were draftees, who had not proceeded further than England or St. Lucia. Up to the time of writing, however, no such recognition has been forthcoming.

The above sets out in most skeletonized form the ordinary duties of H.Q. consequent on the Country being at war, and the

HEADQUARTERS MILITARY DISTRICT No. 6

Port of Halifax being the only port of embarkation and disembarkation for Canadian troops and supplies of war during the most strenuous months of the year.

In addition were the extra responsibilities of caring for troops awaiting embarkation. These troops were not only Canadians but also troops from United States, Australia, New Zealand and some 50,000 laborers from China.

When a contingent passed through the port, either coming in or going out, from illness or other causes some were left behind, and these had to be cared for, often taxing the facilities of the barracks and hospitals to their utmost. In the summer of 1918 when we encamped at Aldershot, some 5,000 United States troops and a whole shipload was suddenly disembarked at Sydney suffering from the "flu."

The temporary derelicts from Canadian troops passing through the City of Halifax were taken care of by being attached to the Composite Battalion, under Lieut.-Col. H. L. Chipman. When ready for Overseas these were attached to another unit going through. The records show the number of such exceeded 10,000 men. Lieut.-Colonel Chipman deserves special mention for his splendid administration of the Composite Battalion and for his wise handling of many difficult problems not to be met in an ordinary Garrison Battalion.

Again, the awful catastrophe which befell the City of Halifax on December 6, 1917, when a ship loaded with high explosives exploded in the harbor, spreading death and devastation broadcast, placed a great burden upon the Garrison and proved its great value in a sudden emergency. Every officer and man of every Military Unit and Department, with all the military facilities of the Garrison were rushed into the work of removing the dead and wounded, fighting fires, preparing shelters, transporting and feeding the destitute, doing police duty and the hundred and one things that came to the hands of a willing, well-trained body of troops.

The Ordnance, under Lieut.-Col. Arthur Panet, opened wide its doors, and one of the first orders issued from H.Q. was for every available man of the 63rd from McNab's and the 66th from York and also every artilleryman of the 1st C.A. from the forts to be rushed to the city and, proceeding to the devastated area by way of the Ordnance Yard, for each to carry with him a blanket for the wounded and destitute. This order was fully carried out, Col. Panet, though himself wounded, travelling continuously to and from the area of most suffering to see that as many as possible were cared for.

Major H. P. Lomas, then at the head of the Department of Supplies and Transport, met the necessities of the sufferers with the same breadth of judgment, bigness of heart and broad interpretation of regulations which marked his most successful administration throughout the war of this the essentially business department of the Service.

Elsewhere in this publication will be found articles dealing with specific work done in this District during the war, so that in this article it is only attempted to give a general idea of who sat at Headquarters during these strenuous times and a general idea of the work they were called upon to originate and supervise; and it must be borne in mind as the detail of this specific work is studied and admired or condemned, the responsibility and the direction was always with that often maligned, seldom praised or congratulated, but nevertheless patient, long-suffering, faithful, headquarters.

This article cannot properly close, however, without mention of the other heads of Departments in addition to those specially mentioned above because of their close association with the matters dealt with, who so heartily and with such great self-sacrifice performed their various duties, each in their turn:

Lieut.-Col. J. A. Grant, Lieut.-Col. McKelvie Bell, and Col. H. S. Jaques as Assistant Directors of Medical Service.

Lieut.-Colonel Houliston, Lieut.-Colonel Benoit, Lieut.-Colonel Van Tuyl, and Major Pringle, Commanding the Royal Canadian Engineers.

Lieut.-Colonel Dean, Assistant Director of Transport and Supplies.

Col. S. J. R. Sircom (Brig.-General upon Retirement), Assistant Director of Pay Services.

Col. J. F. Macdonald, Senior Ordnance Officer.

Major J. A. Proudfoot, District Signalling Officer.

Lieut.-Col. H. F. Adams and Lieut.-Colonel Cram, Clearing Services Command.

CHAPTER II.

THE 6th CANADIAN MOUNTED RIFLES.

THE 6th Canadian Mounted Rifles was recruited from the different Maritime Provinces Militia Cavalry Regiments—" A " Squadron from the 8th P.L.F. (headquarters Sackville, N.B.), and 36th P.E.I. Light Horse (headquarters Charlottetown, P.E.I.); " B " Squadron from the 28th N.B. Dragoon Guards (headquarters St. John, N.B.), and " C " Squadron from the 14th King's Canadian Hussars (headquarters Canning, Nova Scotia).

The establishment of officers and warrant officers consisted of the following:

O.C., Lieut.-Col. R. H. Ryan, South African, Russian-Japanese, American-Mexican Wars; 2nd I.C., Lieut.-Col. A. E. Ings, Militia Long Service Medal; Capt. and Adj., Capt. B. W. Roscoe (later Capt. J. W. Long); Q.M., Major R. A. March; O.M., Major Colin MacIntosh; Chaplain, Capt. G. A. Kuhring; M.O., Capt. F. A. R. Gow; Sig. Off., Capt. H. R. Emmerson; Asst. Adj., Lieut. E. M. Arnold; Vet. Off., Lieut. J. S. Roy; R.S.M., L. W. Long.

"*A*" *Squadron*—O.C., Major A. J. Markham; 2nd I.C., Capt. B. W. Roscoe; Lieut. A. T. Ganong, Lieut. G. N. D. Otty, Lieut. G. R. Barnes, Lieut. W. D. Atkinson, Sqd. Sgt.-Major N. Dawes.

"*B*" *Squadron*—Major C. H. McLean; 2nd I.C., Capt. M. A. Scovil; Lieut. E. J. Mooney, Lieut. E. A. Thomas, Lieut. H. S. Everitt, Lieut. Geo. Morrisey, Sqd. Sgt.-Major J. M. Lamb.

"*C*" *Squadron*—Major T. A. Lydiard; 2nd I.C., Capt. J. C. Gray; Lieut. H. H. Pineo, Lieut. J. P. Knowlton, Lieut. W. J. Brown, Lieut. H. L. Bowness, Lieut. B. M. Beckwith, Sqd. Sgt.-Major George Gill.

Colonel Ryan and many of the officers and other ranks had volunteered at the outbreak of the war but owing to the expected necessity for the employment of mounted troops in the Maritime

Provinces (the 14th K.C.H. having actually received orders for mobilization) their services were not accepted. It was also intimated to Colonel Ryan, who was at Valcartier, when the First Division was mobilized, that in the event of the Maritime Province Cavalry not being mobilized as Militia Units for home service he would be permitted to raise a Cavalry Regiment from these Units and would be given command thereof, owing to his previous service and experience in the field.

Accordingly Colonel Ryan returned to Nova Scotia and in December, 1915, received orders to recruit the Regiment.

AT AMHERST, N.S.

The Regiment was mobilized at Amherst, N.S., mobilization dating from March 17, 1915.

The period during which the Regiment was quartered at Amherst was spent in perfecting the organization, taking on recruits and training the latter, owing to restrictions being largely confined to setting-up exercises, arm drill and route marching with inspections by various Generals.

While at Amherst a draft of two hundred volunteers was sent as reinforcements to the Infantry Regiments in England to make up for the losses sustained by the Canadians in the Second Battle of Ypres. These were replaced by new recruits.

AT VALCARTIER CAMP.

In May, 1915, the Regiment was moved to Valcartier, being brigaded with the 4th and 5th C.M.R.'s, under command of Colonel (later Brigadier-General) C. A. Smart.

Training at Valcartier was intensive and performed on foot, as horses had not been received, the Cavalry formation being however retained. Here the Unit received instruction in musketry and rather prided themselves in their ability in this line.

While at Valcartier and also when at Amherst they were asked if they would volunteer to serve as dismounted troops, and the answer was always that "we will serve in any way we are needed."

THE 6th CANADIAN MOUNTED RIFLES

IN ENGLAND.

The 6th C.M.R. left Valcartier early in July for England, embarking at Quebec on the slow South American cold storage boat *Herschel*. Naturally the accommodations were not of the best, as there were six hundred men and four hundred horses on a boat without practically any passenger accommodation. Their eleven days' voyage ended at Devonport, where they got a great reception. At Exeter they were met at the station by the good ladies of that town and given bags of food and fruit, and had their water bottles filled with hot coffee and tea. Many times since has this been spoken of in grateful words by the men, who were hungry and cold from the long train journey. On arrival at Camp in Dibgate they found themselves once more camping in the sand. As active service in Egypt had been spoken of, the Unit thought the authorities must be trying to accustom it to its future surroundings.

While at Dibgate the Unit received a draft of officers and men from the 8th C.M.R., under command of Lieut. T. D. Johnstone (later Capt. in Command of "B" Co., 5th C.M.R., wounded); second in command, Lieut. H. N. Bate (transferred to R.C.D.'s. when Regiment was broken up). Many of the men who had been sick, owing to the strenuous training, had been transferred to hospital, and when convalescent were sent to the Cavalry Reserve Depot. These had been replaced by the draft of men from the 8th.

IN FRANCE—PLOEGSTEERTE—MESSINES.

The Regiment proceeded to France on October 24, 1915, the Brigade being attached to General Seely's Cavalry Division, operating as Corps Troops in the areas of Ploegsteerte and Messines.

The following officers and warrant officers went to France with the Regiment and saw service at Ploegsteerte and Messines during the fall and early winter months of 1915.

O.C., Lieut.-Colonel Shaw (later O.C. 1st C.M.R., killed in action June 2, 1916).

2nd I.C., Lieut.-Colonel Ings; Adjt., Capt. J. W. Long; Q.M., Major R. A. March (later to 4th C.M.R. Battalion); P.M., Major C. McIntosh (later to Can. Artillery); M.O., Capt. F. A. R. Gow (later to Can. Artillery); Sig. Officer, Capt. H. R. Emmerson (later

Major 219th Infantry Battalion); Vet. Officer, Lieut. J. A. Roy (later to Fort Garry Horse).

"*A*" *Squadron*—Major A. J. Markham (later to Fort Garry Horse), Capt. B. W. Roscoe, Lieuts. A. T. Ganong, G. N. D. Otty, G. R. Barnes, T. D. Johnstone; Sqd. Sgt.-Major N. Dawes.

"*B*" *Squadron*—Major C. H. McLean, Capt. M. A. Scovil, Lieuts. E. J. Mooney, E. A. Thomas, H. S. Everett, George Morrisey; Sqd. Sgt.-Major J. M. Lamb (all later to 4th C.M.R. Regt.).

"*C*" *Squadron*—Major T. A. Lydiard (later to R.C. Dragoons), Capt. J. C. Gray, Lieuts. H. H. Pineo, J. P. Knowlton, B. M. Beckwith, H. N. Bate; Sqd. Sgt.-Major Geo. Gill, D.C.M., later R.S.M. 5th C.M.R.

Lieut.-Colonel Ryan transferred to the Artillery, in which he served with distinction to the end of the war being decorated for conspicuous gallantry in the field.

REORGANIZED AS INFANTRY.

The Division was withdrawn from the trenches in December, 1915, and orders were subsequently received that the 1st and 2nd C.M.R. Brigade should be reorganized into the 8th Canadian Infantry Brigade, consisting of 1st, 2nd, 4th and 5th Battalions of Mounted Rifles. The junior Regiments in each Brigade, namely the 3rd and 6th C.M.R., were split up between the two senior Regiments, thus forming four Infantry Regiments.

The ostensible reason for this was the necessity of relieving infantry in trenches and the unsuitability of the cavalry formation for that purpose. The change in formation necessitated the transfer to England of officers of senior rank.

The command of the reorganized Brigade was assumed by Brig.-Gen. V. A. S. Williams on January 1, 1916, and training in infantry drill and tactics was gone at in dead earnest by all ranks.

This training continued both in the line and out and the Brigade occupied the Ploegsteerte area until March, 1916, when it was moved to the Ypres Sector as part of the newly-formed 3rd Division, commanded by General Mercer, and took over the Hooge-Hill 60 Sector.

THE 6th CANADIAN MOUNTED RIFLES

The disposal of the various Squadrons of the 6th C.M.R. was as follows:

"A" and "C" Squadrons were formed into "D" Company of the 5th C.M.R. Battalion, the company officers and warrant officers being:

Captain B. W. Roscoe (later Major, D.S.O., 2nd I.C. 5th C.M.R. Battalion, wounded June 3, 1916, at Sanctuary Wood); 2nd I.C., Captain H. H. Pineo (later killed in action at Mt. Sorrell, Ypres Sector, July, 1916); Lieuts. A. T. Ganong, G. N. D. Otty, G. R. Barnes; Lieut. J. P. Knowlton (later to record office at Rouen, and received promotion there to Captain); C.S.M. George Gill (later R.S.M. 5th C.M.R. Battalion); "B" Squadron was formed into "D" Company of the 4th C.M.R. Battalion, the company officers and warrant officers being: Major C. H. McLean (later 2nd I.C. 4th C.M.R. Battalion); Capt. M. A. Scovil; Lieut. George Morrisey.

SANCTUARY WOOD.

The first serious engagement in which the Brigade was concerned was the Battle of Sanctuary Wood, which began June 2, 1916.

The disposition of the Brigade was: 1st and 4th C.M.R., front line and close support; 5th C.M.R., Battalion H.Q. and three Companies in support at Maple Copse; one Company in reserve at Zillebeke Bund; 2nd C.M.R. in Brigade reserve near Poperinghe.

The morning of June 2nd was clear with good visibility. About 8 a.m. the Hun started a heavy bombardment, which grew in intensity, and information was received that an attack was in progress on the sector held by the 7th and 8th Brigades. The bombardment continued unabatingly, and about twelve o'clock mines were seen to be blown. The whole of the area held by the two Brigades was being systematically and furiously shelled, and communication with the forward area was impossible.

About 2 p.m. Captain Roscoe received orders to reinforce with his Company, the remainder of the Battalion at Maple Copse. There was no route specified, the officer conveying the order remarking that he hoped they would get through.

The only other officer with the Company at this time was Lieut. G. N. D. Otty, but it developed that the N.C.O.'s had the requisite requirements of leadership and judgment. The Company, led by Captain Roscoe, advanced to the support of the remainder of the Battalion, and in full view of the enemy, through an extremely heavy barrage of fire, reached Maple Copse with few casualties, reporting to Lieut.-Colonel G. H. Baker, then commanding the Battalion.

Orders were then received to connect up with the 7th Brigade on the left, to dig in and hold the Copse to the last. Then it was that the N.C.O.'s showed those qualities of leadership and judgment, which later were to be recognized in a substantial manner.

C.S.M. George Gill, with twenty men was ordered to occupy and hold a strong point whose garrison had been killed. This he did with great bravery, showing much skill in defending the position. Sgts. George Chase, H. McGarry and T. W. Martin led detachments through the Copse and dug in on the edge next the enemy. Lieutenant Otty was absolutely fearless in assisting in the disposition of the Company, refusing to avail himself of anything that looked like shelter. He remarked to the Company Commander that if he was to be killed that would happen and that his men were his first consideration. Unfortunately he was hit and killed within a short time after arrival at the Copse.

The enemy made several ineffectual attempts to break through the line, and at each repulse his artillery fire became more severe. There was absolutely no shelter from his fire, and the Copse was like an inferno. The Company held the position, and were reinforced the next morning by the 2nd C.M.R.'s. After this things quieted down and the remnants of the Company marched out that night.

At the roll-call on relief only one officer (Lieutenant Barnes) and twenty men answered their names, the remainder of the Company which went into action 130 strong, having been either killed or wounded.

Captain Roscoe had been wounded on the morning of June 3rd, after the 2nd C.M.R.'s had arrived, and the command of the Company was taken over by Lieutenant Barnes, who was the Battalion Bombing Officer, and with his bombers had been active in the defence of the position. Lieutenant Barnes made several very daring

THE 6th CANADIAN MOUNTED RIFLES

patrols, practically between the posts of the enemy, who had attempted to push down hill in the long grass. It was through his efforts that the Unit was able to concentrate its rifle fire on the dangerous places and dislodge several machine guns. Lieutenant Barnes afterward got the M.C. for his work on this occasion.

The Battalion, reduced to some 300 all ranks, moved into rest billets, and the losses were filled by a large draft of officers and other ranks from England.

In the reorganization of the Battalion Major D. C. Draper (later Brigadier-General Commanding the Brigade) became O.C. (Lieut.-Colonel Baker having been killed in the engagement); Captain Roscoe was promoted to be second in command, awarded the D.S.O. for his work on the occasion and mentioned in despatches. The command of "D" Company was taken over by Lieut. H. H. Pineo (later promoted Captain), with Lieutenant Barnes, 2nd I.C.

Sergt. Harold McGarry was promoted to C.S.M. in place of George Gill, who was awarded the D.C.M. and promoted to be Regtl. Sgt.-Major for his meritorious services and bravery evinced during the battle. Sergt. Geo. Chase, who was severely wounded, was awarded the Military Medal and slated for a commission.

The 4th C.M.R. Battalion also lost heavily in the battle, and "D" Company of that unit thereafter practically lost its identity as a Maritime Province Company, owing to the casualties suffered.

The command of the Brigade was taken over by Brig.-General J. H. Elmsley, D.S.O. (afterward Major-General), replacing General Williams, taken prisoner in the battle, while the command of the Division devolved upon Major-General Lipsett, D.S.O. (later killed in action), the Divisional Commander, General Mercer having been killed during the action.

The Brigade, and incidentally the Company, under the new command had another very strenuous period of training, and after an initiation trip for the new men the whole Company moved up again to take their place in the line. While in training they had the benefit of the advice of a C.S.M. from the Welsh Guards, which was a great help, especially to the N.C.O.'s. This training showed later on the Somme.

NOVA SCOTIA'S PART IN THE GREAT WAR

THE BLUFF—MOUNT SORELL LINE.

On the first trip in after the June fight, the Unit took over the line on Mount Sorell. The first night in, the Hun started his regular trench mortar strafe. One of the first of these landed on the signallers' dugout, next company headquarters, and buried the men on duty there. Captain Pineo and Lieutenant Barnes, together with some of the men, started in to dig them out. At that time they could still hear the men groaning. Almost immediately afterward the Hun threw over another trench mortar. The men saw it coming by the trail of sparks, and all scattered up and down the trench. Captain Pineo was struck and instantly killed. The work of rescuing the men who had been buried need not have been performed by him. It was his anxiety for his men that cost him his life. Lieutenant Barnes at once took over the command of the Company. Word was here received that the Hun had dug some mines under the trench occupied by the Company, and to be on the lookout. During the night a party who were digging out in front uncovered a mine sap and on pulling up some planks from the roof saw a man with a lighted candle passing under the lines. Explosives were immediately obtained and the sap blown. This evidently put the "wind up" the Hun for he blew the remaining mines, some of which were hardly clear of his wire.

AT THE SOMME.

Shortly after this the Unit left for the Somme, arriving in Albert on September 1st, after a long, hard march, and severe training. They moved up in support and were selected as one of the two Companies to be first over the top. In this engagement, owing to previous officer casualties, the sergeants had to lead Platoons. The attack on September 15th between Moquet Farm and Courcellette was the first occasion in which the Tanks were used. The Unit had wonderful success on this day, losing very few men in the attack. Afterward, out of one hundred and twenty, forty were killed and sixty wounded, holding the trench. Lieutenant Barnes was awarded the bar to the M.C. and his majority for his work on this occasion. No one could speak too highly of the way in which he led his men, and it was largely due to his dash that the attack was so successful. Mention should be made here of Sergeant Lowther, who was left behind with a party of ten men to garrison the trench until relieved by incoming troops. He lost a leg and several of the men were killed and wounded before the relief was accomplished. Sergeant Lowther was awarded the M.M. Sergt.-Major McGarry, who had been recommended for a commission, was killed in this action.

The Unit's next attack was on October 2nd when " D " Company was in support. The objective was Regina Trench, strongly held by two divisions of German Marines, who had just been brought from Ostend to try and stop the Canadians. This was one of the stiffest hand-to-hand fights the Company ever had, and naturally the casualties were very heavy. Several times the Company managed to bomb several hundred yards of trench clear, but each time the Hun would come back with reinforcements. At daybreak, with bombs and ammunition completely exhausted, the few survivors were forced to withdraw to the jumping-off trench. Every officer engaged was either killed or wounded. Sergt.-Major Holmes, who led the Company on this occasion, after the officers were knocked out, was awarded the M.M. Captain Beckwith, who had been detailed as O.C. of the 8th L.T.M. Battery, and had joined the Company for this occasion was wounded in the face. His leadership and energy were of great assistance, and it was largely due to him and his battery who were carrying ammunition that the Company was able to hold on as long as it did.

The remainder of the time at the Somme was spent in relieving and holding front-line positions. The Battalion was complimented by the Army Commander for its fine work while at the Somme, a personal visit being paid by him to Battalion Headquarters for that purpose.

In addition to the decorations mentioned as being won here, many of the officers of the Battalion were cited for bravery and gallantry in the field. Sergeant T. W. Martin was awarded the M.M. and slated for a commission for a daring reconnaisance of the enemy line under artillery fire.

NOVA SCOTIA'S PART IN THE GREAT WAR

ON THE VIMY FRONT.

The Unit's next move was to the Vimy front, where it was soon apparent that preparations were being made for a terrific onslaught on the Hun. Some time was spent here in assisting in the work of preparation, after which the Unit was withdrawn with the rest of the Brigade for a period of intensive training in attack over a taped layout of the enemy trenches. The Unit was then moved up to its part of the line, being in close support to the 4th C.M.R. Battalion.

The Battle of Vimy Ridge will live in history as the great achievement of the war, owing to the position being considered impregnable and the fact that it was captured with inconsequential losses, mainly due to a well considered plan of attack, absolute co-operation between all branches of the service and thoroughness of preparation.

The Company carried on with the usual steadiness during the engagement and rendered valuable assistance, its losses being negligible.

ON THE DOUAI PLAIN.

For some time after the capture of Vimy Ridge it was found impossible to bring up the artillery within range, as the Hun had retired to a line on the outskirts of Lens and Douai. The Company, with the rest of the Battalion, pushed over the Ridge and were in position as a sacrifice Battalion to fight to the last man, in the event of a counter attack being launched to retake the Ridge. Trenches were constructed, deepened and strengthened, but the expected did not happen, and finally the guns were able to get up within range, from which time ordinary trench routine was resumed.

During a tour in the trenches on this front a raid was attempted by the Hun on the Company front. It was unsuccessful, the enemy being repulsed with heavy loss.

Lieutenant Holmes was awarded the M.C. for his work on this occasion, displaying great coolness and gallantry in holding off single-handed, until reinforced, a party of Huns.

The Battalion at this time was under the command of Major Roscoe, D.S.O., who the day following the attempted raid received a message from the Divisional Commander complimenting the

THE 6th CANADIAN MOUNTED RIFLES

Battalion on their steadiness during the attack. A few days after the Brigade was withdrawn from this sector.

The Company, which up until now had been practically all Maritime Province men, under the new reinforcement scheme drew their men from Quebec, and for a while the Company was made up almost entirely of French-Canadians. After Passchendaele, during which the Company gave its usual assistance to the Battalion, the wounded men began to come back as well as some of the N.C.O.'s who had been granted commissions, and once again it became a Maritime Province Company. It was at Passchendaele that Capt. L. C. Eaton was killed, just before going over the top.

In the winter of 1917 the Unit moved back to their old front at Vimy. In March, 1918, the Battalion put on a raid of 250 men. Lieutenants Gillis and Young of the old " D " Company took part in this, and were both awarded the M.C. for their work. Gillis in particular had done some very fine work during the second attack on the Somme. He had come back from hospital with an unhealed wound in his arm, and although it was too late for him to secure a rifle and the necessary equipment, he took a pick-axe handle and joined his Company in going over the top. He brought back the prisoners, sixty in all, taken on that occasion.

After a pleasant spring spent in reinforcing different parts of the line, in August the Unit once again took the road south for Amiens. The work done by the Company during this attack was spectacular. One of their accomplishments was the capture of a 5.9 Battery in action at point-blank range. One of the old 6th men was awarded the D.C.M. for his work on this occasion and Lieutenant Barnstead was awarded the Croix de Guerre for his leadership.

Lieutenant Smith was very seriously wounded during the next scrap in front of Arras, called the Second Battle of Arras. He had been a stretcher-bearer-Sergeant with the old Company and was awarded a commission in the spring of 1917. He was given the M.C. for his work at Arras in the taking of Monchy. He afterwards died of wounds in London. His work all the time he had been with the Battalion had been exceptional and the award of his M.C. was very popular.

The next fight was for Cambrai, which as far as this Company was concerned consisted of a hunt for Huns through the ruins, collecting souvenirs by the way. The Company had a brush with the Bosche on the other side of the town, but they were merely scouts left behind and pulled out as soon as fired upon. The Company was sitting down having dinner when the English troops came

CAPT. L. C. EATON.

CAPT. H. H. PINEO.

LIEUT. G. N. D. OTTY.

LIEUT. GEO. MORRISEY.

through. As there had been no barrage they did not know that the town had been taken. From here the Company went to Valenciennes and then on to Mons. Lieutenant Gillis was wounded at Valenciennes and invalided to England.

The following other ranks of the 6th C.M.R. Regiment, who went to "D" Company of the 5th, obtained commissions with the

THE 6th CANADIAN MOUNTED RIFLES

Battalion for gallantry and devotion to duty on the field: J. W. Lewis, M.C. (later Capt. 8th Bgd. Light Trench Mortars); L. C. Eaton (later Capt. O. C. " D " Company, killed at Passchendaele); A. C. Wiswell, wounded June 2, 1916 (later Div. Bombing Officer, Bramshott); W. O. Barnstead, Croix de Guerre; C. G. Dunham, M.C., wounded June 2, 1916; H. A. Smith, M.C., died of wounds received at Monchy, Aug. 28, 1918; L. J. Young, M.C., wounded June 2, 1916, and at Monchy, Aug. 28, 1918; A. E. Gillis, M.C., wounded three times; A. H. Weldon, wounded June 2, 1916; T. W. Martin, M.M., wounded Aug. 9th at Vimy; W. J. Holmes, M.C., M.M., wounded at Lens, 1916; F. I. Andrews, M.M., wounded June 2, 1916, and November, 1918; Gordon Campbell, wounded twice; C. W. McArthur, M.M., wounded twice; A. H. Whidden, wounded June, 1916; A. Desbrisay, wounded June, 1916, died since returning home.

Cadets undergoing training when Armistice was signed: Duncan Chisholm, Campbell McLellan, Wm. H. Graham, M.M., J. A. Cameron, D.C.M., Walter Anderson, D.C.M.

The following were gazetted to other Regiments: A. Rogers, N. Rogers, D. B. Holman, Stuart Roy, B. Elliott, Geo. Morrison.

"B" Squadron and Headquarters, 6th C.M.R.'s, went to the 4th C.M.R. Battalion and formed " D " Company of that Battalion under the command of Major C. H. McLean, D.S.O (later 2nd i/c 4th C.M.R.'s; Capt. M. A. Scovil, 2nd i/c (seriously wounded and taken prisoner June 2, 1916). Lieut. H. S. Everett, bombing officer 4th C.M.R., was wounded at Sanctuary Wood, May, 1916. Lieut. E. A. Thomas was killed in action at Sanctuary Wood. Lieut. Geo. Morrisey, Intelligence Officer of 4th C.M.R., was killed in action June 2nd, 1916, while attempting to save a comrade's life.

The following N.C.O.'s received commissions from the 4th for gallantry and devotion in the field: C. W. Hicks, wounded June 2, 1916 (afterwards bombing officer, 34th Reserve, Seaford). J. H. Craigie, gazetted to the Imperial Infantry; N. McKenzie, commission with the 85th N.S. Highlanders; J. O. Spinney, commission with the 52nd Battalion; H. B. Fenis, Lieutenant R.A.F.; J. J. Rowland, 4th C.M.R.; J. H. Harris, Depot Battalion, St John; W. C. Wetmore, 236th Battalion.

CHAPTER III.

9th *CANADIAN SIEGE BATTERY, C.E.F.*

THE 9th Canadian Siege Battery was composed of officers and men belonging to the Royal Canadian Garrison Artillery. Most of the N.C.O.'s and men came from Nos. 1 and 2 Companies, R.C.G.A., at Halifax, N.S. A small number came from No. 5 Company at Esquimalt, B.C. All the officers of the original Battery came from the strength of the R.C.G.A. at Halifax.

For months the R.C.G.A. had been mobilized in the Forts for the defence of Halifax; and because the defence of these Forts was a prime necessity, and no other troops being available, it was impossible, in the view of Headquarters, to relieve the R.C.G.A. for service Overseas.

The possibility of an attack from German ships at first kept up excitement, but as the War progressed this soon diminished and the men looked down from the Forts at transport after transport bearing troops Overseas. These were trying days for men keen themselves to go, and it was difficult to make them believe, as they were constantly told, that their duty was here. Volunteers for Overseas were asked for more than once but nothing happened.

Eventually during the summer of 1916 a definite proposal, made by Lieut.-Col. S. A. Heward, then acting C.R.C.A. at the Citadel, to raise a Siege Battery from the R.C.G.A. was granted, on the understanding that men to replace those taken away should be found and trained. This was soon done, and the Battery sailed for England on Sept. 27, 1916.

After a long delay in England the Battery was equipped with six-inch howitzers, and landed in France on March 22nd. The subsequent moves of the Battery after its arrival at the Front is best set forth by the following list of Battery positions:—Mont St. Eloy —Battle of Arras or Vimy Ridge; Hill 131 (Cabaret Rouge): Angres; Hill 70; Frizenberg Ridge—Battle of Passchendaele:

9th CANADIAN SIEGE BATTERY, C.E.F.

Thelus; Calonne; Maroc; Petit Vimy; Les Tilluels; Souchez; Lievin; Villers Cagnicourt—Battle of Canal du Nord; Barrelle Wood; Sauchy Lestree—Battle of Cambrai; Blecourt; Bantiguy; Marquette; Escaudain; Wavrechain-sous-Denain—Battle of Valenciennes; Herin; Valenciennes; St. Saulve; Onnaing; Mons.

During the incessant fighting of all this period it is not known which will be considered as major operations, but the Battle of Arras or Vimy Ridge, Hill 70, Passchendaele, Canal du Nord, Cambrai and Valenciennes will be considered as such as far as the Canadian Corps is concerned, and in all of which the 9th C.S.B. did its part.

After the Battle of Vimy Ridge, the Group Commander showed his appreciation of the work of the Battery by a special letter of recognition for good work done. It had been a very strenuous time. The Battery arrived there only on April 5th. The position was in an open muddy field. There was not much time to get ready. Gun platforms were constructed and camouflage erected, ready to move the guns in at night. All material, as well as the ammunition, had to be carried a long distance. For three nights there was no sleep, but guns were registered on April 7th and the Battery took part in the bombardment on that and succeeding days.

After Vimy the Battery moved forward to a position between Angres and Cité du Caumont. It had a long and memorable stay here during the protracted fighting round Lens. The position was a very forward one for a six-inch Battery, and the Hun machine guns at night seemed very near. Our infantry front line at first was rather uncertain just here and German snipers and posts used to occupy empty houses at night not very far from the Battery. It was a good position. The guns were just behind a hill which screened their flash and were well concealed from aeroplane observation. The men off duty had good deep Hun dugouts, some 600 yards in rear. But the place was shelled continually.

The Battery had wonderful luck, shells day after day dropping all round the guns and B. C. Post. Funk pits were soon constructed near the guns for men to take cover when necessary. It was during one of these enforced cessations of fire that a little episode occurred. The No. 1, on looking out, saw an old gunner (Gunner Forde) calmly sitting on the trail of his gun and quietly using most abusive and lurid language against the enemy. On being asked by him why he did not obey the order to take cover, he said, " There is not a blankety blank Hun living who will make me take cover." It then transpired that he had habitually stayed behind in this manner on such occasions.

One of the chief dangers was from splinters. In trying to get our guns many of the Hun shells exploded on the top of the ridge in front of them, which sent showers of splinters for 800 yards, so that the daily relief going and coming from dugouts to guns had an anxious time. During the stay at Angres many other batteries came to the locality, but did not stay long, leaving for sunnier climes.

It was during one of these visits that the first decoration was awarded to the 9th C.S.B., Gunner Makin getting the M.M. for pulling some gunners belonging to another battery out of the debris in which they had been buried by hostile shell fire. But many others deserved a decoration as well as he and were frequently recommended for it.

In May the Battery had their most unlucky day, one chance shell killing seven and wounding six.

It was in June that a Staff Officer informed the Battery that for the time it had been in France it had (a) fired more rounds than any other Battery, (b) had received more shelling than any other Battery, and (c) was the most advanced Battery on the front.

In October the Battery left Lens area for the North with the Canadian Corps, which was to relieve the Australians in the operations against Passchendaele. It remained in the Ypres Salient till Dec. 13th. The Battery relieved three R.G.A. Batteries in turn, going further forward each time. By a merciful providence the ground was soft, and in consequence many enemy shells were " duds "; otherwise nothing could have prevented heavy casualties. Constant shelling and bombing; the enemy's aeroplanes everywhere: ours not in sight.

The Ypres Salient is the abomination of desolation—one big graveyard. A peculiarly depressing place, nothing can describe it: it has to be felt. A complimentary letter was published from 2nd Division describing the Heavy Artillery's work in the taking of Passchendaele as the " perfection of Heavy Artillery barrage."

9th CANADIAN SIEGE BATTERY, C.E.F.

The Battery moved South again, and for the first time in eight months went into rest at Ham-en-Artois, arriving at that place on Dec. 15th. It seemed almost too good to be true. Jan. 11th found the Battery back in the line again at Petit Vimy. Then followed uneventful moves to Calonne (Feb. 3rd) and Maroc, where there were good cellars for the men.

About this time there was a change in Brigade Commanders. On the new one asking the former one which was the best Battery in the Brigade, the 9th was given a reputation it might well be proud of.

On Feb. 25th the Battery was back again at Petit Vimy position with one section in rear near Les Tilluels. Preparation for the expected Hun offensive was the order of the day. Successive defensive systems were prepared. Batteries were issued with Lewis Guns and were ordered to wire their positions. Many battery positions were prepared and camouflaged. It was hard work for the men who had heavy days and nights of firing to carry out at the same time. Again the Battery found itself the most advanced in the Brigade, and was always being called upon to fire on the most distant target in consequence. In case of a successful Hun attack the position would have been impossible to get out of with the steep Vimy Ridge immediately in rear and all the roads registered and under observation by day. It seemed that the role of the Battery, under such circumstances, was that of a sacrifice Battery. Gradually the infantry in front were drawn in until the line was held by little more than machine gun posts. The field guns took up positions behind and one woke up one night to the unusual sound of our own field artillery shells passing over our heads.

The G.O.C. paid the Battery a visit after a worse than usual "strafe," but he found the men with their "tails up." He said they were doing good work and that was why they were being kept in that position. Three distinct times was the B. C. confidentially warned that the attack was expected on the morrow and three times nothing unusual happened.

March 21st passed and the Huns great attack which was to last nine terrible days commenced. It was to the south of us, and not till the 28th did it reach our neighborhood. But Arras remained firm, and there was no advance worth speaking about on our front.

At 3 a.m. the enemy started shelling the Battery with gas. He attacked persistently with heavy gun fire till 12 noon and again in the afternoon. At night every half hour he put down bursts of harassing fire and concentrations, but the fire of the Battery was kept up in spite of it and gas. The next day the enemy continued his tactics; not a half hour but Battery, billets, roads and railway received his attention. Two of the signallers (Dickey and West) did noble work in repairing our telephone line, nearly a mile, through a regular barrage of high explosive and gas, their job being made more difficult by some defensive wire entanglements which had been recently placed over our line.

Now succeeded several months when the enemy's chief energies were directed to other parts of the Front, and the British Army was recovering from its wounds, filling up its ranks and organizing for the coming glorious advance which was to end the war. During these months the Battery had positions at Souchez and Lievin, neither of these being pleasant spots, but where life was more or less normal; that is, daily and nightly tasks of firing, sometimes counter battery shoots, sometimes destructive shoots, or harassing fire, to all of which the Hun replied in kind. At Lievin he gave us two bad gas bombardments, but the results, had he known them, would have been bitterly disappointing to him, to such an extent had we been educated by this time in anti-gas measures. At Villers Cagnicourt Chère was some heavy firing and obstinate fighting before the enemy was driven across the Canal du Nord. At Barelle Wood the Battery was a day, and at Sauchy Lestree. during the fight for Cambrai, which was very severe, several days were spent. At this place the Huns' night bombers were very active.

But it was now moving warfare in earnest. Blecourt and Batigny were hot places for a day or two. At Marquette and Escaydain a night only was spent in each. Wavrechain-Sous-Denain was easy. At Herin the Battery took part in the very fine artillery preparation for the taking of Valenciennes, and at St. Saulve on Nov. 4th it had its last casualty of one man killed.

During all this moving warfare, conditions were a great contrast to the previous trench warfare. Guns sometimes took up positions in fields almost untouched by shellfire. The laborious gun

9th CANADIAN SIEGE BATTERY, C.E.F.

pit was nearly unknown. The woods and trees were no longer shot to pieces, and occasionally one walked into billets to find cut flowers still fresh on the window sill, or table, left there by the retiring Hun the day before or by its civil occupants who had been forced to leave with him.

9th CANADIAN SIEGE BATTERY.

Authority for organization. H.Q. 1-36-129. Names of original officers with rank: Major (Lieut.-Col.) S. A. Heward, Capt. H. R. N. Cobbett. Lieut. D. W. McKeen, Lieut. D. A. MacKenzie, Lieut. W. E. B. Starr, Lieut. C. B. Thackray, all of R.C.A.

Reinforcements: Lieut. E. S. Hoare, Lieut. H. R. Gunter, Lieut. R. Cruit, Capt. C. MacKay, Lieut. M. A. Wilson. Lieut. E. T. Chesley, Capt. J. E. Lean, Lieut. J. S. Millar, Lieut. W. A. F. Fairchild, Lieut. F. C. Harding, Capt. H. T. Seaman, Major W. G. Scully, all of C.G.A.; Lieut. Warren (Portuguese Interpreter); Lieut. P. Moyara, Portuguese troops; Lieut. J. C. Fraser, C.G.A.

Numerical strength: Officers, 6; W. O. and S. Sergeants, 8; other ranks, 144. Total all ranks, 158.

Date of sailing for Overseas: 27th September, 1916.

Date of return to Canada: May 9th, 1919.

Commissions: Gunners Young and S. Smith to R.O.C. training school for commissions.

Honors: Military Cross, 2; Dist. Conduct Medal, 2; M.S.M., 3; Military Medal, 13; mentioned in despatches, 3.

Total number of battle casualties: Officer, 1; other ranks, 67; total, 68.

CHAPTER IV.

THE 10th SIEGE BATTERY.

THE proposal to recruit a purely Nova Scotian Artillery Unit originated when four young officers had just completed their training with the Royal School of Artillery at Halifax. These young officers were: Lieuts. Wm. Henry L. Doane, 1st R.C.A.; Frederick H. Palmer, 1st R.C.A.; Robert Parker Freeman, 1st R.C.A.; Robert Edward Jamieson, 1st R.C.A..

The proposal was laid before Major J. M. Slayter, R.C.A., and after discussion he agreed to undertake to obtain the necessary authority and to take over, at any rate temporarily, the work of the Battery, if such was approved.

On August 1, 1916, authority was applied for from the General Officer Commanding Military District No. 6 for leave to raise a Battery of Siege in Halifax for service Overseas. On August 12, 1916, the organization of No. 10 Draft Siege Artillery Battery was approved, and on October 1, 1916, authority was received from headquarters for the appointment of the following officers: Major J. M. Slayter, R.C.A. (in Command); Lieuts. Wm. H. L. Doane, 1st R.C.A.; F. H. Palmer, 1st R.C.A.; R. P. Freeman, 1st R.C.A.; R. E. Jamieson, 1st R.C.A.

Barrack accommodation was found for the proposed Battery in South Barracks, and at once the work of active recruiting was taken up. By the end of November, 1916, the Battery was raised to a strength of eighty-five officers and men. Preliminary examinations were completed and as quickly as the men completed their preliminary training, they were passed on to Instructional Courses to qualify as Battery Commanders, Assistants, Signalling and Gun Laying, and all the various specialties that go to make up a Siege Battery. On December 11, 1916, Lieut. W. H. L. Doane was promoted to fill the vacancy of Captain in the Battery. This completed the establishment of officers.

THE 10th SIEGE BATTERY

In accordance with orders received on December 16, 1916, Lieut. Crosby and fifty other ranks were warned to hold themselves in readiness to proceed Overseas. They embarked on the S.S. *Scandinavian* on January 23, 1917. Recruiting continued steadily and on March 26, 1917, Capt. W. H. L. Doane with fifty other ranks proceeded Overseas on the S.S. *Missinabie*.

Capt. F. H. Palmer being now the senior Lieutenant of the Battery was promoted to Captain, March 27, 1917. On April 12, 1917, Lieut. M. B. Archibald, 1st R.C.S., and Lieut. R. D. Lacon, 1st R.C.A., were appointed to the Battery. Lieut. R. P. Freeman and fifty other ranks were warned on May 17, 1917, to hold themselves in readiness to proceed Overseas. They sailed on the *Olympic* on the 28th of May.

On November 5, 1917, warning was received that three officers and two hundred N.C.O.'s and men would proceed Overseas. As the Military Service Act was now about to become law, organizations which had previously handled voluntary recruiting would now completely change their character. Ample man power being available, it would only be necessary to outfit and start preliminary training of men raised under the Act.

In view of this the Draft embarked for Overseas service on November 23, 1917, on the S.S. *Metagama*, consisting of Major J. M. Slayter, Captain Palmer and one hundred and fifty N.C.O.'s and men. Lieutenant Archibald and fifty other ranks proceeded Overseas on the S.S. *Olympic*. Lieutenant Lacon, and some forty men, the latest joined recruits, were left in Halifax to carry on the Depot under the Military Service Act.

As the personnel of the detachment who made up this sailing were of an exceptionally high character, and had had considerable training in specialties, it was hoped that they might be retained as a Battery for service Overseas.

On arrival at Witley, Surrey, England, it was found that there were such heavy demands for reinforcements for Batteries and Brigades already authorized, that it would be impossible to retain the organization as it landed at Witley. Specialists were sent for extra courses, and as these were completed were drafted very largely to the newly-formed 10th, 11th and 12th Siege Batteries, and to the 3rd Brigade of the C.G.A.

The Depot of the 10th Siege Battery at Halifax continued under Major George Oland, with Lieutenant Lacon, Lieutenant McNair and Lieutenant Baird, sending forward drafts and having raised and equipped and sent forward some ten officers and about eight hundred N.C.O.'s and men. The Depot at Halifax was finally absorbed after the Armistice in the 6th Artillery Depot.

These are the bare facts as taken from records, which do not signalize the splendid self-sacrificing work of such officers as Captains W. H. L. Doane, R. P. Freeman, F. H. Palmer, and R. E. Jamieson; and such N.C.O.'s as Jenkins, Fultz and Holmes.

From beginning to end this Unit was marked by the high standard of the men that it drew, the remarkable lack of crime of even the pettiest sort, and the earnestness and whole-hearted manner in which all ranks endeavored to qualify themselves for their duties Overseas.

CHAPTER V.

17th BATTERY (6th BATTERY, C.F.A.)

BY WILFRED HEARN SYDNEY.

THE 17th Battery had the unique distinction of being the only combatant Militia Unit in Nova Scotia to be accepted as a Unit of the Canadian Expeditionary Force for service Overseas in the First Canadian Contingent. On the day that war was declared between Great Britain and Germany, the Department of Militia and Defence wired its acceptance of Lieut.-Colonel H. G. McLeod's offer of the 17th Battery, C.F.A., as a Unit for service Overseas.

The mobilization of the Battery was purely a matter of selection, for many more than the required number applied for enlistment. On August 28, 1914, the Battery left Sydney with the full war strength of 141 officers and men, four guns and 123 horses. The trip to Valcartier was uneventful. Shortly after our arrival there we were disappointed to hear that the Unit would have to be split in order that the new war establishment of six-gun Batteries might be completed. The right section of the 17th was to be amalgamated with the 19th Battery from Moncton and Woodstock, while the left section went with the 21st Battery of Westmount, Montreal. Thus Major McLeod was to command the new 6th Battery, C.E.F., keeping with him Capt. J. Geo. Piercey, while Capt. J. A. MacDonald, our own "Johnnie Angus," was lost to us, and went to the new 5th Battery in the same Brigade.

The two weeks spent in Valcartier Camp were pleasant. The getting used to military routine, drill and ceremonials was not at that early date a hardship. The novelty had not even begun to wear off then. The reviews held by Sir Sam Hughes first and His Royal Highness the Duke of Connaught subsequently, had a certain amount of pleasure for all of us, despite adverse weather conditions. Yet it was not without a certain degree of impatience that we awaited the word to set sail for England.

Eventually, after many false alarms, the word came, and we donned full marching order to set out for Quebec and the waiting transports. What a memorable sight was that Armada congregated at Gaspe Bay! Thirty-three of our largest ocean greyhounds in full steam, ready and anxious to hasten to the assistance of our Mother Country in her hour of need. The order was signalled from the flagship to set out—last letters of farewell were hurried aboard waiting tenders, a lingering last look was taken at the shores of Canada, and the First Canadian Contingent bade farewell to the peaceful land of the Maple Leaf and set its gaze to the East where lay discord and strife.

Ocean trips generally are never very much out of the ordinary, and with the exception of one or two submarine scares, absolutely without foundation, we steamed our uneventful, out-of-the-way course to Merry England—and war. The monotony was relieved by routine, athletic competitions and musical entertainments. It was in the organization of the latter that the popular Canadian composer of present times, Gitz Rice, closely related to the Cape Breton Rices, Brent and Walter, first secured prominence in musical circles. However, if the trip was uninspiring, such could not be said of our reception at Plymouth. Bands playing, throngs cheering, the shores of the city blocked with thousands of people— England certainly did its duty that day in welcoming to its shores her Canadian sons.

Disembarkation lasted a week, but finally the " Old 17th " landed at Devonport and were soon en route for Salisbury Plains. Detrained at Amesbury we were greeted with a downpour of rain, and it was very little else we saw in the weather line during the whole of our stay on that historic plain. Mud, mud, mud, and then more mud; drill, drill, drill, and then more drill, sums up Salisbury Plains, relieved only by brief leaves to London and provincial towns. How we cursed the mud! Finally, however, we were moved into comfortable quarters at Urchfont, where we enjoyed real English hospitality and good cheer. Even the Plains had its pleasant side, though. Our first Christmas away from home was

17th BATTERY (6th BATTERY, C.F.A.)

spent there, and royally did Major McLeod and his fellow officers endeavor to give us a real Christmas.

We spent about a month at Urchfont before the call came for which we had been impatiently waiting. On February 8th, 1915, we left for France. Embarking at Avonmouth we set out for the scene of war. The Allies at that time were being pressed from all sides. The Bases of Calais, Boulogne, and Rouen were seriously threatened. So it was to St. Nazair, a port in the Bay of Biscay, that the Canadians were sent. On February 13th we first set foot in France; on the 16th we detrained within hearing of the guns, at Hazebrouck, marching further in to billets at Borre.

From Borre the 6th Battery moved up into action and took its first position at Fleurbaix on March 1st. The first round was fired into the German front line by Captain Tom Kitchen, then Bombardier, and we took it as a good omen that the second round was observed to have sent our enemy's field kitchen skyward. While at Fleurbaix the Battery played its part in the mix-up of March 10th at Neuve Chapelle, and it was in this same position we underwent our baptism of fire—fortunately with no serious casualties.

On March 29th, the Brigade to which the 6th Battery was attached, was withdrawn to rest—billets at Watou. It was here, on Easter Sunday, that the first intimation of the hardship and danger to be expected at Ypres was given us by our Commanding Officer, Col. J. J. Creelman. The Easter Service was conducted by Rev. Canon Almon, and a feeling of intensity was apparent as he impressed upon us the sad fact, that of those who heard him that day, many would, before long, make that greatest sacrifice. And so indeed it proved. Yet when, on April 18th, we first caught a glimpse of the city of Ypres, then with a population of about twenty thousand, with its shops, estaminets and business places generally in full swing, it was hard indeed for us to believe that our padre could be correct. Little did we foresee that in four short days this city, beautiful, even after its first bombardment, would be a mass of ruins, its population fleeing to safety with a miserable handful of personal belongings, its Cathedral and historic Cloth Hall and invaluable treasures forever lost to posterity. Yet such was to happen.

NOVA SCOTIA'S PART IN THE GREAT WAR

The bombardment of the Second Battle of Ypres commenced on the 21st, and on the 22nd the Hun let loose his devilish fumes of poison gas. The French to our left fell back, exposing our flank, leaving a gap of over a mile. Our own boys held, but at what a price! Reinforcements from our own reserves were hurriedly sent up, and all that was left of our First Division was spread over the whole of a three-mile front. But they held on for that day and the next. On the 23rd, from our position near St. Julien, we took part in what I firmly believe to have been the most dramatic action that the Battery was engaged in during its stay in France and Flanders. Our infantry had fallen back to reform for a counter-attack. The enemy advanced after them at a range of about 1,200 yards from our guns. Two of our latter were immediately switched to the left at an angle of 45° from their original line of fire. The remaining two were galloped over clear country under heavy shell fire to take up a new position.

With approximately only 100 rounds of ammunition, exposed to the heaviest shell fire, we waited until the enemy were sufficiently advanced to come under our "open sights" so that every round might count. So on they came until 600 yards separated us. The order came for us to retire. This Major McLeod ignored, but instead gave the word to open fire. The 7th Battalion charged at the same time, with the remnants of the Kilty Brigade. Round after round we poured into the still oncoming enemy until at last they were held and finally swept back through Langemarck wood. Three new positions were taken up by the Battery that night, and finally we were settled at Indian Hill, near Wieltje, and to the side of Potijze. What a hell-hole it was! Our casualties were fast mounting up, both among the personnel and horses, and unfortunately a number of these were deaths. On May 1st we took up a position on the banks of the Yser Canal, and remained there until the Division was withdrawn for reorganization at Hinges.

On May 19th we were again, as part of the "Flying 7th Division" hustled into hot action at Festubert, and in the following month at Givenchy. It was at the latter place that a gun from the 6th Battery was placed in action in the front line trench, a "stunt" subsequently acknowledged by the General Officer Commanding.

17th BATTERY (6th BATTERY, C.F.A.)

From the "Orchard Position" at Givenchy the Old 17th was sent into action at Neuve Eglise, where for a long time they enjoyed comparative peace, with only occasional casualties, and nothing more than "raiding" work, which was first commenced on this front, to relieve the monotony. It was while here that the 2nd and 3rd Divisions came over and the Canadians became an Army Corps. It was here, too, that we lost our Major.

Major McLeod was of the type of officer most beloved by the Canadian rank and file. Quick, alert, a thoroughly skilled Artillery Officer, he surely would have forced early recognition from headquarters had he been spared to attain it. Terrible was the blow to his "boys," when his body was found in a small pond not many rods from the gun position. His was not even the glory of the death from bullet or shrapnel. Yet his duty had been well done, to his God, to his country, to his fellow officers and men. This brief outline of the Old 17th would be even more inadequate were the writer to omit this humble tribute to a dear friend and beloved Commanding Officer.

LT.-COL. G. H. MCLEOD.

Christmas, 1915, was spent at Neuve Eglise, and again we had to thank our officers for providing the usual Christmas trimmings. Conditions were not as they had been in England, and, unfortunately, many of the old faces were missing. Such were the fortunes of war, and we who had been raw recruits one short year before were beginning to look at things as philosophic veterans.

In the latter part of January the Battery was withdrawn to Caestre for a brief rest, being relieved by one of the Units of the 2nd Division. Early in February we went to Lederzeele, and about March 20th found ourselves in action once more at Neuve Eglise. Just about this time rumors, hitherto vague, became more certain that the Battery was once more to move Ypresward. Rumor became a definite fact on April 4th, and we found ourselves in position at Railway dugouts, a trifle to the south of Ypres City. Here we remained in complete quiet until the 20th, when in the Hill 60 scrap we received our first taste of gas shells.

NOVA SCOTIA'S PART IN THE GREAT WAR

It was during the month of May that the organization of three Howitzer Batteries was undertaken and sub-sections from all the Batteries in the Division were utilized to form these Batteries, and sub-section " C " was separated from the 6th to help form the D, 48th Battery of 4.5's. The complete organization of this Battery had not been consummated before the German hordes again attacked in force, this time at Soisele Hill and Sanctuary Wood. All sub-sections reported back to their own Batteries for duty, and the 6th Battery again played its important part in the Third Battle of Ypres. On the morning of June 13th the Canadians counter-attacked and regained the ground lost in the 2nd of June scrap.

The remainder of the month of June was passed quietly in the Ypres Salient, as was also the month of July, with the exception of a little excitement at " The Dump." About the middle of August the Battery went into billets for rest and tactical drill at Polin Cove and on the 26th entrained at Audruicq for the Somme.

On detraining at Aix la Chateau on the 27th, the Battery, after one day's forced march, went into action at Mesnel on the 28th. On September 3rd the Old 17th supported the attack of an Imperial Corps on Thiepval, which was unsuccessful. We then moved into position at La Boiselle on ground won from the enemy during the fighting there in the early part of July. Glad we were to see at long last ground won from the Hun. Seemingly we were now engaged in driving him back, steadily and surely. The Germans were retreating—the end of the war was in sight—so we thought.

On September 15th the attack on Courcellette was commenced. Who of us that were there can easily forget the glory of that early sunlit September morning! The writer was fortunate enough to be one of a party of Artillery Signallers to " go over " with the second " wave " of infantry and was forward when the signal—dropped from one of our air craft—came to advance. The intensity of the bombardment was overwhelming. It was impossible to hear the loudest shout of the man adjoining you. We were all frantic—cheering, yelling, jumping up and down in our excitement. It was pandemonium let loose with a vengeance—and we were winning. We were advancing. The Sugar Refinery was reached and our Battery was advanced. Courcellette was taken by the 25th and 26th Battalions—and again we were moved forward until we were

17th BATTERY (6th BATTERY, C.F.A.)

practically within two hundred yards of where the German front line had been on the morning of the 15th. This position—Pozieres Wood—had been won by the Australians at a terrible cost some weeks before.

From the 15th until the 26th of September we were kept busy consolidating the ground won from the enemy. On the 26th we were again called upon to take part in a glorious action which won Thiepval for us. We were also successful in our first attack on Regina Trench. Such heavy action was not successfully won without our paying the price, however, and the 6th Battery of October, 1916, little resembled the Old 17th that left Valcartier in September, 1914. Heavy had been the toll of lives and casualties.

It was on October 20th that the last remaining gun brought from Sydney, was condemned after firing 20,010 rounds of ammunition. From this on, the writer (having been wounded at the Somme sufficiently to keep him out of action for the remainder of the war) must depend, not on personal observation, but on information derived from divers sources.

Early in November Desire Support Trench was taken, and a little later on in the same month our wagon lines were again situated at Albert. The march along Bouzincourt, Varennes, Raincheva, Frevent, St. Pol, St. Michel and Marquay was uneventful. On the 30th the Battery stopped at Pernes, for a well-earned rest. Our 1916 Christmas dinner was held here, and mighty well was it celebrated. On January 6th we started out for Bruay, Ruitz, Hersin to Fosse 10 and finally into action at Bully Grenay.

On February 13th the first landing of the Canadians in France was suitably celebrated at noon, by the firing of " Battery cheers " and " Brigade cheers." From then on is merely a series of names, Hersin Wagon Lines, Maisnil-les-Ruitz, Camblain l'Abbe, until the E2 position behind Neuville St. Vaast. On the 25th the Battery was again changed from a four to a six-gun Unit. From Neuville St. Vaast the Old 17th went to Vimy. Who will forget Bentata Tunnel? Who will forget the morning of the 13th when two guns of the old Battery went to form the composite Battery at Bois Carre, to the right of Thelus? On the night of the 16th the Battery went over the Ridge, and from there on the story of the 6th is the same as that of the other Nova Scotia Units that took part at Vimy. From Vimy to late in July was uneventful. On the 22nd of that month our wagon lines were established at Les Brebis. On the 23rd we went into action behind Loos Crassier. Things remained quiet until August 15th when the Hill 70 scrap for Lens commenced. On September 9th we were at Lievin, and remained in that vicinity for about one month.

Around October 1st a move was made to Boyeffles, where the wagon line was established. On the 6th the Battery took up a position behind the cemetery at Lievin, where we remained for some time. On the 24th of October we were again en route for Ypres, our old hunting ground, via Bethune, Morbecque and Godewaersvelde. On the 29th our wagon lines were settled at a spot just south of St. Julien, and on the 1st of November we took up a position, which shall ever be consecrated in memory of our First Canadian Contingent, for the Passchendaele show. On the 23rd we were again en route south, via Bailleul, Strazeele, Haverskerque and Vendin-les-Bethune. On November 26th the Battery was again at the Old Lievin cemetery. Christmas Day, 1917, was celebrated at Haillicourt.

On January 24th the Battery took up a position behind Loos Crassier, where they remained in comparative quietness until March 22nd, when a new position behind the double Crassier was taken. On the 29th we went into action at Ronville Dump between Arras and Achicourt, and from there to the Old Mill at Achicourt on April 1st. On the 8th we were out at Anzin, on the 9th at Musketry Valley position, in front of St. Laurent Blangy. The Battery was withdrawn for rest at Hermanville on May 25th, and on June 1st was inspected with the other Batteries in the Brigade by the Corps Commander. On the 10th Divisional Sports were held, in which the old Battery won its quota of prizes.

On July 15th we went into action at St. Laurent Blangy, and on the 24th were back again at Achicourt—Old Windmill position. August the 1st saw the Unit at Berlincourt, and on the 3rd they entrained at Frevent for Amiens. We detrained the following day at Prouzel and left for Bois de Boves. On August 5th we took up a position at Bois de Gentelles, and on the 8th took part in the "kick off" for the Amiens show with a night position in front of Cayeux. From the 9th until the 16th is simply a sequence of names

17th BATTERY (6th BATTERY, C.F.A.)

that spells the hardest action; Caix Valley, Warvillers, Le Quesnoy, Warvillers. On August 21st the Battery was en route back to Saleux, via Cayeux, Domart and Boves Wood, where they entrained for Aubigny and Dainville Wood.

The "kick off" for the Drocourt-Queant line came on September 2nd. On the 3rd our position was taken up just east of Villers Cagnicourt, and on the 6th the 6th Battery was at Bainville on rest, where they remained for about three weeks. On the 26th the Battery went into action at Buissy, and on the 27th took part in the attack on Canal du Nord and Cambrai. The Old 17th had the honor to be the first Battery to cross the Canal at Inchy, and immediately after took up position just east of the Canal beyond Inchy.

October was merely a repetition of names. The Battery took part in the general rout of the enemy, until November 7th found them at Crespin, in action for the last time. On November the 10th the last round was fired from the Battery in this position by Gunner Malcolm MacDonald of "B" subsection, the very same subsection that fired the first round on March 1, 1915.

At 11 a.m. of November 11th hostilities ceased and the fighting was finished. The "Old 17th," however, marched into Germany as part of the Army of Occupation and completed the work that the original had set out to do. Very few, however, of the original members were left by that time. Yet those of us, who were unable to share in the glorious hour of Victory, were recompensed by knowing that our successors nobly carried on in our places equally as well as, if not better than, we ourselves could have done. The Battery embarked at Southampton on *S.S. Olympic*, and arrived at Halifax on April 21, 1919. It was demobilized the same day and consequently its home city, Sydney, was deprived of the pleasure of welcoming it as a Unit.

CASUALTIES.

```
Officers:    Killed ..........................  5
             Died ...........................  2
                                                    7
Other ranks: Killed ..........................  19
             Died of wounds .................  13
             Died ...........................  2
                                                   34
                                                   41
```

HONORS AND AWARDS.

D.S.O.	3
M.C.	10
D.C.M.	4
M.M.	28
Bar to M.M.	1
M.S.M.	1
Croix de Guerre	1
Despatches	12

CHAPTER VI.

23rd AND 24th FIELD BATTERIES.

IN November, 1914, Lieut.-Col. T. M. Seeley, of Yarmouth, N.S. (O.C. 11th Brigade, C.F.A.), was commissioned to organize the 23rd Battery of Field Artillery, to represent the Maritime Provinces in the 6th Artillery Brigade, C.E.F. The temporary headquarters were at Fredericton, N.B., but recruits were to be drawn from any part of the Maritime Provinces. Many were furnished by the 3rd, 4th and 11th Brigades of the Militia Artillery. An important factor in the new Unit was a group of twenty-five or thirty students who joined from the University of New Brunswick and other universities.

The recruiting proceeded at such a rate that Lieut.-Col. Seeley soon found himself with fifty or sixty men over strength. He appealed to headquarters for authority to have a second Battery formed, which was granted. Lieut.-Col. B. A. Ingraham, R.O., of Sydney, C.B., was commissioned to organize the 24th Battery, also at Fredericton. He took over the surplus from the 23rd, and in addition brought a large detachment of fine men from Cape Breton.

LT.-COL. T. M. SEELEY.

These Batteries trained side by side until February 18, 1915, when they were mobilized with the 21st Battery of Kingston and the 22nd Battery of Montreal, and sent Overseas February 22nd on *S.S. Megantic*, under Lieut.-Col. E. W. Rathburn.

The Mayor of Fredericton, the Premier of New Brunswick, the Earl and Countess of Ashburnham, and the citizens generally were very kind to the artillerymen during their sojourn in Fredericton.

Just previous to sailing there were several changes made in the personnel of the officers. Lieut.-Colonel Seeley was detailed to organization duty in Canada, and Major J. K. MacKay was placed in command of the 23rd Battery. On sailing the staff was: Major MacKay, O.C.; Capt. E. A. Chisholm; Lieuts. J. E. Read and J. N. McEachern. The Staff of the 24th Battery was: Lieut.-Colonel Ingraham, O.C.; Capt. A. T. MacKay (of P.E.I.); Lieuts. G. St. C. A. Perrin and O. Mowatt.

Arriving in England the Batteries received a brief training at Shorncliffe, after which they were drafted to the Second Brigade, C.F.A., and Divisional Ammunition Column in France. A large proportion of the N.C.O.'s and men of these Batteries won commissions and distinctions on the field.

CHAPTER VII.

THE 36th BATTERY, C.F.A.

BY MAJOR D. A. MACKINNON, D.S.O.

THE 36th Battery was formed in Sydney in September, 1915, Major Walter Crowe being the organizer and leading spirit in it. The rush of applications for positions in the Battery was so great that over one hundred had to be turned away. Major Crowe selected his men with great care; and the subsequent achievements of the Battery is evidence that his judgment was good. To Major Crowe must be given a great deal of credit for the splendid record which the Battery achieved Overseas. He remained with it as its Commanding Officer and supervised nearly all its early training, took it Overseas in March, 1916, but on account of being very much over age could not accompany the Battery to France; so the command was given to Major D. A. MacKinnon, of Charlottetown, P.E.I.

MAJ. D. A. MACKINNON, D.S.O.

The Battery arrived in France on July 14th, 1916, and was almost immediately placed in action on the Ypres Salient, which was a very " hot " spot. They were in action only twenty-four hours when they received quite a heavy shelling from the enemy. They remained in this position for about a month, firing day and night, and their quick response to all calls from the infantry was remarked upon. The next move was to Kemmel, which was a nice quiet spot, and the boys enjoyed themselves very much while in that vicinity. Early in October the march for the Somme commenced. It occupied a week; and about the 12th of October the Battery went into action about one thousand yards in the rear of Courcellette. They received considerable shelling but returned one hundred rounds for every one they got. After the Battle of Regina Trench they moved forward in front of Martinpuich, with the expectation of another great battle which never materialized. While in this position they were constantly shelled, the discomforts were terrible, mud and rain preventing any kind of decent accommodation; but the gunners were better off than the drivers at the wagon lines; there the mud was two feet deep, and the trials and sufferings almost unendurable. Nearly all the ammunition had to be carried to the guns by packing it on horses' and mules' backs, taking it up over trails, inasmuch as the roads were death traps, on account of enemy fire. Notwithstanding this the Battery kept up its reputation for activity, having fired on several occasions well over one thousand rounds in a few hours. They were highly complimented for their splendid concealment and for the brave way in which they carried on under very discouraging difficulties. On the 20th of November the Division pulled out of the Somme, greatly to the relief of all.

A week's tramp to the Ecuri Front commenced, the first two days being teeming rain and bitter cold. It was during this march that Sergt. Sam Wilson, one of the most popular men in the Battery, contracted pneumonia and died in a few days, mourned by all. During the following months the Battery stayed in position doing garrison duty, but in February they were forced to leave and made three shifts of positions in three days. The bitter cold, it being the coldest winter in forty years, and the shortage of fodder for the horses, coupled with the hard work which so much moving entailed, caused the death of a great many horses and mules. The hardships of the drivers were also particularly severe, shelter was at a premium, and the winter of 1916 and 1917 will ever remain as a very disagreeable memory.

Early in March preparations commenced for the Battle of Vimy Ridge, the drivers being constantly employed at night hauling vast quantities of ammunition to forward points. The month was very rainy with high winds, and all night the men would be exposed to the rain and winds and return at daybreak tired and exhausted,

THE 36th BATTERY, C.F.A.

cold and wet to the skin. The sufferings which they experienced that winter, and the grim determination with which they carried through their duties will never be forgotten. On the 25th of March the 36th was changed to a six-gun Battery, absorbing one-half of the 29th Battery. It was a splendid consolidation, the new-comers proving very excellent gunners and drivers, and brave men. About the 1st of April, 1917, the Battery moved forward to a little hollow near the Arras road, facing Vimy Ridge. Rude pits had to be constructed for the guns, and these they soon fashioned into a home for the Battery. The Batteries were as thick as flies in this hollow, and we had neighbors on all sides of us. The 2nd of April saw everybody registering on targets in the enemy lines, and one had almost to crawl about to prevent being hit by our own guns. As the enemy had observation of this position they very quickly began to use it, shelling the area with gas and high explosives. It was a most uncomfortable position, and had the battle been delayed a few days longer and the enemy been given a chance to get more heavy artillery, there is no doubt that they would have given us a bad time.

The Battle of Vimy Ridge started at 5 o'clock, April 9th. It was the biggest battle we had ever been engaged in, and every one was quite interested to see how it would pan out. It was a great success, and we quickly got orders to move our position forward so as to be able to range on the retreating enemy. This was accomplished very speedily. The battle practically ended on April 10th, and no further move was made forward. On the 14th we took our guns down into the village of Vimy being, we believed, one of the first Batteries to enter that much shelled village. We were lucky in getting in and lucky in getting our teams out, as the roads were shelled most terrifically. It was three weeks after that before we could bring a wagon of any description down the roads to the Battery. All ammunition and supplies had to be brought on pack horses and mules along trails leading over the ridges, but by the exercise of great care they managed to keep up our ammunition supplies and prevent casualties.

The first two weeks which followed in our position were memorable for the amount of gas which the enemy hurled at us. We wore our masks practically all night. Thanks to a sufficient gas drill and gas protection our casualties were slight. With the energy and resource which characterized our boys they set to work and built a position which was the envy of all. It was so constructed that it was impossible to detect it by aeroplane or other observation. Speaking tubes connected all the gun-pits with the command post, and each pit had a tunnel leading into the other; so that if one was severely bombarded, an escape could be made through the other. The walls of the pits were nicely decorated with captured German material, and the appearance was such as to strike an inspecting officer most favorably. The greatest attention was paid to strengthening each defence, as the shelling was intense both by day and night. It was lucky that all these precautions were taken; for on the 24th of June, just as the Battery had completed firing a trial barrage, the enemy opened up with four batteries of heavy artillery. The bombardment was terrific, and almost all varieties of shell were used, including armorpiercing shell, which went down ten feet in the ground and then exploded. It was marvelous that there was anything left of the Battery, the whole position was covered with shell holes. One of the shells passed through the shelter in which Corpl. John McVicar, of Sydney, was with his gun detachment. The shock instantly killed Corporal McVicar and dazed some of the others. At the same time others had become casualties. The day will be long remembered as one which inflicted great sorrow on the remaining members of the Battery. While we were in this position Corporal Jack and Gunner Wheatley were also wounded, and there were several regrettable casualties among the drivers at the wagon lines.

Early in July the Battery moved to a forward position near Vimy and, while there, was subjected to another terrific bombardment in which they had nearly one thousand rounds of ammunition destroyed. Several of the officers had close calls, and those who are alive will never forget the experience. About the 31st of July the Battery moved to Hill 70, and took up a position behind the double crassier. They constructed a good position in a very short time. The place was alive with Canadian Field Batteries, and it did not take the Hun long to discover the fact. Nearly all the

THE 36th BATTERY, C.F.A.

Batteries were silent; that is, they were not to do any firing until a battle commenced, but the 36th and a few others were selected to do all the firing, including the heavy task of demolishing the wire in the German trenches, so that our infantry could get through. This the Battery did to the entire satisfaction of the infantry, although it was at quite a heavy cost to themselves, as they were constantly shelled day and night, and the position was a most trying one. The battle, which took place about the 14th of August, was one of the bloodiest of the whole war. The Hill was the key to Lens, and the Hun determined to retake it at all costs. In one day there were fourteen counter attacks made by the Hun, and on every occasion the field artillery responded, instantly killing many thousands of Germans. The work of the 36th throughout this engagement was commented on and needs no mention here.

CAPT. F. H. TINGLEY, M.C.

In one day they brought up from the ammunition dump and fired over five thousand rounds of ammunition. For two weeks the gunners had practically no rest, while the drivers that could be spared from the wagon lines came up and assisted in getting ammunition ready. So active had the Battery become that the Hun determined to destroy it and made several attempts but without success. However on the night of the 24th of August, while the Battery was firing an S.O.S., in response to a call from the infantry, they were subjected to a very intense shelling with a new gas, afterwards known as mustard gas. This gas is very much of the nature of sulphuric acid, and the burns made by it are very similar. In a short time several men were struck by the shells, some wounded and some killed; others going to the assistance of their suffering comrades got the gas on their hands and were terribly burned. It was an awful night, and some very gallant deeds were done. The returns next day showed three killed, three officers and twenty-five others gassed. Some of the men who were gassed on that occasion never recovered from it. The effects will be with them as long as they live. It was a very bad night for the Canadian Artillery. Other Batteries suffered, some even more severely, but they received unstinted praise for the gallant way they stuck to their guns. Besides the above, the Battery suffered a great many other casualties while in the Hill 70 Sector. In addition to Lieutenants Teed and Fleet being gassed, Lieutenant Longworth was severely wounded. On the night of the 29th of August we were relieved by a British Battery, but the relief could not be completed in quiet, the Hun shelling the position very severely with gas.

We were all pleased to leave that vicinity, and our next position was on the Vimy Front, which was nice and quiet; and everybody had a very pleasant time until the 10th of October, when the Canadian Corps marched to Passchendaele, a trek that was undertaken with anything but light hearts, for its reputation as a death trap was known to all. On the 21st of October we took over from an English Battery, who were in a very bad way, having been practically shot to pieces. Everything was in very bad shape, only two guns being in action; but with great courage the boys set to work and very soon had the best position in the Salient. They protected their guns and themselves by the use of sand bags; and in that way saved many valuable lives. Conditions were such as to be almost impossible of description. The mud was up to one's knees, and the place seemed to be nothing but shell holes filled with water. The enemy had perfect observation on us from the village of Passchendaele. On the 24th of October we registered our guns on its church, and the battle started on the 26th. During the progress of the battle we were severely shelled, Gunner Ira Stewart, of Charlottetown, being instantly killed. All the gunners carried on very heroically notwithstanding the shelling, and the day ended with a great victory for the Canadians.

A few days later we had moved forward to a position in front of Kansas Cross, and in a short time had prepared a very fine position considering the materials at hand. The artillery programme was a very extensive one, firing starting at 5 o'clock in the morning and continuing at intervals several times through the day and night. The daily expenditure of the Battery ran well over one thousand rounds, and this had to be transported by pack mules a distance of eight miles from the ammunition dump. While on their way to

THE 36th BATTERY, C.F.A.

the guns they were subjected to scattered shelling and to bombing by overhead planes. At night they got no rest either at the guns, or the wagon lines, heavy bombing planes circling over the area and dropping their contents indiscriminately. The casualties of the Canadians in these terrible battles are well known, their sufferings are beyond description. No words of mine can adequately portray the courage, fortitude, cheerfulness and devotion to duty exemplified by the officers and men of the 36th Battery in the terrible battles which culminated in the capture of Passchendaele Ridge. Among the officers it would be unfair to particularize, for all did their part nobly; but I believe that I could speak of Lieut. Andrew Livingstone's three weeks' experience as a forward officer as being the most awful of the lot. Words could not picture the things he saw and what he went through. To Lieut. Chas. Shrieve, of Digby, I always gave the greatest credit for the resourcefulness he displayed in building the positions. For his gallant conduct he was awarded the Military Cross. Lieutenant Teed had previously received the same decoration for similar conduct at Hill 70.

On the 14th of November the most awful experience the Battery ever had was encountered. The night before the enemy had attempted a counter attack but the signal from the infantry had met with such instant response from the field artillery that his ranks were practically decimated. In retaliation he turned every gun he could command on the Batteries of field artillery in front of Kansas Cross. There were probably twenty English and Canadian Batteries within an area of three hundred yards; and on these at 1.30 in the afternoon was placed a bombardment that for intensity has probably never been excelled. Guns and ammunition were blown up at every volley, one entire Battery being wiped out, with all its personnel. The 36th received their share of the shelling, their dugouts being blown up and the gunners and officers buried beneath them. They had, however, suffered very few casualties considering the terrible ordeal passed through; but those who were placed at the guns on that day will never forget the experience.

On the 21st of November they moved out of Passchendaele, the Hun shelling the position just as they were leaving, and the succeeding Battery being practically annihilated within a few days.

A period of recuperation ensued, which did much to recover the morale of the Battery. In January they moved down into the Vimy Front, suffering the ordinary run of casualties, but without any very serious troubles. On the 21st of March, 1918, the Hun put on his famous offensive, and it was feared that he would attempt to take Vimy Ridge. As there was very little chance of getting the guns out if he broke through our infantry lines, it was decided to move the Batteries from the plain to the top of the Ridge, where they were put for defensive purposes. The 36th Battery was selected as a sacrifice Battery and were left in their position in front of Vimy. Their task was to harass the enemy as much as possible, their daily expenditure of ammunition running from a thousand to two thousand rounds. This activity of one Battery did not escape the alert attention of the Hun; and on the 28th of March, when he made his famous attack on Arras, a little to the south of Vimy, he took on the 36th Battery in great style. In three hours it was estimated by observers on the Ridge that over two thousand rounds were fired into the Battery. Guns and dugouts were blown up and a tremendous lot of damage done. Some brave deeds were carried out by members of the Battery, and among the decorations received for this affair were Military Medals by Sergeant Cashen, of Sydney, and Signaller MacKenzie and Bombardier Peter Laforte. All the members of the Battery acted most heroically. That night orders were given to retire the Battery from this untenable position, and in the new one they carried on with much more comfort.

About the 1st of May the Battery went into training for open warfare, and remained in training until July when they went into the line for a few weeks. On the 28th of July they were drawn from the line, and on the first of August started on the famous march to Amiens. The greatest secrecy was maintained regarding the destination of the Canadians, and it was not until the night of the 4th of August that we knew our destination. The nights of the 5th, 6th and 7th were utilized in bringing up thousands of rounds of ammunition and getting ready for the big battle which started on the 8th. The Battle of Amiens was the hand-writing on the wall, so General Ludendorff has told us. On that day the 36th Battery occupied six positions, giving the most splendid aid to our glorious

THE 36th BATTERY, C.F.A.

infantry. At half past four in the afternoon a German aeroplane swooped down on the Battery and killed several horses, wounded some of the men and Lieutenant Manning. The casualties would have been greater but for the bravery and coolness of the machine gunners, who poured a constant volley into the Hun and actually killed him, his plane crashing in a few minutes.

The Battle of Amiens continued for several days with constant advances. On the night of the 13th we were ordered to place three thousand rounds of ammunition in an advanced position for another Battery. Sergt. J. W. Boutillier was given charge of the unloading. While waiting for the arrival of the ammunition his party was subjected to heavy shell fire. Sergeant Boutillier and Sergeant Swift were killed and several others were wounded. Sergeant Boutillier was one of the most outstanding men in the entire Battery and his loss was very keenly felt. For his bravery on this occasion Corpl. A. J. McGillivary was awarded the Croix de Guerre.

On the 19th of August the Battery started on its march for the Battle of Arras, arriving at Arras on the night of the 23rd of August and going into position that same night. The night of the 24th was utilized in bringing up ammunition. On the 25th they rested. On the morning of the 26th the famous Battle of Arras opened. It was a day full of stirring incidents, the 36th Battery suffered severe casualties. The following days were very busy, the Battery constantly moving into new positions, shelling the enemy, and being shelled in return. On the morning of September 1st orders were received to cut wire on the Hindenburg line, and to expend upwards of four thousand rounds for that purpose. The position which the 36th Battery occupied was a very exposed one, and under observation by balloons and other means. The Battery had about completed one task when the enemy started to shell us very severely. At first the rounds fell short. Lieutenant Teed was at the telephone, and thinking that I did not receive the orders at the guns ran down to shout an order to No. 2 gun in charge of Sergeant McKay. Just as he got there an enemy shell landed, instantly killing Sergeant McKay, Gunner John Cornfoot and Lieutenant Teed. These were three of our very best, and the blow was

NOVA SCOTIA'S PART IN THE GREAT WAR

one of the saddest in the 36th Battery's whole experience. Lieut. Lionel Teed was from St. John, and had been with the Battery from its commencement. He was a brave officer, an extremely clever one, and loved by all. Sergeant McKay and Jack Cornfoot were also very popular. The wire cutting was completed. Notwithstanding the shelling the brave boys of the 36th carried on as though nothing had happened. The battle which took place the next day broke the Hindenburg line, the strongest trench fortification ever utilized in warfare.

LIEUT. D. L. TEED, M.C.

A succession of moves forward was then made. The Batteries kept close behind the infantry in their pursuit of the Hun. On the 14th a halt was made, and the Batteries transferred to another section of the Front. They took up a position in the village of Sudemont, which was a very "hot" place, being almost constantly under shell fire. A number of casualties occurred when we were in this position, notably Corpl. John McSween, who lost a leg, and Sergeant Philpott and others. On the 17th the Battery started for the Battle of Cambrai, arriving in that sector on the evening of the 18th. The nights of the 19th and 20th were used in bringing up ammunition to a position in the little town of Inchy, where a battery position had been selected. The ammunition could only be drawn up under the greatest difficulties, for the roads were under heavy shell fire. Some very gallant deeds were done by the drivers and those in charge of them. For one particularly gallant exploit Corpl. A. Morrison received the D.C.M.

The morning of the 21st was beautiful and the battle was wonderfully successful. Before ten o'clock thousands of yards of enemy territory had been penetrated and Bourlon Wood captured. The enemy field artillery recovered and shelled us vigorously, and we suffered several casualties. The battle continued for several days, with constant gain of territory for us. On the night of the 28th, while Lieutenant Livingstone was unloading ammunition, his drivers and the gunners were subjected to heavy shell fire and we

THE 36th BATTERY, C.F.A.

had many regrettable casualties; among the drivers, Frank Hughes, of Charlottetown, and Driver George McDonald, of Sydney. George was one of the most wonderful guides in France, and his loss was a severe one. The next few days saw several moves of positions, and on the 5th of October the 36th Battery was in a position at Raillencourt. On the evening of October 7th orders were issued for the Battery to move up to a position in the rear of St. Olle. The six guns with ammunition and ammunition wagons arrived at the position and were starting to unlimber when a volley of German shells landed directly in them. The casualties were terrific. over 50 per cent. of those present being killed or wounded together with twenty horses. The whole thing occupied only a few minutes, but it saddened a great many hearts. Lieut. Chas. Shrieve was shot through the chest and died instantly. Captain Craig was severely wounded through the hip. Lieutenant Livingstone was wounded in two places and his ankle broken. Twenty-eight N.C.O.'s and men were killed or wounded. Among the killed was the very popular Bombardier John Drysdale. The blow was a demoralizing one, but the undaunted courage of the remaining members of the 36th was equal to the task. Within three hours the guns had been transferred to new positions, and lines of fire laid out, and the Battery ready for action.

CAPT. CHAS. D. 'SHRIEVE, M.C.

The Hill 70 gas episode and the shelling received the night of October the 7th were two of the worst experiences that any Battery had ever been called upon to endure, but the brave boys of the 36th met both with unflinching courage and proved themselves worthy of all the encomiums which had been bestowed upon them. For gallant work on this occasion several members of the Battery were decorated. On the 10th of October Cambrai was captured, the 36th Battery doing its share to make the battle a success.

From Cambrai they moved northward again, occupying various positions with various degrees of fortune until November 1st, when the march towards Mons commenced. This was one long succession of triumphs, culminating in the capture of the celebrated city on the morning of the 11th of November. On the afternoon of the 10th we were in position at Je-Mappes, about one thousand yards from Mons. At 3.30 in the afternoon orders were received to fire on the railway at Mons, and while engaged in doing that several enemy shells were fired into the Battery, one of which instantly killed Lieut. Fred Longworth, of Charlottetown, and wounded Sergeant Dickson and several others. Sergeant Dickson received thirty-two wounds but managed to pull through. On the morning of the 11th at 6.30 word was received that the Armistice was signed, and a March-Past was ordered to take place in the City of Mons. There was great rejoicing at the good news, inasmuch as the suffering of the last three months was beginning to tell on the remaining members of the "Old Guard."

LT. F. J. LONGWORTH, M.C.

I cannot close this account of the doings of the 36th Battery without making reference to the wonderful qualities which the officers, N.C.O.'s and men displayed. It was easy to command a Battery like the 36th. They were everything that could be desired. Loyal, brave and good-humored, with the greatest devotion to duty, they cannot be too highly praised by me. Every man was a hero and every man deserved decorations many times over. I feel that it is but fitting that I should here mention the fact, when speaking about decorations, that the 36th Battery received a very large share of them, including one D.S.O., two Croix de Guerre, eight Military Crosses, one bar for Military Cross, ten D.C.M.'s and twenty Military Medals.

On November 21, 1918, Major D. A. MacKinnon, who commanded the 36th Battery from its arrival in France on July 14, 1916, and who took part with the Battery in all its battles, was granted sick leave to Canada.

The loss of so many brave officers and brave men had been a severe shock to him, and his nerves became greatly unstrung. It

THE 36th BATTERY, C.F.A.

was with sincere regret that he parted with the boys after nearly three years of strenuous fighting. The Battery, after a short stay in Belgium, was transferred to England, demobilizing in March, 1919. On the 36th Battery's return to Sydney, N.S., they were tendered a most notable reception.

LIST OF OFFICERS WHO SERVED WITH THE 36TH BATTERY IN FRANCE, WITH DECORATIONS RECEIVED.

Major D. A. MacKinnon, Charlottetown, P.E.I.... Distinguished Service Order and Croix de Guerre.
Capt. F. H. Tingley (killed), Moncton .... Military Cross.
Capt. A. L. Anderson, Toronto .... Military Cross and Bar.
Lieut. D. L. Teed (killed), St. John, N.B. .... Military Cross.
Lieut. C. D. Shrieve (killed), Digby, N.S. .... Military Cross.
Lieut. R. Fleet, Montreal .... Military Cross.
Lieut. F. J. Longworth (killed), Charlottetown..... Military Cross.
Lieut. J. W. L. Harris, Moncton, N.B. .... Military Cross.
Lieut. A. B. Manning, Toronto .... Military Cross.
Lieut. A. Livingstone, Sydney, N.S. .... Military Cross.
Lieut. I. Alexander, Fredericton, N.B. .... Military Cross.
Lieut. J. O'Grady, Winnipeg ....

CHAPTER VIII.

14th BRIGADE, C.F.A.

THE 14th Brigade, C.F.A., was organized in the spring of 1916 and was part of the 4th Division Artillery, which trained at Petawawa in the summer of 1916. The 14th Brigade, under the command of Lieut.-Colonel John L. McKinnon, of Halifax, N.S., was composed of the following Units: Headquarters, 7 officers, 40 men, recruited in Nova Scotia. Batteries, 55th and 56th, recruited in Guelph, Ont.; 58th, recruited in New Brunswick; 66th, recruited in Montreal. Brigade Ammunition Column, 3 officers, 120 men, recruited in Nova Scotia.

LT.-COL. J. L. M'KINNON.

In addition to the O.C., Lieutenant-Colonel McKinnon, the following other Nova Scotia officers proceeded Overseas with this Brigade: Capt. G. C. Oland, Halifax, Adjutant; Capt. C. V. Trites, Liverpool, Medical Officer, both attached to Brigade Headquarters; Major S. C. Oland, in command of 66th Battery; Lieut. J. Vickery, 58th Battery; Brigade Ammunition Column, Capt. F. S. Burns, Lieut. Herbert Stairs, Lieut. W. M. Ray, Lieut. T. D. Farquahar.

The 4th Divisional Artillery, consisting of the 12th, 13th, 14th and 15th Brigades, and Divisional Ammunition Column, left Canada on September 11, 1916, and completed training in England.

In the fall of 1916 the Imperial authorities for the Imperial Army adopted the formation of six-gun Batteries instead of four-gun Batteries, reducing Brigades in each Division. The Canadian authorities followed in January, 1917, and from the 1st, 2nd and

14th BRIGADE, C.F.A.

3rd Divisions in France a new 4th Divisional Artillery was reconstituted, and the old 4th Divisional Artillery became 5th Divisional Artillery, which later became Corps Artillery.

On the formation of the Nova Scotia Regimental Depot, Lieutenant-Colonel McKinnon was given command and was later appointed Deputy Judge Advocate General, Canadian Forces Overseas.

CHAPTER IX.

THE ROYAL CANADIAN REGIMENT.

THE Royal Canadian Regiment was raised on December 21, 1883, as a Unit of the new Canadian Permanent Force, for the instruction of the Canadian Militia by establishing schools of instruction for officers and non-commissioned officers, and by the formation of a nucleus of officers and non-commissioned officer instructors to assist at the various Militia Camps. The Regiment was first known as the "Infantry School Corps."

In 1885 "C" Company, stationed at Toronto, joined a mixed force of Militia under the command of Lieut.-Col. W. D. Otter, which marched across the ice along the North Shore of Lake Superior to the North-West, to suppress the rebellion of the half-breeds, under the leadership of Louis Riel. The Company took part in the action of Fish Creek and the relief of Battleford on April 24th, and in the action of Cut Knife Hill on May 2nd. It also took part in the pursuit of Chief Big Bear during June and July. It remained in garrison at Battleford from July until October, when it returned to Toronto. This was the first occasion on which Canadian troops had conducted active operations and brought them to a successful conclusion without the aid of Imperial troops.

In 1892 the name of the Regiment was changed to the "Canadian Regiment Infantry," and the following year Queen Victoria approved of the Regiment becoming a Royal Regiment, known as the "Royal Canadian Regiment of Canadian Infantry," and granted permission for her Imperial Cypher, V.R.I., with the Imperial Crown, to be worn as a badge.

In 1899, on the outbreak of the South African War, a second (Special Service) Battalion was raised under the command of Lieut.-Colonel W. D. Otter, and sailed on October 30, 1899, in the *S.S. Sardinian*, arriving at Cape Town on November 30th. In

THE ROYAL CANADIAN REGIMENT

addition to minor skirmishes the Battalion took part in the following actions while in South Africa:

Paardeberg	27th February,	1900
Poplar Grove	7th March,	1900
Dreifontein	10th March,	1900
Israel's Poort	25th April,	1900
Hont's Nek	1st May,	1900
Zano River	16th May,	1900
Doorn Kop	29th May,	1900
Pretoria	4th June,	1900

The casualties in South Africa were thirty-nine killed, twenty-eight died of disease, one hundred and twenty-three wounded.

The Battalion was represented at the annexation ceremony at Pretoria on October 25th by a party specially selected, and on November 7th it embarked at Cape Town for Southampton, arriving on November 29th. The Battalion was inspected by Her Majesty Queen Victoria at Windsor Castle, when she addressed them and thanked them for their services. This was the last official inspection made by the Queen before her death.

On December 11th the Battalion embarked at Liverpool and sailed for Canada, arriving at Halifax on December 23rd, where it was disbanded.

During the South African War the name of the Regiment was changed to the "Royal Canadian Regiment of Infantry." His Majesty King George, then Duke of York, presented colors to the Regiment at Toronto on October 11, 1901, during his tour of the British Empire.

A 3rd (Garrison) Battalion of the Regiment was raised at Halifax to release the 1st Battalion Leinster Regiment (Royal Canadians) for service elsewhere. This Battalion was brought to a high state of efficiency and formed the greater part of the Garrison in the Fortress at Halifax. It was, however, disbanded shortly after being relieved by an Imperial Regiment, the 5th Battalion Royal Garrison Regiment, in September, 1902.

In 1902 the name of the Regiment was once again changed, becoming known by its present distinctive title of "The Royal Canadian Regiment."

In 1904, a special banner, given by His Majesty King Edward VII to commemorate the Regiment's services in South Africa, was presented at Ottawa on October 4th by His Excellency the Governor-General, Lord Minto.

Imperial troops having been withdrawn and the defence of Canada taken over by local troops, the Regiment moved to Halifax, the establishment being raised to ten companies.

On the outbreak of the European War in August, 1914, the Regiment was mobilized at Halifax, occupying the various forts. It was brought up to war strength by a draft of four hundred volunteers, men from the newly formed Camp at Valcartier, for the Expeditionary Force then being raised. Being trained regular troops, and the only ones available for service Overseas, the Regiment, under the command of Lieut.-Colonel A. O. Fages, was sent to Bermuda on September 9th to relieve the 2nd Battalion Lincolnshire Regiment, and were the first Canadian troops to go abroad. In August of the following year, the Regiment having been relieved by the 38th Battalion, C.E.F., proceeded, under the command of Lieut.-Colonel Carpenter, to France, via England, where it was re-armed and re-equipped. It landed at Boulogne, under the command of Lieut.-Col. A. H. Macdonell, D.S.O., on October 31st, and on moving up the line immediately became Corps Troops to the Canadian Corps under Lieut.-General Sir A. E. H. Alderson, K.C.B. It went into the trenches for the first time with the First Canadian Division, opposite Messines.

At the beginning of 1916 it was one of the Battalions composing the 7th Canadian Infantry Brigade under Brigadier-General A. C. Macdonell, C.M.G., D.S.O., of the newly formed 3rd Canadian Division, under Major-General Mercer, C.B. The Brigade consisted of the Royal Canadian Regiment, Princess Patricia's Canadian Light Infantry, 42nd Battalion (Royal Highlanders of Canada) and 49th Battalion (Edmonton Regiment), and, later, the 7th Canadian Machine Gun Company. The Regiment went into the line with the Brigade at Wulvergham, moving afterward to Kemmel and then to Ypres.

The Regiment's first general action was that of the German attack on June 2nd to June 5th on Sanctuary Wood and Hooge, in the Ypres Salient. Here the Regiment, under Lieut.-Col. C. H. Hill, distinguished itself by its steadiness under the heaviest concentration of hostile artillery and trench mortar fire which up to that date had ever been brought to bear on British troops. By its rifle and machine gun fire the attempted infantry assaults against its lines were frustrated, and it was virtually the action of the machine guns, assisted by the 7th Canadian Machine Gun Company, that prevented a great disaster to the whole Ypres Salient. These guns had been unable to get away after being relieved on account of dawn breaking. On June 5th the Germans blew up three very large mines at Hooge, annihilating the Garrison. The guns, which were some distance in the rear, immediately mounted, fully exposed, on the Menin Road, and by their coolly directed fire threw back the German Infantry, thus preventing them from swamping our line and outflanking it both north and south on the Menin Road. The action of June 2nd to 5th exemplified the value of long training. The older men who had been in the Regiment for years, and who were considered as almost past their day, came to the fore wonderfully by their steadiness and discipline. This was shown particularly when during the hostile infantry attacks and intense shelling they remained cool and steady and withheld their fire, only letting forth their perfect deluge of bullets when a good target appeared. This encouraged and gave added confidence to the younger men. It was certainly the old soldier's day.

Between June and August some extremely gallant trench raids and expeditions were carried out by the Regiment. One raid carried out was discovered by the enemy before starting, and came under intense fire from rifles, bombs and machine guns at close quarters. In spite of this the party rushed forward and inflicted heavy losses upon the enemy, but every man except one was wounded. Two officers and some men came out into the open and worked for two hours under fire collecting and bringing in the wounded.

In September the Regiment moved south with the Canadian Corps under Lieut.-General Sir Julian H. G. Byng, K.C.B., K.C.M.G., M.V.O., to the Somme, where until November they took part in very severe fighting at Courcellette, Regina Trench, and elsewhere.

The Battalion performed a very difficult feat on September 15th, when it came up from reserve and occupied a line just after dusk over absolutely strange ground, made unrecognisable by shell fire, and in so doing was obliged to change front twice. They occupied their position on time. Again, on September 16th, two Companies went forward to attack an enemy trench over open ground, in full view of the enemy, in face of deadly rifle and machine gun fire, starting at a distance of over 800 yards and being practically wiped out when less than 50 yards from the enemy's trench.

On October 8th, at Regina Trench, the R.C.R. and one other Battalion were the only Canadian Battalions to capture and for the time hold objectives. There by its gallantry and determination the Battalion held on throughout the day outflanked and unsupported. A Battalion of German Marines was threatening the left, which necessitated a change of front. This was successfully accomplished. The enemy charged the position on three separate occasions, but were driven back with heavy loss each time. This, however, was accomplished only by heavy loss to the Battalion, for, when relieved, it mustered only one officer and eighty-one other ranks: in one Company only five men remained.

On leaving the Somme area the Regiment was so depleted that it was obliged to reorganize. The fighting had been of the bitterest hand-to-hand kind.

The following order was published on leaving the area:

"7th Canadian Infantry Brigade.

"This Brigade has just finished a series of operations of which every member may be justly proud.

"The performance of the 15th September, 1916, when the R.C.R., P.P.C.L.I., 42nd and 49th Battalions, went into an unknown area on four and a half hours' notice, in broad daylight, and under heavy shelling, reached and jumped off on time, not from prepared assembly trenches, but from a battered trench captured that morning, and, changing direction twice, captured and held three different objectives, together with some three hundred prisoners, has been characterized as one of the finest accomplishments by any Brigade in the war.

"No one as time goes on can fail to be more and more impressed with the extent to which each arm of the military machine is dependent upon others for ultimate and lasting success; a Brigade may do better than ever before, and still fail to gain their objective, owing to another arm not having fully accomplished its task.

"The attack on September 16th, 1916, adds to, rather than dims, the glory. Both the R.C.R. and the 42nd Battalion (R.H.C.) knew the barrage had failed, that the Zollern Trench was fully manned, and that the chances of success were slight. Notwithstanding, the attacking companies of these Battalions did their duty, knowing that the attack of the 9th Canadian Infantry Brigade, timed for 6.30 p.m., depended entirely on their capturing their objective. They thrust the attack home gallantly

THE ROYAL CANADIAN REGIMENT

and well, but, under the circumstances, with the odds so heavily against them, it was impossible to make good the Zollern Trench.

"On the 8th October, 1916, Regina Trench was not battered in nor the wire cut, but we all have good reason to be proud of the performance of our Battalions that day—the R.C.R. and 49th Battalion for their attack, the P.P.C.L.I. for their good work in the vacated front line, and the 42nd Battalion (R.H.C.) for cheerfully going in again to take over the defence of the line, although they had been withdrawn a few hours before and were desperately tired. The Machine Gun Company also comes in for its share of the well-earned praise for its excellent barrage work and support of the Infantry.

"We all feel particularly proud of the splendid work of the R.C.R. in driving through to their objective and holding it so long against odds. No one could have done better and few so well.

"A. C. MACDONELL, Brig.-Gen.,
"Comd'g. 7th Canadian Infantry Brigade.

"15-10-16."

In November the Battalion moved north again to Neuville St. Vaast, nothing of much importance happening with the exception of raids. These commenced after Christmas and became almost a daily occurrence. Daring deeds of all degrees were performed by all ranks, with the result that the Battalion was morally and actually master of the situation and owned " No Man's Land."

On April 9, 1917, the Battle of Vimy Ridge commenced. This was one of the most perfectly planned actions that has ever occurred. Every man knew exactly what he had to do and how to do it, and where he was to go. The strong ridge which the Germans had held and fortified to the best of their ability fell into our hands with comparative ease. Many trophies were captured by the Regiment, and all their objectives were taken without any delay or hitch of any kind. This was accomplished in bitter weather and mud knee deep; the ground captured was held intact in spite of the furious and continued attacks launched by the enemy to wrest our gains from us.

After Vimy the Regiment took part in the following major actions:—Avion, June, 1917; Hill 70, July, 1917; Passchendaele, October and November, 1917 (in the latter period eleven hostile attacks were successfully repelled); Amiens, 1918, where the Regiment was on the extreme right successfully operating with the French; Monchy, August, 1918; Cambrai, where Lieut. M. F. Gregg won his V.C.; Forêt de Raisines, Valenciennes; and last, but not least, the dramatic capture of the world famous Mons. The credit for the first to enter Mons has been claimed by the 42nd Battalion. This is a moot point, and is probably due to the fact that a Company of the Royal Canadian Regiment was detached to the 42nd and entered the City from the S.E. The indubitable fact remains that Lieut. W. M. King of the R.C.R. was the first to reach the square, where he was received by the Mayor at the Town Hall with his platoon, and where he signed the Golden Book of Mons, which was given by King Albert to the City on his departure in 1914.

The Regiment returned to Canada and the C.E.F. personnel was demobilized at Halifax on 10th March, 1919.

The following distinctions and awards were gained by the Regiment in the war of 1914-18:—

V.C.	1	M.M.	128
G.B.E.	1	Bar to M.M.	10
C.M.G.	4	M.S.M.	10
C.B.E.	1	Foreign Decorations	15
D.S.O.	11	Mentions	35
O.B.E.	5	Commissions from the ranks:	
M.C.	37	Lieut.-Colonel	1
Bar to M.C.	5	Major	5
D.F.C.	1	Captain	14
D.C.M.	24	Lieutenant	28
Bar to D.C.M.	1	2nd Lieutenant	4

CHAPTER X.

THE 17th BATTALION, C.E.F.

WHEN war clouds lowered on the European horizon in July, 1914, it would have been strange had the men of Pictou County, Nova Scotia, not been among the first to recognize their duty to civilization and the Empire.

On July 31, 1914, the officer commanding the 78th Regiment Pictou Highlanders wired the then Minister of Militia of Canada that his Regiment was ready for service, and received a reply, dated August 1, 1914, expressing the Minister's thanks for the patriotic offer. On August 8th orders were received by wire from the Adjutant-General, Ottawa, as follows: " It is notified for information that not more than 125 men with officers will be accepted from each rural Regiment." This order limited volunteering in Nova Scotian rural corps at once to that number.

On August 20, 1914, 135 officers, non-commissioned officers and other ranks left New Glasgow for Valcartier, being joined at Truro by a full quota of officers, non-commissioned officers and other ranks of the 76th Colchester Rifles and small detachments of the 63rd and 66th Halifax Regiments, a Company from the 75th Lunenburg Regiment under Lieut.-Colonel Andrews, and one from 69th. Passing through Cumberland County the Nova Scotian contingent was further augmented by a roll of officers, non-commissioned officers and men, up to the strength authorized, from the 93rd Cumberland Regiment, with their O.C., Lieut.-Colonel Murray, making in all a total of some five hundred officers, non-commissioned officers and other ranks.

LIEUT.-COL. STRUAN G. ROBERTSON.

NOVA SCOTIA'S PART IN THE GREAT WAR

Had each of the seven Nova Scotia Regiments of Militia been able to send the number authorized the contingent would have been little short of strength as a Regiment. Ottawa had apparently overlooked the fact that both the Halifax Regiments and the 94th of Cape Breton were on garrison duty, making it difficult for them to recruit beyond their then imperative needs or part with the number required.

It was then proposed by the officers on board the troop train that steps be taken to form a Nova Scotian Battalion, so that all might serve together. The three senior officers of the contingent, Lieut.-Colonels Andrews, Cameron and Murray asked Lieut.-Col. S. G. Robertson to undertake the organization and ask that he be given command. Although he had specialized as far as possible in Staff work and felt his services would be of more value in that line than in Regimental duty, the request was difficult of refusal and the proposal was accepted.

From the time of arrival in Valcartier the Nova Scotians remained together until a wire was received from the Minister authorizing the organization of the Battalion. Unfortunately an excessive advertising of the Unit by a too friendly press in Halifax aroused Provincial jealousies and no doubt made fulfilment of the authorization difficult. It undoubtedly made it appear to outsiders that the Nova Scotian officers were doing a lot of advertising, an opinion that was far from the truth. Time dragged on; a few officers and men losing heart joined other Battalions; but their number was small and all had the best reasons for doing so. In most cases it meant promotion.

Shortly before the day of sailing, the raising of two new Units was authorized by Headquarters, to be numbered the 17th and 18th Battalions; and the personnel of the officers was published, which included one, if not two, of the senior Nova Scotian officers. Recruiting, however, showed that there were no available rank and file apart from the Nova Scotians, who, however, absolutely refused to join without their own officers. As all prospect of a Nova Scotian Battalion seemed to have vanished, therefore in order to get the men to join one of the new Units, after consultation with the men Lieut.-Colonel Robertson offered his services as Paymaster in that Unit.

THE 17th BATTALION, C.E.F.

Hardly had his services been accepted by the Officer Commanding than the Premier arrived in Camp and called a meeting of the Nova Scotian officers for the following morning. At the meeting two proposals were made to the officers, who were asked to consider them and report their decision at a later hour. The proposals were to go then as a half Battalion or remain behind to be properly organized and sail later. The meeting of officers decided without dissent that to remain until properly organized was the only course open, in view of the shortness of time and lack of so much that was necessary.

On this report being made to the Premier he stated that it had been decided to send us as a Battalion with the First Contingent, to allow us to recruit as far as possible and if necessary to send drafts later to complete our establishment. The colors of the Battalion were then presented by Lady Borden, with appropriate ceremony.

Within three days sufficient men had been recruited in Cape Breton, Pictou, Colchester and Cumberland Counties practically to complete the strength of a Regiment.

The Premier was no longer in Camp, and transport was refused. Possibly, the momentarily expected sailing of the First Contingent made it impractical, and the Battalion sailed from Quebec on September 30, 1914, with a full strength of officers and non-commissioned officers and 773 other ranks, unbrigaded under strength and under-equipped, but with hearts burning with loyalty, on board the *S.S. Ruthenia*.

Just one hundred and twenty-nine years before the ancestors of many of these men had been disbanded from the 82nd Highlanders in Halifax and given grants of land comprising 20,000 acres in Pictou County. The Regiment had been raised in Perthshire by Col. Alexander Robertson of Struan, then Chief of Clan Donnachie, and was commanded by him. Now commanded by one of the same race and family they were returning to do their part in the world's tragedy.

The nominal roll of officers was as follows: Lieut.-Col. Struan G. Robertson; Majors, Daniel D. Cameron and Daniel Murray; Adjutant, Capt. Charles E. Bent; Asst.-Adjutant, Lieut. L. Ray Cutten.

Captains: W. H. Allen, L. C. Bentley, W. B. Coulter, Alex. Watson, D. C. Sheppard, W. Forbes, Thos. Curwen Reid.

Lieutenants: G. W. Harris, F. M. Bentley, F. M. McDonald, J. E. Christie, E. W. Mingo, C. J. Groggett, J. M. Gillis, Bruce Donald, A. N. Peerless, R. E. Russell, G. A. Ross, G. E. C. Eager, Norman McKee, J. R. Bell, Alister Fraser, Arthur Hunt Chute, B. J. Walker, A. Marlow.

Paymaster, Hon. Capt. Arthur McKay; Quartermaster, Hon. Capt. Robert McMeekin; Medical Officer, Capt. H. Morrell; Chaplain, Paul Goforth; Transport Officer, C. Hamilton Catty.

For five months the Battalion saw service on Salisbury Plain as a Unit. No drafts arrived to bring the Battalion up to strength, but it was attached to one Brigade after another. Some one has said that the ardor of the Highlander springs from internal sentiment, and that the only thing his spirit cannot brook is disappointment.

It has ever been seemingly fated that governments failed to appreciate this characteristic of Scottish soldiers. Broken faith, real or supposed, caused rebellion in even the Black Watch in 1743. In 1795, when it was proposed to break up the Cameron Highlanders by drafting, their Colonel told the Duke of York, then O. in C., " To draft the 79th is more than you or your Royal father dare do!" The Duke of York replied: "The King, my father, will certainly send the Regiment to the West Indies." Colonel Cameron thereupon losing his temper warmly rejoined: " You may tell the King, your father, from me, that he may send us to h—l if he likes, and I'll go at the head of them, but he daurna draft us."

Attempts were made to draft the men of the 17th but as they had been enlisted over three months the Army Act made such procedure illegal, unless voluntary, and the protest of the Officer Commanding, after threatened proceedings, was effectual.

Four Battalions of the First Canadian Contingent, including the 17th, were then made into Reserve Battalions, and the non-commissioned officers and other ranks were drafted into the First Division to make up for the wastage suffered during its sojourn on Salisbury Plain, which then through sickness, desertion and the obtaining of commissions in the Imperial Forces was equivalent to

THE 17th BATTALION, C.E.F.

about ten per cent. of the original total strength of the First Contingent.

As a Reserve Battalion the 17th served throughout the War and practically all Nova Scotian Infantry Drafts passed at one time or another through its ranks. From it were drawn the drafts for the Highland Brigade 1st Division, and latterly those for Nova Scotia Infantry Units in the Field. As a Reserve it outlived many of its enemies.

Of the gallant hearts that left Nova Scotia in August, 1914, many have paid the price and sleep their last sleep on alien soil.

> "And, when the last Great Bugle Call
> *O'er Vimy sounding, throbs,*
> When the last grim joke is entered
> In the big black book of Jobs,
> *And Belgic battlefields give up*
> Their victims to the air,
> I shouldn't like to be the man
> *That played those men unfair."*

CHAPTER XI.

THE 25th BATTALION.

BY CAPT. G. C. M'ELHENNY.

IN endeavoring to write this brief account of the organization, training and operations of the first Battalion of Nova Scotians to be raised and equipped in their own Province and also the first from these "the sea-girt hills and vales," which have contributed more than their quota of soldiers, sailors, statesmen, educators and men of affairs in the past, to man the trenches in France and Flanders, the writer regrets and wishes it understood that he is not writing from personal observations, inasmuch as (and this is what he regrets) he was not a member of the 25th Battalion until the spring of 1917. The substance, then, of the following is compiled from the War Diary of the 25th Canadian Infantry Battalion, and is submitted to the publishers of this volume at their request and with the fullest appreciation of the writer's inability to do justice to the task of chronicling four and a half years of any Battalion's history, least of all the splendid story of the indomitable courage and tenacious striving toward an ideal which were the predominant features of this, in several respects, an unique Battalion in the Canadian Corps.

There are many omissions in the following narrative which the writer regrets are imperative in order to make it of sufficient brevity to allow of its publication in this volume. The nominal roll of officers is as issued by the Department of Militia and Defence on the Battalion's sailing from Halifax on May 20, 1915. The summary of decorations awarded was provided by the Adjutant-General, Canadian Militia, Ottawa, and does not include the medals won by General Hilliam, C.B., and several other

THE 25th BATTALION

officers and some other ranks when with Units other than the 25th Battalion.

It will be interesting to note in the list of original 2nd Division officers who marched across the Rhine at Bonn on December 13, 1918, that only two were commissioned officers on September 15, 1915. They are Major A. W. P. Weston and Lieut. G. M. McNeil, M.C. There were ninety-six other ranks with the Battalion on both the above-mentioned dates.

In the narrative there are many points on which the writer would like to dilate at some length—more especially on some of the deeds of heroism in the different actions. Of these deeds, practically in the earlier days (1915 and 1916), more went unrecognized outside the Battalion than the sum of all the decorations won by the Battalion. To mention more than the few that fit into the narrative is obviously not feasible.

One thing that cheered the 25th Battalion through all their long service in France was the pipe band under Pipe-Major Carson. Major J. W. Logan was responsible for the organization and equipment of this fine band. There was nothing better in the armies in France.

In pursuance of the Canadian Government's scheme to raise a Second Division for service Overseas, Lieut.-Col. G. A. Lecain (69th Regiment), of Roundhill, Annapolis County, was authorized to mobilize the 25th Battalion, Canadian Infantry, in Nova Scotia (October, 1914). Lieut.-Colonel Lecain established headquarters at the Armories, Halifax, and opened recruiting offices in Sydney, Amherst, New Glasgow, Truro and Yarmouth. Recruiting commenced late in October, 1914. The official nominal roll of officers who received appointments to the Battalion is published here and to them is due the credit of the splendid organization and training which enabled these sons of New Scotland to rank second to none with the flower of the British Armies. Mention should also be made of the fine' non-commissioned officers of the Battalion, and those loaned by the Permanent Force, who attended to the details of training with most commendable zeal.

It should be remembered that this was Nova Scotia's first attempt at recruiting and organizing a full Battalion for service in the Great War, and the facilities for the proper fulfilment of such a task were far from perfect. In view of this then Nova Scotians should be, and, I think, are, unanimous in their praise of Lieut.-Colonel Lecain and all ranks of his Battalion for his organizing and so quickly training a Unit which, though many times decimated and only a skeleton of a Battalion left, quickly and smoothly absorbed its reinforcements and carried on with renewed energy and greater deeds toward the high ideal of service for home and humanity.

LIEUT.-COL. G. A. LECAIN.

The writer has often had it suggested to him that it was a pity the deeds of the 25th Battalion were not better known by the people at home. The reply to such a suggestion, on behalf of the Battalion is this: The reputation of the 25th Battalion was safe in the hands of our comrades throughout the Canadian Corps, and our exploits in raiding were the marvel of two armies. These exploits and deeds with their inevitable accompaniment of blood and death were not fit subjects to press-agent into the already over-wrought family circles, which were possibly in receipt of one of those missiles of despair and death—an "official telegram from Ottawa." We gloried in the encomiums of the Brigade, Divisional, Corps and Army Commanders, and still more in the hearty praise of our comrades in the " Y " or the canteens or estaminets. But no one thought of sending an account home. And why? Well, there were a good many Bills, and Jocks, and Toms and so on, who "went west" in that scrap. And what's the use of making it realistic to Mary and Nora and Bessie? "No, Pard, we would rather not."

And there we will leave it and endeavor to adhere to a resolution to make this brief sketch statistically correct.

Before Christmas Day, 1914, the Battalion was at full strength and had the authorized ten per cent. reserve in training in the Armories at Halifax and later on the Common. In April the people of Nova Scotia presented the Battalion with two fine field kitchens and $2,500, the ceremony taking place at the Provincial

THE 25th BATTALION

Building, in front of the whole Battalion on parade and a vast concourse of people.

As evidence of the fine spirit which animated the whole Battalion the following is copied from the official War Diary: " A University Reinforcement Company of the P.P.C.L.I. arrived in the city to embark for England, and the 25th Battalion was called on to supply seven men to bring it up to strength. The Battalion was formed up on the Common and an invitation extended for any who wished to go Overseas at once in this draft to take one pace forward. The whole Battalion, to a man, stepped forward making it necessary to search the records and select seven ex-Imperial service men. Privates Aldridge, Baker, Conroy, Cumberland, Erickson, Kehoe and Leonard were selected."

On sailing for England aboard *H.M.T.S. Saxonia* (Captain Charles, R.N.) on May 20, 1915, Haligonians and many from other points in the Province witnessed many a moving spectacle as bright countenances fought the dimming influence of heavy hearts as they wished the boys of the 25th Godspeed on their journey, and victory in the fight; leaving their safe return or immortalization in the hands of the Creator who deals justly and well in all things. With the 25th Battalion on board the *Saxonia* were those gallant sons of Quebec, the 22nd Battalion. No account of the doings of the 25th Battalion could do justice to its purpose without paying tribute to those noble French-Canadians who were continually associated with the 25th Battalion from embarkation at Halifax on May 20, 1915, to debarkation at the same port on May 16, 1919. Surely there is a lesson for our politicians and religious bigots in the close co-operation which marked the attitude of these two Battalions toward each other throughout the period of their association. Our brave comrades of the 22nd Battalion showed us that the French-Canadian was not only generous in sympathy but quick to collaborate with his fellow Canadians of British descent on the broad principle of national welfare. In battle, in sports, or in argument over the estaminet tables, proof of the whole-hearted camaraderie between the 22nd and 25th Battalions was daily evident and fostered by both Units.

The *Saxonia* docked at Devonport on May 29, 1915, and her valuable human cargo took trains for Westenhanger, in Kent County,

NOVA SCOTIA'S PART IN THE GREAT WAR

where they detrained in the middle of the night and marched to East Sandling Camp, in the Shorncliffe area, to which the 2nd Canadian Division had been assigned for the period of their intensive training.

While this training was being carried out the Battalion took part in Divisional Reviews by H.M. the King, Earl Kitchener, Lieut-General Sir Sam Hughes and General Steele, as well as one in honor of the visit to the area by the Premier of Canada, Sir Robert Borden, and Brigade and Training Inspectors. The 25th Battalion was now a Unit of the 5th (Eastern Canada) Brigade, 2nd Canadian Division, which consisted of four Battalions and details (22nd, 24th, 25th and 26th) drawn from Quebec, Montreal, Nova Scotia and New Brunswick. The Brigade Commander was Lieut.-Colonel (now Major-General) Sir David Watson, and Major-General R. W. Turner, V.C., was Divisional Commander.

After three and a half months of eight hours' training per day, with four hours of practice in night operations frequently, the 2nd Division was ordered to France. The 25th Battalion proceeded by boat from Folkestone to Boulogne on the night of September 15, 1915, and by train on the following day from Pont de Brieques, a few kilometres from Boulogne, to a small station near St. Omer. From here to the front line was the first real test of the Battalion's *morale* and physical condition. Marching for five days with new (Kitchener's) boots over French and Belgian cobblestone roads, the Battalion relieved the King's Own Regiment on the night of the 22nd-23rd of September, 1915, the first Nova Scotia Battalion to face the Hun as a Unit. And not a man had dropped out in the gruelling grind of the last four days. The writer has been told, unofficially, that this was a record for the Division, and though it has never been confirmed, neither has it been denied.

The first few tours in the front lines were spent in the H and I trenches, Kemmel Sector of the Ypres Salient, where the Hun was very active in mining operations. During the Battalion's second tour, which extended over six days, Fritz blew one large and three smaller mines on "B" Company, which killed twelve and wounded twenty, leaving a crater 65 feet by 35 feet and 25 feet deep. This resulted in no advantage to the enemy, inasmuch as the charge was situated so that it must have done considerable damage to his trenches, and the crater was promptly garrisoned by Nova Scotians.

Late in October, 1915, Major E. Hilliam, a 1st Division officer, succeeded Lieut.-Colonel Lecain in command of the Battalion; and, under his soldierly guidance, the 25th began to make the Bosche sit up and notice his surroundings. Under Major (as O.C., Lieut.-Colonel) Hilliam's guidance the Battalion became expert in the little tricks which worried the enemy and made trench life more interesting. Notable among the many episodes which added spice to the daily routine was a raid on the Hun trenches by Lieutenant (now Lieut.-Colonel) Wise, and the stalking of a German patrol in No Man's Land by Corporal (now Captain) "Ernie" Canning, which resulted in the capture of one of their number and the gaining of much information. The small garrison of thirty-five 25th Battalion men, under Lieutenants Morgan, Johnstone and McNeil, holding Nos. 1 and 4 craters at St. Eloi in April, 1915, gave the attacking company of Huns a sample of the unbeatable stuff they are made of.

BRIG.-GEN. E. HILLIAM,
C.B., C.M.G., D.S.O.

In April the 25th Battalion took over the line at St. Eloi where they remained about six weeks. This was beyond a doubt the most trying experience which the Battalion had to that time or has since been called upon to endure. There were no front line trenches. Five mine craters had to be occupied, since the front line trenches were all destroyed, and the men had to occupy most exposed positions. Every hole and every remnant remaining of a trench were used as the only possible cover, and mud, muck and water prevailed. Under continually heavy and harrowing fire and attacks the Battalion endured, though at the price of the loss of hundreds of its personnel. The German artillery fire in the Ypres Salient was the heaviest of the War. With enemy artillery on three sides, the situation may better be imagined than described. One crater that was occupied by the Battalion was attacked no less than five times between dusk and dawn in one night alone. but the crater was held.

NOVA SCOTIA'S PART IN THE GREAT WAR

When the garrison was relieved there were not enough men left to bring out the wounded and a relief party had to be sent in for that purpose. On this front all intercommunication was impossible and isolated parties held the lines. The Battalion was highly commended by the higher command for their excellent work on this front.

The Battalion spent 339 days on the Belgian Front, of which 164 days were spent in actual front line trenches. Many good officers and men were killed or wounded. Among the former was Lieutenant Douglas, who was killed while fighting with the 6th (Western) Brigade in the craters of St. Eloi. Lieutenant Douglas was Battalion Machine Gun Officer and had been loaned with the machine gun section to the 6th Brigade during the furious onslaughts which the Hun was making on the craters. The men with Lieutenant Douglas were all killed excepting five who were captured.

Besides the Kemmel and St. Eloi Sectors, the 25th Battalion were engaged at Vierstraat, Ploegsteerte, Hill 60, Hooge and Messines. And it was here, also, that the Battalion obtained "Robert the Bruce," mascot and veteran of three years' service in the land of his birth. It would be hard for one to see the immense, sleek goat now on the farm of Major Matheson at Baddeck and endeavor to imagine the same animal, two weeks old, hardly bigger than a cat, feeding from a bottle in the hands of Pipe-Major Carson in the kitchen of the band's billet in Locre. But they are one and the same animal. The members of the band bought him from the "Madame" of the house for two francs (40c.), and trained him to "swank" in front of the pipe band, eat cigarettes, drink beer, and demand his blanket at "lights out." He added many other traits and tricks to his repertoire before the Battalion was disbanded, and many a would-be possessor of our mascot has felt the force of his "butt" sufficiently to make them all leave "Robert the Bruce" strictly to his own Battalion.

The 25th Battalion played a leading part in the assault at Courcellette on September 15, 1916. The whole Corps welcomed the relief from the ground-hog tactics of the fray in Belgium and looked forward with keen anticipation to their participation in open warfare tactics on the Somme in Picardy.

The troops marched a good portion of the long distance from Hazebrouck to Albert. The 25th Battalion spent a few days on the way in rehearsing practices in formations for advancing and assaulting and arrived in the brickfields of Albert where the whole Division and units of the 1st and 3rd Divisions were massed under tarpaulins and corrugated iron, a few days in advance of September 15, 1916.

The plan of attack on the immediate front of Courcellette was for the 4th (Ontario) Brigade to open the attack on the morning of the fifteenth (15th) and clear the ground in front of Courcellette and on the sixteenth (16th) the 5th Brigade would carry on the attack into the town. The 4th Brigade had their objectives cleared and consolidated so early in the day that the Divisional Commander decided to put the 5th Brigade over the top at 6 o'clock in the afternoon. Brig.-General MacDonnell (5th Brigade) divided the town evenly, pointed out the objectives to Lieut.-Colonel Tremblay (22nd Battalion) and Lieut.-Colonel Hilliam, explained that the other two Battalions would be in support and reserve and sent the Quebecers and Nova Scotians to it. Both Battalions were led in person by their commanding officers, who set a fine example of leadership and courage to officers and men. The 25th and 22nd Battalions established their line well to the east of the ruined town and maintained their positions in the face of fierce counter-attacks until relieved a few days later.

This operation, brilliant as it was in execution, cost the Battalion some of its most capable officers and men. Lieut.-Colonel Hilliam was wounded in the hand, but refused to leave the line until his Battalion was relieved. He was in evidence everywhere throughout the attack with his long stick cheering his men and by his energy and daring urging them to their best endeavors. In his report to the G.O.C., 5th Brigade, he praised the work of officers and men very highly, and closed with the words, " General, I have the honor of commanding the finest body of men I have ever seen."

Three Company Commanders, Major Tupper ("A" Company), Major Brooks (" D " Company), and Capt. John Stairs (" C " Company), were killed, and the O.C. " B " Company, Major Flowers, was severely wounded. The Adjutant, Captain Dicky, Lieutenants Hobkirk, Howson, Craig and Doane were killed. The wounded included Capt. J. D. McNeil, Major Nutter, Lieutenants Wetmore, Ryan, DeYoung and Dennis Stairs.

NOVA SCOTIA'S PART IN THE GREAT WAR

Before I pass from the doings of the Battalion on the Somme, it is necessary, in order to do justice to the narrative, to record the loss of one of the bravest and most capable officers of the Battalion and one who gave great promise as a fearless and resourceful fighter for high ideals. I refer to Lieut. L. H. Johnstone, who led the 25th Battalion in the fruitless and bloody attack on Regina

CAPT. L. H. JOHNSTONE.

MAJOR J. H. TUPPER.

LIEUT. CHAS. H. HOBKIRK.

LIEUT. C. E. HOWSON.

CAPT. FRASER CRAIG.

CAPT. W. E. E. DOANE.

Trench, October 1st, 1916. While gallantly leading those men into a veritable hell of machine gun and shell fire, the "Iron Duke," as he was nicknamed by the gallant men he was leading, fell to rise no more.

When the Battalion finally moved from the Somme area to be reinforced and recuperated there were less than one hundred of the original crusaders who marched so gaily from Flanders less than one month previously. Though they had received a hard drubbing they made the old nickname of "Herring-choker" one to be respected as long as memory lives and histories are written. Theirs was not the attitude of the torn and mangled dog with its tail between its legs. With reinforcements, which arrived while the remnants of the Battalion rested a few days at Bertrincourt, near Albert, they were transported to Hersin, and immediately went into the line at Bully-Grenay, on the Lens Front, where, with a pugnacity which is typical of the breed, they stirred up a quiet sector until it became the most frequently raided and most heavily shelled of their experience.

The first raid on this front, and one of the most successful, was the enterprise, on Christmas Eve, 1916, directed by Capt. W. A. Cameron and carried out by an officer and twenty men from each Company. The objective took in a point in the enemy lines known as the "Pope's Nose," owing to the peculiar twist in the trench which brought it to within fifteen yards of our line. Each party was successful in gaining entrance to the Hun trenches. In fact, two of the parties encountered no opposition, for Fritz had fled for cover. But the party from "D" Company, under Lieut. (now Capt.) W. A. Livingstone, found their objective strongly manned and the men were able to get in some splendid bayonet and Mills bomb work. They saved seven specimens of German Kultur to tell our Intelligence Staff what they knew about the situation on the other side of No Man's Land.

Captain Cameron, Lieutenants Livingstone and Morris received Military Crosses in recognition of their energy and personal gallantry in the above affair.

Lieut.-Colonel Hilliam, D.S.O., was promoted to the rank of Brigadier-General and appointed to the command of the 10th Infantry Brigade, 4th Canadian Division, in January, 1917. The Battalion at having their C.O. selected for a higher command recognized that no promotion in the Allied Forces was more deserved; but regret at the Battalion's loss was expressed by all ranks. The effects of his soldierly training and administration of the Battalion remained with them throughout the War.

NOVA SCOTIA'S PART IN THE GREAT WAR

In the attack on Vimy Ridge, Easter Monday, April 9, 1917, the 25th Battalion was led by Major J. A. Delancey, M.C., until that brave officer was killed, after which Major (now Colonel) A. O. Blois, of Halifax (who had enlisted as a private in the 40th Battalion, been appointed to a commission in the 64th Battalion, transferred a subaltern to the 25th Battalion and had progressed at that date through the Adjutancy of the Battalion to the rank of Major), took command, and organized and consolidated the objectives which had all been secured by ten o'clock and were extended later in the day.

Two of the Battalion pipers played the boys over the top that wintry morning, and although the German band and our own

LIEUT. J. HALLISEY.

CAPT. J. H. WALLACE.

artillery drowned the skirling notes of the pibroch, our lads were fired with the spirit which prompted these two noble musicians to volunteer and insist on accompanying the Battalion through the muck and mire, the death and destruction which was let loose on that fateful day. They were awarded Military Medals for their splendid example of self-sacrificing disregard for personal safety.

Lieutenant Hallisey, of Truro, was killed while proceeding to the "jumping off" position. Several officers were wounded, and the casualties among the N.C.O.'s and men were very heavy. The death of R.S.M. "Dad" Henchcliffe, M.C., father of all the N.C.O.'s and men in the Battalion, was particularly regrettable; for he was a very efficient warrant officer and a friend to all.

THE 25th BATTALION

Lieut.-Colonel Bauld commanded the Battalion at the taking of Fresnoy and Arleux late in February. While these were only local affairs and confined to a narrow front, they were the cause of some very severe casualties. "D" and "C" Companies suffered very severely at Arleux. Captain Weare, M.C., was severely shell-shocked, Lieutenants Bell and Wallace, two very promising young officers, were killed, and scores of our men caught in the wire, in the darkness, were literally shot to pieces.

Shortly after this affair, two officers' batmen from "C" Company went astray in the darkness with their officers' rations and strayed into the enemy lines. Their whereabouts was a matter of conjecture until the publication of the roll of prisoners of war. In the thirty-eight months during which the 25th Battalion was in contact with the flower of the German War Lord's Legions, only eight of our men were captured alive. The five machine-gunners have already been noted. They were detached from the Battalion at the time of their capture. The two mentioned above were the victims of a dark night and unfamiliar recently captured ground. The eighth man to be captured was taken on the Mericourt Sector early in 1918 during a raid by a party of three officers and ninety Huns on a thinly held portion of the sector. We also succeeded in capturing one of the raiding party who was unfortunate enough to get into our wire entanglements. A great deal of information was gleaned from the captive regarding the training and composition of the raiding party. The man who was captured by the enemy had only joined the Battalion a few days previously. So what information the German Intelligence Staff gleaned from him must have been purely family affairs.

LIEUT.-COL. "STAN" BAULD.

Early in July, 1917, Lieut.-Colonel Bauld obtained leave of absence to visit his home, and the command of the Battalion devolved on Major Blois, D.S.O., who commanded the 25th, until he in turn was granted leave to Canada in May, 1918.

NOVA SCOTIA'S PART IN THE GREAT WAR

The 25th Battalion played a glorious part in the Battle of Hill 70 on August 15, 1917. The boys went over the top from the shell-holes of No Man's Land in front of Cité St. Laurent. ' " A " Company, in the first wave, secured the Hun front line. " B " Company was through them as soon as the creeping barrage permitted and clinched the support line, while " D " Company carried on to the limits of the town. The 24th Battalion then pushed on our positions 600 yards farther to the trench " Nun's Alley." Considering the amount of ground gained and the nature of the fighting, in ruined streets and over demolished buildings, the casualties were very light on the 15th. But the Hun artillery promptly laid down a barrage to cover his counter-attacks, which fell behind the front line and completely churned up the debris formerly known as Cité St. Laurent, where the 25th Battalion was endeavoring to establish a defensive position. The counter-attacks of the Bosche gradually weakened, and by the 18th had ceased; but his artillery strafeing grew more intense as the days passed, causing many casualties.

COL. A. G. BLOIS, D.S.O.

On the night of August 19-20, the 25th Battalion moved from their positions in Cité St. Laurent to the comparative peace and quiet of the front line. At daybreak the 6th Brigade on our immediate right were to attack and tighten the pressure already exercised on Lens. The Hun also divulged his reason for the systematic and furious shelling of our positions during the past six days when he launched an attack in force on the 6th Brigade and extending into our right (" D " Company's front). The O.C. " D " Company, being in an advanced position and close to our own artillery barrage line, was ordered to place his men under cover, which he did, leaving only sentries at the entrances to shelters. Zero hour for the 6th Brigade's and the German attack coincided and both were demoralized by the intensity of the artillery fire they encountered before the assembly positions could be cleared. The result was that neither the 6th Brigade nor the Prussians opposite them left their trenches. But the artillery was not so active on the Front of our "D" Company, with the result that the Huns were throwing grenades down on our dugout steps before our men realized that they were trapped. Lieutenant Dauphinee was killed in a gallant attempt to clear the entrance to the dugout in which the whole Company was sheltered. Captain W. A. Livingstone, M.C., O.C. "D" Company, managed to force his way out by another entrance, and with a Lewis Gun spitting .303 bullets from his shoulder, he managed to clear the trench of those who escaped his fusilade. But the trench was literally filled with corpses from the attacking hordes. Nor was the situation normal as yet. A party of Huns had got in on the right of our boundary, and Lieutenant Spurr and Sergeant Jordan,

CAPT. OWEN C. DAUPHINEE.

after expelling them, organized the survivors of the Company of a Western Battalion, who had lost all their officers and were in a precarious condition. The boys of "D" Company, reinforced by a platoon from "B" Company, which had been led up through the intense shelling by Lieutenant Bell, were busy all day repelling bombing parties which stubbornly attempted to force their way into our lines at the Battalion boundary—the junction of Nun's Alley and Commotion Trenches.

Captain Livingstone, whose work on this day merited the Victoria Cross, was severely wounded in the chest and collapsed immediately after he had cleared the Huns from his trenches, and Lieutenant Spurr commanded his company until relieved by a company of the Royal Canadian Regiment at night. Great credit is due Lieutenants Gibbons and Bell for their skill and judgment in rallying our boys and organizing the defences. The coolness of Sergeant Jordan saved the situation on the immediate right, when he rallied the overwrought survivors of the Western Battalion. Corporal Boudreau, Company Sergt.-Major Bragg, Corporal Veniot.

and Sergt. "Dan" Fraser also distinguished themselves in inflicting punishment on the Hun and by their heroic conduct throughout the day. Company Sergt.-Major Bragg and Sergeant Jordan were awarded Distinguished Conduct Medals for their services on this occasion. Captain Livingstone, M.C., was awarded a bar, and Lieutenant Spurr, the Military Cross.

At Passchendaele, on November 10, 1917, the 5th Infantry Brigade was given the post of honor as a successful assaulting Brigade. The 1st, 3rd and 4th Divisions and the 4th Brigade of the 2nd Division had been engaged in nibbling here and there at the Hun positions and had at length captured most of the Passchendaele Ridge. But the ruined town still remained in German hands. On the morning of the 6th November the 26th Battalion attacked and captured the ruins to the eastern limits of the town and after holding their gains for four days the 5th Brigade was withdrawn from the Passchendaele Sector, and returned to Lens.

The 2nd Canadian Division remained in the Lens-Mericourt Sectors until the latter part of February, 1918. The only notable occurrence, other than the loss of one man to the Huns, as previously noted, was the stealth raid led by Lieut. P. R. Phillips, of Barrington, assisted by a covering party under Lieut. Max MacRae, of Westville. The raiding party of only five crawled over the Lens-Arras Road and made their way among the battered houses of Lens to one of the buildings of Fosse 3 and destroyed a dugout full of "Heinies," bringing the sentry who was on duty at the entrance into our lines. The prisoner proved to be a very observant chap and a great deal of information was gleaned from him. When questioned as to the great offensive which our Staff expected daily, he said no attack would be made on the Canadians. Fritz had probably had his fill of attacking Canucks when he broke his head on them in the First Battle of Ypres, at St. Eloi and the Barrier.

The 2nd Division had completed ten days of what was to be a months' rest when the long-expected Hun offensive broke away south on the British right on March 21st. The 25th Battalion had only started their syllabus of training and recreation when they were ordered south. The northern limits of this effort of the Hun was marked by the southern boundary of the Canadian Corps' front, and here the 2nd Division took over the completely disorganized line of the Imperial troops. The sector was known as the Mercatel-Neuville Vetasse Sector. Here the 25th Battalion was engaged three months in punishing the German Division opposite. Each period of six days spent in the front line was marked by a raid on the enemy outposts, and sometimes our boys penetrated three-quarters of a mile into the Hun lines. So completely terrorized was Fritz by the vigorous onslaughts which occurred almost nightly and several times in broad daylight that no resistance was offered in most cases, and at length the news was gleaned from some of the last prisoners that the whole Division had to be withdrawn for re-equipment.

The 25th Battalion established themselves as the "Master Raiders" of the Canadian Corps, and were called on for some officers and non-commissioned officers to instruct the famous Guards Division in the new and most effective art of keeping Fritz worried. Six of the raids conducted on this front were led by one officer, Lieut. (now Major) Max MacRae, every one of which netted prisoners, besides machine guns and documents. Among the other officers taking part in these raids were Captains Anderson and Holmes, Lieutenants Lounsbury, Hawes, Bell, Johnstone, Holly, Burchell, Spurr, and Wright. It was here that the Battalion established its record of successful raids and became known throughout the 1st and the 4th Armies as the "Raiding Battalion," putting on about thirty raids in this sector.

LIEUT.-COL. J. WISE, D.S.O., M.C., CROIX DE GUERRE.

Lieut.-Colonel (now Colonel) Blois, D.S.O., was granted leave to Canada and handed the Battalion over to Major (now Lieut.-Colonel) Wise in May, 1918.

At the battle of Amiens, August 8, 1918, when the Canadian Corps was first launched into the grand offensive which broke the German morale and brought them begging for peace, the 25th Battalion was on the left of the Canadian Corps and in touch with the dashing Australian Corps on their left. The attack, like that of nearly two years previous at Courcellette, was made with the 4th Brigade taking Villers, Brettonneux, and Marcelcave on the Amiens-Roye Railway, and a considerable stretch of country to the right of those towns. The plans were so well guarded and the assemblage of troops, guns, etc., so effectively concealed, that the enemy was utterly stunned at the suddenness of the attack and the speed with which it was pushed.

After the 4th Brigade had established their line in front of Marcelcave the 5th Brigade carried on the attack through Wiencourt and Guillaucourt. The 25th Battalion encountered considerable opposition in a small wood south of Wiencourt; and it was there that most of the casualties occurred. Lieut. J. W. Holly, of St. John, was killed by machine-gun fire, and thirteen other officers were wounded in ousting the Huns from this wood.

At Guillaucourt, Lieut.-Colonel Wise, who was the first to arrive at the objective, fell, severely wounded by a sniper's bullet. The Adjutant, Capt. N. H. Wetmore, utterly disregarding his own safety, sprang to his O.C.'s assistance and became the target for a better directed bullet from the same sniper and fell, never to rise again.

CAPT. N. H. WETMORE.

Major Day, second in command, who had been acting as a Brigade liason officer during the attack, immediately assumed command of the Battalion and directed it in the advance on the following day when the towns of Vrely and Meharicourt were taken. After having advanced twelve miles in two days, the 2nd Division gave place to the 4th, who carried on to the outskirts of Hallu. This attack was certainly the most successful in which the 25th Battalion had thus far been engaged. An immense area of beautiful country with some important towns had been taken from the Hun, with surprisingly few casualties.

After a few days in the line in front of Hallu, the Battalion was moved to Berneville, near Arras, where the details were left behind and we were into it again—over Telegraph Hill and down the

THE 25th BATTALION

eastern slope to the Cojuel River on August 26th—a distance of four miles—fighting all the way; then across the dried-up bed of the stream on the 27th to Cherisy and past the Sensee River to the heights beyond; and then a tightening up of the Hun resistance, which meant a fruitless hammering at the strongly wired positions in front of Upton Wood and "the Crow's Nest" on the 28th.

The 2nd Division had not rested since the 5th of August, and had penetrated to great depths in the enemy's lines on two fronts. The tired troops could accomplish no more. The writer can testify that men actually fell asleep on their feet on the night of the 28th-29th of August, when a counter-attack was imminent. The state of mind of men when so thoroughly exhausted as our boys were at the end of the third day, is one that cares not·what may happen to a body so completely worn out. It is then that sentiment—love of home, Battalion pride, and the shame of weakness—asserts itself and supports a man when everything tangible is wobbling.

"C" Company lost a splendid officer when Capt. M. L. Tupper was killed. A relative of Major J. H. Tupper, who "paid the price" at Courcellette in 1916, he had shown a fearlessness in the face of the enemy and a conscientiousness in all his duties which well merited his appointment as O.C. "C" Company.

The Battalion had a respite of two days at Hautes Avesnes, on the Arras-St. Pol Road, over the anniversary of the landing in France and the Battle of Courcellette, September 15th, and was then

CAPT. M. L. TUPPER.

continuously in the forward area until after the fall of Cambrai on October 9, 1918, engaging the Hun in the Inchy-Moeuvres and the Marcomg Switch Sectors, and clearing the Hun from the towns of Eseadoeueres and Ievuy, on the northern outskirts of Cambrai. "B" Company, under Lieutenant (now Major) MacRae, M.C. (two bars), did splendid work at Inchy on the 21st and 22nd

September, when they captured seven machine guns, killing the crews and straightening out a kink in our line.

In this wonderful last hundred days of the War, when the Hun had to be dislodged from the positions he had been preparing since his first check at the Marne in 1914, the deeds of valor which were enacted daily and hourly were too numerous to refer to here at any length. But mention may be made of some of the more notable recipients of War Decorations awarded officers, N.C.O.'s and men, who served with the 25th Battalion.

First in the list must come Lieut.-Colonel (now Brig.-General) Hilliam, who won the D.S.O. and two bars for personal gallantry in the field and was mentioned in despatches four times. He was also invested with the insignia of a Companion of the Bath (C.B.) and that of a Companion of the Order of St. Michael and St. George (C.M.G.). Another officer who carries two rows of medals on his breast is Major G. McL. Matheson, D.S.O., M.C., and M.M. Lieut.-Colonel Wise wears the D.S.O. and the M.C., with the French Croix de Guerre. Lieut. M. M. Jordan wears the M.C., D.C.M. and Bar.

Capt. Max MacRae was awarded the Military Cross three times. Company Sergt.-Major Dauphinee and Corporal Leggett each were awarded the Military Medal three times. Regimental Sergt.-Major Hurley was awarded the Military Cross, D.C.M. and French Croix de Guerre. Company Sergt.-Major Boudreau received the Croix de Virtute (Roumanian) besides the D.C.M., M.M. and Bar. Private Mickarek won the Russian Cross of St. George. And many officers and men won Military Crosses, D.C.M.'s, M.M.'s and Bars. A summary of the Battalion's record of awards is given further below.

The last occasion on which the 25th Battalion was in hostile contact with the Hun was at the storming of Elouges, a mining town near Mons, on November 8, 1918. The casualties, though very light, only eleven men being killed, included some of the originals who had seen the thing through to this ringing down of the curtain. Some eleven, including Company Sergt.-Major George Vincent, D.C.M., Corpl. John Morrison and "Billie" Roberts, who had weathered the storm only to be swept over at the harbor's mouth, lie asleep in the little civilian cemetery at Elouges, where their graves will be guarded and cared for by the grateful people of the town, who welcomed the Battalion as liberators.

The boys of the Battalion were enjoying their "lionization" by the populace at Mons when the news was received at 9 a.m. on November 11, 1918, that we had but two hours more of hostilities when the Armistice would become effective.

The remaining three days were given over to celebrating what had been fought for, and prayed for during the last four years—*Victory*. A Thanksgiving Service was held in the little chapel in the town, conducted by the brave chaplain who had stuck to us through the "Last Hundred Days"—Capt. A. J. MacDonald. And the local pastor addressed us in an impassioned Address of Thanks in French, out of which the writer distinguished only the oft-repeated phrase, "Merci beaucoup, nos liberateurs."

On November 19, 1918, the Battalion started on the long march to the Rhine. We crossed the German border near St. Vith at 10.08 a.m., December 5th, with the Union Jack flying at the head of the column. At 10.47 a.m., December 13th, the Battalion crossed the Rhine at Bonn and proceeded to the "Cologne Bridgehead Outpost Line," where we had the satisfaction of telling the Hun how he should act and also the pleasure of enforcing our instructions on him.

After six weeks on the Rhine, during which all ranks had an opportunity of visiting the famous cities of Cologne, Bonn and Coblenz, the Battalion returned to Belgium and went into billets at Arvelais, near Namur. On April 5, 1919, we started for Havre, and on the night of the 9th embarked on the old *Prince Arthur*, formerly of the Boston-Yarmouth service, and on the morning of the 10th arrived at Southampton and proceeded by train to Witley Camp in Surrey, where, after a month's sojourn awaiting documents from the Record Office, we sailed from Southampton on the *Olympic*, May 10, 1919.

On board were the whole 5th Brigade and the 29th Battalion, 6th Brigade. After an uneventful though pleasant voyage, and to the accompaniment of the music of several bands and the shrill whistles of factories, boats and auto horns on both sides of Halifax Harbor, the *Olympic* docked at Pier 2; and after a farewell to the 22nd, 24th, 26th and 29th we lined up for our march to the

NOVA SCOTIA'S PART IN THE GREAT WAR

Armories, which triumphal procession, to the writer, seemed to be but a part of a great dream, as the memory of the exile from home now seems but an hallucination.

TOTAL NUMBER OF DECORATIONS WON IN THE WAR BY OFFICERS AND OTHER RANKS OF THE 25TH BATTALION, NOVA SCOTIA REGIMENT.

Decoration.	Officers.	Other Ranks.
D.S.O.	5	..
M.C.	37	2
2nd Bar to M.C.	1	..
Bar to M.C.	6	..
D.C.M.	..	27
Bar to D.C.M.	..	2
M.M.	..	156
Bar to M.M.	..	25
2nd Bar to M.M.	..	2
M.S.M.	..	8
Croix de Guerre	3	5
Russian Cross of St. George	..	1
Croix de Virtute Militata (Roumania)	..	1
Medaille Barbatie si Credinta, 3rd Class (Roumania)	..	1
Total	51	230

Mentioned in Despatches, officers, 17; other ranks, 15.

LIST OF ORIGINAL OFFICERS OF THE 25TH BATTALION.

Lieut.-Col.	Lecain, G. A., O.C.	Roundhill, Ann. Co.	69th Regt.
"	Sponagle, J. A., M.D.	Middleton, N.S.	C.A.M.C.
Major	Bauld, D. S., "D" Co.	Halifax	66th Regt.
"	Conrad, W. H., 2nd Comd.	"	63rd "
"	Jones, A. N., "A" Co.	"	C.F.A.
"	McKenzie, J. G., "B" Co.	Westville	78th Regt.
"	MacRae, D. A., "C" Co.	Baddeck	94th "
"	McKenzie, L. H., Adjt.	Stellarton	78th "
"	Weston, A. W. P., Jr. Maj.	Halifax	66th "
Hon. Capt.	Graham, E. E., Chap.	Arcadia	C.M.R.
Capt.	Holt, C. W.	Amherst	93rd Regt.
"	Logan, J. W., "C" Co.	Halifax	63rd "
Hon. Capt.	McPherson, D., Chap.	Sydney Mines, C.B.	
Capt.	Margeson, J. W., Paymaster	Bridgewater	75th "
"	Medcalfe, W. B., "B" Co.	Halifax	66th "
"	Purney, W. P., "D" Co.	Liverpool	68th "
"	Tupper, J. H., "A" Co.	Bridgetown	69th "
"	Whitford, W. L., "D" Co.	Chester	75th "
Lieut.	Brooks, E. J., "A" Co.	Falmouth	
"	Bullock, L. N. B., "D" Co.	Halifax	63rd "
"	Cameron, W. A., "A" Co.	St. John, N.B.	
"	Delancey, J. A., "M.G."	Middleton	93rd "
"	Eville, C. K., "B" Co.	Halifax	81st "
"	Grant, J. W., "B" Co.	Amherst	S.A.

THE 25th BATTALION

Lieut.	Grant, J. A., "B" Co......	Halifax	63rd Regt.
"	Johnstone, L. H., "C" Co.	Sydney	81st "
"	Longley, H. G., "Trpt." ...	Paradise	69th "
"	Macaloney, C. W.	Halifax	
"	Morgan, E., "D" Co.	Bear River	69th "
"	Mosher, C. M.	Mahone Bay	75th "
"	Murphy, V. P., "D" Co...	New Ross	75th "
"	McKay, K. L., "A" Co....	Inverness	94th "
"	McKinnon, D., "A" Co...	Woodbine	94th "
"	McLeod, H. A., "B" Co..	Salt Springs, Pic. Co.	78th "
"	McNiel, G. M., "A" Co...	Iona	94th "
"	McNiel, J. D., "C" Co...	Whitney Pier	S.A.
"	Newnham, T. F., "Qmst.".	Halifax	R.C.G.A.
"	Roberts, G. E., "C" Co....	"	....
"	Smith, B. H.	"	.... 66th Regt.
"	Stairs, J. C., "A" Co.....	"	.... 66th "
"	Tanner, F. I., "C" Co....	Pictou	C.F.A.
"	Young, G. R.	Kentville	C.M.R.
67001	R.S.M. Miles, H. F.	Halifax	R.C.R.

Strength of Unit on proceeding to France on Sept. 15th, 1915.
    Officers.   Other Ranks.
      32   1,000

Reinforcements after coming to France.
    Officers.   Other Ranks.
      231   3,829

Wounded and sick to England.
    Officers.   Other Ranks.
      156   2,557

Killed in action and died in hospital.
    Officers.   Other Ranks.
      32   686

Missing.   Prisoners.   Transferred.
Off. O.Rs.   Off. O.Rs.   Off. O.Rs.
 2   64   8   37 682

CHAPTER XII.

THE 40th BATTALION.

THE 40th Battalion was authorized January 1, 1915, under the command of Lieut.-Col. W. H. Gibsone (R.C.R.). As the men were recruited, detachments were formed at McNab's Island, Halifax, Sydney, Glace Bay, North Sydney, Truro, Amherst, New Glasgow, Yarmouth, Lunenburg, Kentville and Digby.

The Battalion was finally mobilized at Aldershot Camp, N.S., on May 11, 1915. Lieut.-Colonel Gibsone proceeded direct to France to become A.A.G. of the 3rd Canadian Division, which was then in process of formation. At Aldershot Camp, N.S., the 40th was first inspected by the Duke of Connaught and Brig.-General H. M. McLean, who commented on their splendid showing. On June 21st, under the command of Lieut.-Col. A. G. Vincent, the 40th Battalion moved to Valcartier Camp, Quebec. Before leaving for Valcartier two drafts were despatched, one of twenty-five men to the 25th Battalion, and another of 250 men and five officers to England, as reinforcements.

At Valcartier strenuous work by all ranks drew special mention of the 40th by Major-General Sir Sam Hughes at a General Review of the Camp a week before sailing. The Battalion was also inspected later at Valcartier by the Duke of Connaught and also by Sir Robert Borden. A week before sailing a third call was made for reinforcements, and again five officers and 250 N.C.O.'s and men, all picked, were despatched to England.

Notwithstanding this great drain, on October 18, 1915, the 40th sailed from Quebec on the *S.S. Saxonia*, with a strength of 1,143

THE 40th BATTALION

all ranks, under the command of Lieut.-Col. A. G. Vincent and the following officers:

Major C. A. Andrews, Second in Command.
Major J. C. Ditmars.
Capt. J. S. Legge, Adjutant.
Lieut. H. Fisher, Q.M.
Lieut. G. M. Sylvester, Assistant Adjutant.
Lieut. A. W. Cunningham, Sig. Officer.
Lieut. H. St. C. Jones, M.G. Officer.
Major Geo. Wood, Chaplain.
Capt. E. Douglas, Medical Officer.
Capt. G. H. Gillis, Paymaster.
Major A. G. Nutter, O.C. " A " Company.
Capt. W. E. Doane, Second in Command.
Lieut. Geo. Campbell.
Lieut. G. W. Anderson.
Lieut. P. W. Freeman.
Lieut. A. S. Allen.
Lieut. J. Harley.
Capt. C. R. Chisholm, O.C. " B " Company.
Capt. H. P. Bell, Second in Command.
Lieut. Mc.I. McLeod.
Lieut. J. D. McIntyre.
Lieut. W. W. Pickup.
Lieut. H. H. Heal.
Capt. A. M. Ross, O.C. " C " Company.
Capt. G. W. Dwyer, Second in Command.
Lieut. G. B. Murray.
Lieut. A. S. Churchill.
Lieut. C. E. Little.
Lieut. L. W. Ormand.
Lieut. D. H. MacKenzie.
Capt. W. Letcher, O.C. " D " Company.
Capt. E. R. Dennis, Second in Command.
Lieut. B. F. Davidson.
Lieut. F. P. H. Layton.
Lieut. R. Jago.
Lieut. L. W. W. Slacke.
Lieut. F. G. Robertson.
Lieut. A. Anderson.

On October 29, 1915, after an uneventful voyage the Battalion landed at Plymouth and proceeded to Bramshott Camp, being the first Canadian Infantry Battalion to enter that Camp, where they took over quarters from the Royal Irish Rifles. At Bramshott the 40th joined part of the then contemplated 9th Brigade of the 3rd Canadian Division, which was under the command of General Lord Brooke.

Owing to the heavy demand for reinforcements, following the disastrous action of June 2, 1916 (the Third Battle of Ypres),

NOVA SCOTIA'S PART IN THE GREAT WAR

the Battalion was moved to East Sandling to become the 40th Reserve Battalion, where drafts were despatched to nearly every Unit in the Canadian Corps. After many moves the 40th absorbed the remnants of the 64th, 104th, 106th and 112th Battalions, and finally returned to Bramshott to become the 26th Reserve Battalion, and was finally absorbed by the 17th Reserve Battalion.

CAPT. E. R. DENNIS
(killed in action at Vimy Ridge. April 5, 1917).

The 40th Battalion has the distinction that practically every officer and man of the original Battalion saw service in France. Ten of the officers were killed in action, viz.:

Capt. A. M. Ross.
Capt. W. E. Doane.
Capt. E. R. Dennis.
Lieut. G. H. Campbell.
Lieut. W. W. Pickup (Major).
Lieut. G. M. Sylvester.
Lieut. A. Allen (Capt.).
Lieut. F. P. H. Layton.
Lieut. H. Fisher.
Lieut. A. S. Churchill.

In addition, nineteen were wounded. Twelve received the M.C., one the D.F.C. Several were promoted and mentioned in despatches for valuable service. It would be a long list to give the names of the N.C.O.'s and men of the original 40th who gave their lives. Several were promoted to commissioned rank in the Field and many others were decorated for valor. Wherever they went they acquitted themselves in such a manner that although never to cross the Channel as a Unit, the 40th always received honorable mention in every fighting Unit in the Canadian Corps.

CHAPTER XIII.

THE 64th BATTALION, C.E.F.

THE 64th Battalion was authorized in June, 1915, and mobilized at Sussex, N.B., August 15th, 1915. It was originally intended that this should be a Highland Battalion raised in Nova Scotia, New Brunswick and Prince Edward Island; and having this in view, the officers were selected from the three provinces proportionately.

When the Unit started to recruit, owing to New Brunswick and Prince Edward Island being still busy completing the 55th Battalion, all the recruits came from Nova Scotia, and eventually, when New

LIEUT.-COL. H. MONTGOMERY CAMPBELL.

CAPT. G. H. MAXWELL (killed in action).

LIEUT. H. M. CAMPBELL (killed in action).

Brunswick and Prince Edward Island began sending their quota, the ranks swelled to over 2,300, whereas the strength of a Battalion was only about 1,100 all ranks.

The 104th Battalion was then authorized as a New Brunswick Battalion, and all the New Brunswick men with some of the officers were transferred to the new Unit.

Lieut.-Col. H. Montgomery Campbell, late 8th Hussars and Commanding Officer 11th Infantry Brigade, Military District No. 6, was appointed Commanding Officer 64th Battalion.

NOVA SCOTIA'S PART IN THE GREAT WAR

The Battalion organized and trained for ten weeks at Sussex, and early in November moved to Halifax, where at Pier No. 2 it went into winter quarters, continuing training till finally sailing on the 31st of March, 1916, for Liverpool on the *S.S. Adriatic*. The following officers proceeded overseas with the Unit:

O.C., Lieut.-Col. H. Montgomery Campbell	Formerly	8th Hussars, N.B.
Second in Command, Major H. Flowers	"	1st C.G.A., N.S.
Junior Major, Major G. H. Maxwell	"	1st C.G. A., N.S.

Company Commanders—
Major Angus W. McArthur	"	78th Regt., N.S.
" G. Guy McLaughlin	"	67th Regt., N.B.
" Guy L. Mott	"	81st Regt., N.S.
" Francis L. Stephens	"	66th Regt., N.S.

Captains—
Anglin, Gerald C.	"	O.T.C., N.B.
Barbour, Roydon McF.	"	O.T.C, N.B.
Bowron, Edward H.	"	78th Regt., N.S.
Fairweather, Frank R.	"	62nd Regt., N.B.

Lieutenants—
Blois, Arthur O.	"	66th Regt., N.S.
Campbell, Herbert M.	"	81st Regt., N.S.
Curren, Reginald H.	"	14th K.C.H., N.S.
Flowers, Eric P.	"	1st C.G.A., N.S.
Gale, John R.	"	62nd, N.B.
Guildford, David A.	"	1st C.G.A., N.B.
Gunn, James D.	"	69th, N.S.
Henry, John D.	"	8th Hussars, N.B.
Hobkirk, Charles H.	"	71st, N.B.
Keswick, Robert McL.	"	73rd, N.B.
McKay, Reary	"	O.T.C., N.B.
McLean, James D.	"	O.T.C., N.B.
McCleave, Harry A.	"	76th, N.S.
Murray, Ralph M.	"	74th, N.B.
O'Leary, Harry	"	73rd, N.B.
Perks, Arthur J.	"	66th, N.S.
Rogers, William M.	"	63rd, N.S.
Russell, Bernard W.	"	C.F.A., N.S.
Watt, William L.	"	73rd, N.B.
Wetmore, Norman H.	"	O.T.C., N.B.
Winslow, Donald B.	"	C.F.A., N.B.

Adjutant, Captain J. Hutton Wallace	"	81st, N.S.
Medical Officer, Capt. Arthur C. Jost	"	C.A.M.C., N.S.
Quartermaster, Captain Samuel S. Wright	"	R.C.G.A., N.S.

Chaplains—
Hon. Capt., Rev. Wm. Fowler Parker	"	........N.B.
Hon. Capt., Rev. Father Patrick McQuillan	"	........N.S.

Paymaster, Hon. Capt. Robert M. Hope	"	C.F.A., N.B.

THE 64th BATTALION, C.E.F.

On arrival in England, April 9th, the Battalion moved to Bramshott, where it remained for four weeks. It then moved to Otterpool for preliminary musketry, proceeding to Lidd for the final training in that branch. During the stay at Otterpool the Battalion was attached to the 6th Training Brigade, being inspected by Major-General Sir Sam Steele, together with the 63rd, 66th and 69th Battalions. After the inspection Major-General Steele informed the troops that they were fully equal to any troops he had ever inspected, but that owing to certain exigencies of the war it was impracticable to send them to the Front as Units. Next day the drafting commenced and 198 were sent to the A.S.C.

After one week at Lidd an order was received to send to Shorn-

CAPT. F. FAIRWEATHER
(killed in action).

LIEUT. REARY MCKAY
(killed in action).

LIEUT. H. A. M'CLEAVE
(killed in action).

cliffe all those who had completed musketry. Five hundred other ranks in charge of Captain Fairweather moved out of camp at 5 a.m. The next week was spent completing musketry, and on the following Sunday the remainder of the Battalion moved back to Otterpool. Other drafts were almost immediately called for of both officers and men.

On July 3rd the last move was made to Caesar's Camp near Folkestone. The remainder of the Battalion was handed over to the 40th Reserve, and the 64th for all practical purposes ceased to exist. The O.C. and Staff were employed in winding up the affairs of the Unit, the other remaining officers being ordered to hold themselves in readiness to proceed to France.

Every officer of this Unit eventually proceeded to France. Of the thirty-nine officers the following paid the supreme sacrifice, namely: Major G. H. Maxwell, Capt. Frank Fairweather, Capt. J. Hutton Wallace, Lieut. Herbert M. Campbell, Lieut. C. H. Hobkirk, Lieut. Reary McKay, Lieut. N. H. Wetmore, Lieut. H. A. McCleave—eight in all. Of the remainder twenty-four were wounded, only seven escaping the casualty list.

This Battalion was undoubtedly one of the best trained Battalions leaving Canada. Many of its N.C.O.'s finally reached the Commissioned Ranks, and the Units in France were always pleased to get a detachment of 64th men.

CHAPTER XIV.

THE 85th BATTALION, NOVA SCOTIA HIGHLANDERS, AND THE 85th BATTALION BAND.

THE first distinctly Highland Battalion to be organized in Nova Scotia for active service Overseas in the late War was the 85th Battalion, Nova Scotia Highlanders. The Battalion was authorized at Ottawa on September 14, 1915, with the appointment of Lieut.-Colonel Allison H. Borden as Commanding Officer. Headquarters for organization and mobilization were first established at the Military Camp, Aldershot, N.S., on September 23, 1915. Recruiting proceeded rapidly, the idea of a distinctly Nova Scotia Highland Battalion having fired with enthusiasm the people of the Province, who, true to their ancestral Highland spirit, were found " deas gu cath " (ready for fight). The success of the recruiting drew an order from Ottawa for Battalion Headquarters to be transferred to Halifax, and for the Battalion to be mobilized in full strength and stationed in the Armories. Mobilization resulted on October 14, 1915, with the 85th Battalion 200 over strength. On that day occurred the first parade of the Battalion—a memorably impressive scene and event, by virtue of its contrasts in personnel: for in all ranks were officers and men who came from every walk of life, professional and industrial and commercial, with farmers and manufacturers amongst the officers, while clergymen, college professors, and teachers paraded shoulder to shoulder in the rank and file.

The 85th Battalion has the distinction of being the senior, and, as it were, the parent Unit of the Nova Scotia Highland Brigade. But with the Brigade as such this chapter is not concerned. Its story has been told incidentally in connection with the other Units which made up the Brigade. It will suffice to remark, however, that this magnificent body of fighting men—" the very flower of Nova Scotia's manhood "—after being noted by the military leaders and authorities in England " as the finest body of troops sent over from Canada," was, under the exigencies of military supervision, finally broken up in England, and reorganized into two Battalions, the 85th Battalion, Nova Scotia Highlanders, and the 185th Battalion, Cape Breton Highlanders. The latter Battalion—" siol nan gaisgeach mora "—became a splendid Unit in the so-called Fifth Division, but was denied the privilege and glory of seeing service

LIEUT.-COL. A. H. BORDEN, D S.O.

in France as a Unit. The record of their compatriots, " D " Company of the 85th Battalion, at Vimy and Passchendaele, a most glorious record, is sufficient proof that had the 185th Battalion, Cape Breton Highlanders, got to France as a Unit, the name not only of Nova Scotia Province but also of the Island of Cape Breton would to-day be shining with still greater glory than that which they now possess for brilliant military achievement in the late War.

THE 85th BATTALION

As it was, however, the records of individual officers and men of the 185th Battalion who had transferred to the 85th and other Units on the 185th being broken up just before the initial drive of 1918, were such as to give a noble name not only to themselves individually, but also to the 185th Battalion and Cape Breton Island, where this splendid Unit of fighting men was recruited.

Reverting now to the 85th Battalion as such, after due training, and many inexplicable disappointments in earlier sailing for Overseas, the 85th Battalion, and the other Units of the Nova Scotia Highland Brigade, broke camp on October 11, 1916, and sailed for England on October 13, 1916, aboard H.M. Transport *Olympic*. The 85th and the Nova Scotia Highland Brigade disembarked at Liverpool on October 19, 1916, and immediately entrained for Witley Camp, Surrey, arriving in Camp the same evening. Following the breaking up of the Nova Scotia Highland Brigade, and the reorganization of the 85th, the Battalion sailed for France on February 10, 1917, going into training for service in the Field at Gouy Servins, Bouvigny, and Bouvigny Wood, from which quarters the Battalion moved up to Music Hall Line, in the reserves, to take part as "a working Unit" in the Battle of Vimy Ridge (April 9, 1917).

Including Vimy, the 85th Battalion was in the following engagements—Vimy, April 9 to 14, 1917; "The Triangle," June 20, 1917; Ontario Trench, June 26, 1917; Eleu dit Leauvette and the Horse Shoe, June 28, 1917; Lens, July to October, 1917; Passchendaele, October 28 to November 2, 1917; Arleux, June, 1918; Fompoux, July, 1918; Amiens, August 8 to 11, 1918; Arras (Drocourt-Queant Line), September 2 to 5, 1918; Cambrai (Bourlon), September 25 to October 2, 1918; Valenciennes, November, 1918; Quievrechain, November, 1918; Honnelle River, November, 1918.

What the Battalion did after the signing of the Armistice is of no military significance. It returned from France to England on May 1, 1919, took part in the Great March of Triumph through London on May 3, 1919; sailed from England for Canada on May 31, 1919; and arrived at Halifax on June 8, 1919, and two days later marched through the City of Halifax, which was *en fête* to give the Unit a memorably joyous welcome home. It was not, however, a welcome from the city, but from the whole Province, and it is estimated that 60,000 outside visitors—friends and relatives—of the returned victors must have been present among the citizens of Halifax to witness the home-coming parade of the 85th Battalion, Nova Scotia Highlanders. A week later (June 15, 1919), a remnant company of the Battalion fell in at Grafton Park, Halifax, and headed by the Royal Canadian Regiment Band, marched with its King's and Regimental Colors to Government House, where the colors were deposited in the presence of His Honor Lieutenant-Governor Grant, Colonel W. E. Thompson, D.O.C., M.D. No. 6, and Staff. On the occasion Lieut.-Col. James Layton Ralston, C.M.G., D.S.O., with Bar, Commanding the 85th, read an address of farewell to the officers and N.C.O.'s and men assembled—and thus the history of the 85th Battalion, Nova Scotia Highlanders, as a fighting Unit, came to an end.

In the proper places there will be explicit observations on the achievements of the Battalion, individual officers, N.C.O.'s and men on the Field. In the meantime, following is a summary of the honors and awards (259 in total) that belong to the Battalion:—

C.M.G.	1
D.S.O.	4
Bar to D.S.O.	1
M.C.	34
Bar to M.C.	3
D.C.M.	15
M.S.M.	4
M.M.	166
Bar to M.M.	12
Croix de Guerre	5
Mentioned in Despatches twice	4
Mentioned in Despatches—Officers	9
Mentioned in Despatches—Warrant Officers	1
Total	259

The first "big show" or engagement in which the 85th Battalion took part was that of Vimy Ridge. Theirs was not at first an envious situation. The Battalion had been substituted for another in the 12th Brigade, but the actual taking over did not ensue till after the Battle of Vimy Ridge. For that engagement the 85th was attached to the 11th Brigade, commanded by Brigadier-General Odlum. For the Battle of Vimy Ridge the 85th moved into position in the reserves, and was to serve as "a working Unit," that is,

THE 85th BATTALION

to follow up the troops in action, and to carry ammunition, build dugouts, keep up communication trenches, clear wire entanglements, and in general, as the phrase is, " to mop up." The 85th, of course, could be called on, as they were, to fight in an emergency. But they were regarded as " green troops," and it was not considered likely by the authorities that the Battalion would be efficient and steady under slaughterous fire. As a matter of fact, all the while between the Battalion's arrival at Gouy Servins till the Unit moved out from quarters into the reserve at Music Hall Line for their part in the Battle of Vimy Ridge, the Commanding Officer, Lieut.-Col. A. H. Borden, the Second in Command, Lieut.-Col. E. C. Phinney, the Adjutant, Major J. L. Ralston, and Assistant Adjutant, Lieut. A. T. Croft, had been preparing the Battalion as much for a fighting Unit as for a working Unit—having had the German lines at Vimy all taped out to scale, and having trained the Unit in every detail of the coming operation, until all ranks knew the precise "lay" of the Vimy Front and how the fighting Units as such would operate in action. Thus considered, the 85th Battalion was not a Unit of " green troops " in the ordinary acceptance of the phrase. They were " ready for fight "—and unexpectedly they got their chance, and achieved to their immortal glory.

The Battle of Vimy Ridge opened in the early morn of Easter Monday, April 9, 1917. At first it was all clear gain for the Canadians. But, at last, toward the evening, word kept coming back that the Canadian advance was being held up, that Hill 145 remained untaken, that it was a "nasty critical situation," because the enfilading of the Huns would destroy attacking troops totally, and that if Hill 145 were not somehow taken, the engagement would fail. Where were there fresh troops who could be sent in to take Hill 145? It is understood that Colonel Hilliam, commanding the 25th Battalion, Nova Scotia's invincible " Shock Troops," recommended that the 85th Battalion be selected for the feat. He assured Brigadier Odlum that even if they were " green troops " they would be steady under fire. The die was cast. Orders came from headquarters that two Companies of the 85th were to go into the line at sundown and assault Hill 145. Lieut.-Col. Borden, Commanding Officer, selected " C " and " D " Companies, and placed Capt.

Percival W. Anderson in command, with Capt. Harvey E. Crowell in command of " C " Company.

At zero hour " C " Company went over the top, followed immediately by " D " Company, but, for good reasons, without the usual barrage. The 85th had *dared*. The question now was on the part of the Units that had been held up, Would the 85th also *DO?* From the moment the Companies went over the top, they proceeded on to their objective, the crest of Hill 145, with the precision and steadiness of inured troops. There is no necessity to describe the assault in detail. But when the Huns first saw the 85th Companies going over the top, they were amazed. As the Companies proceeded forward, steady and indomitable in spite of the gun fire and the hail of bullets from concealed nests of machine guns, the while themselves wreaking destruction on the Bosche, the Germans became alarmed. And when the 85th Companies still kept on, in the same spirit, and with the same effectiveness, the Huns became disconcerted, and at last ignominiously turned and " beat it," leaving Hill 145—the Huns' "pivotal strategic stronghold "—in possession of the 85th Companies and the Canadian Corps. The clearing up of the Ridge and the advance of the 85th Companies to the Lens-Arras Road need not detain us. On the morning of April 14, 1917, the Battalion was relieved by the Royal Sussex, and marched back to rest quarters at Bouvigny Huts.

LIEUT.-COL. E. C. PHINNEY.

There were many acts of heroism on the part of officers, N.C.O.'s and men during the first day of the Vimy Ridge " show " and on later days. One phrase might be applied to summarize the conduct of the Commanding Officer (Lieutenant-Colonel Borden), the Second in Command (Lieutenant-Colonel Phinney), and the Adjutant, Major J. L. Ralston, who had the task of consolidating the line after the taking of the Ridge; not only were they all the time " cool, calm and collected," but the three showed distinct military genius. Outstanding was the conduct of Capt. Percival W. Anderson, who, amongst other exploits, single-handed performed a deed of heroism which won for him the Military Cross (it should have been the V.C.). One of the men in the patrols suffered a bad wound. His groans were heard in "No Man's Land," but he lay where the whole field was raked by rifle and machine-gun fire. Captain Anderson would not ask or command any of his men to attempt a rescue, but went out himself and carried the wounded man back to safety. This splendid soldier and officer was killed at the Battle of Passchendaele, his death profoundly regretted; for he knew no fear, and he was a superb officer and leader of men, a splendid example of the Cape Breton Highlander.

The list of those who turned exploits and won awards at Vimy is too long to admit of detailed accounts. But specially to be mentioned are Capt. H. E. Crowell, Capt. H. B. Clarke, Chaplain, and later Transport Officer (acting); Lieuts. H. C. Verner ("Hell-Fire" Verner), Douglas Graham, Hugh A. Crawley, F. C. Manning; and amongst the privates and N.C.O.'s—Pte. C. A. McLeod, Pte. H. C. Steeves, Pte. A. J. Murphy, Pte. J. S. Westlake, Pte. L. M. Gates, Pte. K. Manoles, Pte. J. C. Taylor, Pte. C. J. Doucette, Runners, Ptes. W. E. Stackhouse, W. W. Pearson and G. B. Peck; Lance-Corporal A. F. MacAree, Lance-Corporal V. M. Lindsay, Lance-Corporal H. W. Hardy, Corporal C. D. Reid, and Sergt. W. U. Martel.

The courage, pluck, indomitableness and resourcefulness of the officers, N.C.O.'s and men of the 85th Battalion at the Battle of Vimy Ridge were instanced not to glorify the Battalion, but to show forth the kind of "stuff" that was the spirit of the Unit. The same kind of spirit was shown in all subsequent engagements— "The Triangle," Ontario Trench, Eleu dit Leauvette and the Horse Shoe and around Lens, up to Passchendaele. The outstanding phase of the long Battle of Passchendaele (October 28 to November 2, 1917) was the recapturing of the front line by "D" Company (Cape Bretoners), commanded by Captain Ross M. MacKenzie— another "saving of the day," as at Vimy, by the 85th Battalion. The 85th was, as decided, to be in the line for a day before going over the top. However, before that move, "D" Company was to take over the whole Battalion frontage, the other Companies to remain at the rear. A Western Canadian Unit was in the line, and just as "D" Company reached the line for the relief of the Western Battalion, the Huns launched a violent and destructive counter-attack. Captain MacKenzie and "D" Company saw that the Western Battalion was falling back, and the Huns advancing in great force. It was a critical situation, and Captain MacKenzie at once offered himself and his Company to reinforce the retiring Unit. The offer was gladly accepted. Captain MacKenzie ordered his Company to drop all kit, and to fix bayonets and advance in true Highland fashion. With huzzas they made for the enemy—dashing upon the Huns with such a rush and momentum, that the Huns became bewildered, next were seized with panic, broke, and "beat it." The situation was saved, and the line recaptured shortly by continued advance to the position from which the Western Battalion was forced to retire. But that advance was costly in casualties, for it was covered by enemy machine guns and snipers' posts. Then it was that the ancient fighting spirit of his Gaelic ancestors shone brilliantly in Captain MacKenzie, and he became the Gaelic Hero Cuchullain in the fight and in death. MacKenzie was shot through the abdomen—some say he was literally riddled—with machine gun bullets, and he fell. But he struggled to his feet and kept on with his Company, bleeding to death, and commanded his men, encouraging them, until he dropped exhausted into a shell hole. Even then, though undone, he would not be attended to, but kept encouraging his Company. Eventually he permitted himself to be placed on a stretcher, and while being borne away, he died—like Cuchullain too, unconquerable in death. There were many other individual examples of heroism on that day and during the days that followed at Passchendaele. But the slaughter was awful: and while the engagement added fresh glory to the 85th Battalion, and is a memorial to the living, it is to be regarded as an apotheosis of all 85th officers, non-commissioned officers and men who fell at that mysteriously ordered engagement —Major P. W. Anderson, M.C., Capts. John M. Hensley, E. R. Clayton, M.C., and Ross M. MacKenzie, Lieuts. Walter U. Martel, M.M., Frank O. Hutchison, Angus D. MacDonald, Norman C. Christie, Alexander D. Fraser, Fred J. Anderson, John R. Mac-Farlane, W. H. Murr and R. Salisman, and the 123 privates and

LIEUT. A. D. FRASER.

MAJOR P. W. ANDERSON.

LIEUT. A. D. MACDONALD.

CAPT. ROSS MACKENZIE.

LIEUT. J. R. MACFARLANE.

LIEUT. N. C. CHRISTIE.

CAPT. JOHN M. HENSLEY.

non-commissioned officers. It was for their bravery and resourcefulness and indomitableness—their sheer invincibility—at Passchendaele that the 85th Battalion won from the other Units in the Canadian Corps and the Imperials the noteworthy, if slangy, complimentary epithet, "The Never Fails."

From Passchendaele to the signing of the Armistice would furnish only repetitions of the records of the 85th Battalion in action. It was all a most honorable and glorious record, quite worthy to stand beside that of Canadian Units which had seen longer service. It would not do, however, to bring this summary narrative to a close without mentioning the characteristics of the outstanding officers, but for whom the 85th would not have been a reality, or would not have achieved so splendidly. First, let it be remembered .perennially that all honor and distinction belongs to Lieut.-Col. Allison H. Borden for conceiving the idea of a distinctly Nova Scotia Highland Battalion, and, later, a distinctly Nova Scotia Highland Brigade. As an officer he always displayed vision and decision, great gifts for organization; and in the Field he was a gallant and resourceful soldier, to whom the loss of men in action was felt as a poignant personal loss. He was awarded the Distinguished Service Order. But posterity will gratefully remember him and honor his name as the Organizer and Commanding Officer of the 85th Battalion, Nova Scotia Highlanders, and the Organizer and Brigadier of the Nova Scotia Highland Brigade. Lieut.-Col. Earle C. Phinney was a young officer, and, in turn, filled several positions from Adjutant to Commanding Officer in Canada and in England, and had the honor of taking the 85th to France, where, though he had voluntarily reverted to Second in Command, he was temporarily in command till the arrival of Lieut.-Colonel Borden. He made a record at Vimy for coolness and resourcefulness in the Field. In a later engagement he was wounded, and was eventually invalided home. Lieut.-Col. J. L. Ralston, who brought the 85th home, as Commanding Officer, also served as Adjutant and as Commanding Officer in the Field. He was his officers' and men's ideal of "the splendid soldier," intrepid and indomitable, and always resourceful. He was wounded several times; and was awarded the D.S.O. and Bar to the D.S.O., and honored by the King with the C.M.G. Lieut.-Col. Joseph Hayes was unique as an

THE 85th BATTALION

officer. He was the M.O. of the Battalion, and a more humane and intrepid M.O. there was not in the Canadian Corps. Though several years past the age limit, he never missed a day from the line from Vimy to Passchendaele, and did much to keep up the morale and fighting spirit of the officers and men of the 85th. In a phrase, Lieut.-Col. Joseph Hayes was a gallant officer, a genuinely brave soldier, and a humane and kind medical expert in the line. The

LIEUT.-COL. J. L. RALSTON, C.M.G., D.S.O.

hygiene of the Battalion, which was a record in the Canadian Corps, was due to Colonel Hayes' rigorous supervision of camp and line sanitation and his meticulous care of the person, food and potables of the officers and men. He was awarded the D.S.O. It is impossible to make a "Homeric Catalogue" of the character and deeds of all the other officers. Suffice it to say that they all were good men and true. The Battalion had the distinction of having Sir Robert Borden, Premier of Canada, as Honorary Colonel.

Killed in Action while serving with the 85th in France and Flanders

LIEUT. O'DONOHUE.

LIEUT. G. F. CANN.

MAJOR IVAN RALSTON.

LIEUT. J. HOLLAND.

LIEUT. GEO. T. LYE.

LIEUT. ERIC LANE.

CAPT. A. M'KINNON.

LIEUT. N. L. CHIPMAN.   LIEUT. CYRIL A. EVANS.   **CAPT. W. T. RUGGLES.** Died after return to Canada.

LIEUTENANT THURBER.   CAPT. T. M. M'LEAN.

LIEUT. F. C. MANNING.   CAPT. M. W. M'KINNON.   LIEUT. J. O. M'LEOD.

NOVA SCOTIA'S PART IN THE GREAT WAR

85th BATTALION BRASS AND REED BAND.

THE literary and the musical professions were well represented in the personnel of the 85th Battalion—by one historian, two poets, and a brass and wood-wind band, an organization of instrumentalists that gave the Battalion additional and peculiar distinction and glory. Lieut.-Colonel Hayes in England and France acted as a free-lance war correspondent and, on arrival home, set to work to prepare the History of the 85th Battalion. He produced an illustrated work of nearly 400 pages—a most readable volume, the first history of any Nova Scotia fighting Unit that had taken part in the late War. It was hurriedly prepared, under very difficult conditions, but despite a minimum of slight and inevitable discrepancies or omissions—every history from Thucydides to John Richard Green has these—it is a well-written and accurate work, a genuine monument to the literary acumen and devotion of that versatile and gallant officer, Lieut.-Col. Joseph Hayes. The two poets were the late Lieut. Frederick C. Manning, a brilliant alumnus of Acadia University, whose "Poems" were posthumously published. They are excellent poems, both in conception and in craftsmanship, and go to prove how great a wastage of brain power and rare spirit was caused by the late War. The other poet was Sergt. J. D. Logan, an alumnus of Harvard University. He was a free-lance war correspondent at the Front. He published two volumes of war poems—"Insulters of Death and Other Poems of the Great Departure" (1916), and "The New Apocalypse and Other Poems of Days and Deeds in France" (1919), besides a series of magazine articles on special phases of the War, a series entitled "From Vimy to Passchendaele" (1918), and before sailing for Overseas a pamphlet on the 85th Band ("Canada's Champion Regimental Band"). All this is mentioned to show that military training for active warfare and actual warfare do not necessarily kill the finer spirit of men or turn soldiers from human beings into brutes. But the chief aesthetic glory of the 85th Battalion was its extraordinary fine marching and symphonic band. Following are the salient facts in its history.

The band was the descendant of the old Albion Mines (Stellarton) Band, established in the '40's of the last century, and having a continuous history of nearly three-quarters of a century to date. It was for years the regimental band of the 78th Pictou Highlanders. Lieut.-Colonel Borden, commanding the 85th, asked Lieut. Dan. Mooney, bandmaster of the Stellarton or 78th Band, to organize a band for the 85th. The original personnel of the 85th Band, the personnel which went Overseas with the Battalion, was: Lieut. Dan. Mooney, Bandmaster; Sergt. J. C. Profitt, Corpls. W. D. MacLeod and Alex. Myers, Ptes. A. H. MacDougall, R. H. Roy, Ronald MacDougall, E. B. Mitchell (did not sail), R. Y. Geddes, C. A. MacDonald, A. J. Fraser, T. R. Roy, J. W. Henderson, T. B. Davidson (died in France), C. W. Appleton, H. P. Barnes, F. T. Freeman, J. J. Gray, T. Mason, C. A. ("Chud") MacDonald, A. R. MacDonald, A. A. MacDougall, J. R. Munro, H. H. Murray, C. E. Purves, G. A. Rackham, W. D. Jamieson, F. A. Ryan, W. P. Cameron, Joseph Smith, James Roy, D. W. Cameron, W. E. Gallagher, F. D. Mooney, A. F. Gallant, W. Dunn (did not sail, died later), Sergt. J. D. Logan.

This band was distinguished in musicianship by *versatility*, *virtuosity* and *brilliancy*. It had acquired a notable reputation for these qualities in Canada, and when Overseas, in England, where it was in demand by towns near Camp Witley, for social functions of a semi-military or war-propaganda nature. The Director of Musical Services, who came to Camp Witley, to hear and conduct the band at rehearsal said of it, in writing: "*It is the best band that has come Overseas from Canada,*" and remarked specially on its precision in attack, its unanimity, its dynamic qualities and nuancing, and its brilliancy.

Now, bands in camp and rest quarters are regarded as good for the morale of Units, but generally were considered as impedimenta (or superfluous baggage) with a Unit active in the Field. But the officers and men of the 85th were insistent in their outspoken demand—" We want our band." The problem was how to keep the band from being broken up, and how to get the bandsmen, with their instruments, into France. It was achieved by the characteristic resourcefulness of the Commanding Officer and officers. When the 85th crossed to France the band was not on the establishment. The bandsmen, however, were brought over on the strength as fighting men, and the instruments came along too, somehow mysteriously, as part of the Quartermaster's stores (Capt. Robert Donaldson was Quartermaster—and a kinder and more resourceful Quartermaster there was not in the Canadian Corps). The bandsmen and their instruments being in France, their fixed place on the establishment of the Battalion was finally adjusted by the authorities.

The fame of this band soon spread throughout the 4th Division and the Canadian Corps, and into England; and it became a matter of perpetual demand for the 85th Band to be present and to play at concert parties and at parades and other functions of the Division and Brigade. This was due more particularly to the versatility of the band in *soloists* and a *group of entertainers* amongst the personnel, who formed a concert party by themselves. It is without question that Thomas Roy, euphonium soloist; Percival Barnes, piccolo and flute soloist; R. MacDougall and D. W. Cameron, cornet soloists; J. C. Profitt and Alex. Myers, clarinet soloists; Alex. ("Attell") MacDougall, trombone soloist, and the trombone quartet (A. MacDougall, J. J. Gray, C. E. Purves, and James Roy) were as expert instrumentalists as the trained ear could wish to hear. They earned for the band its name for virtuosity and brilliancy. The group of entertainers comprised H. H. Murray, George Rackham, Frank ("Hunk") A. Ryan, C. W. Appleton and Ronald MacDougall. Murray was vocal soloist, with band accompaniment, having a rounded cantabile baritone. He was also "the lead" in the theatrical entertainment, sketches and vaudeville, with Rackham as foil. Ryan, Appleton and R. MacDougall were step dancers, and Ryan was noted for his eccentric dancing specialties. The group, assisted by the other members of the band, also produced "The Old Homestead," in costume, at the Front.

On the day of the Great March of Triumph through London, May 3, 1919, the 85th Band made a distinct popular "hit" with

THE 85TH BATTALION.

the Londoners. The Director of Musical Services, noted the fact in the following official communication:

"Argyll House,
"London, W.I.,
"May 5th, 1919.

"To—
"Lt.-Col. G. S. Harrington,
"Deputy Minister, O.M.F.C.,
"34 Grosvenor St., W.I.

"Sir,—I have the honor to bring to your notice the musical report of the bands marching through London:—

"'The 85th Battalion Band, thirty performers, under Lieutenant Mooney, Bandmaster. This famous marching band has been sadly depleted by war losses, but gave a fine, spirited performance, which was much admired.'

"I have the honor to be,
"Sir,
"Your Obedient Servant,
"Jasper Vale-Lane,
"Musical Director."

It should be noted that the band was considerably augmented when in France; and that one member, T. B. Davidson, died, while Ben. Hichens and H. Luscomb were killed in action. It should also be noted that the 85th returned officers and men organized, under the name "The 85th Clansmen," and "The 85th Memory Club," to perpetuate the name of the Battalion and the memory of the fallen by reunions on the days of the engagements in which the Battalion took part.—L.

CHAPTER XV.

106th BATTALION, C.E.F.

THE 106th Battalion, Nova Scotia Rifles, was authorized on November 8, 1915, and recruiting commenced at once. Being the first Rifle Battalion recruited in the Maritime Provinces, it appealed strongly to the members of the various rifle clubs and was soon up to strength.

LIEUT.-COL. R. INNES.

The standards of the Battalion were high. Regimental schools for the training of non-commissioned officers were established. The motto of the Battalion was "None So Reliable," and all ranks sought to make the Battalion worthy to bear such a name.

Headquarters were established at Truro, where two Companies were stationed; the other two Companies were stationed at Springhill and Truro.

LIST OF OFFICERS.

* Killed in action or died of wounds.

Lieut.-Col. Robert Innes	O.C.
Major O. G. Heard	Second in Command.
Capt. C. M. Williams	Adjutant.
Capt. G. M. Bryce	Quartermaster.
Capt. E. L. Miller	Paymaster.
Capt. W. L. Muir	Medical Officer.
Hon. Capt. G. McL. Dix	Chaplain.
*Lieut. H. C. Dawson	Assistant Adjutant.
Lieut. S. D. Morrison	Signalling Officer.
Lieut. R. Flemming	Machine Gun Officer.
Lieut. J. T. Arenburg	Bandmaster.
*Lieut. W. R. McAskill	Base Detail.

LIEUT. W. R. M‘ASKILL
(killed in action).

LIEUT. R. H. SAWLER
(killed in action).

LIEUT. A. H. WALKER
(killed in action).

LIEUT. A. M. O'BRIEN
(killed in action).

LIEUT. P. A. FULTON
(killed in action).

"A" Company.
    *Major E. W. Joy .... O.C.
    Capt. C. B. McMullen .... Second in Command.
    *Lieut. J. F. Hallisey ....
    *Lieut. P. A. Fulton..................
    Lieut. W. R. Cox ....
    Lieut. F. S. Huntley ....

"B" Company.
    Major W. J. H. Moxom .... O.C.
    Capt. F. D. Dodsworth .... Second in Command.
    *Lieut. A. M. O'Brien ....
    Lieut. M. McRae ....
    *Lieut. A. H. Walker ....
    Lieut. F. V. Burgess ....

"C" Company.
    Major J. A. McPherson .... O.C.
    Capt. E. J. Lounsberg .... Second in Command.
    Lieut. H. A. Allum ....
    *Lieut. R. H. Sawler ....
    *Lieut. C. E. Howson ....
    Lieut. G. R. Harrison ....

"D" Company.
    Major J. R. Maxwell .... O.C.
    Capt. T. C. King .... Second in Command.
    Lieut. W. J. Brothers ....
    Lieut. M. J. Dryden ....
    Lieut. W. A. Livingstone ....
    Lieut. G. C. McDermid ....

The Battalion left Canada July 15, 1916, and encamped at Lower Dibgate, Shorncliffe, England. There it met the fate of many other Canadian Units, by being broken up into drafts to reinforce Battalions in the Field.

CHAPTER XVI.

112th BATTALION, C.E.F.

AUTHORITY for the recruiting of the 112th Battalion, with headquarters in the historic town of Windsor, N.S., was granted in November, 1915. Its personnel was composed of officers and men drawn chiefly from the western part of Nova Scotia, embracing the counties of Halifax, Hants, Kings, Annapolis, Digby, Yarmouth, Shelburne, Queens and Lunenburg. Recruiting progressed with unique rapidity and by the middle of April, 1916, the Battalion was at full strength. Over 1,500 men applied for enlistment, and of these about 300 were found medically unfit. The significance of this achievement will be seen when it is considered that it was accomplished without the aid of any extensive recruiting campaign, but by the united effort of each officer and man.

In the early days of the Unit each county was allowed to keep a detachment, providing it numbered fifty men or more, who trained in their own locality until finally mobilized in Windsor in May, 1916. There the Battalion encamped on the hill of Fort Edward, where it was subjected to a rigorous training, and the progress made elicited much praised from Major-General Sir Sam Hughes, then Minister of Militia, who inspected the Unit about the beginning of July, 1916. The period of training at Windsor was one of keen enjoyment to all concerned. Its discipline was stern, its experience was at times hard, but the life was altogether wholesome and profitable, which was evidenced by the improvement in the bearing and appearance of the Unit during its short stay at Windsor.

The Battalion was commanded by Lieut.-Col. H. B. Tremaine. The other officers were: Majors W. F. D. Brennan, second in command; T. M. Seely, M. S. Parker, T. A. Mulock; Capts. R. W. Churchill, O. G. Dauphinee (killed in action), R. T. Christie, J. Flemming (Adjutant), E. S. Spurr, M.C. (killed in action),

NOVA SCOTIA'S PART IN THE GREAT WAR

M. P. Titus (Quartermaster), H. A. MacDonald (Paymaster), John St. C. McKay (Medical Officer), C. R. Cumming (Chaplain), G. R. Martell (Chaplain), Lieuts. J. T. Probert, M.C. (killed in action), R. S. Parsons, W. D. Comstock, J. W. Hughes, J. K. Swanson (killed in action), W. G. Foster (killed in action), G. M. Hebb (killed in action), A. M. Parsons, M.C., R. M. Morris, M.C., R. B. Logan, A. H. Creighton, P. L. Wilcox, J. W. G. Lardner, W. P. Harmon, W. H. Smith, J. C. Lithgow, R. W. Dill, E. W. Bell, C. C. Morash, M. L. Tupper (killed in action), W. J. Sangster, L. E. Langley (killed in action), R. Henshaw, R. M. McGregor (killed in action), O. H. Lunham, G. W. Banks, A. T. E. Crosby, H. L. Gates.

Capt. G. R. Martell, Rector of Christchurch, Windsor, N.S., and Chaplain of the Battalion throughout its organization, did splendid work in recruiting and was beloved by all ranks. Owing to his inability to proceed Overseas, the Rev. Charles R. Cummings was appointed Chaplain and held the position until transferred to hospital duty in England preparatory to proceeding to the Chaplain Services in France in January, 1917. Captain Martell died in June, 1918.

LIEUT. WM. GORE FOSTER.

Colors for the 112th Battalion were made by Mrs. Annie Pratt, of Windsor, Nova Scotia, and were presented to the Battalion by Mrs. Tremaine, wife of the Commanding Officer, on Friday afternoon, July 21, 1916. The Battalion was formed up in mass in front of the bandstand at Victoria Park, Windsor, and addresses were delivered by the Chaplain, Mayor Roach, and others. The next day the colors were deposited in Christchurch, Windsor, where the officers and men attended divine service.

The 112th Battalion embarked at Halifax, July 23, 1916, on H.M.T. *Olympic,* and arrived at Liverpool on July 31st. Here it entrained and proceeded to Oxney Farm near Bramshott. The Unit remained there for about three weeks, after which it moved to Bramshott on the departure of the 4th Division for France. In

112th BATTALION, C.E.F.

Bramshott the Battalion was put through very intensive training, and on October 5th the first draft of 122 other ranks left for France to reinforce the 25th Battalion. On October 10th, 212 other ranks and on October 29th, 40 other ranks were sent to the 25th Battalion, all of whom proved to be a very welcome acquisition to that famous Unit. Other drafts found their way to the Royal Canadian Regiment. Most of the officers were detailed to special schools in various parts of England for a time, after which they were gradually absorbed by the Battalions already at the Front. At one time it was expected that the Battalion would become a Forestry Unit and be sent to France, but for some reason this did not eventuate, and the Battalion was gradually depleted until the remnant was finally merged into the 26th Canadian Reserve Battalion in February, 1917.

CHAPTER XVII.

THE 185th BATTALION (CAPE BRETON HIGHLANDERS)

BY CAPT. ANGUS L. M'DONALD.

IT is a difficult task indeed to compress a history of the 185th Battalion into the space allotted for the purpose in this book. It is a difficult task, because, if we exclude those Battalions that saw active service as complete Units, the history of the 185th is longer than that of any other Nova Scotia Battalion. It is a difficult task because, through this long association and through the high standard of efficiency to which the Battalion attained, there grew up between all ranks a spirit of pride in their Unit and of affectionate regard for each other, which may be fairly said to be almost unique, and which deserves a monument much grander and more enduring than this sketch can hope to raise.

LIEUT.-COL. F. P. DAY.

The origin of the 185th may be said to be in the 85th Nova Scotia Highland Battalion, recruited by Lieut.-Col. A. H. Borden in the autumn of 1915. The enthusiasm with which the people of Nova Scotia hailed the advent of the 85th Battalion engendered the more ambitious idea of a Nova Scotia Highland Brigade, and in the months of February and March, 1916, there was conducted in Nova Scotia a recruiting campaign for the raising of three additional Battalions, to form, with the 85th, a complete Brigade. The remarkable success of that campaign is now part of our Nova Scotian history.

The Island of Cape Breton was given the task of raising a Battalion, to be known as the 185th and to be under the command

THE 185th BATTALION (CAPE BRETON HIGHLANDERS)

of Lieut.-Col. F. P. Day (then Major Day) of the 85th Battalion. Though Cape Breton had already given men to the colors, in numbers far in excess of her due proportion, nevertheless, the prospect of seeing active service with a Unit distinctly and entirely Cape Breton, so fired the imagination of the young men of the Island that in three weeks the Battalion was recruited to full strength.

The sytem of recruiting employed was well calculated to obtain the best results. First, the officers were selected. Some of them were Cape Bretoners, serving with the 85th Battalion, a few came from the Officers' Training Corps of the Colleges, but the majority were drawn from the 94th, the Cape Breton Militia Unit. These officers were sent out into their own native districts to recruit men for their own Companies or Platoons, and the assurance was given that men from the same locality would be placed together in the same Company, Platoon, or Section as the case might be, and under an officer from that locality. That assurance was kept sacredly.

The motto selected for the Battalion was the same as that of the 85th—" Siol Na Fear Fearail "—" Seed of Manly Men." That motto was highly appropriate, for the ranks of the Battalion were in large part filled by descendants of Highlanders—those manly men who peopled Cape Breton in late 18th and early 19th centuries. To the Highland element in the population of Cape Breton the 185th made its greatest appeal, for the promise had been given that the Battalion should wear Highland garb, and the prospect of joining a Unit which should be clad in that picturesque and historic dress undoubtedly touched the Highland imagination. But the other races did not lag behind. The French, Irish and English elements were well represented, and there were not a few recruits of Italian and Russian extraction.

"A" Company of the 185th came from the counties of Inverness, Victoria and Richmond; "B" Company from Glace Bay and New Waterford; "C" Company from North Sydney and Sydney Mines: and "D" Company from Sydney. Broughton, eighteen miles from Sydney, was chosen as a mobilization centre, and there the Battalion assembled during the first week of April, 1916.

At Broughton, three bands, Pipe, Brass and Bugle were organized. The citizens of Glace Bay, the Royal Cape Breton Yacht

NOVA SCOTIA'S PART IN THE GREAT WAR

Club, the "Green Feather" Societies of North Sydney and Sydney Mines, and Mr. Thomas Cantley, of New Glasgow, each presented four pipes and three drums to the Battalion. Money for the purchase of instruments for the Brass Band was subscribed by the citizens of Sydney. For the Regimental March, the stirring Highland air, "A Hundred Pipers," was chosen.

Broughton did not offer a suitable ground for advanced training; and so on May 26th, 1916, the Battalion entrained for Aldershot, N.S., where the Highland Brigade was to spend the summer of 1916, under the command of Lieut.-Col. A. H. Borden, who had recruited and commanded the 85th Battalion. The other Battalions of the Brigade were the 85th, 193rd and the 219th. During the summer the Brigade was reviewed by H.R.H. the Duke of Connaught, Governor-General of Canada; by Sir Sam Hughes, Canadian Minister of Militia; by Major-General Lessard, Inspector-General for Canada. It was twice reviewed by Sir Robert Borden, Prime Minister of Canada. On the last visit of Sir Robert Borden, he was accompanied by Lady Borden, who presented colors to the Battalion. The colors are of beautiful design, rich material and elegant workmanship. They were received on behalf of the Battalion by Major Harrington and Lieutenants Purves and Livingstone, and were blessed by Capt. Michael Gillis, Roman Catholic Chaplain to the Battalion. (The colors were taken to England with the Battalion and after the War were returned to Canada, deposited in the Cape Breton County Court House at Sydney.)

On October 4th the Battalion underwent successfully at the hands of Major-General Lessard its last inspection in Canada. Preparations for embarking for England were begun and on October 11th the 185th bade good-bye to Aldershot and entrained for Halifax. That evening they marched on board "His Majesty's Transport, 2810," the war-time designation of the great steamship *Olympic*.

At five o'clock on the evening of October 13th the *Olympic* steamed out of Halifax Harbor, bearing the Nova Scotia Highland Brigade, surely the most precious cargo that Nova Scotia ever entrusted to the mighty Atlantic. The docks at Halifax were thronged on that day with thousands of people from all parts of

THE 185th BATTALION (CAPE BRETON HIGHLANDERS)

Nova Scotia who had come to say good-bye—in many cases unfortunately a last good-bye—to relatives and friends. Nova Scotia loves her own, sorrows over their departure from her bosom, and watches their fortunes under foreign skies with a fond eye and an anxious heart. I was told in London that, after any battle in which Canadian troops had taken part, there were more enquiries at Canadian Headquarters in London, from Nova Scotians, than from people of any other Province of Canada. I could well believe this to have been so, for in Nova Scotia character, friendship and loyalty to kith and kin are outstanding characteristics.

The officers of the 185th at the time of sailing for England were as follows:

Honorary Colonel .... Col. D. H. MacDougall.
Officer Commanding .... Lieut.-Col. Frank P. Day.
Second in Command .... Major J. G. Johnstone.
Adjutant .... Capt. R. C. Jackson.
Medical Officer .... Capt. J. A. Munro.
Paymaster .... Capt. R. MacDougall.
Quartermaster .... Capt. J. T. Malone.
Protestant Chaplain .... Capt. A. J. MacDonald.
R. C. Chaplain .... Capt. Michael Gillis.
Machine Gun Officer .... Lieut. J. A. Holland.

"A" Company—
  Officer Commanding .... Capt. J. MacIsaac.
  Second in Command .... Capt. A. L. Macdonald.
  Lieutenants .... H. N. Price, John MacKenzie, J. D. MacKenzie, E. M. Johnstone.

"B" Company—
  Officer Commanding .... Major G. S. Harrington.
  Second in Command .... Capt. A. J. MacInnis.
  Lieutenants .... C. MacLeod, W. F. Carroll, J. A. McKinnon, J. H. MacIvor.

"C" Company—
  Officer Commanding .... Capt. W. W. Nicholson.
  Second in Command .... Capt. Alex. MacDonald.
  Lieutenants .... T. D. A. Purves, D. N. MacDonald, L. G. MacCorrison.

"D" Company—
  Officer Commanding .... Major J. W. Maddin.
  Second in Command .... Capt. C. W. Sutherland.
  Lieutenants .... A. M. Fraser, D. M. Wiswell, G. D. Crowell, D. Livingstone.

The voyage from Halifax to Liverpool was made in a little over five days. The Battalion disembarked on the morning of

October 19th, the Pipe Band playing the men down the gangway. Immediately the train was taken to Witley Camp, which was reached after a journey of eight hours. Here the Battalion settled down to work as part of the 12th Canadian Infantry Training Brigade, which name replaced the old name, "Nova Scotia Highland Brigade."

In early December there came tidings which nearly every Canadian Battalion that ever went to England had grown to dread. The Battalion was called on to supply a draft of 192 men for France. The other Battalions of the Brigade had received similar orders, the total number of men required from the Brigade being 800. The call for these drafts seemed to spell the disruption of the Brigade, notwithstanding promises to the contrary in Canada. The strongest protests were made by officers of the Brigade, but to no avail. On December 5th the drafts set out for Southampton whence they were to embark for Havre. The 185th sent 20 men to the 42nd (Montreal) Battalion, and 172 men to the 73rd Battalion, also of Montreal.

Each Battalion of the Brigade had now been considerably reduced in strength, and the Canadian authorities in England decided to amalgamate the 219th with the 85th Battalion, and the 193rd with the 185th Battalion. Officers and men in any one of these four Units who were not physically fit were sent to the 17th Nova Scotia Reserve Battalion at Bramshott. The Nova Scotia Highland Brigade was no more, and the hope in every heart now was that the two Battalions—85th and 185th—which constituted what was left of that Brigade, might reach France as Units.

After the amalgamation of the 193rd, the officers of the 185th were as follows:—

Officer Commanding	Lieut.-Col. F. P. Day.
Second in Command	Lieut.-Col. R. J. S. Langford.
Adjutant	Major J. W. MacDonald.
Medical Officer	Capt. J. A. Munro.
Quartermaster	Capt. F. C. Baird.
Paymaster	Capt. R. MacDougall.
Assistant Adjutant	Lieut. W. E. Macdonald.
Machine Gun Officer	Lieut. J. A. Holland.
Musketry Officer	Lieut. D. M. Wiswell.
Scout Officer	Lieut. H. N. Price.
Bombing Officer	Lieut. J. D. MacKenzie.

THE 185th BATTALION (CAPE BRETON HIGHLANDERS)

"A" Company—
Officer Commanding .... Capt. J. MacIsaac.
Second in Command .... Capt. A. L. Macdonald.
Lieutenants .... John MacKenzie, E. M. Johnstone, T. E. Logan, C. J. Markham.

"B" Company—
Officer Commanding .... Major J. P. LeGallais.
Second in Command .... Capt. F. B. Schurman.
Lieutenants .... J. A. McKinnon, J. H. MacIvor, J. Soy, P. T. Andrews, H. A. Dickson, A. D. Baxter.

"C" Company—
Officer Commanding .... Capt. W. W. Nicholson.
Second in Command .... Capt. Alex. Macdonald.
Lieutenants .... D. J. MacGillivray, H. F. Orman, L. G. MacCorrison, H. D. Cunningham, D. Livingstone.

"D" Company—
Officer Commanding .... Capt. R. C. Jackson.
Second in Command .... Capt. C. W. Sutherland.
Lieutenants .... A. M. Fraser, J. O. MacLeod, J. J. Murray, G. D. Crowell, H. C. Lowther.

About this time the Battalion received permission to use as its official name, "185th Canadian Infantry Battalion (Cape Breton Highlanders)," instead of "185th Canadian Infantry Battalion," as before.

In the spring of 1917, the 5th Canadian Division was organized at Witley Camp, under the command of Major-General Garnet Hughes, who had already won high distinction in France. The 185th was given a place in that Division. The Division was assured that it would be sent to France, and in that hope it set to work with such earnestness that in the summer of 1917 it was regarded as one of the most efficient Divisions that had ever trained in England. The 185th by hard and persevering work had won the reputation of being unexcelled, and by many unbiased observers it was regarded as unequalled, in the whole Division. Certainly, the Battalion was often specially complimented by Inspecting Officers and was often singled out for particular honor. At the great Dominion Day Parade in London, in 1917, the Guard of Honor for the Colors was drawn from the 185th. Again and again its teams won from other Battalion teams in competitions in Musketry, Bayonet Fighting, Physical Training, Drill and Machine Gun Work.

From the first the men had looked forward eagerly to the day when kilts would be issued to the Battalion. Their wish was realized in August, 1917, when kilts of the Argyll and Sutherland tartan were authorized to be worn, and sufficient kilts were sent to the Quartermaster to clothe the whole Battalion.

Reference has been made already to the promise given to the 5th Division that it would go to France intact. That promise was repeated several times, and the hope that it would be kept was the only ground on which men could be induced to remain contentedly in England. But no phrase has done better service during the War than the phrase "military exigencies," and it was invoked once again to justify the disbanding of the 5th Division in February, 1918.

Coincident with the breakup of the Division came the order to the 185th to furnish a draft of two officers and one hundred men to each of the three Nova Scotian Battalions in France—the 25th, 85th and R.C.R. All the men at once volunteered. Sergeants reverted to the rank of private in order to get to France more quickly; Colonels reverted and became Majors; Majors became Captains and Captains Subalterns. The drafts for France were finally selected, and the rest of the Battalion was ordered to be sent to Bramshott, to be absorbed by the 17th Reserve. On February 23rd the Battalion paraded for the last time, the drafts for France stood fast, the draft for Bramshott swung out on the London-Portsmouth Road, the pipers played their last march, and the 185th passed out of existence as an Overseas Unit forever.

It is idle now to lament its unhappy fate, or to deplore the peculiar policy that was pursued toward it and other Battalions of the 5th Division, but Cape Bretoners everywhere will always have difficulty in restraining a regretful sigh over the lot of their own and only Battalion. Let it always be remembered, however, that through no fault of its own did the 185th fail to reach France as a Unit. It kept faith with the people of Cape Breton, and it established a standard which any Battalion might be proud to emulate.

But though there never fell to this Battalion the supreme honor of battle or the glory of triumph, its individual members went forth to war, stronger in training, in discipline, in comradeship and in spirit from their association with the Cape Breton Highlanders.

THE 185th BATTALION (CAPE BRETON HIGHLANDERS)

Every officer of the Battalion saw service in some theatre of war, and five of them now sleep on the field of honor—Lieutenants Fraser, Holland, MacIvor, Livingstone and J. O. MacLeod. Nearly every other officer of the Battalion has been wounded, and several have been decorated for bravery. Of the men it is enough to say that incomplete returns show that 136 of them fell in action. On

LIEUT. A. FRASER
(killed in action).

LIEUT. J. H. M'IVOR
(killed in action).

LIEUT. D. LIVINGSTONE
(killed in action).

CAPT. JOHN T. MALONE
(died on active service)

their graves may the turf lie lightly. Truer hearts or more gallant spirits never fought for any cause, and to them we may be sure that every Cape Breton tongue will apply with heartfelt sincerity the words that have been chosen for the crosses that will mark the graves of British soldiers buried in France—"Their Name Liveth Forevermore."

CHAPTER XVIII.

THE 193rd BATTALION.

THE 193rd Battalion was authorized on January 27, 1916, and John Stanfield, M.P. for Colchester, in the Dominion House of Commons, was gazetted Lieut.-Colonel and appointed Commanding Officer.

For a few weeks following this date the 193rd Battalion was not regarded as a Highland Brigade Battalion, but on February 23, 1916, Lieut.-Colonel Stanfield was officially notified that the 193rd had been selected as one of the Brigade Units.

LIEUT.-COL. JOHN STANFIELD.

Organization for recruiting had already been effected, and the 193rd was in a position to join in the Brigade campaign at once. The territory of the Battalion embraced the six Eastern Counties of the Mainland—Cumberland, Colchester, Hants, Pictou, Antigonish and Guysboro, with headquarters at Truro. Within one month the Battalion was over strength.

On March 24th Capt. J. L. Ralston, of the 85th Battalion, reported for duty as Acting Adjutant. His assistance was invaluable and counted for much in these early days of organization. Capt. J. Welsford MacDonald relieved him on April 7th and was appointed Adjutant. He was later succeeded by Capt. F. B. Schurman.

In February Lieut.-Colonel Stanfield had asked for the services of Capt. R. J. S. Langford, of the Royal Canadian Regiment, Halifax. On April 18th Captain Langford was attached to the 193rd, with the rank of Major, was appointed second in command

THE 193rd BATTALION

and took over the duties of officer in charge of training. The high standard of efficiency to which the Battalion later attained was brought about by Major Langford's enthusiastic and unremitting efforts.

The mobilization of the Battalions of the Highland Brigade at Camp Aldershot in May, 1916, is dealt with elsewhere in this volume. The 193rd arrived in Camp 300 men over strength.

Early in September the Brigadier, Lieut.-Colonel Borden, left for England, and was succeeded in the command of the Brigade by Lieut.-Colonel Stanfield. Major Langford took over the command of the Battalion with the rank of Lieut.-Colonel.

On September 26th, Lady Borden, wife of the Premier of Canada, presented King's and Regimental Colors to the four Battalions of the Brigade.

LIEUT. "TOMMY" LOGAN.
Killed in action.

The distinctive color selected by the 193rd was "Royal Blue."

The Battalion embarked on the *Olympic,* October 12th. The officers at that time were:

```
Lieut.-Col. R. J. S. Langford ....... O.C.
Major J. P. LeGallais .............. Second in Command.
Capt. F. B. Schurman .............. Adjutant.
Capt. F. C. Baird ................. Quartermaster.
Capt. C. S. McArthur .............. Paymaster.
Capt. E. D. McLean ................ Medical Officer.
Capt. J. F. Tupper ................ Chaplain.
```

"A" COMPANY—Major A. T. McLean, Company Commander; Capt. C. A. Good, Second in Command; Lieuts. H. F. Orman, D. J. McGillivray P. Andrews, H. A. Dickson.

"B" COMPANY—Capt. R. K. Smith, Company Commander; Capt. R. G. McKay, Second in Command; Lieuts. N. C. Christie, J. M. Soy, H. C. Lowther, C. F. Wetmore.

"C" COMPANY—Major A. A. Sturley, Company Commander; Capt. A. B. Todd, Second in Command; Lieuts. H. DeW. Cunningham, H. B. Potter, J. A. Ross, C. J. Markham.

"D" COMPANY—Major J. W. MacDonald, Company Commander; Capt. G. McQuarrie, Second in Command; Lieuts. J. O. McLeod, W. E. McDonald, T. E. Logan, J. J. Murray.

A few weeks after arrival at Witley Camp, Lieut.-Colonel Borden returned from the Front and resumed command of the Brigade. Lieut.-Colonel Stanfield, owing to ill-health, was invalided back to Canada. When the Brigade was broken up in December, 1916, the following officers, with 300 other ranks, were transferred to the 185th Battalion: Lieut.-Colonel R. J. S. Langford, Major J. P. LeGallais, Major J. W. MacDonald, Capt. F. B. Schurman, Capt. F. C. Baird, Lieuts. H. F. Orman, D. J. McGillivray, P. Andrews, H. A. Dickson, J. M. Soy, H. DeW. Cunningham, C. J. Markham, J. O. McLeod, W. E. McDonald, J. J. Murray.

The remainder marched to Bramshott, where they were absorbed early in January, 1917, by the 17th Reserve Battalion, and used as reinforcements to the Nova Scotian Battalions in the Field.

CHAPTER XIX.

219th BATTALION, C.E.F.

IN the limited space allowed for this article it is necessary to omit references to the stirring events which marked the recruiting of the Battalions of the Nova Scotia Highland Brigade, the 185th in Cape Breton, the 193rd in Pictou, Colchester, Cumberland and Hants Counties, and the 219th in Halifax and the Western Counties of the Province. Each contributed to the popular enthusiasm, and through the agency of the press any unusual success in one part was heralded throughout the Province and bore fruit in distant sections.

In Halifax and the Western Counties, while there were many agencies at work, too numerous to mention, they naturally centred around the extraordinary series of meetings addressed by Colonel Borden and Captain Cutten, when, accompanied by the 85th Band, they made their historic tour, commencing at Lunenburg on February 26, 1916, and ending at Wolfville on March 12th.

LIEUT.-COL. W. H. MUIRHEAD.

They touched at all the chief points on the Halifax and South Western Railway and returned by the Dominion Atlantic as far as Wolfville. While active recruiting in many places had preceded and prepared for their arrival, the extraordinary enthusiasm aroused by their speeches and by the martial strains of the band formed an epoch in each community.

Recruits enrolled were billeted in their own towns, and detachments marched into Camp Aldershot on June 1st from Lunenburg, Mahone Bay, Bridgewater, Lockport, Caledonia, Shelburne, Clarke's Harbor, Barrington, Yarmouth, Weymouth, Trenton, Digby, Bear

River, Annapolis, Berwick, Bridgetown, Kentville, Wolfville, Dartmouth and Halifax.

The first Battalion orders on record were issued on March 6th by Major E. C. Phinney, who had been placed in temporary command of the 219th. Lieut. C. Holland was appointed Acting Adjutant. For some time the orders were chiefly concerned with the large accessions to the strength of the Battalion, daily reported, as the result of Colonel Borden's successful tour, and the formation of the various detachments. These recruits were now arranged in four companies, "A" in Halifax, "B" comprising the territory from Mahone Bay to Clarke's Harbor, "C" from Yarmouth to Bear River, and "D" from Annapolis to Wolfville.

The first public parade of "A" Company was on May 27th to St. Matthew's Church to attend the memorial service for Lieutenant Campbell, who had been killed in action, and who was the son of Mr. G. S. Campbell, one of the most active spirits in the recruiting campaign.

In the history of the 219th there is a humorous distinction between the first funeral procession and the first actual funeral of one of its members. One night in the early spring a fire occurred in a house in Barrington Street. Unfortunately the inmates could not be extricated in time, and some fatalities resulted. The charred remains of one body was identified as that of Metrofan Meik, a Russian recruit in the 219th. The funeral took place from St. Mary's Cathedral. A firing party was furnished by "C" Company of the 85th. The Last Post was sounded and full military honors paid to the dead. Next morning who should report in the orderly room but Metrofan himself, very much alive and feeling greatly the better for his leave, which had now expired. Who it was that was buried with military honors has never been discovered to this hour.

The first actual funeral of a soldier in the 219th took place on May 2nd, from the Military Hospital in Halifax. The deceased was Private Edwards, a native of England. The services were conducted by Hon. Captain MacKinnon.

It was on Wednesday, February 23rd, that a letter came from Ottawa authorizing the formation of the 219th and granting permission to appoint Major E. C. Phinney, of the 85th as temporary O.C. It was he who had the task of organizing the 219th, and the manner in which he accomplished this is a fine tribute to his executive ability. For the first few days he was assisted by Lieut. C. Holland, who acted as Adjutant. In the beginning of April a rumor was in circulation that the Highland Brigade was not to materialize and that the 85th was to proceed immediately Overseas. Rather than miss this opportunity of going to the Front, Major Phinney relinquished his position as Commanding Officer of the 219th and went back to his former position in the 85th.

On April 8th Lieut.-Col. N. H. Parsons became temporary C.O. of the 219th. He planned a tour of inspection, but his purpose was frustrated by a serious illness. Lieutenant Holland, who afterwards became Staff Captain in the Nova Scotia Highland Brigade, was succeeded as Acting Adjutant by Lieut. John S. Roper. He along with Major Rudland and Lieutenant Wylie had been one of a Military Committee to assist in the formation of the Battalion. He remained Adjutant throughout its whole history.

By May 4th Colonel Parsons felt sufficiently recovered to proceed with his tour of inspection, and during his absence the duties of command devolved on Major H. D. Creighton. But the atmosphere was surcharged with uncertainty and the Battalion was beginning to suffer for want of a permanent head. Lieut.-Col. Parsons returned to the 85th, and, with him, Major Creighton. At last on May 5th, Lieut.-Col. W. H. Muirhead assumed command. Immediately the unrest ceased, and the Battalion settled itself to the business of training.

On the outbreak of the War Colonel Muirhead went at once to the new camp at Valcartier and was given an appointment on the Divisional Headquarters Staff. But being unmarried and anxious to take his part in the actual fighting, he transferred to the Royal Canadian Dragoons before the First Canadian Contingent sailed, reverting to the rank of Lieutenant. Early in May, 1915, he crossed to France in the Canadian Cavalry Brigade, which included, with the Dragoons, the Strathcona Horse and the 2nd King Edward Horse. For nine months he was in the trenches, and witnessed some of the fiercest fighting of the War.

In Canada the idea was gaining ground that new troops should be instructed in the latest methods of warfare, and this could only be done by bringing some of the officers from the Front. Colonel

Muirhead was subsequently appointed second in command of the 112th, which was recruiting at the time, and he returned in January, 1916. As above stated he took over the 219th on May 5th. His keen intelligence, long familiarity with business methods, together with the stern experience he had known at the Front, fitted him in quite an exceptional manner for the command and training of a Battalion.

The Battalions at Camp Aldershot were arranged in order of seniority. Nearest to Aldershot Station was placed the 85th, and then in order the 185th, 193rd and 219th. Beyond the lines of the 219th were quartered the 97th, "The American Legion," made up of men from the United States, who had come to take their share in the fight for the freedom of the world.

Later in the season the waste land beyond the 97th was cleared and became the home of the 246th, the reserve Unit of the Brigade. It might be of interest to mention that the Nova Scotia Highland Brigade wore Balmoral caps with feathers. The feathers were dark gray, but each one of them had a distinctive coloring. In the 85th, it was red; in the 185th, green; in the 193rd, blue; and in the 219th, purple.

Naturally changes took place in the personnel of the officers of the 219th, especially late in the season, when the 246th was formed. But the following list represents with fair accuracy the situation during most of the summer:

Officer Commanding .... Lieut.-Col. W. H. Muirhead.
Second in Command .... Major M. E. Roscoe.
Adjutant .... Lieut. J. S. Roper.
Quartermaster .... Major F. W. W. Doane.
Paymaster .... Hon. Capt. H. D. Henry.
Medical Officer .... Capt. D. P. Churchill.
Chaplain .... Hon. Capt. C. MacKinnon.

"A" COMPANY—Major J. Rudland, Company Commander; Capt. H. A. Kent, Second in Command (Capt. Kent, after going Overseas, became Company Commander of "C" Company); Lieuts. V. G. Rae, E. R. Clayton, A. D. Macdonald, R. D. Graham.

"B" COMPANY—Capt. M. C. Denton, Company Commander; Capt. E. C. Miller, Second in Command (after going Overseas Capt. Miller became Company Commander); Lieuts. W. M. L. Robertson, J. Belyea, A. C. King, E. J. Hallett.

"C" COMPANY—Major A. K. Van Horne, Company Commander; (after going Overseas, Captain Kent); Lieut. G. D. Blackadar, Second in Command (after going Overseas, Capt. H. E. Crowell); Lieuts. H. E. Crowell,

N. L. Chipman, W. J. Wright, Kenneth Campbell, who went over in a draft during the summer.

"D" COMPANY—Capt. G. H. Cutten, Company Commander; Capt. W. Noblett, Second in Command (Capt. Cutten became Major in the 246th and Capt., afterwards Major, H. K. Emerson, recently returned from the front, took command of "D" Company); Lieuts. A. D. Borden, J. P. McFarlane, J. C. M. Vereker and E. R. Power.

In addition to these officers were Lieut. H. A. Love in charge of Signalling Section, and Lieut. W. L. Black of the Machine Gun Section.

During the summer Hon. Captain Father O'Sullivan was added. He was employed most of the time in raising the "Purple Feather Fund," and spent only a week or two in camp.

The Battalion was fortunate in its Sergeant-Major, A. S. Ward, who blended a strict sense of duty with a genial disposition and secured alike the approbation of the officers and the respect of the men.

The Camp had not been long established at Aldershot when it was honored by a visit from Sir Sam Hughes, the Minister of Militia. On June 11th, at 6 a.m. the Brigade was paraded. Although there had only been a few days of united training, the impression produced upon the Minister was quite noticeable, and ever afterwards he showed a kindly appreciation of the Nova Scotia Highlanders.

On August 9th the Camp was honored by another distinguished visitor, Sir Robert Borden, the Premier of Canada, who was accompanied by the Hon. David MacKeen, the Lieut.-Governor of Nova Scotia. The March Past was excellent, and the Premier, a native of the Province, was pleased to speak words of heartfelt appreciation and encouragement. Another inspection was made on August 15th, but this was more of a formal military character and lacked the general significance of the previous reviews.

The red-letter days of the Brigade's whole history at Aldershot were Friday the 25th and Saturday the 26th of August. On Friday the Camp was thrown open to the public, who flocked thither from every part of the Province. The resources of the railway were taxed to the utmost. Fully eight thousand people visited the grounds and witnessed the March Past. They were relatives of "the boys," and nothing revealed more clearly how tenderly the thought

H.R.H. THE DUKE OF CONNAUGHT INSPECTING THE HIGHLAND BRIGADE AT ALDERSHOT CAMP, SEPTEMBER, 1916.

of the Province centred about the rows of white tents, where the flower of its manhood was encamped. By a happy thought the Camp Commandant, Col. W. E. Thompson, added to the ordinary review exercises a short march in column of route, so the men would pass immediately in front of their many friends.

On Saturday morning Field-Marshall His Royal Highness the Duke of Connaught arrived. Exhilarated by the enthusiasm of the previous day, the Brigade excelled itself in its manoeuvres, and especially in the March Past. His Royal Highness, who was too fine a soldier to be guilty of a meaningless expression, declared that he had not inspected anything finer in the Dominion of Canada.

One other function completes the tale of reviews. It was the presentation of colors by Lady Borden to the four Battalions on Monday, September 25th. No little practice was necessary for the involved movements connected with the ceremony. Once again the weather was propitious; the sunbeams kissed the silken colors as they were unfurled to the breeze, and rousing cheers greeted the declaration of the Premier that they would shortly be sent over the seas.

That afternoon a competition was commenced between the various platoons of the Brigade, which resulted in the award going to the " thirteenth platoon " of the 219th, and as a sign that they had won, they were permitted to wear their feathers with the edge trimmed.

On Friday, September 26th, a message arrived ordering the Brigade to be ready to go Overseas in six days, and cancelling all leave for officers and men. The announcement of this approaching embarkation would by itself have been sensational enough, but when it came accompanied by an order that no one should have the privilege of seeing his home again, the men were fairly stunned. All had counted on a " farewell " leave. At first everyone seemed paralyzed. Then their resolution took shape. It was not in the Colonel's power to grant leave but, though a strict disciplinarian, he understood the situation and felt a deep sympathy for the men, and determined that his attitude should be as lenient as possible. The men were resolute to see their homes, many of which were in the vicinity of the Camp. Every effort was made to stop them. Cordons with fixed bayonets were placed around the station at Kentville. But all to no purpose. The majority simply rose and

went. They hired motor cars, mounted horses, or even walked For a moment there was a sense of alarm and humiliation, which quickly changed to confidence and pride as the men came streaming back, satisfied that they had seen their friends and ready to do their duty in facing the foe. This unauthorized farewell furlough was not confined to the 219th but was general in the 185th and the 193rd as well.

The six days' warning was, of course, a mere preliminary measure but definite orders at last arrived for the 219th to march out on the 12th of October at 5 a.m. Never did Halifax seem lovelier than in the bright autumn air as the Battalion marched along Barrington Street and up Spring Garden Road and through South Park Street to the Common, where a vast company of friends and well-wishers had congregated to say good-bye. Ranks were broken and the soldiers mingled freely with the people. The "Fall In" sounded, the band struck up a lively air, and the march was resumed until the gates of the docks closed behind the last file. Opportunities of further adieus were granted in the afternoon within the limit of the dock, and then for the final time the troops climbed the long gangways to the decks of the transport.

All night the *Olympic* lay at the pier. On Friday afternoon she moved up to Bedford Basin. Life belts were passed out and alarms practised. During the afternoon, when rumors that we were doomed to several days' detention in the basin were at their height, the anchor was quietly raised and almost noiselessly the ship began to glide down the harbor. But the movement was quickly noticed on shore, and the tooting of tugs and the cheering of the crowds that rushed to the pier heads showed that the "boys" had not been forgotten by their friends. The shades of night were gathering in as Cape Sambro fell astern, and the twinkle of its kindly light was Nova Scotia's farewell. Betting in New York had run as high as twenty to one that the *Olympic* would be sunk because the notorious German submarine U53, which had committed serious depredations off Nantucket, was reported to be in the vicinity. Whatever anxiety may have been felt by those on the bridge, seemed not in the slightest degree to have reached the troops below, who had a confidence in the British seamanship that was almost sublime.

On Tuesday night two destroyers picked up the ship and acted as consorts. Wednesday morning the coast of Ireland was in view, and Wednesday evening anchor was dropped in the Mersey, the voyage having been completed in four days and nineteen hours. We sailed on a Friday, and the thirteenth at that, but war has exploded the superstitions of the world along with many other things.

Two or three hours were required for the disembarkation. Eight trains were required for the whole Brigade, and they were started at various intervals of time. The last two carried the 219th. It was nearly midnight when the train drew into the siding at Milford Station and, resuming their packs, the men began their two miles' march into Camp.

Witley Camp was situated on Witley Common, a sandy tract covered with scattered pines, known as Scotch fir, and with few houses in the vicinity. Milford Village was a mile and a half away, and Godalming three miles. The nearest town was Guildford, eight miles off. The county was Surrey, and the landscape among the most picturesque in all England.

After the first cold snap that greeted the troops on their arrival, milder conditions prevailed; the air became balmy; the fresh, full foliage on the trees, and the fragrance of the flowers still in bloom seemed to carry summer into December. But as November drew into December cold mists settled into the valley where Witley Camp lay, and caused an acrid chill that seemed to eat into the marrow of the bone. Influenza (known as " flu " or " grippe ") invaded the Camp. The sick parade in the morning increased by leaps and bounds; the general hospital at Bramshott and the sick detention hut of the Brigade were filled and could take no more. A special hut in the Battalion lines was secured and in a few days crowded out, and even the spare accommodation in the medical room was covered with bed boards on which lay fevered and coughing men. December will remain to the troops at Witley Camp something of a nightmare.

No one as yet seriously believed, or at least publicly announced, that the Highland Brigade would not be held together. Had not the Minister of Militia plighted his word to that effect? Had it not been a promise to the men when they enlisted? Towards the

219th BATTALION, C.E.F.

end of November, however, sinister rumors began to filter through and culminated on the 30th November in the call for the first draft for France. Immediately the Camp was in a hubbub of excitement, for the draft required 800 men from the Brigade, and this obviously meant its dismemberment. All reasonable means that might avert the blow were employed, but the order was explicit. No officers were to go except those in charge of drafts, and they were to return from France whenever their duty was accomplished. All non-commissioned officers chosen were to revert to the rank of private. Ultimately 115 went from the 219th under the command of Lieutenant King. The Brigadier addressed a few parting words, and to the strains of martial music and the skirl of the pipes the proud lads marched away leaving a thoughtful Camp behind. What was to be the fate of those who remained? Rumor again became busy, hope revived and old predictions were renewed, when once more with dramatic swiftness the axe fell and when it accomplished its business the Highland Brigade was no more. No one could have attempted to parry the blow more resolutely than the Brigadier. He felt keenly the pledges that had been given and the injustice to Nova Scotia; and his efforts were not without a measure of success. Two Battalions of the four were preserved, the 85th and the 185th. Into the 85th some 350 men, nearly all the Lieutenants and Major Rudland, were drafted from the 219th. A large number from the 193rd were put into the 185th. The 85th received orders to prepare at once to go Overseas, though this was not actually accomplished until February 10th. The 185th was "slated" for the Fifth Division, and it was to remain in Witley Camp. The remainder of the Highland Brigade were to proceed to Bramshott Camp. It was in the last week of December that the large draft, carefully selected and splendidly fit, changed their feathers from purple to red and went over to the lines of the 85th. The officers packed their kits and the happy fellowship of the Mess Room, that had lasted from the happy days of concentration in sunny Aldershot, was dissolved, alas, never in its completeness to reassemble again.

Between five and six hundred of the 219th Battalion still remained. Kits and trunks were packed, adieus paid, our temporary English home broken up, and promptly at 12 o'clock Saturday, December 30th, the Purple Feather ranks, now varied with blue and green and red feathers, moved off headed by the 85th Band. The Battalion settled down in a pleasant part of the Bramshott Camp, on the brow of a hill overlooking the picturesque dale through which flowed a streamlet gathered from the meadows of Haslemere, Shottermill and Hammer. It was the country of George Eliot and of Tennyson's later years. Many travellers had come to it, but never any on so strange an errand.

Presently there appeared in Camp the Old 17th. It had been the first Nova Scotian Unit sent Overseas. Apart from its Commanding Officer, Lieut.-Colonel Cameron, it possessed hardly any Nova Scotians; it was officered and its ranks were filled almost exclusively by Western Canadians. This Battalion, like the famous Minotaur, had fed on the remnants of many others in its time. Would the Highland Brigade succumb to the usual fate or would it prove an indigestible morsel?

At the commencement of 1917 a change of policy was inaugurated affecting all the Canadian Camps in England. Witley was reserved for the Fifth Division. In the others the Training Brigades became reserve ones, which would have a full strength of 8,000 each, and each Reserve Battalion (2,000 in strength) would have some definite fighting Unit at the Front to which it would send reinforcements whenever required. The 17th was made a Reserve Battalion in the 5th Reserve Brigade; it was to reinforce the 25th and 85th and to be distinctively Nova Scotian; it was ordered to take over the 219th and 193rd. Officially the whale swallowed Jonah, but in the curious and unscriptural sequel Jonah took over the control of the whale from the inside. This second transformation was undoubtedly due to the fact that the 17th Reserve was to become a Nova Scotian Unit and naturally Nova Scotians assumed the dominant role; and these were to be found in the ranks of the Highland Brigade. But it was also due to a stubborn and persistent *esprit de corps* that had always characterized the 219th.

The formal transference took place on January 23rd, and that date marks the end of the 219th as a distinct military Unit, and forms a fitting close to this article. It has been the story of a splendid Battalion into which the Western Counties of Nova Scotia poured their best manhood with unstinted patriotism. It represents the finest sacrifice ever made by the loyal enthusiasm of that part of the Province. Fisherman, farmer, lumberman, student, minister, lawyer, doctor drilled side by side in a spirit of comradeship seldom excelled.

It is not given to this bloodless narrative to trace to the field of battle the brave men that filled the ranks, but in the tale of their Battalions they will be found to have played their part in the defence of civilization bravely and·well, and to have left to their country the legacy of an imperishable example.

CHAPTER XX.

246th BATTALION, C.E.F.

THE 246th Battalion was authorized in August, 1916, as a Reserve Unit to supply reinforcements to the Nova Scotia Highland Brigade. It was organized at Camp Aldershot a short time before the Brigade embarked for Overseas, and to it were transferred officers and other ranks who, from various causes, were temporarily unfit for service at the Front. Each Battalion of the Brigade was represented by one Company, " A " Company, the 85th Battalion; " B " Company, 185th Battalion; " C " Company, 193rd Battalion, and " D " Company, 219th Battalion.

The officers were:

Lieut.-Col. N. H. Parsons ....Officer Commanding.
Major G. B. Cutten ....Second in Command.
Major H. H. Bligh ....Company Commander.
Major H. D. Creighton ....Company Commander.
Major M. A. McKay ....Company Commander.
Major W. G. McRae ....Company Commander.
Capt. A. McKinnon ....
Capt. G. E. Roberts ....
Capt. J. Armitage ....Adjutant.
Capt. L. L. Titus ....Quartermaster.
Capt. A. C. Wilson ....Medical Officer.
Capt. C. W. Corey ....Chaplain.
Capt. F. Robertson ....Paymaster.
Lieut. R. V. Harris ....Asst. Adjutant.

Lieuts. F. J. McCharles, A. T. E. Crosby, E. S. H. Lane, H. F. Lockhart, H. L. McInnes, A. W. Rogers, W. B. Ross, E. C. Shields, C. E. Smith, H. R. Theakston, W. M. Bligh, C. E. Baker, G. D. Blackadar, R. S. Edwards, N. Rogers, J. S. Roy.

A detachment of the 246th under the command of Major H. D. Creighton was sent to Trenton to guard the Nova Scotia Steel Company's plant at that point, and was later relieved by a detachment from the Composite Battalion.

During the autumn and winter months recruiting became very difficult, and when the necessity for compulsory service became

246th BATTALION, C.E.F.

evident it was decided to discontinue organization and send the Battalion Overseas in drafts. The first draft, under the command of Lieuts C. E. Baker and W. M. Bligh, embarked in March, 1917, and on June 1st a further draft of 230 men and the following officers were sent Overseas:

Lieut.-Col. N. H. Parsons; Major M. A. McKay; Capt. A. McKinnon, Capt. L. L. Titus, Lieuts. A. T. E. Crosby, R. S. Edwards, E. S. H. Lane, H. F. Lockhart, H. L. McInnes, A. W. Rogers, W. B. Ross, E. C. Shields, C. E. Smith.

On arrival in England the draft proceeded to Bramshott, where one half of the men were sent to the 185th Battalion, then training at Witley with the 5th Division. The remainder together with the officers were absorbed by the 17th Reserve Battalion.

The remainder of the strength left in Canada was transferred to Labor, Forestry, Special Service and other Units, the majority eventually going Overseas.

CHAPTER XXI.

NO. 2 CONSTRUCTION BATTALION.

NO. 2 Construction Battalion was authorized on July 5, 1916. Mr. D. H. Sutherland, of River John, N.S., a well-known railroad contractor, who had enlisted in the 193rd Overseas Battalion, was given command of this Unit with the rank of Lieut.-Colonel.

An Infantry Battalion was not deemed advisable as the population was not sufficient to send the necessary reinforcements; therefore a Construction Battalion was authorized to represent the colored citizens of Canada, who were demanding that their race should be represented in the C.E.F. by a Unit composed of their own people.

LIEUT.-COL. D. H. SUTHERLAND.

The colored citizens of Canada are settled principally in the Provinces of Nova Scotia and Ontario, although of late years a great many have settled in Western Canada. Out of a total population in Canada of 20,000, including men, women and children, Nova Scotia has 7,000; Ontario 5,000; New Brunswick 1,000, and the remainder of the colored population are settled in Western Canada. It is estimated that 200 colored men were engaged in coal mines in Nova Scotia, and therefore not eligible to enlist. The number of men who enlisted in No. 2 Construction from Nova Scotia was 500, so that of the men available in Nova Scotia, the colored citizens sent Overseas in No. 2 Construction Battalion fully 10 per cent. of their population as volunteers.

Recruiting was carried on simultaneously wherever the colored population were located. A detachment of sixty men, under command of Capt. W. A. McConnell, was raised at Toronto and

No. 2 CONSTRUCTION BATTALION

latterly joined the detachment at Windsor, Ont., under the command of Capt. A. J. Gayfer. The Ontario recruits in all numbered 350. About fifty recruits volunteered from Western Canada. The headquarters was first located at Pictou, N.S., and later transferred to Truro, where more barracks room was available.

No. 2 Construction Battalion was the only volunteer Unit to engage in war-work before proceeding Overseas. A Company of 250 men, under command of Capt. Kenneth A. Morrison, was employed during the months of January, February and part of March lifting rails from the Grand Trunk sidings at Moncton, Nappadogan and Edmundston, N.B., to be shipped Overseas for the Western Front.

Following is a list of officers of this Unit:

```
D. H. Sutherland ............... Lieut.-Colonel and O.C.
Kenneth A. Morrison ............. Capt. and Second in Command.
John Sidney Davie ............. Capt. and Adjutant.
Walter Adam McConnell ........ Captain.
George Peter McLaren ........... Captain.
A. J. Gayfer ..................... Captain.
James Stuart Grant ............. Captain and Paymaster.
David Anderson ................ Captain and Quartermaster.
Russell R. McLean ............. Lieutenant.
James Bertram Hayes ...........'.. Lieutenant.
Roderick Livingstone ............ Lieutenant.
Halton Fyles .................... Lieutenant.
William L. Young ............... Lieutenant.
L. Bruce Young .................. Lieutenant.
Isaac Logan Banhill ............. Lieutenant.
Attached Officers ............... Capt. Dan. Murray, Medical Officer.
                                  Hon. Capt. William A. White,
                                  Chaplain.
```

Mr. Harry B. McLean, of the Cook Construction Company, and Wheaton Bros., presented the Unit with a set of band instruments. Mr. Andrew Wheaton also assisted the Unit financially. Mr. H. B. McLean was appointed Honorary Lieutenant-Colonel on account of his interest in and assistance to the Battalion.

The Unit embarked at Halifax, March 25, 1917, on board the troopship *Southland;* in all there were 3,500 troops on board. The ship was in command of Captain Morehouse, and the troops in command of Lieut.-Col. D. H. Sutherland. The convoy arrived at Liverpool April 8th. During the passage great precautions were taken to guard against enemy submarines. No lights were shown.

no bugles blown and a constant watch was kept day and night for floating mines and submarines. This period was the worst in the history of submarine warfare, as more ships were sunk during the week April 1 to April 8, 1917, than at any time during the War.

The Unit entrained at Liverpool Sunday noon, April 8th, and left for Seaford, travelling by special troop train through a very picturesque country. Arriving at Seaford the Unit was escorted by a British band to our Camp under canvas, about two miles from the depot. All troops arriving from Canada at this time were segregated ten days, to avoid the introduction of contagious diseases. The Unit was taken on the strength of the Canadian forces at Seaford, under command of Col. G. S. Gardiner.

Before proceeding to France, it was necessary for any Unit to have the full quota of men in accordance to the establishment of the Unit. As No. 2 Construction was 300 under strength, the Unit was reorganized into a Construction Company of 506 men and ten officers. As there was no provision on the establishment for a Lieutenant-Colonel, Lieut.-Col. Sutherland, Officer Commanding, reverted to the rank of Major to proceed to France in command of the Unit.

While at Seaford, from April 8 to May 17, 1917, the Unit was detailed into working parties and employed in building trenches for the troops in training and in building and repairing roads within the bounds of the Canadian command. Permanent air picket was detailed about May 1st, to be in readiness in the event of air raids, which were of frequent occurrence. During the Sports' Day Competition among the Canadian Forces at Seaford, the members of No. 2 Construction won a silver cup presented for competition by the British Y.M.C.A.

The Unit was ordered to France on May 17th, and entrained at Seaford at 2 a.m., May 17th, arriving at Folkestone and proceeding direct to the Channel troopship at the pier. The crossing occupied two hours. The Channel boats carrying troops were well escorted by British destroyers on port and starboard sides, while the *Silver Queen*, a small-sized dirigible airship, escorted our troopship overhead to sight for enemy submarines. Arriving at Boulogne at 3 p.m. the Unit was escorted to a rest camp; twenty-four hours

No. 2 CONSTRUCTION BATTALION

later, on May 18th, the Unit entrained at Boulogne and travelled by special troop train by Etaples, Paris, Dijon, Dole, Mouchard and arrived at our destination, La Joux, Jour Mountains, on May 21st.

The Unit was attached to No. 5 District, Canadian Forestry Corps, under command of Lieut.-Col. Geo. Johnson. There were four Forestry Companies consisting of 170 men, 40 teams, logging and sawmill outfit, located within one-half mile radius from No. 2 Construction Company's Camp. The officers and men of No. 2 Construction were detailed into working parties and paraded daily to assist in the logging, milling and shipping operations of the Forestry Corps.

The officers were employed as follows:

Major Sutherland was in command of the Unit and kept a general supervision over the different working parties.

Capt. J. S. Grant was employed as officer in charge of shipping for No. 5 District, and all lumber sawn by the four Companies was shipped at La Joux Station by No. 2 Construction men. A detachment of fifty men, under command of Lieut. H. Fyles, assisted No. 22 Company, C.F.C., in logging and in the construction of a narrow gauge railway to transport saw-logs to the mill. The roads were kept in repair by Capt. David Anderson, No. 2 Construction, with a party of 100 men. A road plant consisting of a rock crusher, steam drill, motor lorries and steam roller, was employed, and the roads were kept in a good state of repair where the heavy traffic demanded the best roads possible.

The water to supply the Camp had to be pumped to an elevation of 1,500 feet by means of force pumps in relay. Lieut. Bertram Hayes was officer in charge of pumping stations and water lines. Capt. R. Livingstone was Transport Officer for No. 5 District, assisted by Lieut. Russell McLean, both of No. 2 Construction Company.

On December 30, 1917, Capt. K. A. Morrison left La Joux for Alencon, in command of 180 other ranks to report to the O.C. No. 1 District, C.F.C.; Lieut. S. Hood was Adjutant of this detachment. Fifty other ranks were despatched to 37th Company, C.F.C., near Peronne.

NOVA SCOTIA'S PART IN THE GREAT WAR

A few items, as follows, taken from the War Diary of this Unit July 1, 1918, will be of interest;

Dominion Day celebrated by the eleven Forestry Companies and No. 2 Construction Company, composing No. 5 District, in field sports held at Chapois. The four Companies from La Joux, namely, No. 22, 40, 50 and No. 2 Construction paraded to the grounds under the command of Major Sutherland. During the day, the band of this Company, by their excellent music, greatly assisted in entertaining the crowd and making the holiday a success.

July 7, 1918: Camp inspected by Lieut.-General Sir Richard Turner, V.C., accompanied by Major-General A. MacDougall, G.O.C. Canadian Forestry Corps, and Lieut.-Colonel Johnson, O.C. Jura Group. The interior economy and general tidiness were favorably commented upon.

July 13, 1918: Hon. Capt. W. A. White, Chaplain, returns from visiting the Alencon detachment.

July 14, 1918: Sunday, no work. The Mayor of Salins invited the Canadians in this district to send a detachment to Salins to take part in a review in which American and French troops were participating. Major Sutherland represented Lieut.-Col. G. M. Strong, D.S.O., O.C. No. 5 District, C.F.C., who was absent on duty, and acted as reviewing officer of the Allied Troops at Salins, in commemorating the National Day and to do honor to the French Republic. The band of this Company, under the leadership of Sergt. G. W. Stewart, played the National Anthem and a programme and greatly assisted in making the event a memorable one.

July 15, 1918: Camp inspected by General Bouillard, Commanding 7th Army Division, French, and Lieut.-Col. G. Johnson, O.C. Jura Group.

April 3, 1918: The following telegram sent to the D.T.O., C.F.C., France, from the O.C. No. 2 Construction Company:

"Will you please recommend my Unit which is organized for construction work for transfer to Western Front."

In April, 1918, Colonel Strong, D.S.O., O.C. No. 5 District, C.F.C., recommended that No. 2 Construction Company be given the establishment of a Battalion. This recommendation was approved

No. 2 CONSTRUCTION BATTALION

by the G.O.C., General White, and General MacDougall, but held up for lack of reinforcements.

Shortly after the Armistice, orders were received for this Unit to report at the General Base Depot, Etaples. The Unit left La Joux, December 4th. One hundred and fifty Russian soldiers, who had been attached to No. 2 Construction Company during 1918, were taken over by No. 40 Company, C.F.C. No. 2 Construction arrived at Etaples December 7th, and was joined by the detachment from Alencon and fifty men from 37th Company, C.F.C. The Unit sailed from Boulogne, December 14th, with 600 attached troops, under command of Major Sutherland, and arrived at Bramshott Camp. The Unit was attached to the Nova Scotia Regimental Depot, and from there dispersed to the several military camps representing the various military districts in Canada, to which the men would be forwarded for demobilization. The different drafts composing this Unit sailed the latter part of January, 1919, for Halifax.

A letter was received by Major Sutherland from Major-General MacDougall conveying the thanks of the Canadian Forestry Corps to the officers and men of this Unit for their valuable and faithful services while attached for duty and discipline to the Canadian Forestry Corps.

CHAPTER XXII.

THE CANADIAN FORESTRY CORPS.

ON February 15, 1916, the Colonial Secretary cabled to the Governor-General of Canada, H.R.H. the Duke of Connaught, the following message:

"H.M. Government would be grateful if the Canadian Government would assist in the production of timber for war purposes. Owing to the very serious shortage of freight for munitions, food, forage and other essentials, which is a matter of the gravest concern to H.M. Government, it is impossible to continue to import Canadian timber on a sufficiently large scale to meet war requirements, and arrangements must therefore be made for felling and converting English forests.

"Chief difficulty is finding sufficient skilled labor, fellers, haulers and sawyers. One thousand five hundred men are urgently needed, and H.M. Government would suggest that a Battalion of lumbermen might be formed of specially listed men to undertake exploitations of forests of this country. If proposal commends itself to Canadian Government, would beg very early action. Suggest that men be enlisted into Canadian Expeditionary Force and despatched in small companies under competent supervision. Government is aware that lumber season is now in progress, but feel sure that men would enlist even at sacrifice of present employment if the reason of appeal were made known to them. Incidence of cost will be arranged as agreeable to Canadian Government."

A further cable was sent on February 29th. So quickly did the Canadian authorities make up their minds, that on March 1, 1916, a cable was sent stating that the Battalion asked for would be provided with the least possible delay. The raising of Units in this Corps exemplified the readiness of the Canadian Government to assist in the most unexpected direction.

The 224th Battalion, under Lieut.-Colonel McDougall, arrived in England, April 28, 1916, and the 230th, 238th and 242nd Battalions followed within six months.

Nova Scotia's quota in this branch of the Service was about 525 officers and men, known as the Nova Scotia Forestry Draft,

THE CANADIAN FORESTRY CORPS

composed of three Companies with a personnel of officers as follows:

Staff.—Major M. C. Denton, Officer Commanding; Major E. J. Stehlen, Second in Command; Capt. J. G. Pierce, Adjutant.

"*A*" *Company.*—Capt. M. D. McKeigan, O.C.; Lieut. A. Roy, Lieut. Parker McDonald, Lieut. David Neal.

"*B*" *Company*—Capt. G. D. Blackader, O.C.; Lieut. N. P. McKenzie, Lieut. C. B. McDougall, Lieut. C. F. Kinney.

"*C*" *Company.*—Capt. H. B. Verge, O.C.; Lieut. George Harding, Lieut R. S. Shreve, Lieut. W. V. R. Winters.

Authorization for this Unit was granted in March, 1917. Recruiting and organization work began immediately by Companies, under the direct supervision of the Company Commanders in the various counties as follows: "A" Company in Pictou, Cape Breton, Victoria and Inverness; "B" Company in Halifax, Cumberland, Colchester and Prince Edward Island; and "C" Company in Shelburne, Queens, Lunenburg, Yarmouth and Digby; "A" and "B" Companies mobilized at Truro;

MAJOR M. C. DENTON, Forestry Corps.

"C" Company at Yarmouth; and on May 29th all Companies proceeded to Aldershot to complete the work of organization, after which they embarked on the White Star Line Transport *Justicia*, and arrived in England, July 4, 1916.

The Base Depot for the Corps was at Smith's Lawn, Sunningdale, Berkshire, within the confines of Windsor Great Park. This site was given to the Corps by His Majesty the King in December, 1916.

About the middle of August the entire draft was broken up, a portion of the officers and men were absorbed into other Forestry Units, operating in England, Scotland and the South of France. Officers that were not disposed of in this manner transferred to the Flying Corps, Canadian Railway Troops, Infantry and Labor Battalions, subsequently getting over to France.

It is difficult to conceive the multitude of ways in which timber was used for war purposes. At the Front, the Army very largely walked on timber, lorries drove on timber, railways, light and heavy, required huge numbers of sleepers or ties. Underground no less than above ground was timber used for dugouts, and all the complicated contrivances connected with trench warfare. From huts to ammunition boxes, from duckboards to stakes for barbed wire entanglements, the uses of timber ranged. The general specifications for a Company's operation in this Corps was the production of Sawn Lumber, Fuelwood, Pickets, Hurdles, Fascines, Faggots, Continuous Rivetting and Parry Sticks.

In order to save time, and for other reasons, it was arranged that Canadians should bring with them their own machinery and equipment of the kind to which they were accustomed, with the necessary modifications to adapt it to the conditions in Britain and France. The work of the Forestry Corps was thus not only of the utmost assistance in meeting the need of timber for the War, and in saving tonnage, but was of permanent value in that it has knit more closely together the people of Great Britain, with their compatriots scattered throughout Canada.

CHAPTER XXIII.

NO. 6 DISTRICT DEPOT.

DURING the early part of 1918 when the Germans were making their last great drive, few people realized that preparations were already made for the demobilization of the Canadian Corps. These preparations were due to the foresight of Headquarters Staff. Accordingly when the organization of No. 6 District Depot was completed on the 18th of April, 1918, a District Depot was established in each Military District of Canada, each Depot being designated by the number of the Military District in which the Depot was situated.

Lieut.-Col. B. W. Roscoe, D.S.O., was first appointed Officer Commanding, and he had under him a small but efficient Staff, with Capt. J. S. Davies, M.C., as Adjutant, headquarters being at Leith House, Hollis Street, Halifax.

The functions of District Depots at first were many. Besides carrying out ordinary discharges, all personnel in the different hospitals had to be looked after, and in addition to this all casualties who became fit for further service were allotted to the different Service Companies and Battalions in the District and to their own Units Overseas.

No. 6 District Depot differed from the other Depots in so far that it had an Embarkation Casualty Section which handled all casualties, on embarkation; that is to say, when troops were proceeding Overseas from the different districts of Canada, who for various reasons could not embark at the appointed time, they were taken on the strength of No. 6 District Depot and forwarded by some future sailing.

This work was carried on by Lieut.-Colonel Roscoe until June, 1918, when Lieut.-Col. D. A. MacRae, 25th Battalion, was appointed Officer Commanding, with Capt. G. T. Shaw, 31st Battalion, as Adjutant, headquarters being removed to Wellington Barracks.

From this time on the work began to increase owing to the great number of men returning from England to be demobilized. Demobilization went on very rapidly, and when the Armistice suddenly came it was realized that more speedily to carry out demobilization No. 6 District Depot would have to be enlarged. With this in view two Dispersal Stations known as "A" and "B" were added to the Depot, these Dispersal Stations being situated in Charlottetown and Halifax, and commanded by Major J. S. Stanley and Major J. G. Johnstone, respectively. To these officers was allotted the greater part of the organization of their respective stations which was carried on in such a manner that great credit was reflected upon the Depot as well as upon the officers commanding.

Everything was now in readiness to handle very speedily troops arriving for demobilization, so that when the first complete Unit, the Royal Canadian Regiment, arrived at the Port of Halifax early in March, 1919, it was demobilized in less than a day. This was made possible by the hard work of the Officer Commanding Dispersal Station B, Major J. G. Johnstone.

This work was kept up by the stations throughout Canada until late in July, 1919, when it was found that the Canadian Corps had practically been demobilized. At first it was thought it would take two years to complete demobilization of our forces, but the whole work was carried on so speedily that the feat was practically accomplished in six months. This in itself speaks well of the splendid organization of the Depots.

No. 6 Depot, besides demobilizing the Maritime troops, demobilized a great number of troops from other districts, viz., the Cavalry Brigade, Engineer and Forestry Units, Railway Troops and several Hospital Units. The work of No. 6 Depot was highly praised by Gen. John Hughes during his tour of inspection, when he stated that No. 6 District was one of the best organized throughout Canada.

One will realize the immense amount of work done by No. 6 District Depot by the results obtained; that is to say, the total number of discharges from April 18, 1918, until the latter part of May, 1920, were one thousand five hundred and seventy-eighty (1.578) officers and twenty-seven thousand eight hundred and

No. 6 DISTRICT DEPOT

ninety-six other ranks (27,896), made up as shown in the table below:

Reasons.	Officers.	Other Ranks.
1. *Medically Unfit.*		
(a) Disability due to or aggravated by service	76	2,983
(b) Requiring further medical treatment of long duration or vocational education	38	507
2. *Demobilization.*		
All discharged other than above	1,462	24,299
3. *Struck off Strength.*		
Deaths	2	17
	1,578	27,896
Transferred to other Districts	8	58

It will be very gratifying to Nova Scotians to know that the whole Staff of No. 6 District Depot were made up of Nova Scotia officer ranks, all of whom saw service at the Front, and it is sure when the records of the District Depots are compared that No. 6 District Depot will be well to the forefront.

Officers on strength No. 6 District Depot when organized:

Officer Commanding..........Lieut.-Col. W. B. Roscoe, D.S.O.................C.M.R.'s.
Second in Command..........Major A. B. Bucknell......15th L.H.
Adjutant......................Capt. J. L. Davie, M.C..... 21st Bn.
Assistant Adjutant............Lieut. J. A. Ross..........85th Bn.
Quartermaster................Capt. A. A. Clark.........139th Bn.

June, 1918.

Officer Commanding..........Lieut.-Col. D. A. MacRae..25th Bn.
Second in Command..........Major J. L. Davie, M.C....31st Bn.
Adjutant......................Capt. G. T. Shaw.........21st Bn.
Assistant Adjutant............Lieut. A. F. Ferguson......10th R.R.T.
Quartermaster................Capt. A. A. Clark .... 139th Bn.
Records Officer...............Lieut. B. E. Elliott........ C.E.

Leave and Furlough Section.

Officer Commanding..........Capt. M. S. Hunt......... 5th Bn.
Second in Command..........Lieut. J. Harley..........25th Bn.

Details Company.

Officer Commanding..........Capt. F. A. Ladd..........7th Bn.

NOVA SCOTIA'S PART IN THE GREAT WAR

Casualty Company.

Officer Commanding..........Major L. D. V. Chipman...13th Bn.
Company Officers.............Capt. A. G. Foster ....7th Bn.
                             Lieut. W. H. Whidden..... Composite Bn.
                             Lieut. H. A. Crawley......85th Bn.
                             Lieut. A. A. Crawley......R.C.G.A.

Discharge Section.

Officer Commanding..........Capt. R. W. Dill ....25th Bn.
Section Officers...............Capt. J. A. Gunn.......... 13th Bn.
                              Capt. F. A. MacAloney.....R.A.F.
                              Capt. W. Fisher............25th Bn.
                              Lieut. G. W. Banks........38th Bn.
                              Lieut. I. C. Banks......... Composite Bn.

Hospital Section.

Officer Commanding...........Major J. A. Mackenzie.... 85th Bn.
Section Officer................ Capt F. T. DeWolfe.......C.G.A.

Dispersal Station "A," Chalottetown.

Officer Commanding.......... Major J. W. Stanley......C.G.A.
Second in Command..........Capt. J. S. Bagnell........C.G.A.
Company Officers.............. Lieut. R. Richie........... C.G.A.
                              Lieut. H. E. McEachern....50th Bn.
                              Lieut. J. McDonald........C.G.A.
                              Lieut. J. White............C.G.A.

Dispersal Station "B," Halifax.

Officer Commanding.......... Major J. G. Johnstone.....85th Bn.
Second in Command..........Capt. M. S. Hunt..........5th Bn.
Company Officers..............Capt. R. L. Billman........C.G.A.
                              Lieut. J. Bonner...........85th Bn.
                              Lieut. B. E. Nicks .... 13th Bn.
                              Lieut. J. H. E. Jones.......C.E.

CHAPTER XXIV.

THE ARMY SERVICE CORPS.

IN the lexicon of the Army Service Corps, the word "impossible" does not exist. It was this spirit, insistently inculcated since the organization of the Corps in 1902, that made the accomplishment of the seemingly "impossible" possible by the Canadian Army Service Corps in the Maritime Provinces when the Kaiser let roar his terrorizing thunderbolts in August, 1914.

Blatant glory has seldom perched on the escutcheon of this hard-worked Corps, but, on the other hand, the capable work of the Army Service Corps has frequently been the means of attracting this coy bird to a resting place on the banner of many a Unit whose prowess fills the pages of history.

Briefly, it is the efficient service of the Army Service Corps that makes possible the achievement of great things by the army.

LIEUT.-COL. E. C. DEAN.

It is impossible to record the history of the Canadian Army Service Corps in the Maritime Provinces throughout the duration of the Great War—and after—without beginning at the basis of the structure, namely, No. 4 Detachment of the Canadian Permanent Army Service Corps, now known as No. 6 Detachment of the Royal Canadian Army Service Corps, having its headquarters at Halifax.

On August 4, 1914, No. 4 Detachment was officered by five officers of the Canadian Permanent Army Service Corps, two attached officers of the Active Militia, and one officer of the Imperial Army Service Corps, attached. The Detachment was administered by Major E. C. Dean, who was attached to the Staff of Military

District No. 6 as an Assistant Director of Supplies and Transport (now Lieut.-Colonel E. C. Dean, Senior Supply and Transport Officer, attached to the Staff of M.D. No. 6). He was also Commandant of the Canadian Army Service Corps School of Training. In command of the Detachment was Major R. O. Marks, an officer of the Imperial Army Service Corps, temporarily loaned to the Canadian Sister Corps. He was also Adjutant of the School of Training. The other officers of the Permanent Force were Lieut. H. O. Lawson (now Major Lawson, Senior Supply and Transport Officer, M.D. No. 3, Kingston, Ontario); Lieut. Keith MacDougall (now Major MacDougall, in charge of No. 6 Detachment, R.C.A.S.C.); Lieut. J. A. Gwynne (who proceeded Overseas as Adjutant of the Second Divisional Train); and Lieut., now Capt., George Simms, District Barracks Officer—a most efficient, hard-working officer, whose capability went a long way towards making possible the quartering and comfort of many thousands of troops in the Maritime Provinces. The splendid services rendered by this officer—his absolute devotion to his arduous duties, his zeal and tireless efforts in behalf of the C.E.F., and, at the same time, his careful supervision of all matters pertaining to the financial interests of the public purse—are well worthy of recognition.

The two attached officers of the Active Militia were Lieut. (now Major) H. R. Hendy, of Esquimalt, B.C., and Capt. H. J. B. Keating, of No. 6 Company, Canadian Army Service Corps. Captain Keating is now stationed at Quebec.

The rank and file of the Detachment numbered less than fifty—scarcely sufficient to care for the needs of Halifax Garrison in peace time. The available transport comprised about a half-dozen horses, two time-worn Ford passenger cars, two steamboats, and a "dumb" lighter. Practically the whole of the land transport was carried out by horses and wagons under a civilian contractor—Mr. George E. VanBuskirk.

The Supply Depot, including grocery store, bakery, and meat shop, was located within the confines of Glacis Barracks—the headquarters of the Army Service Corps at Halifax—in a small brick building which, under the regime of the Imperials, had been used as a school for the senior children of Imperial soldiers in garrison at Halifax. Under peace conditions this building was inadequate

THE ARMY SERVICE CORPS

for the purposes for which it was used, and, needless to say, under war demands its continuance as such was out of the question. All flour, bread, groceries, meat, and other supplies, had to be taken in and out of one small door.

To meet war requirements, the garrison gymnasium—situated about fifty feet from the old senior school building—was taken over and converted into an ideal Supply Depot. The former grocery store was then opened up to enlarge the bakery, which was modernized by the introduction of electrically-operated machinery and new and enlarged ovens. The meat shop was also improved, the chill room enlarged and modernized by the addition of a "trolley" system for the expeditious handling of meat. Thus in a short time the handicap with which the Army Service Corps labored at the outbreak of war was quickly overcome.

The most serious difficulty, however, which had to be combatted was that of obtaining sufficient men to carry out the increased work thrown upon this Corps by the sudden strengthening of Halifax Garrison, and the calling out of troops to guard various points in the Maritime Provinces. This was a real and trying hardship. The other Permanent Force Units forming Halifax Garrison could not spare men to assist the Army Service Corps, as every man was needed within his own Unit. The problem was partly solved by calling up a number of non-commissioned officers and men of No. 8 Company, Canadian Army Service Corps, commanded by Capt. F. W. Wickwire, with headquarters at Kentville, N.S. No. 7 Company, commanded by Major A. L. Massie, with headquarters at St. John, also supplied a few. Later on Lieut.-Col. I. W. Videto, commanding the 63rd Halifax Rifles, and Lieut.-Col. A. King, commanding the 66th Princess Louise Fusiliers, very generously loaned a number of splendid men, whose ready adaptability made it possible for the Army Service Corps to "carry on." As time advanced enlistments made the Corps more or less self-sustaining, but the fact remains that never throughout the duration of the War were sufficient men actually enlisted in this branch of the Service to render it indepedent of other Units. This condition was probably due to the fact that the possibility of getting Overseas was greater by enlisting in other Units.

Mention has been made of Nos. 7 and 8 Companies of the Canadian Army Service Corps. Both these Companies played important parts in the Great World War, at home and abroad. Major Massie took Overseas the Second Divisional Train, and all the officers and practically the whole of the rank and file of No. 7 Company accompanied him. Captain Wickwire, of No. 8 Company, after a short period as Deputy Assistant Director of Supply and Transport, M.D. No. 6, also went over to France with this Train, and rendered very efficient service with it in the fighting zone.

The strengthening of the Garrison of Halifax made possible the fulfilment of the plans of defence, which had long since been carefully laid down. This, and the summoning of troops for guard purposes at various points in Nova Scotia and New Brunswick, threw a vast amount of work on the Army Service Corps, for not only had these troops, scattered over a wide area throughout the three Provinces, to be housed, and their daily wants in the matter of food, water, light, fuel, straw for bedding, transport and necessary services arranged for, but it was also required, following a preconceived plan, to provide for them against the possibility of their being cut off from their source of supply. To do justice to the amount of labor involved in the organization and administration of this task would require a volume greater in size than this one. so all that can be done is to give a brief outline of the general scheme followed.

When the Royal Canadian Regiment, with its supporting artillery, were ordered to garrison points in the Island of Cape Breton and Canso, they left Halifax self-sustaining for fourteen days; that is, they carried with them reserve rations sufficient for fourteen days for all ranks. In addition they carried rations for current consumption sufficient for all ranks for a further fourteen days, but minus meat, butter and bread. Lieut. J. A. Gwynne, of the Army Service Corps, and one clerk, accompanied the Regiment to Sydney to make necessary supply and other arrangements. The tasks this officer had to attend to may be judged when it is known that he had to make contracts, and to arrange to supply the wants of troops located at nine different points, covering a frontage of about fifty miles, and requiring travel by train, steamship, street car and automobile to reach the various posts. So capably was the duty performed that the troops had never to go without a meal, their

THE ARMY SERVICE CORPS

rations being arranged with practically the regularity which prevailed in Halifax under peace conditions. When Lieutenant Gwynne was summoned for service Overseas, he was replaced at Sydney by Lieut. Horace Westmoreland. Later on this officer went to France as Transport Officer of the Royal Canadian Regiment, being replaced at Sydney by Lieut. Cecil Sircom. These three officers belonged to the Permanent Force, and received their training at Halifax.

As the Supply and Transport Officer at Sydney found it impossible to give any attention to the troops stationed at Canso, the work there incidental to the Army Service Corps was performed by the Officer Commanding the Guard, who received the necessary instructions by telegram and telephone from the Assistant Director of Supplies and Transport at Halifax, an Army Service Corps' Clerk being sent to Canso to attend to the necessary accounting.

An incident might here be related as exemplifying the difficulties that had to be overcome from time to time by the Army Service Corps. Certain heavy guns had to be transported from Prince Edward Island to points in Nova Scotia. Every effort was put forth to obtain the services of a ship capable of carrying these guns, but without success. Finally, after a delay of several days, Lieut.-Colonel Arthur Peake telephoned from Charlottetown to Halifax to say that a ship was then approaching Charlottetown Harbor which might be suitable. The A.D. of S. & T. at Halifax instructed him to approach the captain of this vessel and explain to him the situation, and if he was not agreeable to undertaking the task of transporting these guns, Colonel Peake was to commandeer the ship and move the artillery to the places directed. Whether it was Colonel Peake's persuasiveness or his war-like demeanor that had the desired effect cannot be stated with certainty. Time was spent only in removing sufficient of the ship's cargo to make it possible to load the guns, which were then transported with despatch. Meanwhile other arrangements had been made by the Army Service Corps to carry these guns to the points in Nova Scotia where they were required.

The troops forming the actual defence force of Halifax and environments were supplied on the same basis as those sent to Cape

Breton, so that in the event of necessity they could sustain themselves for fourteen days, and by the addition of tinned meat and biscuit, the period could be extended another fourteen days.

Meanwhile troops had been summoned for the defence of St. John, N.B., which necessitated calling out a portion of No. 7 Company of the Canadian Army Service Corps, under the command of Major A. L. Massie. This detachment took up its headquarters in the Armories, and from there efficiently ministered to the wants of the troops on duty and in training at St. John and adjoining points. Lieut. J. Key, who had been trained at Halifax, was sent to St. John to take up the duties as District Barrack Officer, carrying out these duties very satisfactorily. Lieut. Arthur Biggar, who was also trained at Halifax, was despatched to St. John as Officer in Charge of Supplies, a position he filled very creditably until called for duty in France. The troops doing duty at St. John and adjacent points were also rationed on the same basis as were those on duty at Halifax, Cape Breton, and other points.

It will be remembered that early in the War a Capt. Von Weghorn, an officer of the Prussian Army, startled the civilized world by an attempt to destroy the International railway bridge spanning the St. Lacroix River, between McAdam Junction, on the Canadian side, and Vanceboro, on the United States' side. A suitcase filled with dynamite was placed between the piers of the northeast corner of the bridge on the Canadian side. The attempt failed, the bridge being only slightly damaged and traffic not delayed. It was considered expedient, however, to place an armed guard on this bridge on the Canadian side. To Lieut.-Col. E. C. Dean, A.D. of S. & T., M.D. No. 6, fell the duty of making the necessary supply and other arrangements for this guard.

A similar guard was placed over the new railway bridge spanning the St. John River at St. Leonards.

Guards were also established over the Marconi Wireless Towers at Newcastle, N.B., and Barrington Passage, the latter under command of Lieut.-Col. T. M. Seeley. These guards required the usual attention on the part of the Army Service Corps. To maintain the guard at Barrington Passage was a cause of anxiety, as it was stationed at a point some miles off the main road, in the midst of a wilderness, and could be reached only in good weather, as the road

THE ARMY SERVICE CORPS

leading to the Wireless Station from the main highway was—well, simply impossible.

Permanent guards were also maintained at Louisburg, Glace Bay, Whitney Pier, Sydney, North Sydney, Sydney Mines, Cranberry Head, Chapel Hill, Canso and various other places.

Incidentally troops were gathering at Valcartier to form the First Contingent and the quota from the Maritime Provinces had to be transported to the place of rendezvous. The manner of the arrangement of this transportation was unique. Recruiting was being carried on in practically every city, town, village and hamlet in the Maritime Provinces. Movements were made when it was known that sufficient numbers of men had been recruited to justify sending them forward. On the A.D. of S. and T. rested the task of making train arrangements to get these recruits to Valcartier. It was done in this manner: Instructions were sent to various recruiting centres to have certain numbers of recruits entrain on a certain train on a certain day. Thus, for instance, the first lot might entrain at Louisburg, and others along the line as far as Sydney; probably some would be brought over from Sydney Mines and North Sydney to Sydney. At the latter place two, three or four special coaches would be attached to a regular train, and as this train proceeded towards Truro, the number of recruits would be augmented, until on its arrival at Truro it might have from two to three hundred on board. Meanwhile, a sufficient number would be run up from Halifax, and a special train would then be made up at Truro and run to Levis, P.Q., where a transfer would be made for Quebec and Valcartier. At other times Moncton would be made the point at which a special train would be made up, in which case St. John supplied the completing quota to make up the train load of 500 or thereabouts. It must be borne in mind, however, that the whole movement was planned ahead of time, and the transport scheme carried out on a definite plan.

Obviously it was impossible to send out transport warrants to cover the movement of these various groups, so an arrangement was made whereby the railway authorities agreed to accept temporary interim receipts from officers or non-commissioned officers in charge of these groups, on the presentation of a telegram or letter of instruction from either the A.D. of S. & T. or any other Staff officer. These receipts were issued in duplicate, one copy of which was kept by the ticket agent and the other mailed to the A.D. of S. & T. Upon receipt of the latter, covering transport warrants were mailed to the ticket agents concerned. By this means some thousands of troops were moved expeditiously from the Maritime Provinces to Valcartier.

New Units of the Canadian Expeditionary Force were forming in various parts of the Maritime Provinces, and it behooved the Army Service Corps to quarter them, arrange for supplies, water, light, land transportation, barrack equipment, and a thousand and one details incidental to the requirements of newly-formed military organizations, and of which only a trained soldier has the faintest conception. These new Units, or in some cases reinforcements, were scattered throughout the length and breadth of the three Provinces, at such places in Nova Scotia as: Halifax, Windsor, Truro, Pictou, New Glasgow, Antigonish, Sydney, North Sydney, Sydney Mines, Broughton, Glace Bay and Amherst.

When the Malleable Iron Works at Amherst, were converted into a domicile for the involuntary reception and entertainment of adherents of the doctrines of the Kaiser and his admirers, a small detachment of the Army Service Corps was sent there to attend to their well-being. The late Capt. P. F. Keating was in command of this detachment which had also to look after the needs of the recruits quartered in Amherst. Captain Keating was trained at Halifax and later proceeded Overseas in command of No. 4 Company of the Third Divisional Train. This Company was recruited at Halifax, having its headquarters in the old Medical College Building at the corner of College and Carlton Streets.

Shortly after the outbreak of war, Canadian horses began to find their way Overseas. In the first winter of the War the number shipped from the Port of Halifax was something like 17,000. On the Army Service Corps rested the duty of embarking these animals. The absence of forewarning of train loads of horses being en route for Halifax was sometimes the cause of great anxiety. At five o'clock one Easter Sunday morning a telephone message from a railway official conveyed the tidings that there were three train loads of horses in the freight yards consigned to the Assistant

THE ARMY SERVICE CORPS

Director of Supplies and Transport. As this was the first intimation received of the movement of these horses, naturally no arrangements had been made for their reception, and as the ships by which they were to be conveyed Overseas were not in the harbor, it became necessary to arrange for their disentrainment without loss of time. Mr. M. McF. Hall, Secretary of the Halifax Exhibition, was called out of bed by telephone, the situation explained to him, and arrangements completed to detrain and stable the horses at the Exhibition Grounds. Every available man of the Army Service Corps was aroused from bed and marched to the Exhibition Grounds, there to care for these horses instead of proceeding to church to take part in Easter Sunday Service. Later, a detachment of artillerymen was told off to take on the responsibility of these horses. At least on two other occasions consignments of horses reached Halifax under similar circumstances.

Another "job" of the Army Service Corps at Halifax was to receive, account for and send forward Overseas thousands upon thousands of parcels of "comforts" for the troops at the Front, these parcels coming from all parts of Canada, comprising everything in size from an envelope containing a handkerchief to packing cases and barrels of comforts of every description. Every parcel received was given a number, registered, and then despatched Overseas.

Arrangements for the embarkation of complete Units and reinforcements of troops during the early part of the War also fell to the lot of the Army Service Corps, the A.D. of S. & T. being the responsible officer. He had a most capable and efficient assistant in the person of Capt. S. A. Doane, of Army Service Corps, whose knowledge of steamship matters is unsurpassed, and who carried out practically all the details incidental to the embarkation of troops at Halifax.

The Barrack Services under Capt. George Simms was a hardworked branch, the pressure on which did not cease until long after peace had been declared.

It is worthy of mention that throughout the War thousands of contracts for supplies were made and carried out by the Army Service Corps in the Maritime Provinces, involving the expenditure of millions of dollars, the accounting for which was also one of the many duties of the Army Service Corps, yet not in a single instance was there the breath of scandal discernible, a single transaction questioned, or a suggestion of deviation from the ethical pathway of rectitude. Truly a glorious record and heritage for the Canadian Army Service Corps in the Maritime Provinces, with headquarters in the Metropolis of Nova Scotia.

The statement has been made that at the outbreak of the Great World War there were stationed at Halifax eight officers of the Army Service Corps. Most of these were soon cleared out and proceeded Overseas. Major Marks, Lieutenants Lawson and MacDougall were summoned to Valcartier and accompanied the First Contingent. Lieut.-Colonel Dean was called to take command of the First Divisional Train, but as his services at Halifax could not then be spared, he was not permitted to go. Later on he was given the command of the Second Divisional Train, but again he was held back, Major A. L. Massie of St. John being given the command. Col. W. A. Simson, a Nova Scotian, was placed in command of the First Divisional Train, which proved to be the "first" Train in more senses than one, inasmuch as it was conceded to be the best Train in France, barring none.

On the establishment of an Army Service Corps Training School at Toronto, Capt. H. R. Hendy, of Halifax, was appointed Adjutant. On proceeding Overseas, he was replaced by Capt. Cecil R. Sircom. Both of these officers received their training at Halifax, as did also upwards of one hundred officers, all of whom "made good" in Flanders Fields, bringing credit to themselves, the Army Service Corps and the Metropolis of Nova Scotia, where they were trained.

Among Nova Scotia officers of the Army Service Corps who were trained at Halifax and saw service at the Front were: Capt. G. A. Redford, of New Glasgow; Lieut. D. A. Starr, of Halifax; Capt. "Ted" Foster, of Bedford; Capt. G. W. Underwood, of New Glasgow; Capt. Walter Taylor, of Halifax, who transferred his affections to the Army Medical Corps; Lieut. Frank S. Brennan, of Halifax, later transferred to the Flying Corps; Lieut. A. B. Dewberry, of Halifax. In addition Lieut. L. Pierce, of No. 8 Company, saw service in France, while Lieuts. J. A. Rose, G. H. Applegate, W. J. V. Tweedie, H. S. Crowe and F. D. Doyle, also of No. 8 Company, all Nova Scotians, performed meritorious service

THE ARMY SERVICE CORPS

in Canada. Lieut. J. G. Ryan, of Kentville, received his training at Halifax and filled many important appointments at Sydney, Amherst, Aldershot, Ottawa and elsewhere. Physical unfitness rendered him unable to partake in the campaign Overseas.

The Headquarters Company of the Fourth Divisional Train was organized at Halifax, the 200 members being recruited almost entirely from Nova Scotia. The Train was mobilized and trained at Halifax. It was commanded by Lieut.-Col. E. C. Dean, who took it Overseas. Of this Unit a Canadian officer in high position in England said it was one of the best trained bodies of men that Canada had contributed to the Great War.

On the departure Overseas of Lieut.-Colonel Dean, the duties of A.D. of S. & T. were taken over by Major A. P. Lomas, of No. 6 Company of the Army Service Corps. This officer very efficiently administered the Army Service Corps affairs in the Maritime Provinces for nearly three years, and rendered the British Empire invaluable service. He was ably seconded by Major E. E. Wood, who commanded the local C.P.A.S.C., now developed into a Company of upwards of 200 men, having about fifty horses and forty motor vehicles.

The Permanent Detachment of the Army Service Corps at Halifax contributed very materially in personnel to the various Army Service Corps Units proceeding Overseas, the Detachment being made up largely of Nova Scotians. The training and disciplining these men received at Halifax had the effect of leavening the Overseas Units with which they became associated.

When the casualties began to return from France, they came in ship loads, about ninety per cent. returning through the Port of Halifax. Sometimes as many as three vessels a week arrived. Most of the well-known big ships were engaged in bringing home these war-scarred veterans, among the number being the *Olympic*, *Aquitania* and *Mauretania*. In this work the Army Service Corps played an important part, as they made all train, berthing and feeding arrangements, as well as issuing all ranks with the necessary tickets for transportation. The Army Service Corps worked out each train "consist," gave the completed train schedules to the railroad officials, who made up the trains in accordance therewith.

Lieut.-Col. E. C. Dean, who had just returned from France, was appointed Chief Transport Officer. Other Army Service Corps officers employed on this important work were: Major F. W. Wickwire (who later succeeded Colonel Dean as Chief Transport Officer), Capt. S. A. Doane, Lieut. Ken. Love, Capt. L. Prickler, and Lieut. George H. Edgar. Also assisting were eighty train conducting officers, one of whom was placed in charge of each troop train to look after the comforts of the men, see that they were properly fed, and that the train was run through to its destination without undue delay.

Troops were disembarked at the rate of 1,000 under one hour: the *Olympic* and *Aquitania*, each carrying 5,500, were cleared in five hours. About twelve to fourteen trains on an average were required to despatch this number of men homeward, and the fact that over a quarter of a million men were thus entrained, ticketed, berthed and fed en route without a single mishap or complaint serves to illustrate the almost perfect system that prevailed. Troops were entrained at the rate of 1,000 an hour, which meant that a troop train departed every half hour, which may be considered quick work even from a railroad standpoint.

Though he was not connected with the military in any way, at the same time a word of praise is due Mr. Ernie Cameron, now Superintendent of the Dining and Sleeping Car Department of the Canadian National Railways at Halifax, for the very able, efficient co-operation he gave the military authorities in making up trains, providing most excellent meals for the men en route and in many ways doing his bit to make the home-coming of the warriors a happy one.

The Maritime Provinces, and Nova Scotia in particular, may justly be proud of the part played in the Great War by their sons who wore the badges of the Army Service Corps. The highly creditable achievements of this organization—a Unit usually little heard of, but which accomplishes big things—has shed lustre on the names of the three Provinces down by the sounding sea.

CHAPTER XXV.

THE CANADIAN ORDNANCE CORPS.

ON the outbreak of hostilities the Canadian Ordnance Corps had a strength of four officers, fifty-five other ranks and thirteen civilians. It was very soon apparent that the Ordnance Depot would have to be kept working twenty-four hours per diem. All ranks therefore were immediately placed under canvas within the Depot, and shifts arranged so that work of the Ordnance Depot could be continued the whole period of twenty-four hours.

The armament of the Fortress and the Royal Canadian Engineer Defence electric lights were immediately equipped up to war scale. All fighting equipment necessary for the Royal Canadian Regiment, the 63rd and 66th Regiments, and 1st Regiment Canadian Garrison Artillery was immediately issued. Companies of the 94th and 78th Regiments were later clothed and equipped for duty at various strategic points in Nova Scotia.

With the manning of all Forts it became necessary to place a highly trained mechanic, known as an Armament Artificer, in each, to keep all guns and machinery in repair, and ready for immediate action. These were provided by the Canadian Ordnance Corps.

As soon as the Camp opened at Valcartier, it fell to the lot of the Canadian Ordnance Corps at Halifax to ship forward the bulk of the stores for equipping the Units being mobilized at Valcartier. Day after day, night after night, it was one continuous loading of cars to rush forward to Valcartier Camp. Special efforts were made to complete the 17th Battery, C.F.A., Sydney, with clothing and equipment before proceeding to Valcartier.

Prior to the departure of the 1st Division from Valcartier, an advance party from the Canadian Ordnance Corps was being sent to England to prepare for the arrival of the Canadians in England. Conductor J. D. Pitman and three non-commissioned officers and men left Halifax with seventy minutes notice and proceeded to England as part of the Canadian Ordnance Corps advance party The party were each in possession of a haversack and water bottle as their kit. Conductor Pitman received promotion to the rank of Major, and held Staff appointments on the various Divisions in France, finally being made Chief Ordnance Officer, Canadian Overseas Military Forces, and was awarded the D.S.O.

As the Imperial Government was, during the early stage of the War, urgently in need of guns and ammunition, all guns and ammunition which could be spared from this district were immediately shipped away direct to the Royal Arsenal at Woolwich.

Two Armament Artificers also left Halifax to proceed with the Canadian Artillery Brigades of the 1st Division, and of these two, Armament Q.M.S. Smith, it is regretted, after having greatly distinguished himself in action, died of the result of wounds.

In October, 1915, the Halifax Detachment of the Canadian Ordnance Corps sent Overseas a nucleus of an Ordnance Mobile Workshop required by the Canadian Corps for the inspection, repair and upkeep of guns and vehicles of all kinds in the Field. This Unit was placed under the command of Major A. S. Buttenshaw, Inspector of Ordnance Machinery. This officer was afterwards Chief Inspector of Ordnance Machinery, Canadian Forces, and was awarded the D.S.O. Other ranks of the Detachment were moved away from time to time Overseas as ordered from Ottawa. Owing to the enormous amount of work required in the clothing and equipping of C.E.F. Units in the district, it was necessary to more than treble the Staff, recruits enlisting being trained for their duties by the few permanent men who, though much against their own wishes, were kept in Halifax, and even then all ranks were working day and night. The explosion which occurred in Halifax, December, 1917, also added to the work, various temporary hospitals being equipped by the Canadian Ordnance Corps.

In August, 1918, one officer and nine other ranks of the Halifax Detachment, C.O.C., were ordered to Vancouver as part of the Siberian Expeditionary Force. Several cars were loaded at Halifax with stores for this force and sent forward. The Halifax Detachment, with Ordnance men from other districts, arrived in Russia

THE CANADIAN ORDNANCE CORPS

at Vladivostock and at once opened up a complete Ordnance Depot, where work was carried on in the usual smooth manner.

Several hundred thousand tons of ammunition, arms, equipment and clothing have been handled by the Canadian Ordnance Corps at Halifax during the period of the War, both coming from and going to England. The Ordnance Workshops at Halifax carried out an enormous amount of repair work, and in addition manufactured large quantities of military stores which were unable to be purchased. Tradesmen enlisting in the C.E.F. in various parts of Canada, such as wheelers, blacksmiths, saddlers and armorers, who were required to accompany troops Overseas, were sent to the Canadian Ordnance Corps, Halifax, for training. The Ordnance Department was also called upon to carry out all repairs and testing of ammunition for the Naval Services, both Imperial and Canadian, in addition to that of the Land Service. This work has to be done by experts, and necessitates very long hours, as certain cordite tests have to run continually day and night for several days at a time.

Since the War, all the equipment, including ammunition, for the new Reorganized Active Militia, is being handled at Halifax and reshipped to the various military points in Canada.

The following officers and senior warrant officers of Canadian Ordnance Corps have served with No. 6 Detachment, Canadian Ordnance Corps, during various periods of the War:—

Colonel J. F. MacDonald; Lieut.-Colonels A. H. Panet and M. C. Gillin; Majors A. S. Buttenshaw, D.S.O., and J. D. Pitman, D.S.O.; Captains E. M. Cartmer, J. H. MacQueen, S. V. Cooke. A. M. Simons, J. N. Gibson, and R. N. C. Bishop; Lieut. G. E. J. Ball; Conductors J. A. Villard, E. V. Hessian, A. Bentley, D.C.M., and A. Lable.

In recognition of services rendered during War 1914-1918, His Majesty the King has graciously approved the grant of the title " Royal " to the Canadian Permanent Ordnance Corps, and hereafter this Corps is permitted to bear the designation of " The Royal Canadian Ordnance Corps."

LIEUT.-COL. JOSEPH HAYES, D.S.O., C.A.M.C.,

Twice mentioned in dispatches; M.O., 85th Infantry Battalion 30-10-15 to 19-12-17; M.O., 4th Divisional Train, 19-12-17 to 14-4-18; S.M.O., Central Group, C.F.C., 15-5-18 to 1-1-19; O.C., No. 2 Canadian Stationary Hospital, 7-1-19 to 17-5-19. Author of "The 85th in France and Flanders."

CHAPTER XXVI.

NOVA SCOTIA MEDICAL SERVICES IN THE GREAT WAR.

BY LIEUT.-COL. JOSEPH HAYES, D.S.O., C.A.M.C.

> "Men whisper that our arm is weak,
> Men say our blood is cold,
> And that our hearts no longer speak
> That clarion note of old;
> But let the spear and sword draw near
> The sleeping lion's den,
> Our Island shore shall start once more
> To life with armèd men."

THE medical men of this Province were no less ardent in their desire to serve their country in the War than all the other professions, trades and callings. It was a contagion in the air that got into the blood. Sooner or later everybody got it and responded to it according to their own notion of service or opportunity. Medical men were needed at home as well as abroad. There were recruits to be examined and young soldiers in training requiring medical and surgical attention and the country could not be stripped of medical service. No sooner were Units formed than there was a clamor for medical appointments. Some medical men even joined the combatant ranks, although they were soon returned to the medical service owing to the demand for medical officers. Also many Nova Scotia medical men went direct to England, or were already abroad, and joined up with the Royal Army Medical Corps. Many of these, with many regimental medical officers, owing to their isolation from the great body of medical men associated with Canadian Hospitals, will be overlooked in narratives of the doings of the medical fraternity.

Before describing in detail the medical work done by Nova Scotians during the War, it will be useful to give a brief outline of the activities of the Medical Service in war.

NOVA SCOTIA'S PART IN THE GREAT WAR

Medical attention is required all the way from the recruiting and training camps at home, and those in England and France and along the lines of communication, up to the front areas and fighting Units in the firing line, No Man's Land and the hand-to-hand encounter in the enemy trenches. But perhaps the function of the Medical Service which calls for the greatest vigilance and most thorough care is the prevention and control of epidemic and contagious diseases.

The most strenuous efforts of the Medical Services are exerted to rescue the man who is wounded in action, and to give him such prompt attention as will prevent him, as far as possible, from bleeding to death or dying from shock or exposure and to hasten him to a place where the best surgical skill can be exercised to save his life and limbs.

The primary aid is under the direction of the Regimental Medical Officer who is assisted by sixteen stretcher-bearers and two orderlies whom it is his duty to keep in a constant state of efficiency by careful training, as unskilled men, during active operations, are constantly being added from the ranks to make up wastage. One Nova Scotia Regiment lost thirty-three per cent. of its stretcher-bearers in two hours in the Vimy Ridge engagement.

This little coterie goes into the trenches with the Unit. The Regimental Medical Officer selects a Regimental Aid Post (R.A.P.) well to the front and as far as possible out of the direct line of enemy fire, so that the wounded may be safely cared for and promptly evacuated. The stretcher-bearers are detailed four to each Company, and these go with their Companies into action and accompany them wherever they go. They are the most exposed men in an engagement; for while the combatants may advance in rushes and seek shelter as they go, the stretcher-bearer is constantly exposed, going back and forth to the relief of the wounded. As a result of the efficiency these men attain, their dressings, applied on the battle-field during action, often can go untouched until they reach the hospital.

At the Regimental Aid Post further treatment is given by the Regimental Medical Officer, food and hot tea or coffee are given and the wounded are rolled in blankets and made as comfortable as possible before being sent out. All cases are tagged, usually a white tag showing the man's name, number, Regiment, the nature of his injury, and any special treatment or remedies that may have been given. In dangerous cases a red tag is used, which secures the right of way in rapid evacuation and immediate attention.

As soon as casualties are ready for evacuation from the R.A.P. they are handed over to the Bearer Section of a Field Ambulance to be carried to their Advanced Dressing Station. As it is practically never possible to establish the Main Dressing Station sufficiently far forward to convey stretcher cases to it in one relay, and at the same time have it accessible to motor ambulances, light railways and other means of rapid evacuation, Advanced Dressing Stations are set up as near the front as can be evacuated to the Main Dressing Station by horsed ambulances with reasonable safety by day as well as by night. The evacuation of the wounded up to this point must usually be done at night on account of enemy observation; though the walking wounded are often able to take advantage of lulls in the hostile fire and make their way out during the day. Usually arrows are put up along the route pointing the direction for "walking wounded."

The Main Dressing Station of the Field Ambulance is provided with facilities for attending to cases requiring immediate operation as the only means of saving life. It must be remembered that this Unit is on the field of actual operations and within reach of the direct fire of the enemy. The sick and wounded are here sorted, classified and evacuated as soon as possible to the Casualty Clearing Station (C.C.S.). The few mild cases that can be returned to the line or sent to near-by rest camps after twenty-four or forty-eight hours are held at the Field Ambulance, it being necessary to conserve, as much as possible, the man-power for the line.

The Casualty Clearing Station affords the next relief. This is the first Unit completely equipped for urgent, formal major operations, and some have X-ray apparatus and electrically-heated operating tables. Although cases are not carried to a finality of treatment, and are only kept until fit to move after relief is given, practically all wounds are dressed at the C.C.S. After emergent operations wounds are often packed with dressings and hurried on to a general hospital in the Lines of Communication. It must be remembered that these Units are within range of enemy guns and liable to get short notice from the enemy, by concentrated high explosive shell-fire, to vacate, or they may have to advance with the advance of their own troops. Constant action is therefore necessary to maintain rooms for the steady stream of wounded which they must always be prepared to handle. It is only the most urgent operations that are performed, such as wounds of the abdomen, chest and brain, or such wounds as are liable to become hopeless through infection or complications before reaching the base. The C.C.S. is usually located at a rail head and has access to ambulance trains for evacuation. These trains are wonderfully equipped with an emergency operating room, kitchen, dining room for up-patients and Staff sleeping berths, dispensary, medical officers, nurses and orderlies.

Now comes the first real hospital treatment. All along the coast of France and at suitable places were hospital centres such as Calais, St. Omer, Le Treport, Le Havre, Rouen, Etaples and Boulogne, with General and Stationary and Special Hospitals. These centres were under an A.D.M.S., who was informed usually twice daily by the different hospitals what empty beds were available. From this information convoys (hospital trains) were dispatched from the C.C.S. to the different hospitals. These were notified by telegraph of the approximate time of arrival so that ample provision could be made to transfer by motor ambulance the patients from the train, on arrival, to the hospital.

These hospitals were all splendidly equipped with X-ray departments and pathological laboratories, and were well staffed with medical and surgical specialists, highly trained nurses and orderlies. When satisfactory progress had been made here, patients were transferred to England to similar, though more highly specialized, hospitals and convalescent homes, and finally, where necessary, were invalided home to Canada.

The difference between a General and a Stationary Hospital was only in size, the former being primarily about twice the size of the latter.

Nova Scotia contributed its quota to all these varied services, including three complete Medical Units.

NOVA SCOTIA MEDICAL SERVICES IN THE GREAT WAR

NO. 1 CANADIAN CASUALTY CLEARING STATION.

The first Nova Scotia Unit to be accepted and mobilized for Overseas Service with the First Contingent was a Medical Unit, No. 2 Clearing Hospital, which had recently returned from annual training at Sussex, N.B. Its headquarters was at Halifax and its Commanding Officer Major F. L. S. Ford, who afterwards became Colonel Ford, C.M.G., and was three times mentioned in Sir Douglas Haig's despatches.

COL. F. L. S. FORD, C.M.G.

This Unit afterwards became No. 1 Canadian Casualty Clearing Station and had a most brilliant record, going through the whole war service of the Canadian Corps.

Immediately after Great Britain entered the War on August 4, 1914, Major Ford telegraphed to Ottawa offering his Unit for Active Service, and on August 10th its mobilization was ordered at Liverpool, N.S. On August 12th a recruiting meeting occurred in the Town Hall, Liverpool, which was one of the first, if not the first, public recruiting meeting held in Canada. This meeting was addressed by Major Ford, the mayor of the town, and a number of other citizens. There was a great deal of enthusiasm, and then and there the Unit was recruited up to peace-time strength, and in a few days orders were received to entrain on August 20, 1914, for Valcartier Training Camp, via Halifax.

When the people of Queens County saw this first draft of the flower of their young manhood march away in the King's uniform for service on the battle-fields of Europe, they felt that the War was a real thing and had already reached their erst-while quiet, peaceful homes. The send-off was appropriate to the occasion and the people were proud of their noble sons who so promptly responded to the call of Empire and bore themselves splendidly as they marched away amidst the acclaim of their friends and comrades.

This Unit had always been recruited principally from Queens and Annapolis Counties, but had members on its strength from all over the Maritime Provinces and during the period of Active Service had on its roll men from all parts of Canada.

At 11 a.m., August 22nd, the Unit arrived at Valcartier with six officers and forty-one other ranks, who were soon mixed up in the moil and swirl and grind of military training in that big Camp with some thirty thousand others.

The officers, N.C.O.'s and men who went to Valcartier from Liverpool were: Major F. S. L. Ford, Commanding Officer; Capt. H. T. M. McKinnon, Capt. C. Harold Dickson, Capt. G. B. Peat, Lieut. H. A. Pickup, Q.M., Lieut. G. W. McKeen, Staff-Sergt. F. Burnett, Staff-Sergt. E. Dexter, Staff-Sergt. E. Hunt, Q.M.S. R. Robar, Staff-Sergt. R. Brown, Sergt. J. Fiendel, Sergt. McLeod: Privates—A. Crouse, J. Gardine, L. Keating, P. Joudrey, A. Morris, N. Neily, M. Reid, L. Frost, W. Joudrey, W. Murray, H. Harnish, E. Conrad, G. McGill, H. Rafuse, C. Fraser, C. Holden, E. McGowan, C. Robart, W. Bernadine, J. Hallett, W. O'Reilly, H. Oickle, C. Jollimore, S. White, A. Trefry, B. Smith, A. Joudrey, L. Brooks, H. Lantz, J. Downer, G. Conrod, R. Bell.

On arrival at Valcartier this Unit took over No. 2 Camp Hospital, and carried on as a Field Hospital. The Staff was kept pretty busy with the usual run of camp sickness among new recruits, camp diarrhœa, acute indigestion, fevers, camp accidents, and the usual P.U.O.'s and N.Y.D.'s thrown in.

While at Valcartier, the O.C., Major Ford, was gazetted Lieut.-Colonel. Capt. G. W. O. Downsley, Capt. C. E. Cooper Cole, and forty other ranks of No. 1 Clearing Hospital of Toronto were taken on the strength as well as Major H. A. Chisholm, Capt. R. H. McDonald and Capt. J. M. Stewart. Lieut. G. W. McKeen was transferred as Medical Officer to an Army Service Corps and Captain Cole was retransferred to No. 2 General Hospital.

At 4.30 p.m., September 25th, the Unit left by train for Quebec and embarked on the *SS. Megantic* at 6 p.m. The other Units to embark on this ship were: The 15th Canadian Battalion (48th Highlanders), Lieut.-Col. John Currie; The 1st Divisional Ammunition Column, Lieut.-Col. J. Penhole; No. 1 Canadian Field Ambulance, Lieut.-Col. A. E. Ross.

After lying in the stream for five days the ship weighed anchor at 10.30 p.m. on September 30th and proceeded down the St. Lawrence River to the rendezvous in Gaspé Bay, for there were thirty-one troopships in this grand fleet which was to convey the Canadian Army of thirty thousand safely over the ocean to Old Mother England.

As the good ship *Megantic* glided quietly down the river the stars shone brightly, the silvery moon was high in the heavens, and the clear frosty tang of early autumn was in the air. As the shimmering waters of this great river glistened and danced in the moonlight all nature seemed to have an air of serene quietude and universal confidence. The scene might have been committed to canvas as an emblem of peace; but this was a first stage in the great adventure of war, the fullest bitterness of which many of that gay company were destined to taste.

At 3 p.m., October 3, 1914, this great flotilla weighed anchor and put to sea, led by *H.M.S. Eclipse*, immediately followed by the *Megantic*, containing the first Nova Scotia Medical Unit. There were a number of torpedo boat destroyers, and among the battleships were the *Queen Mary* and the *Glory*. After an uneventful voyage of eleven days this great flotilla arrived at Plymouth on October 14th. The reception given the Canadian Contingent everywhere was wonderful. The sentiment back of it all seemed to reach every heart. A splendid army of sturdy Anglo-Saxons from a new and great country had come three thousand miles over the seas to join the forces of the Mother Land within two months from the time she had entered the War.

After lying in the stream for two days the *Megantic* docked and on October 16th the 1st Canadian Casualty Clearing Station disembarked and marched midst cheering throngs through the streets of Plymouth together with the other Units, and entrained for the land of winter slush and mud at Salisbury Plains. At 2 a.m. on a pitch dark October morning the Unit detrained at Patney and Chirton Station and marched to West Down North, where they arrived tired and weary after a sleepless night and a long march, at 7.30 a.m., October 17th.

NOVA SCOTIA'S PART IN THE GREAT WAR

Major H. A. Chisholm was called for duty to the office of the A.D.M.S. Canadians shortly after arrival. Major Chisholm belonged to Antigonish, and was a member of the Permanent Army Medical Corps. He had a distinguished career Overseas and attained the rank of Colonel and was mentioned in despatches and awarded the honors of C.M.G. and D.S.O. He also held the important positions of D.A.D.M.S. 1st Canadian Division; A.D.M.S. 4th Division; A.D.M.S. attached to the office of the D.G.M.S. Canadians, London, and D.D.M.S., O.M.F.C., London.

The unusually heavy autumn rains of 1914 converted the rolling downs of Salisbury Plains into seas of mud, through which the Unit wallowed and bathed and boated in its efforts to follow field training. The troops were all under canvas at this time.

Lord Astor, then Major Astor, had a palatial residence and spacious grounds at Cliveden, near Taplow, Bucks, the grounds of which he offered for hospital purposes. In December No. 1 Canadian C.C.S. was sent to Cliveden to establish a hospital, and for six weeks the entire personnel was busy in these preparations. This hospital, established by No. 1 Canadian Casualty Clearing Hospital of Nova Scotia, ultimately developed into the great Duchess of Connaught Hospital, afterwards officially known as No. 15 Canadian General Hospital, upon which thousands of Canadians, Australians, New Zealanders, South Africans and other Britishers can look back with grateful memories for the skilful and successful treatment and great kindness for which this hospital became noted.

A Casualty Clearing Station is a field unit, and consequently when the 1st Canadian Division was ordered to France this Unit received a move order and preceded the Division to France, landing at Le Havre at 10 a.m., February 3, 1915, on *S.S. Huanchaco* from Southampton. On the same ship was another Canadian Hospital Unit—No. 1 Canadian Stationary, commanded by Lieut.-Col. Lorn Drum (now Colonel Lorn Drum, C.B.E., Inspector of Military Hospitals for Canada). These, however, were not the first Canadian Units in France, as they were preceded in November, 1914, by a No. 2 Canadian Stationary Hospital, which was commanded in its last days in France and brought back to Canada by the writer. This was really the first Canadian Unit of any description to function in France as a Unit and the only one in France in 1914.

After some six weeks stay at Le Havre the Unit was transferred to Boulogne, where it arrived at 9.45 a.m., February 26, 1915.

Motion was usually rapid in France and changes made at short notice. Within a week this Unit had orders to proceed from Boulogne to First Army Headquarters at the Town of Aire-Sur-La-Lys, where it arrived Saturday morning, March 6th. On arrival the Unit was assigned to Fort Gassion, which had been a French prison before the War but was now occupied by British troops as a rest camp, and there was also a Motor Ambulance Convoy billeted there. The work assigned to No. 1 C.C.S. was to take over this old prison and make it immediately ready for the reception of patients.

The old buildings were filthy and in a dilapidated condition, and required a great deal of work to prepare them for patients, and all the equipment had to be unpacked and placed. The whole Unit went to work with diligence and determination and within forty-eight hours they brought order out of chaos and on Monday morning admitted and comfortably housed fifty patients.

The Battle of Neuve Chapelle was in progress and was the source of most of the patients during the week.

Heroic work was done by the six nursing sisters who had been attached to and had come over to France with this Unit. They were:—Vivian Tremaine, M.V.O., R.R.C., Frances M. Frew, M. U. Riverin, Amy Howard, Minnie Follette.

Nursing Sister Follette, of Great Village, Colchester County, afterwards lost her life with the sinking of the hospital ship *Llandovery Castle* by the Germans.

No. 1 Canadian C.C.S. was the only Canadian Unit in action during the Battle of Neuve Chapelle. It was one of six C.C.S.'s attached to the First Army. Before the War was over there were sixteen. This Unit showed such prompt action and capacity that it received the special commendation of Major-General Sir W. G. MacPherson, Director Medical Services, First Army, and in June the O.C., Lieut.-Colonel Ford, was awarded the C.M.G., the first awarded to Canadians in France.

During this engagement Capts. C. H. Dickson and G. W. O. Downsley and a party of twelve orderlies were hastily sent to Merville to assist a British C.C.S., and at the Second Battle of Ypres, Captain Downsley and Captain J. M. Stewart, of Halifax, with Nursing Sister Follette and twelve orderlies were assigned to duty at Hazebrouck to assist another British C.C.S.

There was heavy fighting throughout the summer of 1915 in the Bethune Sector, and No. 1 Canadian C.C.S. did a lot of heavy and trying work, and in addition detailed a section under Major W. T. M. McKinnon and Captain C. H. Dickson for duty with No. 2 British C.C.S., which was located at the Village of Choques.

This Unit continued its headquarters at Aire, and in May, June and September took its full share in the herculean task of evacuating the wounded from Festubert, Givenchy and Loos. During the battle of Loos over sixty thousand casualties were evacuated from the British Front by the various clearing stations in four days.

One of the outstanding distinctions of No. 1 Canadian C.C.S. is that, when His Majesty King George V was seriously injured near Bethune in August, 1915, by his horse falling and rolling over on him, one of the nursing sisters of this Unit, V. A. Tremaine, was selected by the Director Medical Services of the 1st Imperial Army for personal attendance upon the King. His Majesty was cared for in a chateau near Aire until he was able to be moved to England. Sister Tremaine and a second nurse who had been selected, Nursing Sister E. K. Ward, Q.A.I.M.N.S. Territorials, accompanied the Royal patient and nursed His Majesty through convalescence at Buckingham Palace.

When Sister Tremaine finished her duties the King conferred upon her the M.V.O. and personally presented her with the insignia of that Order and made a personal gift of an exquisite brooch of gold and enamel set with diamonds. Her Majesty the Queen gave her autograph copies of the royal photographs.

The Unit continued to operate at Aire until January, 1916, when it was transferred to Bailleul and opened up in a very fine pavilion of the Asylum for the Insane. This splendid building was subsequently destroyed by German shell fire and bombs. The Unit saw much strenuous work here, and had its first experience with gassed cases. Sixty of these out of eight hundred died within the first twenty-four hours after being brought in.

Major Edward Archibald, of No. 3 (McGill) Canadian General Hospital, was attached to the Unit as a surgical specialist, and Major W. A. McLean, of Glace Bay, N.S., was transferred from

No. 1 Canadian General Hospital as his assistant, and afterwards succeeded Major Archibald. Major McLean was killed during the summer of 1917 while at work in a C.C.S. in the northern sector of the British line. He was considered one of the most brilliant surgeons in the British Army.

In June, 1916, Colonel Ford was appointed Deputy Assistant Director of Medical Services of the Canadian Corps and Lieut.-Col. T. W. H. Young succeeded to the command. Later Colonel Young was succeeded by Major C. H. Dickson, who was promoted to the rank of Lieut.-Colonel.

There was a great deal of activity on the Arras Front in the early spring of 1917, and preparations were being made for the drive for Vimy Ridge. At this time the Unit was transferred to Aubigny, behind Arras. Under the energetic administration of Lieut.-Colonel Dickson this Unit was very much increased in strength and did valuable work during the Battle of Vimy Ridge and throughout the operations on the Arras Front.

In the summer of 1917 the Unit was again moved to a position near Nieuport and arrived just as the Germans had broken through and made a nasty salient in the British line. Amidst this confusion, uncertainty and fierce fighting, the Commanding Officer, Colonel Dickson, quickly located his Unit and did such splendid work in the evacuation of the wounded that he was mentioned in despatches and awarded the D.S.O.

The Unit remained at Nieuport for a few weeks only when the position became untenable for hospital purposes, owing to almost constant shelling and nightly bombing. Lieut.-Colonel Dickson was called to London for Staff duty, the command was taken over by Lieut.-Colonel A. G. H. Bennett, O.B.E., and the Unit was transferred again to the Arras-Vimy Front.

During those anxious days of the early spring and summer of 1918, while the Germans battered themselves hopelessly against the impenetrable wall of steel erected by the Canadians along the Arras Front this Unit did fine work in caring for and clearing the seriously sick and wounded and also got many casualties from that memorable drive of the Germans against the 5th British Army in March, 1918, as all the Ambulance and C.C.S. Units in that area were quickly put out of commission.

When preparations were made for the final victorious Canadian drive which commenced at Amiens on August 8, 1918, this Unit was moved to that sector and followed the Canadian Corps through those strenuous days to final victory and accompanied the 1st Canadian Division on its victorious march into Germany. At Bonn No. 1 Canadian Stationary Hospital took over the famous St. Martin's Hospital, which was located on one of the loftiest hills in Bonn, and but two weeks before had dukes and scions of the leading aristocracy of Germany as patients, for it had been one of the most exclusive hospitals in Germany. Now it became the haven of the sick Canadian Tommy.

It seemed like the realization of a fantastic dream to the medical Staff and nursing sisters, as well as the rank and file, to find themselves in a modern and well-equipped hospital with luxurious appointments and surroundings, as compared with four long years of mud and mire under canvas, in huts, and often broken-down buildings on the edge of the battle-fields of the Somme, Ypres, Vimy, Passchendaele, Amiens, Bourlon, Cambrai and Valenciennes, Mons, and then glorious victory.

The following is an incomplete list of the battle casualties of this Unit:—

KILLED IN ACTION.

Major Walter Maclean; Nursing Sisters Mae B. Sampson and Minnie Follette, both killed on Hospital Ship *Llandovery Castle;* Pte Proctor, Pte. Vere Mason.

WOUNDED.

Lieut.-Col. F. S. L. Ford, seriously, by piece of bombshell (fracture base of skull); Capt. E. C. C. Cole, seriously; Capt. R. H. MacDonald, Sergeant M. Neilly, seriously.

NO. 7 CANADIAN STATIONARY HOSPITAL.

(Dalhousie Unit.)

Dalhousie University was early inspired with patriotic fervor. Within a month after the outbreak of war between Great Britain and German, Dalhousie University offered to the Government the personnel of a Casualty Clearing Station. This offer was renewed in the spring of 1915. It was not known until later that this type of Unit was not in demand, and it was decided to offer the personnel of a Stationary Hospital.

So anxious was Dalhousie to have a definite, tangible part in the more strenuous service of the nation in this great struggle, that a delegation was sent to Ottawa on August 13, 1915, representing the Governors and Faculty of the University. So well were the claims of Dalhousie presented that the offer was now accepted of a Stationary Hospital, to be known officially as " No. 7 Canadian Stationary Hospital." Definite authority for this was received on September 27, 1915.

COL. JOHN STEWART, C.B.E.

When it came to the selection of a Commanding Officer everybody turned instinctively to that great outstanding factotum in Medicine and Surgery in Nova Scotia, Dr. John Stewart, whose name inspired enthusiasm, confidence and respect.

Halifax was taxed to its utmost in supplying accommodation for troops. All the old military barracks were full, the Armories were occupied by infantry Battalions, the sheds on No. 2 Pier were also occupied, and there was consequently some delay in finding accommodation for the mobilization and training of this Hospital Unit. Dalhousie University came to the rescue and gave the old Medical College building on the corner of Robie and College Streets, and Principal Kaulbach, of the Maritime Business College, gave the use of the dining room and kitchen of the Business College restaurant as a mess room. By November 1st the old Medical College had been converted into an adequate barracks and orderly room.

The selection of the medical and nursing personnel and the recruiting of other ranks then commenced in earnest and the response was wonderful. For a Stationary Hospital only twelve medical officers and twenty-seven nursing sisters were required: but thirty medical men and eighty nurses applied. The material was all so excellent that it was a delicate and difficult task to select. Preference was given, however, to Dalhousie graduates and those connected with the University; and among the nurses preference was given to graduates of the two outstanding Nova Scotia nurses training hospitals, the Victoria General Hospital, Halifax, and St. Joseph's Hospital, Glace Bay, as these were the only general hospitals in the Province with the necessary number of beds to meet the requirements of the Military Service in the matter of training.

Just before orders were received to proceed Overseas in the latter part of December, 1915, the Unit was inspected by General Benson, G.O.C. of this Military District, Colonel A. H. Powell, D.A.A. & Q.M.G., and Colonel Grant, A.D.M.S. These officers were very generous in their praises of what the Unit had already accomplished in the way of training and establishing a snappy military organization. Their sturdy Commanding Officer, with his sixty-seven years of youth, had shown his magnificent qualities of body as well as mind and character. When Colonel Stewart set the pace on their route marches the youngest and most athletic had to let himself out. Colonel Grant, the A.D.M.S., referred to the splendid work already done in the service by members of the Staff, and mentioned particularly the work done by Major E. V. Hogan as Chief of Surgery at Cogswell Street Military Hospital and Major L. M. Murray as Chief of Medicine; and also expressed his regret at losing his Deputy, Capt. F. V. Woodbury, but congratulated the Unit on what it had gained thereby.

The time set for leaving Halifax for Overseas was December 31, 1915, via St. John, N.B. The departure at one time of so many professional men and women, who stood high in the confidence of the people of Halifax and Nova Scotia, was a poignant reminder of the serious proportions assumed by the Great War.

On the evening of the last day of 1915, when Dalhousie Unit entrained at North Street Depot, a large concourse of people were assembled, not only of Halifax but from many other parts of the Province. The bands of the 1st Canadian Artillery and 63rd Rifles, as well as the pipers, joined the citizens of Nova Scotia in a fitting farewell. Their train pulled out amidst music and cheers.

The Unit arrived at St. John at 6 a.m., New Year's Day, and went aboard His Majesty's Troopship *Metagama*. At noon the officers were entertained at luncheon by the medical profession of St. John at the Royal Hotel. The Unit sailed at 9 o'clock on the evening of January 1, 1916, with several other Units, with Col. H. C. Bickford as Officer Commanding troops.

Sea voyages are pretty much alike. There are those who like their beer and poker, or bridge, and those who like to laze and read and sleep and sleep and read and laze, or sit and think, or simply sit, while others wish they had taken the advice of the poet—"Praise the sea but keep on land." A convoy of torpedo boat destroyers was met at noon on the eighth day out, and at 3 a.m. on January 10th the Unit landed at Plymouth and disembarked at 9 a.m.

The personnel on arriving in England was as follows: O.C., Lieut.-Col. John Stewart; Majors E. V. Hogan and L. M. Murray; Captains M. A. MacAulay, V. N. MacKay, K. A. MacKenzie, E. K. Maclellan, S. J. MacLennan, D. A. MacLeod, J. A. Murray, John Rankine, Frank V. Woodbury, Karl F. Woodbury (Dental Officer), Lieut. S. R. Balcom, Dispenser; Lieut. Walter Taylor, Quartermaster; Miss L. M. Hubley, Matron, and twenty-six Nursing Sisters; one hundred and twenty-three N.C.O.'s and men.

The officers, non-commissioned officers and men entrained at once for Shorncliffe, where they arrived in the evening, while the matron and nursing sisters proceeded to London and were temporarily quartered at Bonnington Hotel. They were afterwards distributed for duty between the hospitals at Westcliffe, Moore Barracks and Ramsgate.

On the 11th the Unit was inspected by Lieut.-Col. F. W. E. Wilson, of Niagara, Ontario, A.D.M.S. Shorncliffe area.

Billets were secured and the medical officers were employed on medical boards or as medical officers to various Units in the training camps, while the non-commissioned officers and men were assigned to various duties.

On January 17th Capt. F. V. Woodbury was stricken with that dread disease among troops, cerebro-spinal meningitis. For some days there was great anxiety on his account, but he made a rapid and complete recovery.

On February 5th Colonel Stewart, O.C. of No. 7 Canadian Stationary Hospital, was given command of Shorncliffe Military

Hospital, with the forty subsidiary hospitals of the Dover area, in succession to Lieut.-Col. R. J. Blanchard, No. 3 C.C.S., of Winnipeg. He immediately recalled the nursing sisters and reassembled his Unit, and with his reorganized Staff manned Shorncliffe Military General Hospital and the Helena Hospital for officers. The Shorncliffe Hospital alone had 800 beds, and altogether there were some 10,000 beds in the hospitals taken over. Colonel Stewart and his Staff had a pretty busy time administering the hospitals of this large area. Sir Frederic Eve visited these hospitals periodically.

During this time there were some changes in personnel: Corpls. G. S. Mitchell and Eric Grant left to take commissions; Capt. S. J. MacLennan went to Westcliffe Eye and Ear Hospital. Capt. E. Douglas joined the Unit during the latter part of the period here and sixteen other ranks were taken on strength.

There was much excitement and anticipation when it was announced that the Unit was to proceed to France. The impression got abroad somehow that the Unit was to go direct to the Arras and Somme areas, where they would be in close contact with actual warfare. This was the source of a good deal of enthusiasm. The Unit left Shorncliffe and proceeded to Southampton on Sunday, June 18, 1916, embarked there on the *City of Benares* and landed at Le Havre the same day. On arrival the Unit received orders to take over the Hotel des Emigrants at Le Havre from No. 2 Imperial General Hospital, which contained 400 beds. This was somewhat disappointing to the men after their anticipations of proceeding at once to the Front. However, all ranks settled down to steady work, and in a few weeks orders were received to establish a subsidiary tented hospital Unit at Harfleur, about six miles from Le Havre, to consist of 400 additional beds. This meant that the existing Staff had to man two hospitals of the same size, thus bringing a very heavy strain on the entire personnel, especially the nursing sisters and other ranks. Major L. M. Murray was placed in charge of the Harfleur Division.

The main hospital was used for German wounded prisoners being sent back from the forward areas and for local sick from various Imperial Units at Le Havre. The subsidiary hospital was used for camp sick and accidents from the Canadian Base and several Imperial Units.

As soon as these extensions were completed and in operation an urgent request was sent in for more men. Eventually a much larger number were sent than were required of P.B. men. (Permanent Base men are those who are no longer fit for service in the front areas.) These were with the Unit only a few days when orders were received to despatch to hospitals in another area a draft larger in number than the one received. This took away several old members of the Unit and left it shorter handed than ever, but the Unit "carried on" and did its work under difficulties.

Constant changes were taking place in the staff. Capt. J. M. Stewart, nephew of the O.C., came to the Unit shortly after arrival in France from No. 1 C.C.S., and in August, 1916, Capt. F. V. Woodbury, Capt. M. A. MacAulay, Capt. John Rankine and Capt. Edgar Douglas were posted to other duties. Capt. E. K. Maclellan was posted to another hospital in March, 1917. Numerous officers from other parts of Canada were detailed for duty with this Unit from time to time. One of the most popular of these was Captain Ireland, of Ontario, who afterwards received the M.C. and was killed in action.

On December 31, 1916, the hospital at Le Havre was handed over to the Royal Army Medical Corps and the personnel of Dalhousie Unit, which had been carrying on there, marched to Harfleur and joined the balance of the Unit. Once more the whole Unit was united and experienced a very general sense of satisfaction. Ample provision had been made for quarters, mess, dental offices and orderly room.

In January and February, 1917, the weather was very severe, with steady, keen frost and a good deal of snow, "But," as Colonel Stewart puts it, "the bitterest memories are the indescribable mud, deep, tenacious and slippery." As spring approached it looked as if the summer were to be spent in the beautiful Lezard Valley, in which Harfleur was situated, and consequently potatoes and other vegetables were planted, shrubs set out and other work done with a view to beautifying the grounds. It was beginning to seem quite like home here. All the troops coming to France en route to the Front came through this base, and many Nova Scotians were met and old acquaintances renewed. Also a good many Nova Scotia boys trickled in to the hospital, and when they did they were lavished with attention, and all the nurses and orderlies wanted to wait on them, and the pipers, too, would manage to make themselves heard and many a lad's eye was made brighter when he heard again the skirl o' the pipes.

There was no abiding place in France, and it was just as one got nicely settled down that he had to move, and at this very time the Unit got orders to proceed to the front areas and take over a hospital at Arques, which is a suburb of the City of St. Omer. Headed by the pipers the Unit marched off to the station Saturday evening, May 12th, but did not entrain until daylight the next morning when a special train was provided for the Unit and its hospital equipment.

The hospital at Harfleur was taken over by a Welsh Unit, the 40th Stationary Hospital, R.A.M.C.

The route was through Yvetot, Amiens, Abbeville and over the Somme, past the former battle-field of Crecy, through Boulogne and Calais to St. Omer and to the little suburban town of Arques, which was reached at 2 a.m., May 14, 1917. The rumble of the artillery could now be plainly heard, and the eastern sky was aflicker with the flashings of guns. The Unit was now within thirty miles of the trenches. A noble old French Chateau with spacious grounds, and a canal running through them, was to be the domicile of the hospital. This same chateau had been occupied by the Duke of Wellington after the campaign of Waterloo.

Tents were pitched on the grounds to supply the additional accommodations required, and the hospital equipment was soon unpacked and placed; but there was considerable delay in getting the necessary supplies for the erection of kitchens, bath houses, pavilions, and material for other necessary alterations and accommodations.

The first convoy was received on June 8th and consisted of wounded German prisoners of war. There were 13 officers and 379 other ranks. This was a large order for the first while not yet completely ready, and tested the resourcefulness and agility of the Unit. They rose to the occasion and handled the situation with great skill. Many of the men were only slightly wounded, and were soon discharged to prison camps.

NOVA SCOTIA MEDICAL SERVICES IN THE GREAT WAR

From this time on everybody was kept busy. Wounded came by ambulances, hospital trains and hospital barges down the canal. There were Imperial, Canadian, Australian, New Zealand, East Indian and Portuguese troops.

Dominion Day, 1917, will long be remembered by the inhabitants of St. Omer and vicinity. The Unit engaged a large field and advertised an athletic meet, and sent invitations to all the Units in the area. They all responded, for when July 1st came, bright and sunny, the whole countryside turned out, including the civilian population. A splendid programme of sports was carried out, and No. 7 carried off a goodly share of the honors. In the shade of the trees of the chateau grounds in the evening tables were spread and the Unit sat down to a " family party " and enjoyed a season of conviviality and good fellowship.

The next afternoon all patients who were able to be up, or to be carried out, were given a special tea on the lawn in honor of Dominion Day. While this was going on His Majesty the King with H.R.H. the Prince of Wales paid the Unit a surprise visit, His Majesty was particularly gracious in his felicitations to patients and Staff, by all of whom the honor of this visit was greatly appreciated.

During the summer the enemy aeroplanes were very active in bombing raids on the back areas, especially on moonlight nights. The first real bombing raid this Unit experienced was on September 30th. Enemy aeroplanes came over this area in great force shortly after sundown and began dropping numerous bombs. The loud swish of the bombs coming through the air followed by the fearful crash of the explosion was terrifying; but everybody, nursing sisters and all, " stood to " at their post of duty. Although No. 7 escaped there were serious casualties. Four men were killed and several wounded at the British Hospital just across the river, and four nursing sisters and sixteen men were killed at the Scottish Hospital in St. Omer, only two miles distant.

On October 8th H.R.H. the Duke of Connaught visited and inspected the Unit.

The first word of the terrific explosion at Halifax was received on December 8th, and many anxious days were spent awaiting definite word and to know just what had happened.

The Commanding Officer, Lieut.-Colonel Stewart, was called to the higher and more important duties of Surgical Consultant to hospitals in England and left the Unit, greatly to the regret of the entire personnel, on Thursday, March 7, 1918. The command of the Unit was taken over by Major E. V. Hogan, who was promoted to the rank of Lieut.-Colonel.

March and April, 1918, brought still more busy days to the Dalhousie Unit. Being so near the Front they received a very large number of wounded, many straight from the field of battle. Although this hospital had only 400 beds it frequently had 800 severely wounded soldiers to look after.

The final titanic struggles of 1918 had been ushered in when the fate of the world hung in a balance and men spoke hoarsely and with bated breath of the possible outcome. The Germans had smashed through the Fifth British Army in front of Cambrai and then hurled themselves against the Canadians on the Arras Front, only to be checked and beaten off. Then they sought a more vulnerable sector and attacked the Portuguese on the Bailleul Front. The Portuguese troops gave way and the enemy rapidly advanced towards Aire and got within less than three miles of this strategic point and were able to put shells into St. Omer, Arques and all sections of that hospital area, so that shelling became more or less constant and bombing raids were a nightly occurrence. There were a number of casualties among patients and Staff at some of the hospitals. Word was hourly expected that Aire had been taken and that the Germans were marching on Hazebrouck and St. Omer. It was therefore considered that this area was no longer tenable for hospital purposes and orders were issued for all hospitals to evacuate at once. Dalhousie Unit entrained on April 18th for Etaples.

The Unit had received orders to promptly open up a large tent hospital at Etaples; but these orders were subsequently cancelled, greatly to the disappointment of the Staff, and the entire personnel was posted to various other hospitals in that area.

The Germans seemed to have acquired a special fancy for bombing and shooting up hospital areas, and on May 18th subjected Etaples to a very severe aerial bombardment by sixty planes. Casualties among officers, nursing sisters and men amounted to over a thousand. Dalhousie Unit lost two men killed—Pte. F. W. Laidlaw and Pte. Takanayagi (Jap)—and two others wounded, including the Commanding Officer, Lieut.-Col. E. V. Hogan, and Pte. W. G. O'Tulle.

Etaples had been a large hospital centre, but was now abandoned as such and the various hospitals were withdrawn to other places. The Dalhousie Unit was moved to Rouen, which was the largest base hospital centre in France. Here the officers and personnel were distributed and attached to various British Hospitals and had a further enriched experience, as there were very many casualties constantly coming in direct from the field of battle, owing to the demoralization of the hospital service in the front areas during the period of the German drive. Most of the nursing sisters had been allowed to go on leave, and some were sent to England.

A special Canadian Hospital was to be established at Camiers, between Etaples and Boulogne, and Dalhousie Unit was ordered, in September, 1918, to reassemble and proceed to Camiers and take over a hospital of 1,000 beds at a site formerly occupied by No. 42 British Stationary Hospital. In the five months that followed this hospital was crowded and the patients were all Canadians.

It was during this period that the Armistice came with its relaxing influences, its glorious sweets of victory, and happy dreams of home. Christmas also brought its good-cheer and was most pleasantly celebrated by the patients as well as the Staff with a splendid Christmas dinner and other festivities.

Early in February, 1919, the Unit received orders to hand over to the Nova Scotia sister Unit, No. 9 Canadian Stationary Hospital —the St. Francis Xavier Unit—and proceed to Le Havre en route to England and Canada. The Unit sailed from Le Havre on March 17, 1919, for Southampton, arriving there in the afternoon. The stay in England lasted only a month, but this was ample time for all the members of the Unit to visit different parts of the British Isles.

During its service the Dalhousie Unit treated some 60,000 sick and wounded, 10,000 in England and 50,000 in France.

On April 17, 1919, a happy group of Nova Scotians assembled on the docks at Liverpool and boarded the good ship *Belgic* with

3,500 other Canadian troops for Home, Sweet Home. On April 23rd that goodly company landed in Halifax and were greeted by a people proud of their noble sons returned with the laurels of victory. That happy group of Nova Scotians now assembled on the pier at Halifax and were given an ovation and cheered to the echo as they marched through the streets to the Armories to be demobilized. These were they who had gone in the honored name of Old Dalhousie. Well did they guard the honor of that name, and long may Dalhousie and Nova Scotia be proud of the record and deeds of the Dalhousie Unit.

The following casualties occurred among the members of the Unit:

Killed in Action: Ptes. Wm. Beck, B. E. Fraser, J. F. McLellan, Horace Grant, S. J. Dick, F. W. Laidlaw, Sergt. F. J. Howley, Ptes. J. C. Sutherland, P. L. Findlay, C. P. Wright, C. J. A. Guymer, Takanayagi (Jap).

Died from Service Disability: Pte. C. J. McCarthy.

Wounded: Lieut.-Col. E. V. Hogan, C.B.E.; Major D. A. MacLeod, Ptes. W. H. Chase, F. F. Choote, Dawson (twice), Bugler J. E. Doyle (twice), Sergt. P. D. MacDonald, Pte. W. G. O'Tulle (twice), Sergt. F. H. Pond.

The following Nova Scotia medical officers were at different times attached to the Dalhousie Unit: Gerald Grant, M.C.; J. M. Stewart, A. E. Mackintosh, A. H. McKinnon, F. B. Day, J. A. Munro, E. D. McLean, E. D. Douglas, M.C.; J. E. Ellis, Seymour MacKenzie, K. Blackadar, A. M. Covert, A. Ellis, J. I. O'Connell, Andrew Love, W. H. McDonald.

The following received commissions in the Field: H. B. Archibald, Wm Beck (killed in flying), R.F.C., G. Dawson, M.C. (wounded and awarded M.C.), Geo. Edgar (awarded commission, Embarkation Officer in Halifax), C. W. Holland, A. R. McPherson, W. H. Pool, D. H. Sutherland, M.C., J. D. Vair, Horace Grant, G. Wright, M.C., C. C. Armstrong, H. C. Lewis, C. F. Moriarity, J. C. Sutherland (killed), P. R. Tingley, A. W. Webber, C. Glennister, C. E. White, C. P. Wright, G. C. Beazley, J. F. McLellan, M.M., G. H. Morrison, H. B. Titus, T. H. Whelpley, C. J. A. Guymer, D. H. Windsor.

NOVA SCOTIA MEDICAL SERVICES IN THE GREAT WAR

Promotions and Awards: Lieut.-Col. John Stewart became Colonel and received the C.B.E., and later was Surgical Consultant to Canadian Hospitals in England.

Major E. V. Hogan assumed command of the hospital on the promotion of Colonel Stewart. He was promoted to the rank of Lieutenant-Colonel, received the C.B.E. and was wounded in the Etaples raid.

Major L. M. Murray became heart specialist to Special Canadian Heart Hospital at Bushey Park.

Capt. M. A. MacAulay, promoted to Major, left the Unit and was in command of various Units and Field Ambulances. After his return home was in command of Cogswell Street Military Hospital.

Capt. V. N. MacKay, promoted to Major and was retained in England for special laboratory work.

Capt. K. A. MacKenzie, promoted to Major on leaving the Unit at Arques in the summer of 1917 and was detailed for duty at Colchester Heart Hospital as Heart Specialist. Subsequently he became Officer in charge of Medicine at Bramshott Military Hospital.

Capt. E. K. Maclellan, promoted to Major, afterwards returning to Canada where he became Officer in charge of Pine Hill Military Hospital, and later President Standing Medical Board. In winter of 1917, Acting Officer in charge Surgical Service No. 12 Canadian General Hospital.

Capt. S. J. MacLennan, transferred to Westcliffe Eye and Ear Hospital, on arrival in England, for special duty. Invalided home from England.

Capt. D. A. MacLeod, mentioned in dispatches, wounded at Passchendaele in September, 1918, promoted to Major, and on return to Canada became Registrar at Camp Hill Military Hospital.

Capt. J. A. Murray, promoted to Major, and on return to England from France in summer of 1917 became Officer in charge of Clarence House Canadian Convalescent Hospital.

Capt. John Rankine, left Unit in summer of 1916 and went as Medical Officer to No. 1 Entrenching Battalion. Was attached to No. 4 Field Ambulance, returning to Canada for duty in the fall of 1917.

Capt. Frank V. Woodbury went to one of the Entrenching Battalions and was later attached to the Staff of the 3rd Division, recalled to England for Staff duty. Received promotion to Majority and subsequently promoted to rank of Lieutenant-Colonel.

Capt. Karl F. Woodbury served continuously and returned to Canada with the Unit, with much credit to himself and the Unit, as Dental Officer.

Lieut. S. R. Balcom returned to England in July, 1917, became Quartermaster No. 12 General Hospital and promoted to Captain. He returned to Canada and took over duties as Officer in charge of Medical Stores, Military District No. 6.

Lieut. and Quartermaster Walter Taylor, promoted to Captain, served continuously with the Unit until recalled home at the time of the Halifax explosion in December, 1917, having had three children killed in the explosion and losing his property. Later became Quartermaster Cogswell Street Hospital.

Matron L. M. Hubley served continuously with the Unit until April, 1918, subsequently attached for duty to No. 3 General Hospital and No. 8 Stationary Hospital, and Westcliffe Eye and Ear Hospital, returning to Canada, March, 1919. On returning to Canada she was employed as Matron of Cogswell Street Military Hospital. In December, 1916, Matron Hubley was awarded the Royal Red Cross, 1st Class.

Nursing Sister S. A. Archard served continuously with the Unit, with the exception of a short time at a Forestry Corps Hospital. She was awarded the Royal Red Cross, 2nd Class.

Nursing Sister R. S. Calder, invalided to England in October, 1916, served with Canadian Hospitals in England during the rest of the War and was awarded the Royal Red Cross, 2nd Class.

Nursing Sister E. A. Cooke served continuously with the Unit in England and France, returning home with the Unit. She was mentioned in dispatches and was awarded the Medal of Queen Elizabeth of Belgium.

Nursing Sister A. M. Johnston, mentioned in dispatches.

Nursing Sister MacDonald, mentioned in dispatches and awarded the Royal Red Cross, 2nd Class.

Nursing Sister F. A. Rice, awarded Royal Red Cross, 2nd Class.

Sergt.-Major G. T. Brown, recalled to England in June, 1917, receiving a commission as Quartermaster of C.A.M.C. General Depot, later being promoted to captain's rank and receiving the O.B.E.

Sergt. P. D. MacDonald was transferred to the R.C.R. and was wounded in action.

Sergt. F. J. Howley received a commission in service. While home on leave was killed in the Halifax explosion.

Sergt. A. F. McGregor, recalled from Shorncliffe to Canada to complete medical studies at McGill. On graduating received commission and later served again Overseas. He was promoted to Captain.

Sergt. F. H. Pond obtained commission with an Infantry Battalion and was severely wounded and invalided to Canada.

Sergt. T. H. Robinson succeeded Sergt.-Major G. T. Brown, being promoted to warrant officer.

Sergt. C. G. Sutherland, recalled from Shorncliffe to Canada to complete medical studies at McGill. On graduating received commission and later served again Overseas, having been promoted to Captain.

Corpl. E. McN. Grant left Unit in Shorncliffe, receiving commission in 13th Battalion. Later invalided to Canada.

Corpl. G. S. Mitchell promoted to Captain, later became Chaplain of the Unit. Invalided to Canada in October, 1917.

Bugler J. E. Doyle, transferred to No. 1 Field Ambulance, promoted to Sergeant, wounded twice and awarded D.C.M.

NO. 9 CANADIAN STATIONARY HOSPITAL

(St. Francis Xavier College Unit).

With characteristic enterprise St. Francis Xavier College decided, as the War went on, that it should stand side by side with other Universities of Canada in direct representation. In the autumn of 1915 the President and Governors offered a Medical Unit for Overseas. This seemed the most fitting service for a great Christian and humanitarian institution, and it was understood that hospitals were in demand.

NOVA SCOTIA'S PART IN THE GREAT WAR

Dr. H. P. MacPherson, President of the University, took the matter up direct with the Government of Canada, and in April, 1916, authority was given for the acceptance of No. 9 Canadian Stationary Hospital from St. Francis Xavier.

This announcement was received with great enthusiasm, and it was decided not to send the Unit away empty-handed. A subscription list was opened and friends of the University were given an opportunity to subscribe to a fund to provide for some special equipment and to organize a band. The response was most generous, and in a very short time an ample amount of money was secured. Besides private subscriptions, liberal donations were received from the Red Cross, Daughters of the Empire, Knights of Columbus and other societies.

LIEUT.-COL. R. C. M'LEOD.

Busy days followed in selecting the personnel and organizing the Unit. No recruiting campaign was necessary. The loyal sons of St. Francis and daughters of Antigonish, and many others everywhere, were offering their services. As the brokers would say: " The stock was over-subscribed." And it was a matter of selection.

The command was given to Lieut.-Col. Roderick C. McLeod, who had already enlisted in the C.E.F. and was daily expecting orders to proceed Overseas. Colonel McLeod was a graduate of St. Francis Xavier and had attained a wide reputation as a successful medical practitioner of North Sydney. He was a man of a most genial personality and beloved by all who knew him. His appointment to the command of this Unit was hailed with universal satisfaction.

Colonel McLeod was assisted in the work of organization by Major H. E. Kendall as second in command, an outstanding surgeon of Cape Breton; and Major J. S. Carruthers, an energetic Militia officer, was appointed adjutant.

The enthusiasm among nurses for service in this Unit was remarkable. Applications poured in from every Province in

NOVA SCOTIA MEDICAL SERVICES IN THE GREAT WAR

Canada and from many parts of the United States, by mail and telegraph. Miss S. C. MacIsaac, a graduate of Mt. St. Bernard Convent, of Antigonish, was chosen as Matron. Miss MacIsaac was trained as a nurse at St. Joseph's Hospital, Glace Bay, in which institution she had charge of the operating room for three years. She had taken a post-graduate course at Mercy Hospital, Chicago, and when war broke out she was Assistant Matron at Mt. Zion Hospital, San Francisco. Miss MacIsaac therefore came to her new, important and strenuous post well qualified.

The organization of the Unit was completed at the University Town of Antigonish, the seat of the mother College, St. Francis Xavier. The college authorities and citizens of Antigonish vied with each other in extending an enthusiastic reception to the volunteers as they came, and everything was done to make their stay pleasant.

Orders were issued from headquarters for the Unit to mobilize at Halifax in the spring of 1916. The officers took the C.A.M.C. Training Course at Cogswell Street Military Hospital, and the nursing sisters were also posted there, and faithful work was done in a general course of preliminary training.

The original personnel was as follows:

Lieut.-Col. Roderick C. MacLeod, Commanding Officer; Major Henry E. Kendall, Second in Command; Major J. Stewart Carruthers, Adjutant.

Medical Officers: Capts. Alex. R. Campbell, J. F. Ellis, T. A. Lebbetter, A. H. MacKinnon, J. I. O'Connell, L. D. Densmore, Hon. Capt. J. L. Johnson, Capts. R. MacCuish, J. A. McCourt, L. J. Violette, Hon. Lieut. Leo F. Fry.

Nursing Sisters: Emma Ella Barry, Laura Emily Campbell, Sarah Catherine Chisholm, Monica Connell, Isabel Helen Dawson, Helena Margaret Ellis, Florence Mary Kelly, Nellie King, Annie MacDonald, Annie Helen MacDonald, Catharine Chisholm MacDonald, Catharine Eileen MacDonald, Catharine Tulloch MacDonald, Jessie MacDonald, Minnie Frances MacDonald, Flora MacDougall, Mary MacGrath, Sadie Catharine MacIsaac (Matron), Christena Mary MacKenzie, Dora MacKenzie, Annie Tremaine MacLeod, Marcella Agnes O'Brien, Catharine Regina

Shea, Edith Alexander Thompson, Mary S. Walsh, Anna Teresa Young.

The Unit was not long in receiving orders to proceed Overseas, and on June 19, 1916, set sail per *S.S. Missinabie*. After ten days' sail on typical summer seas a landing was made at Liverpool Here the jolly family group was divided and the officers and men were sent to Shorncliffe and attached for instruction and duty to Shorncliffe Military Hospital, while the matron and nursing sisters entrained for London, where they were detailed, by the Matron-in-Chief, for duty to various hospitals in England.

This was a sort of a period of orphanage; but in exactly three months, September 29, 1916, the Unit was again reassembled for the purpose of taking over the Bramshott Military Hospital, No. 12 Canadian General Hospital, which served the large military training camps of Bramshott and Witley. This was a splendid experience and training for the entire personnel. A great deal of excellent work was done. The Medical Division was taken charge of by Major Charles Hunter, of Winnipeg, and Major H. E. Kendall was in charge of the Surgical Division, assisted by Capt. K. A. McCuish.

CAPT. K. A M'CUISH.

While acting as the Medical Officer of the 5th C.M.R.'s Captain McCuish received wounds at Passchendaele, from which he died. He was buried in the Military Cemetery at Remi Siding, near Poperinghe, Belgium, in a hero's grave, and now "sleeps where poppies grow in Flanders fields."

The winter of 1917 taxed the capacity of the hospital to the utmost, as well as the endurance of the Staff, owing to a very severe outbreak of influenza in the Bramshott area. The splendid manner in which the Unit rose to the great demands made upon it and coped with the serious condition that arose, called for special commendation from Major-General Foster, Director-General of the Canadian Medical Services.

NOVA SCOTIA MEDICAL SERVICES IN THE GREAT WAR

Here the first great sorrow came to the Unit in the illness and death of their beloved Commanding Officer, Lieut.-Colonel MacLeod. He contracted anthrax poisoning, from which he died January 4, 1917. With military honors and amidst a large concourse of sorrowing comrades he was laid to rest in the cemetery at Bramshott.

Command of the Unit was taken by Major H. E. Kendall, who was promoted to the rank of Lieut.-Colonel. Lieut.-Colonel Gilmore of Toronto took charge of the surgical section.

The spring of 1917 was a very hard period, as was also the fall of 1917. The damp and chilly English climate was very trying to new Canadian troops, and there was a large amount of sickness. A good many battle casualties were also received from France.

A call came from France for more Canadian hospitals, and No. 9 Canadian Stationary Hospital was selected. The Unit was ordered to proceed to France, and sailed from Folkestone in December, 1917, landing at Boulogne the same day with the following officers: Lieut.-Col. H. E. Kendall, Officer Commanding; Major Charles Hunter, Major Adair, Quartermaster; Capt. J. Williams, Pathologist; Capt. H. L. Reazin, Capt. J. W. Lord, Capt. Andrew Love, Capt. W. F. MacIsaac, Capt. A. F. Slayter, Capt. D. A. Webb, Capt. J. Wilfred, Hon. Capt. J. O. Ralston, Chaplain; Hon. Capt. P. White, Chaplain.

Major Adair was subsequently Quartermaster at No. 3 Canadian General Hospital at Boulogne, where he died suddenly of uræmia following influenza in the spring of 1919.

On arrival in Boulogne the Unit received orders to proceed to Longuenesse, near St. Omer, and open a hospital of four hundred beds. Here everything was found to be in readiness. There were hutted wards of corrugated iron, wooden administration buildings complete in every detail and ready for occupation. There was an excellent, well-lighted, well-ventilated and **thoroughly-equipped** operating room. The quarters provided for officers, nursing sisters and men were all that could be desired.

It was only a few days before the Unit was ready to carry on, and early in January, 1918, the first convoy was received, consisting of over one hundred wounded soldiers from the Front. Excellent and steady work then continued.

In February instructions were received from headquarters to enlarge the hospital to nine hundred beds. With willing hands and enthusiastic workers this was soon completed, and during the month of March a great many surgical cases were dealt with. Capt. A. Loos and Capt. A. F. Slater were the surgical specialists at this time. On account of the large number of surgical cases application was made for assistants. Capt. T. MacGregor, a noted Scotch surgeon of Glasgow, was sent for temporary duty. The officer in charge of the Medical Division was Capt. H. L. Reazin, a successful and well-known practitioner of Toronto.

During the spring of 1918 the St. Francis Hospital Unit carried on under precisely the same conditions of harassing shell fire and nightly bombing as described in connection with the Dalhousie Medical Unit.

The nursing sisters and hospital Staff displayed great courage all through these trying times, remaining at their posts in the operating room and hospital wards. No pen can describe the nerve-testing and nerve-wracking experience of hearing the swish through the air of those terrible and deadly bombs, then the terrific explosions and rocking and trembling of the earth which meant destruction and death to many. The way those splendid young women carried themselves was magnificent. Without a quiver or the slightest hesitation they kept right along with their work and soothed and encouraged and ministered to their patients. They were the same living contradiction here as elsewhere to all logical relations, and the harmony of things. They would jump up on the operating table and scream at the suggestion of a mouse or trench rat; but would go out into the storm and darkness and fire to give a drink of water to a wounded soldier.

The Unit was making preparations to still further expand the bed capacity of the hospital when orders were issued for all hospitals in the area to evacuate at once. The wounded were sent by ambulance trains to the base, the equipment was packed up, and on April 19th the Unit moved to Etaples, which is a fishing village about twenty miles from Boulogne. It was a large hospital area and there were 25,000 available beds.

On the outskirts of the town near the village of Le Faux a site was provided for the St. Francis Unit. The nursing sisters were

NOVA SCOTIA MEDICAL SERVICES IN THE GREAT WAR

detailed for duty to No. 1 Canadian General Hospital and No. 7 Canadian General Hospital. The officers and men were under canvas.

The Unit was under instructions to open a tent hospital of 600 beds, and the work was progressing rapidly when that terrible air raid came at 10 o'clock in the evening of May 18th and continued for nearly two hours. The casualties were very heavy and every hospital suffered. A number of live bombs dropped within the small area occupied by the St. Francis Unit. Two men were instantly killed and thirteen wounded. The killed were Sergeants MacMillen and Taylor. They were buried in the Military Cemetery at Etaples. Seventeen hospital marquees of the Unit were destroyed during this raid. It was fortunate that the Unit had not commenced receiving patients.

One of the medical officers, Capt W. F. MacIsaac, of Antigonish, was badly wounded, and succumbed to his injuries in No. 1 Canadian General Hospital on June 3rd. He was a young man of brilliant attainments, exemplary character and a promising young surgeon. He too was buried in the Military Cemetery at Etaples. The whole Unit was in attendance at the funeral.

COL. R. ST. JOHN MACDONALD.

Since a large part of the hospital equipment was destroyed it was decided to move the Unit to another area. All the railways were congested and every other means of transportation taxed to the utmost; consequently no means of moving the equipment could be obtained, and it remained packed for several months. Most of the officers and men were detailed for duty to other hospitals.

Lieut.-Col. H. E. Kendall was recalled for duty to England on August 28, 1918, and command of the Unit fell to Major R. St. J. MacDonald, who had been posted to the Unit a few months previously.

The Unit was instructed to be in readiness to open up a Convalescent Hospital for the Canadian Corps. But before this was carried out the Germans made an unconditional surrender which they were allowed to call an Armistice.

Hopes were now high for an early, in fact, immediate return home, and this became the all-absorbing topic of conversation. Capt. A. Sterling, Capt. S. MacKenzie, Capt. G. Zwicker, Capt. G. Phillips and Capt. S. Whitehouse arrived from England on November 20th and joined the Unit. Capt. Sterling had gone Overseas as a combatant officer with the R.C.R.'s and saw considerable fighting. Owing to the scarcity of medical officers in the summer of 1917 he was asked to transfer to the Medical Corps, which he did, and was posted to the Canadian Special Hospital at Etching Hill, where he remained until joining No. 9 Canadian Stationary.

Major S. L. Walker was posted to this Unit on November 25, 1918, and was afterwards promoted to the rank of Lieut.-Colonel. He had been on active service with various Units since the spring of 1915. Colonel Walker was an excellent administrative officer and added strength to the Staff as second in command.

The Unit received instructions to take over the special hospital at Camiers from the Dalhousie Unit, which had received orders to proceed to England en route to Canada. This change took place on February 8, 1919, and St. Francis Unit took over the hospital with 900 patients.

In a short time the number of patients increased to 1,100 and St. Francis Unit had the honor of being raised to the status of a General Hospital. This gave an opportunity for some well-merited promotions among the officers, non-commissioned officers and men.

At this time the Staff was as follows:

```
Col. R. St. John MacDonald Officer Commanding.
Lieut.-Col. S. L. Walker....Second in Command.
Major H. G. Murray.......In charge Medical Division.
Major A. Sterling..........In charge Surgical Division.
Major R. F. Slater..........Registrar and Paymaster.
Major J. R. MacRae........
Major G. S. Gordon........
Major S. Sprague..........
Hon. Capt. H. E. Law .....Quartermaster.
Hon. Capt. A. E. Hagar ....Chaplain.
Capt. S. P. H. Morlatt......Dental Officer.
Capt. F. Hinds.............Dental Officer.
Capt. J. F. Elkerton........
Capt. J. D. MacDonald......
Capt. W. M. MacDonald....
Capt. A. R. Campbell.......
Capt. G. Phillips...........
Capt. S. Whitehouse........
Capt. G. Zwicker...........
```

NOVA SCOTIA MEDICAL SERVICES IN THE GREAT WAR

The stay at Camiers was made more pleasant for the personnel and patients by the attention paid to recreation and amusements. A baseball league was formed for the area and many good games were played, in which there was a great deal of enthusiastic interest. There was also much interest taken in tennis and quoits. A moving-picture theatre was constructed and equipped by the Canadian Y.M.C.A., under Capt. A. E. Hagar, which was an unfailing source of pleasure to the patients and personnel. The Y.M.C.A. also established a canteen and furnished a reading room. The Red Cross too, through its representative, Major F. Murphy, contributed very largely to the success of the Unit by providing comforts for the patients and a large amount of sporting equipment.

A thrill of pleasant anticipation ran through the Unit when on May 20th orders were received that the patients were to be evacuated at once with a view to demobilization and return to Canada. As soon as the patients were evacuated no time was lost in turning the hospital equipment and supplies in to Ordnance Stores. This was completed on May 28th and on May 30th the Unit moved to Boulogne, crossed to Folkestone the same afternoon and arrived at Witley Camp, Surrey, the next day.

After a very pleasant month in England, occupied mostly with leave-taking and renewing old acquaintances, the Unit proceeded to Southampton and embarked on the *S.S. Olympic* for Halifax on July 2nd, together with No. 7 Canadian General Hospital (Queens) and No. 4 Canadian General Hospital (Toronto).

On July 8th at 6 p.m., after a voyage of only six days, these happy home-comers were docked at Halifax. The Unit was met by representatives of St. Francis Xavier College, whose name it had the honor of bearing, led by Dr. J. J. Tompkins. Dr. Tompkins invited the officers, non-commissioned officers and men to a reception as well as farewell banquet at the " Green Lantern." Other guests present were Governor Grant, Hon. R. E. Faulkner, Hon. Senator Crosby, Col. John Stewart, Lieut.-Col. E. V. Hogan and John Neville. After an excellent supper the Unit was welcomed home in a very happy manner by Dr. Tompkins, Governor Grant and others. Col. R. St. J. MacDonald and Lieut.-Col. S. L. Walker replied on behalf of the Unit.

The following morning, July 9th, the Unit was demobilized after over three years' service Overseas.

The entire personnel had changed since leaving Halifax for Overseas, and on demobilization was as follows:

Col. R. St. J. MacDonald.
Lieut.-Col. S. L. Walker.
Major A. Sterling.
Major H. G. Murray.
Major G. S. Gordon.
Major A. F. Slater.
Hon. Capt. A. E. Hagar, Chaplain.
Hon. Capt. F. Kelley, Chaplain.
Capt. A. H. Haugh.
Capt. J. D. MacDonald.
Capt. W. M. MacDonald.
Capt. G. Zwicker.
Capt. G. Phillips.
Capt. S. Whitehouse.
Capt. W. H. P. Lavell.
Capt. W. B. Surleton.
Capt. M. MacKay.
Capt. J. MacBeth.
Capt. S. P. H. Morlatt.

Following is a list of honors received by original members of No. 9 Canadian Stationary Hospital, as far as can be ascertained at the moment of writing:

Lieut.-Col. R. St. John MacDonald.. Mentioned in dispatches.
Capt. A. R. Campbell .... M.C.
Capt. L. D. Densmore............ M.C.
Matron S. C. MacIsaac .... Mentioned for valuable services, 20-10-17; R.R.C., 2nd class, 1-1-19; R.R.C., 1st class, 31-7-19.
Nursing Sister F. Kelley......... R.R.C., 2nd class.
Nursing Sister C. E. Chisholm.... Mention, 20-12-18; mention, 11-7-19.
Nursing Sister Annie MacDonald. Mentioned for valuable services, 20-10-17.
Nursing Sister C. M. MacKenzie.. Mentioned for valuable services, 20-10-17.
Mentioned for valuable services, 9-9-19.
Nursing Sister C. R. Shea........ Medaille Militaire des Invalides.

MISCELLANEOUS MEDICAL SERVICES.

Less than half the Nova Scotia medical men who went Overseas served with the Nova Scotia Medical Units. This narrative would therefore be very incomplete without reference to the major portion.

Many of these had distinguished service with the Royal Army Medical Corps (R.A.M.C.) and with other Canadian and Imperial Hospitals, as well as with the fighting Units as Regimental Medical Officers and other general and special duties.

NOVA SCOTIA MEDICAL SERVICES IN THE GREAT WAR

Be it said to the honor of Nova Scotia that the organizing and directing genius of the Canadian Army Medical Service was supplied by two Nova Scotians, Major-Gen. Guy Carleton Jones, C.M.G., who was born in Nova Scotia and practised his profession in Halifax, and Major-Gen. G. L. Foster, C.B., who was born in Nova Scotia and also practised his profession in Halifax.

General Jones went Overseas with the First Canadian Contingent as A.D.M.S. and shortly after arrival in England was made Director of Medical Services, Canadian Expeditionary Force, with headquarters in London, which he organized and administered with great ability until he was made Medical Inspector, Canadian Expeditionary Force, in 1917. Later he became D.M.S. in charge of hospitals in Canada.

General Foster succeeded General Jones as D.M.S. Canadian Expeditionary Force and later was made D.G.M.S., O.M.F.C., and successfully carried on the duties of that high and difficult office until the end of the War and the demobilization of the Canadian Army.

Another outstanding Nova Scotia Medical Officer was Lieut.-Col. H. M. Jacques. When the First Contingent left, Colonel Jacques became Acting D.G.M.S., Ottawa. He was A.D.M.S. 2nd Canadian Division in France; he was three times mentioned for distinguished service in Sir Douglas Haig's dispatches and was promoted to the full rank of Colonel and awarded the D.S.O. and Bar for distinguished and gallant service in action.

The nursing service has also brought great credit to Nova Scotia, and it is a further honor to the Province that the Canadian Army Nursing Service was under the direction of a Nova Scotian. The Matron-in-Chief was Miss Margaret C. MacDonald, of Bailey Brook. She was mentioned for distinguished services and awarded the R.R.C. She had seen active service in the Spanish-American War and was selected to accompany the Second Canadian Contingent to South Africa..

The following is a synopsis of the Military Services of Nova Scotia medical men not previously mentioned, as far as can be obtained. It has been impossible to get a complete authentic record, and although every medical man on the Medical Register for the Province, who was known to have been in the military service, was written to personally for information, only thirty replies were received to 150 letters. The list is therefore liable to some errors and omissions.

MILITARY MEDICAL SERVICE OVERSEAS.

ARCHIBALD, MAJOR THOMAS DICKSON—Went to England as a combatant officer with the 8th Canadian Mounted Rifles in 1916. On this being broken up, a Canadian Cavalry Field Ambulance was formed, which Captain Archibald joined as a Medical Officer. He was in the Somme fighting, was two years in France, and was promoted to the rank of Major.

ATLEE, MAJOR H. BENGE.—Enlisted in R.A.M.C. in London, England, November, 1914. Appointed Medical Officer, Royal Munster Fusiliers. Served in Gallipoli, the Suvla Bay expedition, No. 19 British Hospital, Alexandra, Egypt, the 69th Ambulance, Salonika. Was awarded the M.C. and promoted to the rank of Major.

BAULD, LIEUT.-COLONEL W. A. G., D.S.O.—Enlisted 1914. Demobilized June, 1919. Served in England, France and Salonika. Twice mentioned in despatches. Awarded D.S.O.

BARRACLOUGH, CAPT. WILLIAM—Enlisted C.A.M.C. 20-12-16. Demobilized 12-12-19. Served in Canada :0-12-16 to 23-3-17, England 27-3-17 to 15-6-18, France 15-6-18 to 19-5-19. Was Neurological Specialist in Camp Hill Hospital, Halifax, 27-5-19 to 12-12-19.

BARSS, CAPT. G. A.—Enlisted Captain R.A.M.C. in England 29-8-15. Posted to Durham Light Infantry, with which he went to France in January, 1916. Served also with Scots Guards. Mentioned twice in despatches for services in the Somme, 1916, and Cambrai, 1917. Demobilized 29-8-18.

BLACKADAR, CAPT. K. K.—Enlisted 5-1-17. Demobilized 21-7-19. Served in Canada, England and France.

BLACKETT, CAPT. ARTHUR E.—Enlisted Capt. C.A.M.C. 9-8-15. Demobilized 23-6-19. Served in Canada 9-8-15 to 18-6-16, England 18-6-16 to 4-5-17 and 2-9-18 to 18-1-19, France 4-5-17 to 2-9-18.

BORDEN, CAPT. R. F.—Enlisted 1-7-16. Demobilized 27-4-19. Served in Canada, England and France.

BURGESS, CAPT. HARRY C.—Served Overseas. No particulars available.

BURNS, CAPT. ARTHUR S.—Enlisted 19-2-16. Demobilized 23-12-19. Served in Canada, England and France.

CAMPBELL, CAPT. DONALD ST. C.—Captain C.A.M.C. Enlisted 23-12-16. Demobilized 29-12-19. Served in Canada, England and France.

CAMPBELL, CAPT. JOHN G. D.—Enlisted 26-12-16. Demobilized 29-11-19. Served in Canada, England and France.

CARRUTHERS, LIEUT.-COL. J. S.—Enlisted 30-6-15. Returned 26-1-19. Served in Canada, England and France.

CHISHOLM, CAPT. JAMES STANLEY—Enlisted 8-5-15. Demobilized 30-9-19. Served in Canada, England and France.

CHURCHILL, CAPT. L. P.—Enlisted 15-2-16. Demobilized 11-3-19. Served in Canada, England and France. M.O. 219th Battalion. Served in France with 5th Field Ambulance, 3rd British General Hospital, 47th British General Hospital, 7th Canadian General Hospital, 1st Canadian Mounted Rifles and R.C.R. Awarded M.C. for gallant services at Battle of Arras.

COCHRANE, CAPT. WILFRED N.—Enlisted 13-11-16. Demobilized 1-1-19. Served in England and France; in France with No. 7 Canadian Stationary Hospital (Dalhousie Unit), 8th Canadian Field Ambulance and 3rd Division Train.

COCK, MAJOR J. L.—Enlisted 9-3-15. Demobilized 12-1-20. Served in Canada, England and France.

COFFIN, CAPT. WILLIAM V.—Overseas Service. No particulars available.

COLLIE, CAPT. JOHN R. M.—Overseas Service in the Navy. No particulars available.

COVERT, CAPT. ARCHIBALD N.—Enlisted 7-3-20. Demobilized 12-6-19. Served in Canada, England and France.

CREIGHTON, MAJOR THOMAS McCULLY.—Was in England when war broke out and enlisted in the British Navy July 30, 1914. Was posted to *H.M.S. Argonaut,* transferred to Hospital Ship *China* and went to Salonika. Later joined the Army and went to France. On returning to England became D.A.D.M.S. Demobilized September, 1919.

NOVA SCOTIA'S PART IN THE GREAT WAR

CROLL, LIEUT.-COL. ANDREW—Enlisted 1-4-15. Demobilized 4-11-18. Served in Canada, England and three years in France.

CURRY, MAJOR WILFRED A.—Enlisted in R.A.M.C. in England. Had three years' service in France as Surgical Specialist to No. 44 C.C.S. and No. 34 C.C.S. On returning to England was attached to Shepherd's Bush Orthopædic Hospital, London. On demobilization was appointed Orthopædic Specialist to Department of Soldiers' Civil Re-establishment for Nova Scotia and Prince Edward Island.

DAVIDSON, CAPT. VICTOR DAVID.—Overseas Service. No particulars available.

DAY, CAPT. FREDERICK B., M.C.—Enlisted 5-10-15. Demobilized 30-4-19. Service in Canada, England and France. In France served with No. 7 Canadian Stationary Hospital, 13th Field Ambulance. In trenches as M.O. 54th Canadian Infantry Battalion until wounded twice by shrapnel. Awarded M.C. for gallant services in action.

DOBSON, CAPT. WM. L.—Enlisted 16-9-17. Demobilized 25-7-19. Served in Canada and England.

DONOVAN, CAPT. OSCAR C.—Enlisted 11-19-15. Demobilized 25-2-20. Served in Canada, England and France. Was a Surgical Specialist in France, and after returning to England was attached to Shepherd's Bush Orthopædic Hospital, London. Was awarded the Croix de Guerre by the French.

DOUGLAS, MAJOR EDGAR, M.C.—Enlisted 17-8-14. Demobilized 29-9-19. Served in Canada, England and three years in France. In France served with No. 7 Canadian Stationary Hospital, No. 1 Canadian C.C.S., No. 11 C.C.S., R.A.M.C., 4th Canadian Field Ambulance, No. 13 Canadian Field Ambulance. Was wounded in head and hand at Lens, and wounded in left shoulder at Passchendaele. Awarded M.C. for gallant service at Lens.

DOULL, CAPT. JAMES ANGUS, M.C., Croix de Guerre— Served in England and France. Particulars not available.

DWYER, CAPT. THOMAS R.—Enlisted 12-5-17. Demobilized 10-11-19. Served in Canada and England.

DYAS, CAPT. ALEX. D.—Enlisted 10-8-16. Demobilized 8-10-19. Served in Canada, England and France as Ear, Nose and Throat Specialist. Wounded by shrapnel at Arras.

EAGAR, MAJOR WILLIAM H.—Service in Canada, England and France as X-ray Specialist.

EATON, CAPT. PERRY B.—Enlisted 13-3-17. Demobilized 11-9-19. Served in Canada and England.

FREEMAN, CAPT. E. H.—Enlisted 11-5-15. Demobilized 31-1-19. Served in England, France, Salonika, Palestine and Egypt.

FREEMAN, CAPT. NELSON P.—Enlisted 1-10-16. Demobilized 15-6-18. Served in Canada and England. Invalided home with paralysis, one side.

GASS, CAPT. CHAS. L.—Served Overseas. Particulars not available.

GITTLESON, CAPT. PHILIP M.—Served Overseas. No particulars available.

GODFREY, CAPT. HARRY M.—Overseas. No particulars available.

GODFREY, CAPT. ALEX. T.—Enlisted 22-10-16. Demobilized 4-6-18. Served in Canada and England.

GOUTHRO, CAPT. H. P.—Enlisted 26-11-16. Demobilized 12-1-20. Served in Canada, England and France.

GOW, MAJOR F. A. R.—Enlisted 14-10-14. Demobilized 15-5-20. Served in Canada, England and France. 1914-15 Star.

GRANT, CAPT GERALD W.—Enlisted 7-11-16. Demobilized 15-7-19. Served in Canada, England and France. Awarded M.C. for gallantry in action, and the 1915 Star.

GREEN, CAPT. FREDERICK WILLIAM—Served Overseas. No particulars available.

HAYES, LIEUT.-COL. JOSEPH, D.S.O.—Enlisted 24-9-15. Demobilized 16-5-19. Served in Canada, England and France. Served in France with 85th Canadian Infantry Battalion, 4th Divisional Train, No. 10 British General Hospital, Facture Detention Hospital, S.M.O. Central Group C.F.C., O.C. No. 2 Canadian Stationary Hospital. Was twice mentioned in dispatches and awarded D.S.O.

HART, CAPT. EDWARD C.—Served Overseas. No particulars available.

NOVA SCOTIA'S PART IN THE GREAT WAR

HEAL, JAMES G. F.—Served Overseas. Particulars not available.

HEMMEON, MAJOR JAMES A. M.—Enlisted 1-3-16. Demobilized 6-8-19. Served in Canada, England and France.

HENDERSON, CAPT. CHARLES S.—Enlisted 18-4-18. Demobilized 12-1-20. Served in Canada 18-4-18 to 7-12-18 and 1-9-19 to 12-1-20, and in England 7-12-18 to 21-8-19.

HINES, CAPT. ARTHUR—Enlisted 31-5-16. Demobilized 31-8-19. Served in Canada, England and two years in France. Was awarded M.C. for gallantry in Battle of Amiens, August 8th, 1918.

JOST, MAJOR ARTHUR C.—Enlisted 6-3-16. Demobilized 1-8-19. Served in Canada and England. On demobilization held the temporary rank of Lieut.-Colonel.

JOHNSON, CAPT. ARTHUR M.—Highfield House, Bury, England. Served Overseas. No particulars available.

JOHNSON, CAPT. JAMES MacGREGOR, Highfield House, Bury, England. Served Overseas. No particulars available.

JOHNSON, STEPHEN R.—Served Overseas. Particulars not available.

KEAY, CAPT. THOMAS—Enlisted 24-1-17. Demobilized 11-7-19. Served in Canada, England and France.

KENNEDY, CAPT. GEORGE B.—Enlisted 7-16-15. Demobilized 12-6-19. Transferred from C.A.M.C. to R.A.M.C., July, 1915. Served in Canada, England, Malta (in St. Andrew's Hospital), Fort Manuel, France, April, 1916, with 77th Field Ambulance, No. 16 General Hospital, 5th Field Ambulance, 3rd Cavalry Field Ambulance, No. 2 Stationary Hospital, No. 223 Brigade, R.F.A., No. 7 Stationary Hospital, Boulogne, etc.

KENNEDY, CAPT. WILLIAM F.—Enlisted 18-8-18. Demobilized 1-3-20. Served in Canada, England and France in various arms of the Service.

KENNY, CAPT. W. F.—Enlisted 28-6-15. Demobilized 28-2-20. Served in Canada, England and France.

LYONS, CAPT. JAMES N.—Served Overseas. No particulars available.

MacAULAY, CAPT. DANIEL A.—Enlisted August, 1918. Demobilized 5-3-19. Served in Canada, England and France.

McAULAY, MAJOR MURDOCK A.—Enlisted August, 1915. Demobilized on disbanding of C.E.F., but continued in service of C.A.M.C. as O.C. Cogswell Street Military Hospital, Halifax. Also served in England and France.

MACKASEY, CAPT. WM. P.—Served 31 months in the R.A.M.C. Was on service in England 6-9-15. Demobilized in Canada 4-5-20. Africa 1916. Chief Surgeon on Ambulance Ship in the Mediterranean.

MEECH, CAPT. LLOYD R., M.C.—Served Overseas and was awarded the M.C. for gallant services. No particulars available.

MILLAR, MAJOR J. ROSS—M.O. German Prisoners of War Camp at Amherst, March, 1915. Joined R.A.M.C. July, 1915, and proceeded to England. Joined No. 2 British General Hospital, France, in September, 1915. Posted to No. 37 C.C.S. in November, 1915. Sent to Italian Front with No. 37 C.C.S. in November, 1917. Transferred as Surgical Specialist to No. 9 C.C.S., January, 1918. In charge Advanced Operating Centre, Asiago Plateau. On returning to England assigned to duty with Shepherd's Bush Orthopædic Hospital, London. On returning to Canada was appointed Orthopædic Specialist to D.S.C.R. for Nova Scotia and Prince Edward Island, which position he resigned to resume private practice.

MORRIS, LIEUT.-COL. CLARENCE H.—Enlisted August, 1914. Demobilized 11-11-19. Served in Canada, also England, 5-10-14 to 1-1-15; France 1-1-15 to 1-8-15; Gallipoli 5-12-15 to 5-2-16; Egypt 5-2-16 to 6-2-17; Macedonia 15-4-17 to 17-10-17. Mentioned in Sir Ian Hamilton's dispatches, November, 1915. On return to Canada was O.C. Camp Hill Hospital, Halifax, and later D.A.D.M.S., M.D. No. 6.

MORTON, CAPT. LEWIS M.—Enlisted 11-10-15. Demobilized 28-8-19. Served in Canada, England and France.

MUIR, CAPT. WALTER H.—Enlisted 16-11-15. Demobilized 13-12-19. Served in Canada, England and France. Joined Staff of No. 7 Canadian General Hospital in France at Etaples 7-8-17. Sent to forward areas 28-8-17 for duty with No. 5 Canadian Field Ambulance. M.O. 6th Brigade Canadian Field Artillery 14-4-18. Was in all the activities of 2nd Division from Passchendaele to the Rhine.

MUNRO, CAPT. JOHN A.—Enlisted 15-2-16. Demobilized 31-3-19. Served in Canada, England and France.
MURRAY, CAPT. DAN.—Enlisted 26-2-17. Demobilized 1-8-19. Served in Canada, England and France.
MURRAY, CAPT. DUNCAN.—Enlisted 4-11-16. Demobilized 13-6-19. Served in Canada, England and France.
McCURDY, CAPT. DEXTER S.—Enlisted 23-12-16. Demobilized, 12-7-19. Served in Canada, England and France.
MacDONALD, LIEUT.-COL. T. HOWARD—Enlisted 1914. Served in England and France. He was appointed O.C. of the ill-fated Hospital Ship *Llandovery Castle,* on her last voyage, on which he was drowned
MacDONALD, CAPT. NATHANIEL—Enlisted October, 1915. Demobilized 28-12-18. Served in Canada, England and France. Was mentioned in Sir Douglas Haig's dispatches.
MacDONALD, CAPT. JOHN CLYDE—Served Overseas. No particulars available.
MacDONALD, MAJOR P. W. S.—Enlisted early in 1915. Served in Canada, England and France. Was on D.M.S. Staff, London. Died of influenza in England.
MACDONALD, MAJOR WILLIAM HENRY—Enlisted 25-9-16. Demobilized 4-6-19. Served in England on Surgical Staff, Kitchener Military Hospital. Went to France 10-10-17 and joined No. 7 Canadian Stationary Hospital as Second in Command. Surgical Specialist Staff of No. 3 Canadian C.C.S., 4-1-18 to 14-8-18. On Surgical Teams No. 19 and No. 38, British C.C.S., and No. 32 British Stationary Hospital. Was in retreat of 5th Army and escaped with small surgical outfit.
MACDONALD, CAPT. WILFRED M.—Enlisted February, 1917. Continued in C.A.M.C. after dispersal of C.E.F. Served in Canada, England and France.
MacINTOSH, CAPT. ARTHUR E.—Enlisted 30-6-15. Demobilized 15-7-19. Served in Canada, England and France. Served in France with No. 7 Canadian Stationary Hospital.
McKAY, CAPT. JOHN ST. C.—Enlisted 25-11-15. Demobilized 13-6-19. Served in Canada, England and France.
McKAY, CAPT. MURDOCK—Enlisted 4-1-17. Demobilized 12-7-19. Served in Canada, England and France.

MacKENZIE, CAPT. SEYMOUR G.—Enlisted 12-11-17. Demobilized 28-8-19. Served in Canada, England and France.
MacKINNON, CAPT. HUGH A.—Enlisted 3-5-16. Demobilized 15-7-19. Served in Canada, England and France.
McLARREN, CAPT. PHILIP D.—Enlisted 30-5-17. Demobilized 12-1-20. Served in Canada, England and France.
MacLEAN, CAPT. E. D.—Enlisted 14-2-18. Demobilized 21-2-19. Served in Canada, England and France. Went to England with the Highland Brigade. On going to France was attached to No. 7 Canadian Stationary Hospital.
McLEOD, CAPT. JOHN KNOX—Enlisted 25-5-17. Demobilized 31-5-19. Served in Canada, England and France. On returning to Canada was appointed O.C. Ross Moxham Hospital, Sydney.
O'NEIL, MAJOR FREEMAN—Enlisted April, 1914. Demobilized 15-7-19. Served in England 18-11-18 to 4-5-19; France 19-6-19 to 30-6-19.
McRAE, CAPT. DUNCAN R.—Overseas. No particulars available.
MacRITCHIE, CAPT. JOHN JAMES—Overseas. No particulars available.
PARKS, CAPT. JOHN E.—Enlisted 20-7-15. Demobilized 15-6-19. Served in Canada, England and France.
PARKER, CAPT. VERNON H. T.—Enlisted 31-3-17. Demobilized 26-8-19. Served in Canada, England and France.
PATTON, CAPT. WELDON W.—Overseas. No particulars available.
PENNINGTON, CAPT. JOHN W.—Overseas. No particulars available.
POTTER, COL. JACOB L.—Canadian Permanent Army Medical Corps. At outbreak of War was A.D.M.S., Military District No. 3. Called to office of D.G.M.S., Ottawa. Became acting D.G.M.S. and afterwards Deputy D.G.M.S. Went to Siberia with the Canadian Stationary Hospital.
PORTER, CAPT. SYDNEY E.—Enlisted 30-7-17. Demobilized 31-5-19. Served in Canada and England.
PATRICK, CAPT. IVAN YOUNG—Enlisted 19-4-18. Demobilized 21-7-19. Served in Canada and England.

NOVA SCOTIA'S PART IN THE GREAT WAR

PEAKE, CAPT. EDGAR P.—Enlisted 3-7-17. Demobilized 31-7-19. Served in Canada, England and France.

PICKUP, CAPT. WILLIAM A.—Enlisted 16-7-14. Demobilized 1-7-17. Served in Canada, England and France.

ROBBINS, CAPT. WELTON H.—Enlisted 15-9-17. Demobilized 25-11-9. Served in Canada, England and France.

SLAYTER, MAJOR JOHN HOWARD—Enlisted 8-6-16. Demobilized 21-11-19. Served in Canada, England and France. Awarded M.B.E.

SPARROW, CAPT. CECIL J.—Enlisted 6-9-15. Demobilized -7-18. Served in Canada, France and the Balkans.

SPONAGLE, LIEUT.-COL. J. A.—Enlisted 20-11-14 as M.O. 25th Infantry Battalion, which proceeded Overseas 20-5-15. Was M.O. 1st Canadian Divisional Train in France. Went through Battles of Lens and Passchendaele with this Unit. In England held numerous important appointments—among them: Pensions and Claims Board; O.C. of C.A.M.C. Training Depot; Duchess Connaught Canadian Red Cross Hospital; O.C. Canadian Hospital, Hillingdon House, Uxbridge. Had twenty-seven years' previous experience in the Canadian Militia. Received Colonial Auxiliary Forces Officers' Decoration for long service. Was demobilized February 16, 1920.

SUTHERLAND, CAPT. COLIN G.—Enlisted 1-6-17. Demobilized 9-6-19. Served in Canada and England.

SUTHERLAND, MAJOR ROBERT H.—Enlisted 5-8-14. Demobilized 21-7-19. Served in Canada, England, Egypt and Salonika with No. 1 Canadian Stationary Hospital.

TRITES, CAPT. CHARLES B.—Enlisted 18-4-16. Demobilized 5-5-19. Served in Canada, England and France.

WHITMAN, CAPT. GEO. W.—Overseas service. No particulars available.

WILSON, CAPT. ARTHUR A. C.—Served in Canada and England.

WISWELL, CAPT. GORDON B.—Enlisted October, 1915. Demobilized 6-2-19. Served in Canada, England and France. Was awarded M.C. for gallant service in action and was mentioned in dispatches.

NOVA SCOTIA MEDICAL SERVICES IN THE GREAT WAR

WYLDE, CAPT. CHARLES F.—Served Overseas. No particulars available.

ZWICKER, CAPT. W. D.—Enlisted 24-1-17. Demobilized 12-1-20. Served in Canada, England and France.

MILITARY MEDICAL SERVICE IN NOVA SCOTIA.

Capts. W. B. Almon, Hugh O. Blauvelt, William J. Barton. Thomas I. Byrne, Barry H. Calkin, Allister Calder, Michael J. Carney, Prof. John Cameron, George M. Campbell, John L. Churchill, Major James R. Corston, Capts. Allan R. Cunningham. John A. Davis, Lieut. David Drury, Capts. Charles S. Elliott, Guy S. Goodwin, John W. Gannon, W. H. Hattie, B. A. LeBlanc, Roy D. Lindsay, Vernon L. Miller, Major Ernest F. Miller, Capt. Angus M. Morton, Major Leander R. Morse, Capt. John A. Murdoch. Major Donald McDonald, Capt. Dan. F. McInnis, Lieut. Joseph W. McKay, Capts. Donald J. MacKenzie, John M. McLean, Majors Geo. J. McNally, A. G. Nichols, Lieut.-Col. Albert A. Schaffner, Capt. W. H. Schwartz, Lieut. Sieniewicz, Major Dugald Stewart, Lieut. Clarence W. Thorne, Capt. Solomon J. Turel, Major Philip Weatherbe, Major H. B. Webster.

NURSING SERVICE.

In connection with the Nova Scotia Hospital Units reference has been made to only a few Nova Scotia nurses. No account of the humanitarian service of the medical organization in the Great War should fail to give prominence to the noble work of the nursing sisters. What they have done to lighten the weary hours of the wounded, war-sick and homesick soldier has been stamped indelibly on hundreds of thousands of hearts throughout the world.

Every effort has been made to get a complete list of all the Nova Scotia nurses who served in the Great War and where they served. The nearest approach to it is an official list of nurses who either enlisted or were demobilized in Nova Scotia at the headquarters of No. 6 Military District. This has been supplemented by submitting the list, for revision, to some thirty active service nurses and also a number of Medical Officers. Even now there will undoubtedly be some omissions and errors.

NOVA SCOTIA'S PART IN THE GREAT WAR

MILITARY SERVICE OF NURSES ENLISTED OR DEMOBILIZED IN NOVA SCOTIA.

England, France and Salonika.

Clarke, Catherine Parker.
Condon, Margaret.
McKenzie, Elizabeth Margaret.

MacIntosh, Mary Catherine.
McKay, Alice Lettie.

England and Salonika.

Brennan, Emily Lorraine.

England, France and Russia.

Cotton, Dorothy M., R.R.C.

England and France.

Archard, Sarah Ann, A.R.R.C.
Allan, Ann Doctor, R.R.C.
Arbuckle, M. B.
Benvie, Ada.
Black, Amy Isabel.

Bayers, Gladys Fuller.
Beers, Vivian Gertrude.
Cameron, Josephine Christine.
Connell, Monica.
Cooke, Elizabeth Ann; mentioned in dispatches.

Nova Scotia was as prominent in the Nursing as in the Medical Service, and is said to have contributed during the War more Matrons in France than any other individual Province in the Dominion. It gave the Matron-in-Chief of the Canadian Forces, Miss Margaret C. MacDonald, R.R.C., M.M. des I (French Army). Miss MacDonald had previously seen active service in the Spanish-American War and the South African War.

The other Nova Scotia nurses who were Matrons in France during the war were: Miss Georgina Pope, R.R.C. (Senior Matron in Canada), who went with the Canadian Contingent to the South African War as Matron; Miss Harriett Graham, R.R.C.; Miss L. M. Hubley, R.R.C.; Miss K. C. MacLatchy, R.R.C.; Miss S. C. MacIsaac, R.R.C.; Miss Elizabeth B. Ross, R.R.C.; Miss A. C. Strong, R.R.C.

Calder, Jennie Squair, A.R.R.C.
Cameron, Annie May.
Campbell, Laura Emily.
Chisholm, Christena Elizabeth; mentioned in dispatches.
Chisholm, Sarah Catherine.
Churchill, Sarah.
Davidson, Jessie Ann.
Dawson, Isabel Helen.
Dempsey, Mary Catharine.

Doyle, Elizabeth C. (Mrs.)
Drew, Margaret Currie.
Duthie, Edna Craig.
Edgecombe, Lillian Grace.
Ellis, Helena Margaret.
Etherington, Ethel B.
Fitzgerald, Lillian Mary.
Follette, Minnie (drowned *Llandovery Castle*).
Fraser, Annie Margaret.

NOVA SCOTIA MEDICAL SERVICES IN THE GREAT WAR

Fraser, Edith Morrow.
Fraser, Pearl (drowned *Llandovery Castle*).
Genders, Sarah Elizabeth.
Gillan, Ina Gertrude.
Gordon, Eleanor McLaren, A.R.R.C.
Graham, Harriet M. (Matron), R.R.C.
Gray, Dorothy Louise, R.R.C.
Gray, Marguerite Olive.
Guild, Effie Jean.
Gunn, Mary Catharine.
Haliburton, Marion Frances.
Hazard, Mary Elizabeth.
Howard, Alice Maud.
Hubley, Laura May (Matron), R.R.C.
Irwin, Eliza Blanche.
Johnstone, Alice May; mentioned in dispatches.
Johnstone, Margaret A., R.R.C.
Kelly, F. M., R.R.C.
Kendall, Helen Mary.
King, Hazel Mary.
Lamplaugh, Mary Edith, R.R.C.
Landells, Margaret Jane.
Lynch, Mary Theresa; Belgian decoration.
MacAulay, Lorinda.
MacDonald, Annie; mentioned in dispatches.
MacDonald, Annie Belle; French decoration.
MacDonald, Annie Helen.
MacDonald, Catherine Chisholm.
MacDonald, Catherine Tulloch.
MacDonald, Helen Catherine.
MacDonald, Hilda Havergill.
MacDonald, Janet MacGregor, R.R.C.
MacDonald, Jessie Belle.
MacDonald, Jessie Helen.
MacDonald, Louise, A.R.R.C.
MacDonald, Margaret, A.R.R.C.
MacDonald, Margaret Clothilda (Pr. Matron, C.E.F.), R.R.C. (Florence Nightingale decoration).
MacDonald, Mary Margaret.
MacDonald, Mary Simpson.
MacDonald, Minnie Frances.
MacDougall, Annie Claire.
McCuish, Elizabeth Margaret.
McDonald, Catharine Eileen.
McDonald, Nellie Elizabeth.
McDougald, Flora.
McDougald, Margaret; French decoration.
McGrath, Mary.
McInnis, Florence Louise.
McIsaac, Sarah Catherine (Matron), R.R.C.
McKay, Helen Barbara, A.R.R.C.
McKeel, Theadora, R.R.C.
McKenzie, Charlotte.
McKenzie, Christina Mary.
McKenzie, Dora.
McKenzie, Margaret Eliza.
McKenzie, Minnie Hannah.
McKinnon, Euphemia.
McLatchey, Katherine O. (Matron), R.R.C.
McLean, Catherine.
McLean, Elizabeth Isobel.
McLean, Marguerite.
McLean, Mary Rachael.
McLeod, Annie Tremaine.
McLeod, Winifred G.
McLeod, Isabella Gordon.
McLeod, Margaret Christena.
McNeill, Mary Belle.
Moreshead, Eleanor Gorrill.
Mosher, Eva Maud.
Mulcahy, Grace.
Mutch, Florence Sarah.
Myers, Olga.
Nicholson, Elsie Sarah.
O'Brien, Marcella Agnes.
Paget, Catherine White.
Paton, Florence May.
Patton, Mary Steele.
Pidgeon, L., R.R.C.; mentioned in dispatches.
Pope, Georgina, (Matron), R.R.C.
Rice, Frances Augusta, A.R.R.C.
Richardson, Edith Louise.
Rose, Lenora E.
Ross, Elizabeth Belle (Matron), R.R.C.
Schurman, W i n i f r e d Dobson; French decoration.
Shannahan, Mary Catherine.
Shea, C. R.
Smith, Sarah Catharine.
Stevens, Louise Myrtle.
Strong, A. C. (Matron), R.R.C.
Stuart, Evelyn Mary.
Tait, Mary.
Thomas, Lalia E.
Thompson, Wilhelmine Irene.
Thompson, Edith Alexandra.
Urquhart, Lottie.
Veits, Caroline Winifred.
Walsh, M. S.
Walters, Emma Jane.

NOVA SCOTIA'S PART IN THE GREAT WAR

Watson, Mabel Margaret.
Watson, Maud.
Waugh, Belle.
Waughan, Belle.
White, Catherine M.

White, Helen St. Clair.
White, Katherine Elizabeth.
Williams, Maysie Ellen.
Young, Anna Teresa.
Young, Rose Olga.

England.

Anderson, Minerva Blanche.
Bain, Margaret Winnifred.
Barnes, Ellen Caroline.
Bentley, Olla May.
Clarke, Edith Esther.
Campbell, Annie May.
Campbell, D.
Coates, Dora Evelyn.
Cameron, Elizabeth Vena.
Cameron, Mary Lillian.
Cameron, Sarah Belle.
Colter, Bessie Long.
Connors, Florence Marguerite.
Cray, Bertha Geraldine.
Currie, Alice Margaret.
Desmond, Mary.
Davies, Margaret Emily.
DeWolfe, Annie Clark.
Dunlop, Laura Alice.
Ellis, Marion Dean.
Fife, Lillian Jessie.
Fraser, Lavinia Flora.
Fraser, Flora Mathilda.
Harrison, Eunice Knapp.
Hallisey, Catherine Martina.
Hillcoat, Anna Rebecca.
Hubley, Jennie Mable.
Hartling, Mabel.
Howard, Mary Munroe.
Jennex, Lenna (died).

Layton, Adrianna R.
LeDrew, Annie May.
Mack, Beatrice Helena.
Mombourquette, Katherine.
Morrison, Daisy Dean.
Mutch, Helen Frances.
Murray, Ann Elizabeth.
Murray, Emma Blanche.
McCarthy, May Charlotte.
McCuish, Harriet Mary.
MacDonald, Jessie.
MacDonald, Georgina Emily.
MacDonald, Margaret Catherine.
McInnes, Dorothy Jean.
MacIntosh, Margaret Isabel.
McLeod, Sadie Isabel.
McLean, Sadie Ethel.
McNeill, Margaret Blanche.
Morrison, Myrtilla Grey.
Morrison, Jean Augusta.
Payne, Sarah.
Smith, Mabel Eliza.
Sedgewick, F. M.
Skerry, Annie Adelaide.
Stewart, Margaret Wood.
Stevens, Annie Jane.
Thompson, Ethel Elaine.
Torr, Alice.
Tout, Dora Olivia.
Urquhart, Lottie.

Canada.

Anderson, Roberta.
Andrews, Edith.
Barnaby, Agnes Gertrude.
Bearisto, Mary Kier.
Bissett, Barbara Beatrice.
Boland, Florence.
Bauld, Muriel.
Burton, Mary Elizabeth.
Campbell, Jean Marion.
Cook, Gertrude Pauline.
Coolen, Anasthasia Muriel.
Coolen, Mary Ellen.
Davies, Edith Maria.
Doull, Jessie Cameron.
Dunbar, Lillian Campbell.
Farry, Lucy.

Fitzgerald, Edith Maria.
Fraser, Florence Amelia.
Fraser, Frances Margaret.
Gates, Sarah Gladys.
Gilchrist, Marion L.
Gillis, Christine Anna.
Graves, Laura May.
Haverstock, Laura Grace.
Hayden, Mary Josephine.
Holloway, Eva.
Hunt, Minnie Hannah.
Hunt, Myrtle C. (died).
Keith, Gertrude.
Kennedy, Margaret.
LaPierre, Mary Ann.
Larking, Nora Evelyn.

Jarvis, Jessie (died).
LeJeune, Mary.
Lester, Olla Dell.
Logan, Caroline.
Manning, Myra Ayer.
Mills, Ethel Rosamund.
Morrison, Anna May.
McCrea, Theresa Ann.
MacDonald, Evangeline.
MacDonald, Harriet Helen.
MacDonnell, Mary Elizabeth.
McInnis, Ellephallie Carrie.
McKenzie, Helen Gertrude.
McKinnon, Ruth.
McLean, Josephine.
McManus, Laura.

McManus, Lila Theresa.
McNeill, Mary Eleanor.
O'Callaghan, Mary.
O'Leary, Catherine.
Prest, Violet Ella.
Ross, Vivian Russell.
Schaffner, Marion Parker.
Schaffner, Muriel Campbell.
Steeves, Ina Maud.
Sullivan, Mary Margaret.
Sutherland, Roberta.
Talbot, Frances Elizabeth.
Trivett, Jean Dorothy.
Urquhart, Susan Hope.
Whidden, Mary.
Young, Josephine M.

Military Service—No Particulars Available.

Benjamin, Vera Louise.
Christie, Freda Hope.
Fraser, Elda Jean.
Fyfe, Hannah G.
Harrison, Jena Augusta.
Hill, Eliza Victoria.
Jones, Helen.

Kelley, Margaret Neill.
Mosher, Lydia T.
MacDonald, Anna Bula.
McKenzie, Jean Annie.
McLeod, Marion.
Perry, H. H.
Purcell, Mary Louise.

CHAPTER XXVII.

THE CANADIAN ARMY DENTAL CORPS.

THAT Dental Services are a necessity in the army is one of the many lessons taught us by the War and it has been amply proved that the Canadian Army Dental Corps was responsible for placing at least 10 per cent of the Canadian and British troops at the Front who, but for the excellent dental services provided, would not have been there.

LIEUT.-COL. B. L. NEILLY.

Members of the dental profession in Nova Scotia were among the first to offer their services, and in August, 1914, three of them, Drs. B. L. Neilly, F. W. Bruce Kelly and H. L. Mitchener, were on duty at Valcartier Camp. Drs. Neilly and Kelly proceeded Overseas and were the first dental surgeons at the Front. So far as can be learned these were the only dental surgeons with the Canadian troops at that date, Captain Bentley of Ontario reporting early in September.

For eight years previous to the War a Committee of the Canadian Dental Association on "Dental Services in the Army" repeatedly approached the Federal Government with regard to a definite Army Dental Association to be administered by the Medical Services or otherwise, but were finally informed that the organization then existing, which consisted of twenty-six Dental Officers attached to the Army Medical Corps as Honorary Captains and Lieutenants, was quite saisfactory.

On the outbreak of the War members of the profession throughout Canada, realizing the necessity of dental services for recruits, voluntarily provided dental treatment for thousands of men who, otherwise, could not have been accepted.

THE CANADIAN ARMY DENTAL CORPS

The attention of the Minister of Militia, Sir Sam Hughes, was directed to the importance and value of this work by Generals Fotheringham, Lessard, Loggie and others as well as by a subcommittee of civilian dentists from Toronto, who proceeded to Ottawa early in 1915 under the direction of Dr. George Kerr Thomson of Halifax, Chairman of the Canadian Dental Association's Committee on "Dental Services in the Army," with the result that the Minister immediately issued orders for a Dental organization, similar to that of the Medical, but entirely separate.

To this action by the Minister is due the fact that Canada was the first country in the world to organize an Army Dental Corps separate and distinct from other military organizations. Dr. Thomson was first recommended by the Toronto Committee and the dental profession for Director of Dental Services, but Dr. Armstrong of Ottawa received the appointment, and in June, 1915, proceeded Overseas with thirty-five officers, thirty-five N.C.O.'s and thirty-five privates. This organization was increased from time to time until there were over one thousand Dental Officers and other ranks on duty Overseas.

It was realized that while it was necessary to provide dental services for men Overseas, it was even more important that they be made dentally fit before sailing; and in October, 1915, the Home Service organization was authorized with a Director at Ottawa and an Assistant Director in each Military District together with a strength of one officer, N.C.O. and private for each 1,000 men. This necessitated an organization of at least sixty of all ranks in Military District No. 6, which at that time included New Brunswick, Prince Edward Island and Nova Scotia.

Members of the dental profession in the three provinces responded notably to the call of duty, and, while it does not come within the scope of this history to mention the services of men in other provinces, it is desirable to put on record great appreciation of the excellent services rendered by members of the dental profession in New Brunswick and Prince Edward Island who were on duty in Military District No. 6. One of the most prominent practitioners in St. John, N.B., Dr. James M. Magee, ex-President of the Canadian Dental Association and Dominion Dental Council

THE CANADIAN ARMY DENTAL CORPS

and a member of the Nova Scotia Dental Association, who, before the War, was attached as Honorary Captain to the Army Medical Corps, was one of the first to join the Home Service organization in Military District No. 6.

Major Thomson was appointed A.D.D.S., Military District No. 6, on November 1st, 1915. During his absence at Valcartier Camp in the summer of 1916, Captain Magee acted as A.D.D.S. in Military District No. 6 and later was appointed A.D.D.S. of Military District No. 7 when New Brunswick became a separate Military District.

The C.A.D.C. in Military District No. 6 was administered on a most economical and business-like basis, and at the Camp Hill Army Dental Surgery, one of the finest and best equipped in the world, many thousands of men were made dentally fit, not only before going Overseas, but also on their return to Canada, when a great many of them needed extensive restorative dental appliances.

For several weeks after the great explosion, which occurred on December 6, 1917, the Staff of the Camp Hill Dental Surgery rendered services and co-operated with the medical officers, part of the dental surgery being used as an operating room for the eye specialists. Some of the dental officers on duty were severely but not seriously injured, and during the first thirty-six hours after the explosion rendered valuable first aid to the injured, with whom Camp Hill was overcrowded.

In 1916, at Aldershot Camp, two appendicitis operations were successfully performed in the Camp Dental Surgery, which was completed long before the Camp Hospital. These cases would probably have proved fatal had it not been for the foresight of the dental Staff in expediting the construction of this dental surgery.

Through the efforts of Dean Frank Woodbury arrangements were carried out by the Dental Faculty of Dalhousie University for rendering dental services to the men of the navy before the work was performed by the Dental Corps.

The following is a list of dental officers who served Overseas and at home:

CANADA.—Major G. K. Thomson, Major H. E. Mann, Capts. H. L. Mitchener, H. G. Dunbar, W. W. Woodbury, G. Tingley, J. M. Magee, A. G. Wicks, J. E. Sewell, J. B. Brown, J. E. Blanchard, F. C. Bonnell, I. K. Farrar, F. A. Godsoe, F. E. Burden, W. H. Steeves, L. O'Leary (Q.M.), J. E. Jewett, A. Gasson, R. I. Robertson, F. W. Johnson, H. S. Allen, G. R. Smith, F. T. Bowness, Y. E. Gaudet, McIntyre, F. G. Mann, F. W. Barbour, R. I. Irving, Lieuts. A. J. Cormier, H. Adamson, Guy Stultz, L. M. Finigan, A. K. Wade, A. J. Couglin, F. W. LeFugery, A. B. Crowe, H. C. McIntosh, Regtl. Sergt.-Majors, F. E. Fahie, I. K. Jackson, F. B. Miller, Quartermaster Sergts. J. M. Blanchard, Laurie Blanchard, L. H. Jenkins, G. Sommers, Staff Sergts. A. H. Churchill, J. H. McLaughlin, E. S. Dexter, Sergts. A. W. Allen, L. M. Withrow, C. W. Burgoyne, Staff Sergts. E. E. Hatfield, Neil Flannery, F. H. Phinney, Sergts. J. L. Sears, R. H. Wilby, Cox, C. R. McLellan, R. C. Wall, J. St. C. Smith, C. E. Cantelope, T. Ranford, W. Hazelwood, Percy Rennels, W. R. Gunn, Quartermaster Sergt. L. McGuire, Company Quartermaster Sergt. W. H. D. Bence.

OVERSEAS.—Lieut.-Col. B. L. Neilly, Major F. W. B. Kelly, Major C. E. McLaughlin, Capts. R. J. McMeekin, Karl Woodbury, C. D. Desbrisay, S. S. Harvie, E. A. Randall, H. Clay, E. S. Millett, H. O. Harding, Arthur Viets, T. E. Robins, R. W. Frank, W. R. Fraser, Karl Damon, Otto Nase, J. P. Gallagher, J. McDonald, McNeil, W. R. Wilkes, R. C. Crosby, E. A. Randall, K. C. Dobson, H. C. McDonald, Staff Sergts. J. E. Fraser, C. Garrett, R. B. Horton, Sergts. S. W. Hatfield, C. A. S. Carlow, H. O. Lord, F. A. McGarrigle, G. Lowine, Phillips, G. A. Barter, W. Dyer, Raymond King, W. Joy, J. McLean, McGibbon, J. L. Rogers, I. D. S. Ross, G. E. McDonald, H. E. Grey, V. D. Crowe, Collier, Jones, Butterworth, Doucette, Quartermaster Sergt. Richards.

CHAPTER XXVIII.

CANADIAN ARMY PAY CORPS.

BEFORE the outbreak of the War in 1914 the Canadian Army Pay Corps had only sufficient Staff to deal with the small permanent force, of which it was an integral part. When the Canadian Expeditionary Force was organized, and troops mobilized for home defence, the C.A.P.C. was called upon to undergo the same strain and expansion demanded of every branch of the service. Outside of the army little is known of the responsibilities suddenly thrust upon this department. It had to deal with all finances, pay, separation allowance, assigned pay, civilian employees, tradesmen's accounts, etc., and, as will be seen by the statement at the end of this article, No. 6 Detachment stationed at Halifax alone disbursed $53,357,388.08 between August, 1914, and July, 1920.

In August, 1914, No. 6 Detachment, whose territory at that time included New Brunswick and Prince Edward Island, as well as Nova Scotia, consisted of the following officers and non-commissioned officers: Lieut.-Col. S. J. R. Sircom (now retired with rank of Brigadier-General), Capt. J. L. Regan, Sergt.-Major J. Turner, Quartermaster Sergt. G. H. Saunders, Staff Sergt. G. T. Allum, Staff Sergt. C. A. Chew, Staff Sergt. B. A. Spink, Sergt. E. R. Kelly, Sergt. A. V. Chase, Sergt. W. A. Coyne, Sergt. F. A. Chew.

This Staff was increased until at one time 14 officers and 120 non-commissioned officers and men were employed. Some of these served in No. 6 Detachment throughout the whole period of the War. Others were transferred to various Units, went Overseas, or took their discharge.

NOVA SCOTIA'S PART IN THE GREAT WAR

Every soldier, from a Tommy to a full-fledged General, will admit that as far as organization and administration were concerned the Canadian Army Pay Corps was beyond criticism. As soon as a man enlisted he received his pay regularly, no matter where he was—in Canada or in England, in the Field, in hospital or on furlough; and when he returned to Canada for demobilization the cheque for balance of pay due was handed to him on the day he was discharged. In addition to this monies were forwarded to his dependants on account of Separation Allowance, and assigned pay, settlement made for clothing and equipment, which he purchased from stores on repayment, for Victory Bonds which he purchased during his services, remittances to his friends and other payments.

All this entailed an enormous amount of work. Ledger sheets had to be kept up to date, pay books checked up, remittances looked after, cheques written, documents made up and sent along with the soldier from one place to another until he finally returned to Canada, bearing with him like documents from England. Every officer, non-commissioned officer and man knows the amount of detail work which this involved.

BRIG.-GEN. S. J. R. SIRCOM.

Of the original Staff, Col. S. J. R. Sircom, affectionately known to the troops in this district as the "Grand Old Man," endeared himself to all ranks with whom he came in contact by his urbanity and kindly consideration. Colonel Sircom commenced his military career early in life. He joined the Halifax Garrison Artillery as a 2nd Lieutenant in 1878, and the 63rd Regiment, Halifax Rifles, in 1885. He transferred to the Militia Staff with the rank of Major in 1905, and on January 1, 1907, was appointed to the C.A.P.C. with the rank of Lieutenant-Colonel, and became Paymaster of the 6th Divisional area. He was promoted to the rank of Colonel on May 24, 1916. He proceeded to London as a representative of the Paymaster-General the latter part of 1918, and on his return from Overseas was retired to Pension with the rank of Brigadier-General.

CANADIAN ARMY PAY CORPS

Capt. J. L. Regan proceeded Overseas with the First Contingent as assistant to Col. W. R. Ward, then Chief Paymaster Canadian Expeditionary Force. Captain Regan was largely responsible for the organization of the Canadian Pay Services in France and England. He was later promoted to the rank of Colonel and appointed Deputy Paymaster-General. He was awarded the C.M.G., and on his return to Canada became Director of Pay Services at Ottawa.

COL. J. L. REGAN, C.M.G.

Quartermaster Sergt. J. Turner transferred to the Highland Brigade as Captain and Quartermaster. He was seriously injured in the Halifax explosion and is now invalided to Pension. Staff Sergeant G. T. Allum, now Sergeant-Major, is retired to Pension. Quartermaster Sergeant G. H. Saunders was promoted to the rank of Captain. Captain Saunders remained with No. 6 Detachment during the whole period of the War, and the admirable manner in which this Unit met all demands upon it, particularly during the trying months of demobilization, was largely due to his energy, efficiency and foresight.

Staff Sergts. C. A. Chew and B. A. Spink proceeded Overseas and both returned with the rank of Captain. The former was discharged to Pension; the latter is employed at Militia Headquarters. Staff Sergt. A. V. Chase went Overseas with the Clearing Services Command and returned with the rank of Captain. He will be remembered by all returning officers and men who passed through or had dealings with the Clearing Depot, Halifax, as a very efficient officer. Sergt. W. A. Coyne proceeded Overseas as Captain Clearing Services Command and is now struck off strength. Sergt. F. A. Chew proceeded Overseas with the 25th Battalion, returned as a Captain in the C.A.P.C., and is now struck off strength to Pension.

Capt. G. C. Sircom, son of Brigadier-General S. J. R. Sircom, after return from Overseas, was employed in the Pay Office, and now has a commission in the Permanent Army Pay Corps.

Lieut.-Col. J. A. C. Mowbray, when war was declared, offered his services and was detailed as Paymaster to the 2nd Brigade, C.F.A., proceeding Overseas with that Unit. After serving in France for about one year he was recalled to London to fill a post in the Pay Office Headquarters. He became Deputy Assistant Paymaster-General, was awarded the O.B.E., and later was transferred to Canada to fill his present position, which is designated as Senior Pay Officer for Nova Scotia.

LIEUT.-COL. J. A. C. MOWBRAY, O.B.E.

The following are a few of the officers who did good work in this Division during the War, either before proceeding Overseas or returning from Overseas on demobilization or as Paymasters of Units:—Major J. Taylor, Major M. H. Morrison, Major R. H. Humphrey, Major J. D. Murphy, Major Colin MacIntosh, Capt. H. Powis Herbert, Capt. G. C. Milsom, Capt. W. W. Brignell, Capt. C. S. Simpson, Capt. R. Bartholomew, Capt. H. A. MacDonald, Capt. J. L. Melanson, Capt. R. H. Hardwicke, Capt. A. A. Cameron, Capt. Tait Scott, Capt. H. W. Ireland, Capt. Walter Ruggles, Capt. W. C. L. Bauld, Capt. R. MacDougall, Lieut. H. S. Major, Lieut. W. E. McDonald, Lieut. H. A. Allum, Lieut. H. S. Simpson, Lieut. W. J. O'Donnell.

To show the vast amount of work carried out by this Detachment the following statement of monthly expenditure is appended. This does not include disbursements for clothing and equipment, horses, transports, camp supplies, wagons, etc., but purely pay and allowance of troops and their upkeep. Considering the amount of cash handled it is satisfactory to know that not one cent was lost to the public by misappropriation or otherwise.

CANADIAN ARMY PAY CORPS

	1914.	1915.	1916.	1917.	1918.
Jan. ...	....	$482,294 94	$896,549 00	$666,896 18	$557,736 27
Feb. ...	....	470,046 71	976,053 25	644,126 11	518,971 86
Mar. ..	....	662,605 50	1,153,944 98	675,447 01	726,882 97
Supp. ..	....	287,295 99	868,515 21	5,506 91	18,643 78
Apr. ...	....	573,994 33	926,836 11	747,234 96	700,400 20
May ..	....	589,433 57	1,140,637 41	691,321 20	600,590 53
June ...	....	460,883 20	1,269,057 73	679,157 80	745,238 77
July ...	....	421,362 69	928,319 09	579,265 37	940,247 42
Aug. ..	$161,021 38	418,878 19	911,739 50	571,727 69	709,107 18
Sept. ..	314,031 19	447,655 00	849,942 58	550,065 71	595,238 78
Oct. ...	307,412 29	533,383 39	819,436 00	745,190 00	614,166 48
Nov. ..	342,922 32	602,738 82	752,020 66	697,784 22	610,452 05
Dec. ...	459,147 34	867,574 05	683,957 09	535,004 98	671,840 28
Total ..	$1,584,534 52	$6,818,146 38	$12,177,008 61	$7,788,728 14	$8,009,516 57

	1919.	1920.
Jan. ...	$683,909 27	$657,541 08
Feb. ...	872,284 08	402,801 20
Mar. ...	1,176,278 36	347,439 80
Supp. ..	26,683 87	60,765 01
Apr. ...	1,113,762 96	142,518 83
May ...	1,208,976 54	121,399 76
June ...	1,378,733 64	145,981 25
July ...	1,596,356 84	132,327 77
Aug. ...	1,638,684 02	
Sept. ...	1,505,466 80	
Oct. ...	1,727,033 48	
Nov. ...	1,178,085 30	
Dec. ...	862,424 00	
Total ..	$14,968,679 16	$2,010,774 70

Summary.

1914	....	$1,584,534 52
1915	....	6,818,146 38
1916	....	12,177,008 61
1917	....	7,788,728 14
1918	....	8,009,516 57
1919	....	14,968,679 16
1920	....	2,010,774 70

Total expenditure to
July, 1920 .... $53,357,388 08

CHAPTER XXIX.

THE ROYAL CANADIAN GARRISON ARTILLERY.

LORD KITCHENER once remarked—in reply to a question—"The Front is where a soldier is ordered to be." In accordance with this, those men whose duties necessitated their being retained in connection with the Coast Defences, were made to abide by the decision of those responsible for the strategy of the defence of Canadian shores.

After the War, the Permanent Force, of which the R.C.G.A. form a part, are the only persons in uniform; and the imputation of not being an Overseas Unit is not a good advertisement to attract recruits. Moreover, the imputation is not only unjust, but untrue, as the following will show:

In July, 1914, relations between the British Empire and the Central Powers were very strained, and on July 30th, four days before the War was officially declared, the R.C.G.A. were ordered to man the most important forts as a precaution, since it is an axiom in naval warfare that, if possible, a surprise attack is the first and best declaration of war.

On August 5th Fortress Orders contained the following:—"War having broken out with Germany, the Halifax Defence Scheme comes into force herewith."

On the 6th August, the 1st Regiment, C.G.A., mobilized and proceeded to the Forts to complete the manning, since the R.C.G.A. alone were too few in number completely to man more than the two largest forts.

The first portion of the annual training for the year had just been completed, and one can truthfully say that Halifax was as well able to repel a raid as any other fortress in the Empire at that period.

THE ROYAL CANADIAN GARRISON ARTILLERY

It was thought by most people in the early days of the War that the War would last only a few months, and the personnel of the Defences had to find accommodation where they could, until well on into the winter; for coast forts in peace time are not provided with accommodation for lengthy occupation; consequently, both officers and men had a far from comfortable time until wooden huts were constructed.

None of the Artillery Units allotted to the Fortress were for any length of time up to full strength, so that barely sufficient men were available to form the necessary reliefs for the guns.

Night and day, all through the War, from July 30th, 1914, until after the signing of the Armistice, November 11, 1919, enough men to work the guns had to be near them and alert, while on each gun was a sentry, who was relieved every hour, and whose duty was to watch seawards for the approach of any hostile craft. Not a very arduous task at first sight, but enough to make most men long to be Overseas after a few months of it.

Fortunately the Germans were not very enterprising, and considered that the presence of the Coast Defences was too great a risk to run, so that Halifax did not have to go through the horrors of a bombardment as well as the explosion, though, had the city been undefended, it would, no doubt, like several English towns, have received a few shells from time to time.

In March, 1915, the 3rd Regiment, C.G.A., from St. John, N.B., came for training, as St. John was about to be fortified, and a portion of this Unit was retained to reinforce the Units already doing duty in the Forts. In April, 1915, No. 4 Company, P.E.I., C.G.A., came for training. Some of these men had already been on duty with heavy field guns at Canso and Sydney. When trained they remained in Halifax, sending drafts Overseas from time to time, and proved themselves efficient gunners.

In June, 1915, a number of N.C.O.'s and men sailed for the Front, but all efforts of others to do so were in vain, though several N.C.O.'s and men took their fate in their own hands and stowed away on transports conveying infantry. Some of these got as far as France, but discipline had to be maintained, and all were brought back. This incident will show that the men of the R.C.G.A. did not remain in Halifax from choice.

In July, 1916, authority was at last obtained for the R.C.G.A. to form a Siege Battery, and this was quickly done; in it were some of the best N.C.O.'s and men in the Corps, and the whole Battery were of splendid physique. This Battery left for Overseas in September, 1916, under the command of Major S. A. Heward, R.C.A. It arrived in France on the 22nd March, 1917, and took part in many big fights, including Vimy Ridge, Hill 70, Passchendaele, Cambrai and Mons. Men of a Siege Battery get plenty of heavy work and little chance of heroic deeds as individuals, but the Battery has to its credit the following decorations:—Military Cross, 2; Distinguished Conduct Medal, 2; Military Medals, 16; Meritorious Service Medals, 3; while several other officers from the R.C.A. in Halifax were awarded the D.S.O. and M.C.

As soon as the Battery left for Overseas, preparations for raising another were immediately made, and those officers and men who were unable to go in the previous one vied with each other to get a place in this, but it was not authorized, and drafts only were found as reinforcements to the one already authorized. Moreover, it was deemed advisable that certain specially trained officers and men were essential for the efficient working of the Home Defence, and these could not go, even in drafts, unless they had others to replace them.

It takes some time to make an artilleryman, particularly a garrison gunner, who is expected to know every type of gun from a light field piece to the heaviest coast defence gun, or siege howitzer, all of which form part of the armament of a coast fortress, so that, although no doubt if the War had lasted long enough all would eventually have been replaced, these men had to remain.

A number of R.C.A. officers went over in charge of drafts of the R.C.G.A. or other Units.

The 1st Regiment, C.G.A., sent over many officers and men in drafts to infantry units and to an Ammunition Column.

The P.E.I. C.G.A. Detachment also formed an Ammunition Column.

THE ROYAL CANADIAN GARRISON ARTILLERY

Early in 1915 the British Government decided to re-arm St. Lucia, and the Units at Halifax, with some additional personnel from Esquimalt and Quebec, were called upon to furnish men for this purpose. The first draft went in March, 1915. They had to mount the guns (some of which were of French pattern and quite strange to them), and generally organize the defences.

In the autumn of 1917 and spring of 1918 the enemy submarines raided the Atlantic coasts of the United States and Canada, and it was very essential that the important port of Sydney, N.S., should be more strongly defended, so new guns of heavier calibre were sent from Halifax and mounted there. This necessitated additional men, and drafts from Toronto and British Columbia were detailed for this purpose.

These men, some of them called under the Military Service Act, were an exceptionally good type and quickly made efficient specialists and gunners. Some were sent for training as officers and would have relieved those officers in the Forts who had been unable to get away. Unfortunately for them the Armistice was declared and hostilities ceased, so that this scheme did not materialize, though some of these men obtained probationers' certificates.

An important branch of the R.C.G.A. in Halifax is the Royal School of Artillery (Coast Defence and Siege) and this School, the only Siege Artillery School in Canada, was responsible for the training of most of the Siege Artillery Officers and Specialists, as well as several Batteries and Drafts that went Overseas after the First Contingent.

In addition to this, a gun practice at Halifax, Sydney and St. John was carried out under the supervision of the R.S.A. Staff, while courses for officers and specialists, Coast Defence Artillery, were also given.

The establishment of Instructors was one officer and three other ranks, but as one N.C.O. Instructor was stationed at St. John, this was increased by a N.C.O. from the 1st Regiment, C.G.A. Officers from the C.G.A. were attached as assistants for varying periods.

In June, 1915, the I.G., now Lieut.-Col. W. G. Beeman, D.S.O., R.C.A., went Overseas, and in 1916 his successor, Major H. R. N.

Cobbett, R.C.A., went over with No. 9 Siege Battery. In 1918 one Warrant Officer Instructor was permitted to go; he was immediately appointed Instructor at the Canadian School of Gunnery, Witley, England, and it was only with great difficulty that he managed to reach France, where he again was utilized as an Instructor.

The rest of the Staff felt most keenly the fact that they had to be retained in Canada, as their position after the War, when dealing with classes who had seen Overseas service, would not be at all enviable. It was very unfortunate that arrangements had not been made to replace them, so that they might go to the Front even for a short time, because although it is a fact that good teachers are born, not made, there is a tendency to think that anyone with long experience in the fighting line must be a good instructor.

Officers from all parts of Canada took courses at the R.S.A., and it speaks well for the training which they received that on reaching England further training, other than three weeks' at Lydd, was considered unnecessary in most cases, and at Lydd these officers usually took first place in the examinations held there.

Many of them, who were unable to get positions in the C.E.F., were given commissions in the British Artillery, and in several cases commanded Batteries.

Owing to the smallness of Staff and limited demand for siege artillery the actual numbers trained were not as large as those in other Artillery Schools, but with small classes the training was naturally very thorough.

Among the Units trained may be mentioned:—

Coast Defence.	Siege.
1st Regiment, C.G.A.	2nd Montreal H'y B't'y.
3rd Regiment, C.G.A.	McGill Siege B't'y and Drafts.
P.E.I., C.G.A.	3rd C.G.A. Siege B't'y and Drafts.
Drafts from Toronto and B.C.	R.C.G.A. Siege B't'y and Drafts.
And 10 courses for officers and specialists lasting two months each.	Halifax (10th) B't'y and Drafts.
	And 9 courses for officers and specialists, lasting two months each.

Total number trained by R.S.A., exclusive of Batteries:

Officers.	Men.	Officers.	Men.
190	301	122	258

THE ROYAL CANADIAN GARRISON ARTILLERY

SUMMARY OF PERSONNEL WHO WENT OVERSEAS.

R.C.G.A.

Officers.	Other Ranks.	Sphere of Operations.
13	288	Western Front.
..	60	To St. Lucia.
1	36	To C.E.F., Siberia.
8	..	British Mission, Siberia.
Total.. 22	384	

1st Regiment, C.G.A.

Officers.	Other Ranks.	
48	625	Western Front and St. Lucia.

P.E.I. C.G.A.

Officers.	Other Ranks.	
3	110	Western Front.

On mobilization these units had:

	Officers.	O.R.
R.C.G.A.	17	336
1st Regt., C.G.A.	20	230
4 Coy., P.E.I., C.G.A.	3	72
Total	40	638

Altogether about 80 officers and 1,500 N.C.O.'s and men of the Artillery Units (including 10th Siege Battery) stationed in Halifax were sent Overseas, and the majority of those mobilized in 1914 who did not go were unable to do so either through being specialists, over age or low category.

When it is realized that these Corps had great difficulty in obtaining recruits, owing to the fear that men would be retained for Home Service, the numbers shown are considered very creditable.

CHAPTER XXX.

THE CANADIAN ENGINEERS.

THE Corps of Canadian Engineers has no local connection with any Province in the same way that Infantry Regiments and Battalions have. At the end of the War in France it consisted of some twelve Battalions, together with other small Engineering Units with Administrative Staffs, etc., which Units were recruited from all parts of Canada, and no particular Engineering Unit was sent from the Province of Nova Scotia.

A great many individual officers and men were sent to the Engineers from this Province, and did very excellent work, but were posted to various Overseas Units, hence the impossibility of describing particularly the work and services of Nova Scotia Sappers.

As far as service in Canada is concerned the defence of the Fortress of Halifax was a very important matter, and the services of a very large number of officers and other ranks of the R.C.E. Permanent Force and Canadian Engineers, Active Militia, were employed at this Fortress throughout the War. Their strenuous duties and long hours in connection with the continual operation of electric lights and maintenance of fortifications were carried out untiringly and most conscientiously.

Practically every officer and other rank in these two Corps not only volunteered for Overseas service, but also took very strenuous measures to get to France, by hook or by crook, and a great many of them were successful. Others unfortunately were retained in Halifax for the defence of that Fortress.

CHAPTER XXXI.

MILITIA UNITS ON HOME SERVICE.

THE following memorandum was prepared to bring to the attention of the Minister of Militia and Militia Council some facts and figures respecting the services of the Militia of Canada *in Canada,* and particularly the Fortress of Halifax, Nova Scotia, and the Atlantic Seaboard, who although they repeatedly volunteered for Overseas were not allowed to go because their duties were held to be supremely important by those in authority.

1st—Halifax has always been a Military and Naval Station of the Empire, and confidential instructions have always been in existence and a comprehensive scheme of defence in the hands of officers commanding Units, to be put in force immediately on declaration of war. Therefore, the following Halifax Fortress Order was issued by the G.O.C. M.D. No. 6, August 5, 1914:

No. 681. "War having broken out with Germany the Halifax defence scheme comes into effect forthwith."

In accordance with this order all Halifax Units were immediately mobilized and remained on duty in defence of Halifax practically for the duration of the War. The 94th Regiment was also mobilized for the defence of the Canso cable station, Cape Breton wireless station, etc., and other detachments were placed on active service at various points in the district.

2nd—The importance of Halifax as a Military and Naval Station in British North America in the eyes of the Imperial and Canadian authorities is borne out by the following facts:

(*a*) The immense amount of money spent in fortifications.

(*b*) The inauguration of an examination service whereby all vessels were examined before being allowed to enter the harbor.

(*c*) Halifax was the examination port for North America, and at times there were upwards of 200 large ocean-going vessels lying at anchor in the harbor.

(d) The manning of the Port War Signal Station, by which all British and Allied warships were passed in under secret signals and codes.

(e) All guns in the various forts were kept loaded, and the crews were kept standing by day and night, ready for instant action.

(f) The infantry continually patrolled the coast, guarding the approaches to the city, and protecting cable landings and wireless stations.

(g) When orders were issued to reduce the strength of the defences in September, 1914, the British Admiral on the Station informed Headquarters that if this order were carried out he would withdraw his fleet and mine the harbor, which would mean closing the harbor to all shipping.

(h) A Hydroplane Station was established, and patrolled the coast daily during the latter part of the War.

(i) Owing to the protection afforded by the defences of Halifax, the authorities were enabled to dispatch from this port in the vicinity of 300,000 Canadian troops, in addition to many thousand Colonial and Allied troops, including Australians, New Zealanders, Bermudians, Fiji Islanders, Americans, and some 50,000 Chinese labor troops.

(j) By means of its defence Halifax afforded shelter for a large number of merchant vessels that were driven in by German raiders early in the War.

It should also be noted that submarines were frequently in the vicinity of the harbor, and on one notable occasion a large oil tanker was sunk two hours after she left her pier, and several fishing vessels were sunk off the coast, and other large transports and cargo vessels were driven ashore at the entrance of the harbor. The transport *City of Vienna* became a total wreck. Preparations were made and orders issued to provide against possible landing parties from German raiders. Stringent orders were issued providing for the screening of all lights in the city and prosecutions were issued for neglecting to carry out this order.

The foregoing is enumerated with the object of showing the importance of Halifax Harbor as a War Station and the necessity of having it properly defended by maintaining the Garrison at full strength.

CHAPTER XXXII.

THE FIRST REGIMENT CANADIAN GARRISON ARTILLERY.

THIS Unit was organized in 1869 for the purpose of assisting the Regular Forces of the Garrison of Halifax in manning the Forts. The Regiment has always been at a high state of efficiency, due to the superior class of men it has been able to attract to its ranks.

From the date of its organization the Regiment has been commanded by many prominent citizens. The following is the list in order of service: Lieut.-Col. A. G. Jones (late Lieutenant-Governor of Nova Scotia), Lieut.-Col. Wm. Creighton, Lieut.-Col. George Mitchell, Lieut.-Col. Thomas Mowbray, Lieut.-Col. A. E. Curren, Lieut.-Col. F. H. Oxley, Lieut.-Col. A. G. Hesslein, Lieut.-Col. H. Flowers, and, in 1914, at the outbreak of war, by Lieut.-Col. J. A. Marshall, followed at the completion of his term of service by Lieut.-Col. A. W. Duffus, who commanded up to the cessation of hostilities.

LIEUT.-COL. A. W. DUFFUS.

On August 3, 1914, Capts. A. N. Jones, S. C. Oland, and George Brew were detailed for duty at the examination Battery. On August 4th the Commanding Officer received orders to mobilize, and on August 6th the Regiment was detailed to and occupied its various posts in the Batteries of the Fortress of Halifax. All officers and men in the city reported for duty; those absent were summoned by wire and letter, and joined the Unit within a few days.

NOVA SCOTIA'S PART IN THE GREAT WAR

The following officers remained with the Unit during the War, but did not proceed Overseas, because the Department at Ottawa claimed their services could not be dispensed with:

Lieut.-Col. J. A. Marshall, Lieut.-Col. A. W. Duffus, Major A. M. Bauld (Q.M.), Capts. J. M. Allen (Adjt.), W. C. Bauld (P.M.), L. J. Donaldson (Chaplain), Major H. E. Gates, Major P. O. Soulis (transferred to H.Q. M.D. No. 6), Capts. C. Churchill, A. F. Haliburton, L. L. Harrison, Lieuts. O. A. M. Wilson, G. B. Isnor, W. J. O'Connell, J. E. Rutledge, A. H. Thomson, Leo Esther, G. W. Carmichael, W. E. Forsythe, C. R. Hoben, H. C. Frame, P. L. Whitman, D. A. Forsythe, R. M. Fielding, F. A. Grant, W. E. Stewart, E. K. Fielding, H. H. Miller, W. Mitchell, A. J. Haliburton, C. H. Crosby, F. S. Thomson.

The Department of Militia and Defence at first ruled that no officer or man of the Fortress could proceed Overseas, as his services were required here and he could not be spared. Later on this ruling was somewhat modified and officers and men were relieved as soon as they could be replaced by new men and permitted to join various Units. Many, however, were not accorded this privilege, much to their chagrin.

Six hundred and twenty-five men and the following officers were permitted to go Overseas at various times and with various Units and branches of the service, taking any chance that offered rather than remain at home:

Lieut.-Col. E. V. Hogan, Major G. H. Maxwell, Major J. L. MacKinnon (now Lieut.-Colonel), Major A. N. Jones, Capts. L. N. Seaman, E. L. Miller, S. C. Oland, G. M. Brew, F. S. B irns, G. B. Oland, G. A. Medcalf, P. B. Stairs, Lieuts. J. R. Curry, W. M. Ray, F. B. Sharp, G. A. Gaherty, R. W. Churchill, D. J. Maxwell, E. P. Flowers, D. A. Guildford, E. A. Bell, H. R. D. Lacon, R. F. B. Campbell, T. DeW. Farquhar, H. M. Stairs, E. S. Thomson, F. H. Palmer, R. P. Freeman, C. H. Coll, J. D. Smith, W. P. Potter, F. G. Hayden, H. W. L. Doane, W. M. Marshall, A. G. Wooten, H. St. G. S. DeCarteret, E. G. Dickie, A. E. Horne, R. G. Crosby, F. M. Blackett, R G. McAloney, W. R. Harris, M. B. Archibald, H. B. Bell, T. H. Whelpley, O. R. Crowell.

And from the Reserve of Officers, Lieut.-Col. H. Flowers and Major Allister Fraser, M.C. Of these Major G. H. Maxwell,

OFFICERS OF THE 1ST REGIMENT, C.G.A.

Capt. Philip B. Stairs, Lieuts. E. G. Dickie and R. G. MacAloney made the supreme sacrifice.

It is impossible to give a list of the many non-commissioned officers and men who were a credit to their Regiment on the fields of Flanders. Their records appear with the records of the Units in which they served.

It is supposed by many that the troops of the Garrison lived in comparative luxury, whereas the contrary was the case. Many hardships were undergone and, apart from the fact that the Hun raiders gave Halifax a wide berth, knowing that an attack would mean a waste of ammunition, which could not be replaced this side of Zeebrugge, conditions generally were often not so good as in France, owing to the severity of our climate. The casements in which the men were supposed to be quartered in time of war were entirely unfit for occupation as, owing to long disuse, they were in a very damp and unsanitary condition. The Unit was, therefore, placed under canvas, and it was late in December before any attempt was made to provide proper and suitable winter quarters. Owing to a fine distinction made between the Militia and Overseas forces, which only an army man can understand, the men were not provided with a full kit, even boots being denied them until many of them were actually barefoot. Underclothing and other necessaries had to be purchased by the men themselves, until at last the responsible authorities awakened to the fact that there was a real war on.

About August 16, 1914, the first Canadian Contingent commenced mobilizing at Valcartier, and orders were received calling for volunteers from the Garrison. The 1st C.A. were to provide one officer and twenty-five other ranks. Capt. George M. Brew proceeded to Valcartier with the draft, and on arrival was told he was not wanted and ordered to return to Halifax. This officer was so disappointed that he resigned his commission and travelled to England at his own expense, where he joined a Unit of the Imperial artillery and served with it during the greater part of the War.

In September, 1914, it was considered unnecessary to keep the Units on garrison duty at full strength, and a reduction was proposed. The naval authorities, however, insisted that a fully garrisoned fortress was necessary as a protection for the Naval Base.

FIRST REGIMENT CANADIAN GARRISON ARTILLERY

and no reduction was made. Later on the artillery forces were increased. All of which shows the importance placed on the Fortress by the Imperial authorities during war time.

From time to time the Commanding Officer offered the services of the Unit for Overseas, and asked permission to form Batteries of heavy and field artillery, but without result. Small detachments were allowed to volunteer as emergencies arose, such as artillery Units being short of men, on account of casualties occurring, while passing through Halifax, and then only on condition that men were found to replace them. It was not until 1917 that permission was given to form an ammunition column, and immediately on its completion a second one.

Much might be written of happenings during the war period which, while of interest to the officers, non-commissioned officers and men, were all in the day's work and of no historical value. It is sufficient to say that this Unit with the other Units of the Garrison performed their duties well and satisfactorily.

CHAPTER XXXIII.

THE 11th BRIGADE, C.F.A., AND COMPOSITE ARTILLERY COMPANY.

THE 11th Brigade was the junior Artillery Brigade of the 6th Military District. It comprised in addition to the Headquarters Staff, the 27th (Digby) Battery, the 28th (Pictou) Battery and the 29th (Yarmouth) Battery. Although the Brigade was not ordered out on active service, it contributed possibly more than its original strength in personnel to the prosecution of the Great War. Almost the first day of the War the Commanding Officer (Lieut.-Col. T. M. Seeley, of Yarmouth, N.S.) wired the offer of services to headquarters and the Battery officers busied themselves with looking to the details of organization.

Capt. F. W. Pickles, O.C. 29th Battery (Yarmouth), joined the 17th Battery of Sydney, one of the first Units on the march, with a detachment of eighteen non-commissioned officers and men from his Battery. Subsequently every artillery Unit and many of the Infantry Battalions had on their strength representatives of the 11th Brigade. This was made possible largely by the untiring efforts of a few senior officers, who for some good reason or other, were unable to proceed Overseas. Prominent among these were Majors H. S. Hamilton, of Pictou; D. C. McKay, of Digby, and A. K. Van Horne, of Yarmouth.

The services of the officers of the 11th Brigade, summarily put, were: Lieut.-Col. T. M. Seeley, O.C., was successful in organizing the 23rd Battery, C.E.F.; a Company for guard duty at Barrington Passage, Radio Station, and a Company in the 112th Battalion,

THE 11th BRIGADE, C.F.A.

C.E.F., under Colonel Tremaine, with which the latter crossed the Atlantic. Capt. A. A. Durkee, Adjutant of the Brigade, organized at Valcartier the first Ammunition Unit in the C.E.F., and proceeded Overseas with the First Contingent. He was early at the Front, and was promoted to Major and Lieut.-Colonel, and commanded, in turn, a Brigade Ammunition Column, a Battery, and a Brigade of Artillery. He was mentioned in dispatches and was awarded the D.S.O. Lieut.-Col. Durkee is also a South African War veteran. Capt. V. F. Connor, C.A.M.C., was on duty through the greater part of the War, and rendered valuable service at the time of the great explosion in Halifax, December, 1917.

The 27th Battery contributed to the C.E.F. Capt. Glidden Campbell, of Weymouth, who went over with the 85th Battalion, and who was awarded the M.C.; Lieuts. C. D. Shreve, M.C., killed in action in the artillery; K. V. Schurman and H. A. Marshall.

The 28th Battery had to its credit in the C.E.F., Major J. K. McKay, of Pictou, who went over in command of the 23rd Battery, C.E.F. He commanded a Battery and a Brigade of Artillery at the Front, being latterly promoted to the rank of Lieut.-Colonel. He was severely wounded and received the D.S.O. From the 28th, Lieuts. C. E. Churchill, H. P. MacKeen, J. E. Read, J. D. Hickman, H. P. MacKenzie, and possibly others, entered the C.E.F. Capt. V. C. Johnson, Corps Reserve, was Overseas.

The 29th Battery furnished (in addition to Adjutant Durkee, already mentioned) Capt. F. W. Pickles, who commanded a section of a Divisional Ammunition Column at the Front; Lieut. Ralph P. Harding, who rose to the command of a Battery, with the rank of Major, and returned with the M.C. and the D.S.O.; Lieuts. W. Arthur Porter, G. St. C. A. Perrin, E. J. Vickery, G. O. Rogers, E. J. Stekelin, who became Major; H. E. Crowell, who became Major; S. C. Hood, Jr., who became Captain, and M. B. Davis. The 29th Battery claims the honor of having had in its membership at one time Brig.-General W. O. H. Dodds, C.M.G., D.S.O., now of Montreal.

COMPOSITE ARTILLERY COMPANY

IN April, 1915, detachments from the 27th Battery (Digby) and the 29th Battery (Yarmouth) and No. 1 Siege Company (Mahone), were assembled at Yarmouth, under Lieut.-Col. T. M. Seeley, for preliminary training, and in May following proceeded to Barrington Passage for guard duty at the Radio Station. Among their duties was the construction of a road three miles long through a very difficult country. Practically the whole strength of this Company transferred to Overseas Units. Officers, in addition to the O.C.: Capt. W. T. Ernst, and Lieut. C. Melvin.

CHAPTER XXXIV.

THE 63rd REGIMENT HALIFAX RIFLES.

THE 63rd Regiment, Halifax Rifles, was first organized as a Regiment in 1860, under the title of "The Halifax Volunteer Battalion." The Volunteer Companies which then composed the Regiment had previously been acting as independent bodies. The first Colonel was Sir Willian Fenwick Williams, of Kars, and on March 16, 1860, Capt. William Chearnley (late of H.M. 8th King's Regiment of Foot), who was in command of the Chebucto Greys, was by an order from Adjutant-General's Office appointed Captain Commanding the Halifax Volunteer Battalion. This was the official date of the organization of the Unit, better known as the 63rd Halifax Rifles.

The Companies comprising the Regiment at its formation were the Scottish Rifles, Chebucto Greys, Mayflower Rifles, Halifax Rifles, Irish Rifles, and Dartmouth Rifles. In 1862 the Dartmouth Engineers joined the Regiment, which mustered seven Companies.

On November 10, 1862, the Halifax City Council presented the Regiment with its first set of colors. The presentation was made by the wife of the Mayor, Mrs. P. C. Hill. On the same date, Lady Mulgrave, wife of the Governor of Nova Scotia, in the name of the ladies of the City of Halifax, presented the Regiment with a silver bugle, which was to be shot for each year. This bugle is still in the possession of the Regiment.

In January, 1865, Captain Chearnley was appointed Lieut.-Colonel and the Battalion reorganized, two of the Companies, the Irish Rifles and Dartmouth Engineers, disbanding. The Halifax Rifles, which was double strength, took the place of the Irish Rifles—the muster now being six Companies. This Regiment had its first call for service in 1866, doing garrison duty during the alarm caused by the Fenian Raids into Canada. The service lasted from June 6th to July 31st.

NOVA SCOTIA'S PART IN THE GREAT WAR

In 1868 the Regiment was transferred from the Volunteer Force to the Active Militia, and was officially designated as the Halifax Volunteer Battalion of Rifles, and on May 13, 1870, the Militia Department having been regularly organized, the name changed to the 63rd Battalion of Rifles, and later to 63rd Regiment, Halifax Rifles, which name it retained up to and during the late Great War.

Successive Commanding Officers were as follows: Lieut.-Col. Chearnley, 1865 to 1871; Lieut.-Col. Andrew MacKinlay, 1871 to 1872; Lieut.-Colonel Pallister, 1872 to 1879; Lieut.-Col. J. W. Mackintosh, 1879 to 1890; Lieut.-Col. J. D. Walsh, 1890 to 1892; Lieut.-Col. T. J. Egan, 1892 to 1898; Lieut.-Col. John Crane, 1898 to 1903; Lieut.-Col. J. T. Twining, 1903 to 1908; Lieut.-Col. C. A. Gunning, 1908 to 1913; Lieut.-Col. I. W. Vidito, 1913 to 1917; Lieut.-Col. C. A. Mumford, 1917 until demobilized 1918.

The 63rd furnished 109 officers and men for service during the North-West Rebellion. Major Walsh was in command, with Capts. Hechler, Cunningham and Fortune and Lieutenants Silver, James, Twining, McKie, Fletcher and Fiske. Captain Corbin was appointed Quartermaster of the Provisional Battalion. They entrained for the West on April 4, 1885, and returned to Halifax and rejoined their Unit July 24 of the same year. The Regiment also furnished sixty-one officers, non-commissioned officers and men for service in the South African War.

On the declaration of the Great War, August 4, 1914, the 63rd Regiment, Halifax Rifles was ordered out for service in defence of the Fortress of Halifax. One hundred men under the command of Capt. H. N. Clarke, with Capt. J. W. Logan, Lieut. E. R. Dennis and Lieut. F. H. M. Jones, proceeded at once to Wellington Barracks, and the remainder of the Unit was at once mobilized and proceeded under command to the various war stations assigned to it.

By August 5, 1914, the mobilization of the Unit being completed, the Regiment paraded in full strength under Lieut.-Col. I. W. Vidito, with Major W. E. Thompson Second in Command, and Capt. D. R. Turnbull, Adjutant, and proceeded to their new quarters, Wellington Barracks, where the Composite Company under Capt. H. N. Clarke was absorbed, the officers and men rejoining their old Companies.

THE 63rd REGIMENT, HALIFAX RIFLES

On August 12th "B" Company proceeded to McNab's Island under the command of Capt. C. A. Mumford, with Lieuts. C. N. Bennett and W. E. Doane. "D" Company, under Capt. H. F. Adams and Lieut. C. J. Roche, proceeded to York Redoubt. On August 18th "G" and "H" Companies proceeded to the Eastern Camp Site, Dartmouth. These two Companies were under the command of Major W. H. Conrod. "G" Company (Capt. E. A. Vossnack, Lieuts. G. S. Kinley and G. C. Sircom) occupied York Farm; "H" Company (Capt. H. N. Clarke and Lieuts. E. C. Phinney and J. W. Grant) occupied Kuhn's Farm. On August 25th "D" Company under Capt. H. F. Adams moved from York Redoubt to Camperdown, and on the same date "A" Company (Capt. F. C. Kingdon, Lieut. R. C. McDonald); "C" Company (Capt. H. G. DeWolfe, Lieut. H. J. Stech) and "F" Company (Capt. J. W. Logan, Lieuts. G. M. Sylvester and F. H. Jones) moved to McNab's Island. "E" Company (Capt. E. K. McKay, Lieuts. O. Vossnack and E. R. Dennis) moved to Lawlor's Island. The last four Companies were under the command of Major W. E. Thompson. On August 30th headquarters and regimental details moved to McNab's Island.

Immediately on arrival at their stations each Company started the work of digging trenches, placing wire entanglements, constructing blockhouses, dugouts, etc. The men were driven at top speed at this work, officers and men working all day as well as doing picquet duty at night.

During the early days of the War H.M. ship *Suffolk,* then engaged in hunting for the enemy cruiser *Karlsruhe,* called at Halifax in urgent need of coal, and was coaled in record time by the 63rd Regiment.

On August 22nd the first Overseas draft was called for and twenty-four non-commissioned officers and men under command of Lieuts. A. F. Major and G. L. Stairs, proceeded to Valcartier Camp. On November 25, 1914, forty-eight non-commissioned officers and men were transferred to the 25th Battalion, C.E.F., which was then being organized, and on December 6th Major W. H. Conrod, Lieuts. L. N. B. Bullock, G. C. Sircom and J. A. Grant were transferred to that Battalion.

Major W. E. Thompson was called in by Headquarters Military District No. 6 in December, 1914, to take over the work of Inspector of Outposts and Detachments throughout the district, with the rank of Lieut.-Colonel.

On May 20, 1915, Capt. Wm. Taylor, Lieuts. C. J. Roche and J. A. Watters, with thirty-three other ranks proceeded to Jamaica on military duty. On August 13, 1915, thirty-six other ranks were transferred to the 40th Battalion, then in training at Valcartier. In September, 1915, an Overseas Company was formed to which officers and men given permission to go Overseas were attached for training. From this time, all drafts from the 63rd for Overseas Units were taken from this Company.

An Overseas draft of 100 other ranks with Lieuts. W. D. Simpson, H. D. Hilton and C. D. Llwyd were struck off the strength of the 63rd Regiment on February 25, 1916.

Major H. F. Adams was appointed Officer Commanding Discharge Depot, Halifax, from July 1, 1916. A draft of eighty-eight other ranks under command of Lieuts. H. A. Creighton and Benj. Taylor embarked for Overseas on July 15, 1916. The Regiment was inspected by Field-Marshall H.R.H. Duke of Connaught on August 24, 1916.

The 63rd was placed on a four Company basis from November 1, 1917. The Company officers were: "A" Company, Capt. F. C. Kingdon, Lieuts. J. A. Watters, H. V. Wier, G. W. Churchill, H. S. Holloway. "B" Company, Capts. H. J. Steck, D. W. Kennedy, Lieuts. F. A. Taylor, C. S. Innes, H. R. McCaughin, G. R. Forbes. "C" Company, Capts. E. Ricketts, G. S. Kinley, Lieuts. T. L. Parkman, J. E. Milsom, C. N. Innes. "D" Company, Capts. O. F. Vossnack, W. Taylor, Lieuts. E. G. McMinn, W. R. R. Tayler, H. H. Irwin.

Lieut.-Col. I. W. Vidito was transferred to the Reserve of Officers on July 1, 1917, and was succeeded in the command of the Regiment by Lieut.-Col. C. A. Mumford. On the morning of December 6, 1917, five officers and 143 other ranks were detailed for relief work following the explosion at Halifax. On April 16, 1918, the 6th Battalion Canadian Garrison Regiment was authorized, and in May the 63rd Regiment was relieved from duty. The following named officers were transferred to the 6th Battalion: Lieut.-Col.

THE 63rd REGIMENT, HALIFAX RIFLES

C. A. Mumford, Capts. E. Ricketts, H. J. Steck, E. K. McKay, G. S. Kinley, Lieuts. H. V. Wier, J. A. Watters, E. G. McMinn, G. W. Churchill, J. E. Milsom, H. R. McCoughin, G. R. Forbes, R. J. Colwell.

The undermentioned officers were transferred to the 1st Nova Scotia Depot Battalion: Lieuts. H. A. Wilson, W. R. R. Tayler, H. S. Holloway, Majors A. R. McCleave and H. N. Clarke, Capts. F. C. Kingdon, J. D. Monoghan and Lieut. T. Parkman were relieved from active service.

On the organization of the First Canadian Contingent the Regiment volunteered for service Overseas, but much to the disappointment of all ranks had to continue its allotted duties in the defence of the Fortress of Halifax. Owing to the heavy demands on the Ordnance Department for clothing and equipment needed by troops preparing for embarkation the requirements of troops on Home Service could not be met until late in 1914, and for some time clothing was patched with flour sacks or any other material available, and worn out soles of boots were reinforced with shingles. In spite of all discouragements the 63rd faithfully performed the tasks assigned it, and when at last it was permitted to send drafts Overseas it became the ambition of all ranks to obtain a transfer to the Overseas Company. Altogether the Regiment supplied 70 officers and 815 other ranks for service at the Front.

The following is a list of officers who served with the Regiment at various times during the War. Those who went Overseas are marked *: *Lieut. A. B. Anderson; Capt. H. F. Adams (now Lieut.-Col. R. O.); *Lieut. A. A. Allenback; *Lieut. W. B. Arthur; *Lieut. H. P. Bell (Captain C.E.F.); *Lieut. C. W. Bennett (killed in action); *Lieut. L. N. B. Bullock (D.S.O. and Bar— Lieut.-Colonel C.E.F.); *Lieut. F. A. Brewster (M.C.); *Lieut. G. A. Campbell (killed in action); *Major W. H. Conrod; *Major H. N. Clarke; Lieut. J. H. Congdon; Lieut. G. W. Churchill; *Lieut. W. L. Coleman; Lieut. H. J. Crosskill; *Lieut. R. J. Colwell; *Lieut. T. F. Campbell; *Lieut. C. H. Colwell; *Lieut. A. H. Creighton; *Lieut. H. A. Creighton; *Lieut. B. Currie (Captain C.E.F.); Capt. H. G. DeWolf; Lieut. W. H. Dennis; *Lieut. E. R. Dennis (M.C., killed in action); *Major F. W. W. Doane; *Lieut. H. W. L. Doane; *Lieut. W. E. E. Doane (killed in action); *Lieut. S. Downer; *Lieut. J. S. Davie (M.C., Major C.E.F.); Lieut. R. F. Davison; *Lieut. A. C. Delacroix; *Lieut. E. R. Eddy; Lieut. R. G. Forbes; *Lieut. W. G. Foster (killed in action); *Lieut. P. W. Freeman; Lieut. L. A. Gastonquay; *Lieut. G. H. Gillis (D.F.C., Captain C.E.F.); *Lieut. J. A. Grant; *Lieut. W. P. Grant; *Lieut. R. J. Harris (died); *Lieut. J. A. Harris; *Lieut. H. E. Hilton (killed in action); *Lieut. H. S. Holloway; *Lieut. W. A. Hendry; *Lieut. E. J. Hallett (M.C.); *Lieut. E. A. Hartling; Lieut. H. H. Irwin; *Lieut. C. S. Innes; *Lieut. Colin Innes; *Lieut. F. H. Jones (M.C.); Capt. R. J. Huston; *Lieut. A. E. Jubien; Capt. F. C. Kingdon; *Lieut. A. L. A. Kane; Lieut. D. W. Kennedy; Lieut. A. W. Kidner; *Lieut. G. S. Kinley (Captain C.E.F.); *Lieut. G. H. Keeler (M.C.); Lieut. J. H. LeBlanc; *Lieut. C. D. Llwyd (M.C., killed in action); *Major J. W. Logan; *Lieut. G. R. Leslie; *Lieut. O. W. Lingham; *Lieut. A T. Lewis (M.C., Captain C.E.F.); *Lieut. A. F. Major (killed in action); Lieut J. E. Milson; Capt. R. A. Milson; Lieut.-Col. C. A. Mumford; Lieut. J. D. Monaghan; Capt. A. R. McCleave; Capt. E. K. McKay; *Lieut. R. C. McDonald; Lieut.-Col. J. W. McMillan (Chaplain); *Lieut. Geo. O. McDonald (drowned); Lieut. E. J. McMinn; Lieut. H. R. McCoughin; *Lieut. A. T. McDonald (Major C.E.F.); Lieut. T. L. Parkman; *Lieut. P. R. Phillips (M.C.); *Lieut. E. C. Phinney (Lieut.-Col. C.E.F.); *Lieut. G. C. Pickford; Capt. E. Ricketts; *Lieut. C. Roche (killed in action); Lieut. G. B. Robertson; *Lieut. W. M. Rogers; *Lieut. J. S. Roy; *Lieut. C. E. Scarfe; *Lieut. W. D. Simpson; *Lieut. G. C. Sircom; *Lieut. W. J. Stairs; *Lieut. G. L. Stairs (killed in action); Lieut. H. J. Stech; *Lieut. E. S. Smith; *Lieut. G. M. Sylvester (killed in action); *Lieut. B. A. Taylor (killed in action); *Major W. E. Thompson (Colonel D.O.C., Military District No. 6); Capt. W. Taylor, Lieut. J. F. Taylor; Lieut. F. A. Taylor; Capt. D. R. Turnbull; *Lieut. W. R. R. Tayler, Lieut.-Col. I. W. Vidito; Capt. E. A. Vossnack; Capt. O. F. Vossnack; Lieut. J. A. Watters; Lieut. H. V. Wier; *Lieut. H. A. Wilson; Lieut. P. J. Webb; Lieut. R. E. Wellard; Lieut. H. H. Westbrooke; Lieut. A. B. West.

CHAPTER XXXV.

THE 66th REGIMENT PRINCESS LOUISE FUSILIERS.

FOLLOWING Great Britain's declaration of war against Germany on August 4, 1914, the 66th Regiment, Princess Louise Fusiliers, immediately paraded at the Halifax Armories and the same evening sent an advanced party of four officers and one hundred other ranks in command of Capt. D. S. Bauld to Wellington Barracks, where the balance of the Unit under its Commanding Officer, Lieut.-Col. H. L. Chipman, followed, and established its headquarters on August 7, 1914. Preparations were immediately made to place the 66th Regiment on a war footing, and excitement ran high because it was felt by all ranks that, this being one of the oldest Units in the Province, the 66th Regiment would be among the first to see real service; but the fact that it was never sent Overseas caused in the later years of the War a feeling of bitter disappointment, particularly among those who were destined to carry on tame and unattractive garrison duty throughout the War.

LIEUT.-COL. A. KING.

The "Halifax Defence Scheme" unfortunately condemned it to this uninteresting work, and although the Regiment repeatedly volunteered for service Overseas its requests were ignored. The defence of Halifax was altogether a thankless task, and the often repeated assurance that the Regiment was performing the duties required of it brought little consolation to the officers and men whose sole ambition was to join their comrades in the Field.

NOVA SCOTIA'S PART IN THE GREAT WAR

The personnel of the officers who turned out with the Regiment at the time of the declaration of war was as follows:—

Lieut.-Col. H. L. Chipman.........Officer Commanding.
Major and Bt. Lieut.-Col. A. King..Senior Major.
Major R. B. Simmonds.............Junior Major and Acting Adjutant.
Capt. F. L. Stephen................Acting Quartermaster.
Lieut.-Col. M. A. Curry...........Medical Officer.
Lieut.-Col. W. J. Armitage........Chaplain.
Major R. H. Humphrey............Paymaster.

Company Officers.
Capts. A. W. Weston, G. W. Murray, J. McFatridge, D. S. Bauld, H. H. Bligh, R. W. Frost, C. E. Dowden, J. R. Glazbrook; Lieuts. W. B. Medcalfe, G. W. Stairs, G. H. Liddell, C. A. Fages, J. C. Stairs, J. R. Simmonds, G. Dwyer, W. C. Borrett, J. H. Crosskill, B. H. Smith, R. F. Studd, F. H. Marr, F. R. Heuston, D. Stairs, G. E. Creighton, L. E. VanBuskirk.

Later two officers reported for duty from the Corps Reserve, and during the period of the War twenty-five additional officers were granted commissions in the Regiment. The Regiment at the outbreak of the War was on an eight Company basis, and it was not until December 6, 1915, that the double Company system was adopted.

The first move of importance was the sending of a detachment, on August 11, 1914, of four Companies, B, E, F and G, and the Regimental Machine Gun Section, all under command of Major R. B. Simmonds, to Chain and Long Lakes, with instructions to prepare a system of trenches, blockhouses, etc., and arrange generally for the defence of Halifax City from any possible attack from the West. This force was designated the "Chain Lakes Detachment," and with interchanges of officers and other ranks remained on duty at this post until January 15, 1917, when it proceeded to York Redoubt.

The headquarters of the Regiment was moved from Wellington Barracks to York Redoubt on August 29, 1914, and remained there until the demobilization of the Unit on May 1, 1918. In January, 1915, Lieut.-Colonel Chipman was seconded from the Regiment and took over command of the Composite Battalion, which had been organized for garrison duty, and Lieut.-Col. A. King was gazetted O.C 66th Regiment, and continued so until the Unit was relieved from active service in May, 1918.

THE 66th REGIMENT PRINCESS LOUISE FUSILIERS

About December 1, 1915, authority was granted for the Regiment to organize a reinforcing draft, five officers and two hundred and fifty other ranks. The South Barracks on Sackville Street were immediately taken over, and recruiting and organization work in connection with the draft was proceeded with. The draft finally sailed for England on January 22, 1916. This draft was commanded by Capt. R. F. Studd, the other officers accompanying it being Lieuts. T. F. Morrison, W. K. Fraser, L. J. Atkinson, and W. S. Fielding.

During the War the 66th Regiment was inspected by His Royal Highness the Duke of Connaught, His Excellency the Duke of Devonshire, Major-General Gwatkin, Chief of the Canadian General Staff, Major-General Lessard, Inspector-General of Eastern Canada, and by many other distinguished soldiers, and was at all times most highly complimented on its excellent state of efficiency.

This Unit played a prominent part in the relief work following the great explosion of December 6, 1917, which devastated a large portion of the City of Halifax, caused the loss of some seventeen hundred lives and entailed untold suffering among so many families for months following. Lieut.-Col. R. B. Simmonds was in command of all military and naval relief parties engaged in rescue work in the devastated area, and later was placed in charge of a committee to procure relief for dependants of all men who were serving at home or Overseas. It was the duty of this committee to find food, clothing and shelter for the families of all soldiers who had suffered in the explosion. A large number of mechanics were placed under the direction of this committee and the work of relief practically completed by May 1, 1918.

LIEUT.-COL. R. B. SIMMONDS.

That the duties of this committee were all carried out it might be mentioned that it effected practically permanent repairs to over one hundred and sixty houses, besides looking after the needs of many suffering families, for which it was complimented by the Minister of Militia and received the thanks of the Halifax Relief Commission.

Notwithstanding that the Regiment was kept in Canada, it was, nevertheless, called upon to perform various and arduous duties at all times. That the Regiment also assisted in a very tangible way in winning the War is proved by the fact that the 66th Regiment, Princess Louise Fusiliers sent fifty-four officers and eight hundred and fifty men to swell the ranks of various Overseas Units of the Canadian Expeditionary Force, a large number of whom are now sleeping their last sleep in the fields of Flanders, having upheld the honor of their Regiment and proved their belief in its motto, "Fideliter."

CHAPTER XXXVI.

94th VICTORIA REGIMENT, ARGYLL HIGHLANDERS.

MUCH has been written of what was done by Canadian Units in France and Belgium, but little has been said of the Units compelled to remain on home service, which had to content themselves with performing garrison duties and supplying reinforcements to the army in the Field.

The 94th Victoria Regiment, Argyll Highlanders, with Headquarters at Baddeck, Cape Breton, was at the commencement of hostilities perhaps the most distinctively Highland Battalion in the forces of the Empire, inasmuch as the Gaelic language was the mother tongue of eighty per cent. of its personnel. As a rural Battalion it is recognized as having sent more officers and men Overseas than any other similar Unit in Eastern Canada. All its original members, excepting those over age or physically unfit, were transferred to C.E.F. Units; many of them paid the supreme sacrifice, and a number of them were decorated for distinguished service.

At 9.30 a.m., August 4, 1914, the Officer Commanding the Battalion, Lieut.-Col. J. D. McRae, received mobilization orders. The marching-out strength, including the Canso detachment, was 377 all ranks. The eight Companies were commanded by the officers, and proceeded to their different stations, on the dates named below:

"A" Co., Capt. D. P. McRae, Whitney Pier, Sydney ....7th Aug.
"B" Co., Capt. D. A. McRae, Marconi Towers, Glace Bay....6th "
"C" Co., Capt. A. J. McNeil, North Sydney.................5th "
"D" Co., Capt. M. A. McLeod, Marconi Towers, Glace Bay..6th "
"E" Co., Capt. M. D. McKeigan, Louisburg..................5th "
"F" Co., Capt. R. Y. McKenzie, Lloyd's Cove, Sydney Mines..7th "
"G" Co., Capt. J. G. Johnstone, Canso......................5th "
"H" Co., Capt. W. D. McKenzie, Sydney ....7th "
Regimental Staff to Headquarters, 33 Charlotte St., Sydney...7th "

Regimental Staff.

Lieut.-Col. J. D. McRae........,Officer Commanding.
Major J. S. McLean............Second in Command.
Major A. D. McRae............Junior Major.
Capt. W. G. McRae............ Adjutant.
Lieut. A. J. McInnis............Instructor of Musketry.
Lieut. G. M. McNeil............Signalling Officer.
Major M. A. J. McDonald......Quartermaster.
Major Dan McDonald..........Medical Officer.
Capt. M. H. Morrison..........Paymaster.

Lieutenants.

"A" Co., P. W. Anderson and J. A. Kiley.
"B" Co., W. W. Nicholson and F. J. McCharles.
"C" Co., A. J. McDonald and J. A. McDonald.
"D" Co., N. J. McDonald and A. N. McKenzie.
"E" Co., J. L. McKinnon and D. McKenzie.
"F" Co., D. McKinnon and D. McKenzie.
"G" Co., K. L. McKay and J. McIsaac.
"H" Co., A. McKinnon and J. D. McRae.

Captain C. C. McIntosh was Chaplain of the Unit, but was not called out for service with it.

During the years 1914 to 1918 the following officers, sixty in all, were transferred to C.E.F. Units:

Majors.
M. W. Morrison and J. G. Johnstone.

Captains.

D. A. McRae.	J. McIsaac.	W. W. Nicholson.
K. L. McKay.	W. G. McRae.	D. McKinnon.
M. D. McKeigan.		A. McKinnon.

Lieutenants.

A. J. McInnis.	J. A. McKinnon.	S. D. Morrison.
G. M. McNiel.	J. A. Rankin.	C. W. Sutherland.
J. D. McIntyre.	C. Campbell.	D. N. McDonald.
W. J. Brothers.	A. W. McLean.	W. H. McConell.
C. McDermid.	W. A. Livingstone.	B. Campbell.
G. B. Morley.	T. D. A. Purves.	F. J. McCharles.
J. W. Maddin.	R. A. Pertus.	J. A. Holland.
J. H. McIvor.	G. D. Crowell.	M. W. McKinnon.
C. F. Gallant.	C. R. McKenzie.	H. C. Verner.
A. E. Wilcox.	W. E. Beaton.	T. C. King.
S. Schoefield.	M. J. Dryden.	R. M. McDonald.
J. A. McDonald.	Alex. McDonald.	M. J. McRae.
David Neil.	A. H. Walker.	A. S. Henry.
P. W. Anderson.	C. Holland.	D. S. Carey.
J. D. McNiel.	R. Flemming.	J. B. Fraser.
D. H. McKenzie.	W. R. McAskill.	Theodore Chisholm.
L. G. McCorrison.	A. M. Fraser.	

94th VICTORIA REGIMENT, ARGYLL HIGHLANDERS

From a total of 344 other ranks who came out with the Battalion at the commencement of the War, 311 volunteered for service Overseas. It took time to train a sufficient number of recruits to replace these men, but within six months all had been transferred to C.E.F. Units and were on their way to France. Altogether the Battalion during its period of service sent 3,632 men to the Front, and it was a difficult matter at all times to retain a sufficient number of men to perform the necessary duties.

The eight Companies of the Battalion were called upon to perform Garrison Guard and Outpost duties at important shipping points, wireless and cable stations, not only in Cape Breton but also at Canso. For defence purposes the troops at Marconi Towers, Glace Bay, Louisburg and Canso erected blockhouses and wire entanglements, built redoubts and dug trenches, in addition to carrying into effect a syllabus of training designed better to fit the men for their more strenuous work with the Expeditionary Force.

The Battalion was demobilized June 29, 1918, and the following officers were transferred to "F" Company, 6th Battalion, Canadian Garrison Regiment, who assumed the duties previously performed by the 94th:—

Capt. A. J. McNiel.

Lieutenants.

J. A. McDonald.	J. D. McRae.	Bert Campbell.
L. E. McDonald.	A. J. McDonald.	J. R. Fraser.
	Dan McKenzie.	

Major M. J. McDonald, Quartermaster, was employed as the representative of the A.D. of S. & T. in Cape Breton, and Major D. McDonald, Medical Officer, was attached to the A.D.M.S., Military District No. 6. The undermentioned officers were relieved from duty and returned to their homes:—

Lieut.-Col. A. D. McRae.
Major W. G. McRae.
Major J. Darke (attached from 4th P.E.I. Heavy Battery).
Capts. D. P. McRae, D. McKenzie, J. A. Kiley, J. L. McKinnon.
Lieuts. S. A. Reeves, J. D. Aucoin.

N.C.O.'s and men in Class 1 of the Military Service Act, and those who were willing to be transferred, were handed over to "F" Company, 6th Battalion, C.E.F., for duty in Cape Breton.

NOVA SCOTIA'S PART IN THE GREAT WAR

The following 94th officers transferred to C.E.F. Units were awarded decorations:—

Major P. W. Anderson..................Military Cross.
Major M. D. McKeigan.................French Croix de Guerre.
Capt. W. A. Livingstone................Military Cross and Bar.
Capt. G. B. Morley......................Military Cross.
Lieut. G. M. McNeil..................... Military Cross.
Lieut. W. E. Beaton.....................Military Cross.
Lieut. A. S. Henry...................... Military Cross.
Lieut. J. D. McIntyre....................Military Cross.
Lieut. A. E. Wilcox..................... Military Medal.

The following officers were killed in action or died of wounds:—

Major P. W. Anderson, M.C.
Capt. M. W. McKinnon.
Capt. W. E. Beaton, M.C.
Capt. Aubrey McKinnon.
Lieutenants A. H. Walker, W. R. McAskill, J. A. McDonald, J. H. McIvor, J. A. Holland, A. M. Fraser, R. A. Pertus.

It is impossible at the present time to obtain a nominal roll of the N.C.O.'s and men who fell on the field of honor. The list is a long one, and in many Cape Breton homes, mothers, wives, sisters and sweethearts mourn with proud resignation the lads who will not return. Neither is it possible to obtain a complete list of decorations awarded. The summary that follows has been compiled from incomplete, unofficial sources:

D.S.O. 1
M.C. 14
Bar to M.C. 2
D.C.M. 15
M.M. 79
Bar to M.M. 10
M.S.M. 4
Despatches 3
Croix de Guerre 2

The undermentioned N.C.O.'s and men obtained commissions:

Sergt. G. McL. Matheson (Major, 25th Bn.) D.S.O., M.C., M.M., Despatches.
Pte. Jas. A. Anderson (Capt., 85th Bn.).... M.C.
Corp. C. J. Oram (Lieut., 25th Bn.)........M.C.
Corp. D. A. Livingstone (Lieut., 25th Bn.)..M.M.
Corp. K. Morrison (Lieut., Can. Eng.)..... M.M. and Bar.
Pte. Thos. Toone (Lieut., Can. Eng.).........M.C., D.C.M., M.M.
C. S.-M. R. Roberts (Lieut., 25th Bn.)......D.C.M.
Pte. J. R. Burchell (Capt., 85th Bn.)........M.C. and Bar.
Pte. H. N. McNeil (Capt., 85th Bn.)........M.C.
Pte. W. V. McKinnon (Lieut., 25th Bn.)...M.M.
Pte. M. Gray (Capt., Can. Eng.)...........M.C., M.M.

94th VICTORIA REGIMENT, ARGYLL HIGHLANDERS

Under the reorganization scheme of 'the Canadian Militia the 94th Regiment is wiped off the slate and is succeeded by the 1st Battalion, Cape Breton Highlanders (85th Battalion, C.E.F.). The officers, N.C.O.'s and men of the old Regiment, who served in it for years before the fateful summer of 1914, cannot view its passing without a certain measure of sadness and regret. The spirit of comradeship that existed among all ranks encouraged them to carry on through many difficulties in years of peace and enabled them at a few hours' notice to proceed in full strength to their allotted stations, on the declaration of war.

Inspired by the Regiment's ancient motto, "Dileas d'on Bhrataich" ("True to the Flag"), every man who was physically fit, and many who were not, volunteered for service Overseas. They did their duty nobly and gave their country a full and overflowing measure of splendid service. The memory of our comrades whose mortal remains sleep in the stricken fields of France and Flanders will be held in affectionate recollection as long as life lasts. Of them the soldier poet of Nova Scotia, Dr. J. D. Logan, a sergeant of the 85th Battalion, who served with many officers and men transferred to that Unit from the 94th, writes:

> "They gave the All that men can give;
> They gave themselves that men might live,
> They are Christ's heroes. Lo, on their brows Love's diadem!
> O God of Righteous Battles, let it be well with them."

CHAPTER XXXVII.

THE COMPOSITE BATTALION.

THE Composite Battalion was formed at Halifax from Companies drawn from the Militia Regiments of Nova Scotia, New Brunswick and Prince Edward Island to replace the Royal Canadian Regiment, which was transferred to Bermuda shortly after the outbreak of hostilities.

Companies consisting of three officers and fifty-six other ranks were supplied by the 67th, 69th, 71st, 74th, 75th, 76th, 82nd and 93rd Regiments, and arrived at Halifax on September 8th and 9th, 1914, taking over at once garrison duties from the 66th Regiment, P.L.F., which proceeded to York Redoubt for outpost duty.

LIEUT.-COL. H. L. CHIPMAN.

The following guards were furnished: Quarter Guard, Wellington Barracks; Gun Wharf; King's Wharf; Lumber Yard; Station Hospital; Grain Elevator; North Ordnance; Dry Dock; Richmond Pier and Rockhead Hospital. Weekly Guards were also mounted at Fort Clarence, Fort Cambridge, Fort Ogilvie and Point Pleasant Battery.

The Battalion was commanded by Lieut.-Col. A. E. Carpenter, R.C.R., with Capt. M. E. Roscoe as Adjutant:

The Company officers were:—" A " Company (67th Regiment) —Capt. C. G. McLaughlin, later transferred to 64th Battalion, C.E.F.; Lieut. C. Rideout, 145th Battalion, C.E.F.; Lieut. C. E. Williams, 55th Battalion, C.E.F. " B " Company (69th Regiment) —Major Whitman, resigned and replaced by Capt. M. S. Parker, 112th Battalion, C.E.F.; Lieut. S. McNeil; Lieut. J. C. Willett, 165th Battalion, C.E.F. " C " Company (71st Regiment)—Capt.

THE COMPOSITE BATTALION

H. Woodbridge, 55th Battalion, C.E.F.; Lieut. C. A. Good, R.F.C.; Lieut. B. Wade, resigned and replaced by Lieut. F. Fitzpatrick, 55th Battalion, C.E.F. "D" Company (74th Regiment)—Capt. S. S. Wetmore, 55th Battalion, C.E.F.; Lieut. J. A. Sproul, resigned; Lieut. M. P. Gillis, 112th Battalion, C.E.F. "E" Company (75th Regiment)—Capt. W. L. Whitford, 25th Battalion, C.E.F.; Capt. A. Berringer, resigned; Lieut. C. C. Morash, 112th Battalion, C.E.F. "F" Company (76th Regiment)—Capt. H. Dickie, resigned and replaced by Capt. W. H. J. Moxsom, 106th Battalion, C.E.F.; Lieut. O. G. Heard, 106th Battalion, C.E.F.; Lieut. C. Major, 40th Battalion, C.E.F. "G" Company (82nd Regiment)—Major F. Boulter, later transferred to 105th Battalion, C.E.F.; Lieut. A. McLeod, 105th Battalion, C.E.F.; Lieut. G. E. Full, 40th Battalion, C.E.F. "H" Company (93rd Regiment)—Major G. R. Oulton; Capt. J. N. McDonald, 106th Battalion, C.E.F.; Lieut. D. Anderson.

In addition to the duties already enumerated, Guard was mounted over prisoners of war at the Citadel and at the Detention Barracks, Melville Island. The prisoners were German officers and men capturd on the high seas, with a sprinkling of civilians, some of whom were found on captured ships; others were residents of Canada whom it was found necessary to intern.

In March, 1915, the Interment Station at Amherst was opened, and two and one-half Companies under command of Major G. R. Oulton, with Capt. J. N. McDonald, Lieuts. Davidson and Sproul, were sent there, and were replaced by one Company from each of the following Regiments:—78th Regiment—Capt. J. A. McKenzie, later transferred to 85th Battalion, C.E.F.; Capt. J. R. Maxwell, 106th Battalion, C.E.F. 81st Regiment—Capt. E. S. Doering; Lieut. J. H. Wallace, 64th Battalion, C.E.F., killed in action; Lieut. W. W. Slack, 40th Battalion, C.E.F. 93rd Regiment—Capt. J. A. McPherson, 106th Battalion, C.E.F.; Lieut. P. Boucher, 165th Battalion, C.E.F.

Lieut. E. W. Joy reported for duty to replace Lieut. C. S. Major, transferred to 40th Battalion, and assumed the duties of Fortress Intelligence Officer. Other officers on duty were Major F. S. Heffernan (93rd), Quartermaster; Lieut. Keith Rogers (C.S.C.), Signalling Officer; and Lieut. R. Innes (81st), Musketry Instructor, afterwards O.C. 106th Battalion.

Previous to July, 1916, each Company Commander had his own account with the District Paymaster and was responsible for all payments to his officers and men. When the Battalion was recognized as a Unit it was allowed a Paymaster. Capt. H. B. Verge received the appointment and retained it until transferred to the Nova Scotia Forestry Battalion in June, 1917, when Capt. W. S. Brignell took over his duties.

The Battalion suffered considerably in the explosion of December 6, 1917, losing six men killed and 87 per cent. of the N.C.O.'s and men injured. One officer and two N.C.O.'s died in hospital from injuries received. The more serious injuries were received by men on guard at Richmond Pier, North Ordnance and Dry Dock. All the men killed, excepting one, who was killed in the barrack room, were members of these Guards. A snowstorm with high wind which raged for thirty-six hours after the explosion made the barracks almost untenable, as windows and doors were gone and no fires could be laid until the chimneys were inspected. The morale of the men was good during this period. Many N.C.O.'s and men had their families living near the barracks, a large number of whom were killed and injured.

The first draft of one hundred men from the Composite Battalion was sent Overseas in January, 1916, under command of Lieuts. W. S. Brown and O. Thorne. A second draft of fifty-six men, under command of Lieut. W. R. Clark, sailed on June 26, 1916. A number of men were transferred to the R.C.R. Base Depot from time to time and were included in Overseas drafts sent by that Unit.

When the Military Service Act came in force in 1918, 125 men in the Composite Battalion, who came under its provisions, were sent Overseas. The remainder were transferred to the 6th Battalion, Canadian Garrison Regiment. All the senior officers were transferred to their Militia Units, with the exception of Major J. E. Morse, who was transferred to the 6th Battalion, C.G.R. The junior officers were transferred to the Depot Battalion, 1st Nova Scotia Regiment, excepting Lieut. W. H. Whidden and Lieut. I. C. Banks, who were taken on the strength of No. 6 District Depot and appointed respectively O.C. Casualty Company and Discharge Section.

THE COMPOSITE BATTALION

The following officers were on duty when the Unit was disbanded:—Lieut.-Col. H. L. Chipman, Officer Commanding; Major G. R. Oulton, Second in Command; Major E. K. Eaton, R.C.R., Adjutant; Lieut. W. B. Arthur, Assistant Adjutant; Capt. W. W. Brignell, Paymaster; Major F. S. Heffernan, Quartermaster; Major D. G. Mossmain, O.C. "A" Company; Major F. Boulter, O.C. "B" Company; Major J. E. Morse, O.C. "C" Company; Capt. G. L. Whidden, O.C. "D" Company; Capt. S. L. McNiel, Lieut. W. L. Coleman, Lieut. R. J. Colwell, Lieut. H. C. Crosby, Lieut. C. McLellan, Lieut. J. R. Campbell, Lieut. W. E. Mitchell, Lieut. W. H. Whidden, Lieut. I. C. Banks.

Other officers who had served with the Battalion in 1916 and 1917 were as follows:—Lieut. C. A. Vaughan, later transferred to 106th and resigned; Capt. A. Stirling, 145th; Lieut. W. Ross, 38th Battalion; Lieut. S. Rogers, R.C.R.; Lieut. St. C. Stayner, unattached; Lieut. S. Bradford, R.F.C.; Lieut. H. F. Arthur, R.N.A.S.; Lieut. R. Asher, R.F.C.

The following officers of the R.C.R. also served: As Adjutant, Lieut. G. L. P. Grant Suttie, who replaced Capt. M. E. Roscoe, transferred to the 219th Battalion, being later relieved by Capt. V. W. S. Heron, who in turn was relieved by Major Eaton.

CHAPTER XXXVIII.

THE 1st DEPOT BATTALION NOVA SCOTIA REGIMENT.

THIS Unit was authorized on September 25, 1917, for the purpose of looking after the draftees under the Military Service Act. Lieut.-Col. H. Flowers, formerly of the 64th and 25th Battalions, C.E.F., was appointed to command, with Lieut.-Col. D. S. Bauld, 25th, Second in Command. The original officers of this Unit were all officers with service at the Front in France, invalided home, and unable to return on account of various disabilities. It was due to this experience that they were able to handle this Unit, which eventually reached the proportions of a Brigade with credit to the Province of Nova Scotia and themselves.

LIEUT.-COL. H. FLOWERS.

The strength of a Battalion is roughly 1,000 all ranks, and at times the strength of the 1st Depot Battalion, Nova Scotia Regiment, reached over 5,000.

The original senior officers were:

    Major F. L. Stephens...................... 64th and 14th.
    Major O. G. Heard........................ 106th and 8-th.
    Major W. McPherson..................... 112th and 87th.
    Major G. L. Mott.......................... 64th and 13th.
    Major Stanley............................. C.F.A.

Later the following were attached:

    Major Inman.. 105th.
    Major W. Grant.. 25th.
    Lieut.-Col. N. H. Parsons............................ 246th.
    Adjutant, Captain Simpson.......................... 85th.
    Paymaster, Capt Geo. Farish....................... 25th.
    Quartermaster, Capt. W. St.C. Ingraham........... 25th.

THE 1st DEPOT BATTALION, NOVA SCOTIA REGIMENT

From time to time new officers who had not seen Overseas service were attached, and these were sent Overseas with drafts as soon as they could be gotten ready. The real work of the Unit commenced about February 1, 1918, because quarters for mobilization were not available earlier, on account of the destruction of property caused by the Halifax explosion in December, 1917. The work was carried on at the Armories, Halifax, under most trying conditions. "A" Company was quartered at Charlottetown to take care of the Prince Edward Island draftees, and remained there doing this work until demobilized. "B" Company was moved to Amherst early in March, 1918, remaining there until May 16th, when it joined the Battalion at Aldershot, Nova Scotia, the Companies in barracks at Halifax having moved to Aldershot on May 13th.

From that date the work of the Unit was extremely strenuous. Draftees were ordered in at the rate of 250 daily, and the Camp soon assumed the appearance of a Brigade. The men were medically examined, inoculated, vaccinated, and their dental troubles administered to. They were clothed, trained, and when they had become sufficiently expert to form fours, were equipped and sent to England to complete the training so well begun here.

This Unit dealt with all men coming under the Military Service Act, who were either ordered to report or were arrested for some default under the Act, and in this way about 14,000 men passed through the files of the Unit. Of course, there was considerable shrinkage, because many did not come up to the necessary physical standard, and because others became casualties. In all some 5,000 recruits were sent Overseas.

The largest draft was one of 1,700. This draft paraded at 8 p.m. on August 3, 1918; the roll was called, documents checked, etc. The men were then dismissed and ordered to parade and entrain at 4.30 a.m. on August 4th. Every man of the 1,700 answered the roll call but one. He was late for parade but in time to entrain. His excuse was that he had been married after being dismissed the night previous. Under the circumstances the O.C. forgave his tardiness. This was the last draft to be sent. The War in Europe began to take on a more cheerful aspect; the farmers and fishermen were required for harvesting, etc., and some leave was given.

In September the Unit moved back to the Halifax Common for winter quarters. November 11th the Armistice was signed, and almost immediately the welcome order to demobilize was received. By March, 1919, all the affairs of the Unit were a matter of history.

CHAPTER XXXIX.

"B" UNIT, M.H.C.C.

IN the spring of 1915, when the casualties of the Canadian Overseas Forces commenced returning to Canada, the best methods of dealing with them had to be considered. The first men to return were not for medical treatment. They were dealt with by the Discharge Depots at Halifax and Quebec. At these points the men received their discharge from the army, their tickets to their homes, a suit of civilian clothes, and the balance of pay due to them.

Towards the fall of 1915 the sick and wounded commenced returning, at first in small numbers; and they were also dealt with by the Discharge Depots. Those not requiring further medical treatment were discharged and sent to their homes, with three months' pay, paid in three monthly instalments. Those who required further medical treatment were also discharged, but were sent to the Convalescent Home nearest to their homes. These Convalescent Homes were small, and most of them were placed at the disposal of the Government by private individuals. They were all equipped by the Red Cross, I.O.D.E., and other local societies organized throughout Canada by the women of Canada. In the autumn of 1915 the Military Hospitals Commission was created, with authority to accept and administer these Homes. The powers of this Commission were almost unlimited as to their control, administration, and creation of Hospitals and Convalescent Homes for the treatment of Canada's troops returning from Overseas.

In the spring of 1916 the sick and wounded returned in great numbers, and the Military Hospitals Commission having foreseen this, was well prepared to receive them, having provided large Hospital and Convalescent Home accommodation throughout Canada from coast to coast.

The question now before the Government was how were the men to be kept under discipline in these Hospitals and Convalescent Homes when the men were no longer soldiers, having received their discharge from the army when passing through the Discharge Depots at ports of arrival. It was finally decided that those who required further medical treatment would not receive their discharge on arrival, but would be forwarded to the Hospital or Convalescent Home nearest to their homes and these men would receive their discharge from the army when their medical treatment was brought to a finalty.

MAJOR J. F. TAYLOR.

To take charge of the administration and discipline of these men, in the various Hospitals and Homes throughout the country, the Military Hospitals Commission Command was created in June, 1916, " B " Unit being the Unit charged with the administration of the Hospitals and Homes throughout the Maritime Provinces. The Officer Commanding this Unit during the whole period of its existence—two years—was Major J. F. Taylor, of Halifax, an officer who had done excellent service in the Pay Branch, and who was selected to command the Maritime Province Unit on account of his tact and business knowledge. Major Taylor organized and administered the affairs of " B " Unit in a highly efficient manner at all times, showing great sympathy to the men under his command. Owing to his great tact and business ability, the Unit was second to none in Canada.

The duties performed by " B " Unit were manifold. Military discipline was adopted to a certain extent in all M.H.C.C. Institutions, but had to be administered with regard to circumstances. The officers saw only the aftermath of the terrible cataclysm enacted " over there," and their hearts were absorbed in the work of repairing broken humanity.

The personnel of the Staff of " B " Unit on March 1, 1917, was as follows:

    Major J. F. Taylor........................Officer Commanding.
    Capt. C. M. Mosher......................Adjutant.
    Capt. F. A. R. Gow......................Medical Officer.
    Captain Clarke..........................Quartermaster.
    Capt. A. A. Peachy......................Paymaster.

"B" UNIT, M.H.C.C.

On November 1, 1917, Capt. C. M. Mosher resigned as Adjutant and Capt. Walter Whitford was appointed to that office and carried on until " B " Unit was dissolved. In November, 1917, Capt. H. C. Sircom, a returned officer, was appointed Paymaster to succeed Capt. Peachy, who had been transferred to the Discharge Depot Command.

The Hospitals and Convalescent Homes that were turned over to " B " Unit by the Military Hospital Commission consisted of the following:—

   The Parks Convalescent Hospital........St. John, N.B.
   Ross Convalescent Hospital..............Sydney, N.S.
   Clayton Convalescent Home.............Halifax, N.S.
   Dalton Sanitarium......................North Wiltshire, P.E.I.

Ross Military Convalescent Home was presented to the M.H.C.C. by Commander and Mrs. J. K. L. Ross, of Sydney, C.B., on June 1, 1915.

The personnel in each of these Hospitals were transferred to the M.H.C.C., and, with the exception of a few minor transfers, carried on in the same efficient manner that had characterized them from the organization of the M.H.C.C. By constructing and taking over other large buildings, the M.H.C.C. soon made adequate arrangements for dealing with the large number of soldiers returning from Overseas. Pier 2 having been taken over by the Militia Department for a Clearing Hospital, it was transferred to the M.H.C.C., February 15, 1917. Necessary alterations delayed the opening of this Hospital until April 1, 1917. Its worth as a Hospital was well demonstrated both while under the command of the M.H.C.C. and later under the command of the Clearing Services.

CAPT. WALTER WHITFORD.

Pine Hill Presbyterian Theological College, Halifax, was taken over by the M.H.C.C. as a Convalescent Hospital on March 1, 1917, and Capt. M. S. Hunt was placed in charge, with Major Philip Weatherbe, Senior Medical Officer, and Capt. John Cameron, Resident Medical Officer. Capt. Dexter McCurdy was also a member of the Medical Staff but was transferred on Overseas service in

August, 1918. This Hospital, situated as it was, on the shores of the Northwest Arm, Halifax, proved a great boon to the returned convalescent soldiers. Its location adjoining Point Pleasant Park was an ideal one for the care and comfort of convalescent soldiers. There was an abundance of pure air, shady trees, and pleasant walks, and though quite removed from Halifax City and its noisy traffic, it was still sufficiently near to permit men able to walk to get a tram car running into the city, where they could enjoy a few hours with friends at a theatre or elsewhere. At the rear of the Home the waters of the Northwest Arm gave the men ample opportunity for boating, bathing and various other water sports, of which they took full advantage during the summer months. It is the unanimous opinion of the returned soldiers that Pine Hill was the *Ideal* Convalescent Hospital in Nova Scotia.

In May, 1917, the Moxham Convalescent Hospital at Sydney, C.B., was opened, with Major F. O'Neil in command. Major O'Neil who had been in command of the Ross Convalescent Home from December, 1916, was an efficient officer and discharged his duties in a very satisfactory manner.

During the latter part of July, 1916, an arrangement was made with Dr. F. A. Miller, of the Kentville Sanitarium, to deal with tuberculosis patients; for a great number of the men returning from Overseas were pronounced tubercular. Within a very few days Kentville Sanitarium was full of patients, and although from time to time large additions were built to the Sanitarium, it was always taxed to its utmost capacity. In fact during the summer of 1917, many hospital tents were erected on the Sanitarium grounds, for the accommodation of tubercular patients, and when autumn with its cold winds became too severe, many patients had to be sent to their own homes, to be treated until room was available at the Sanitarium, when they were recalled. Great credit is due to Dr. Miller for the splendid manner in which he dealt with the patients under his control. Capt. A. G. Forster, a returned officer, was in charge of Administration and Discipline of the Kentville Sanitarium and was a conscientious, hard-working officer.

On July 1, 1917, " B " Unit had on its strength 1,886 officers and other ranks all receiving medical treatment. About 50 per cent. of this number were out-patients, with home leave. These men

"B" UNIT, M.H.C.C.

were recalled to the Hospital from time to time as their physical condition demanded.

About this time New Brunswick became a separate Military District, and it was decided to organize a separate M.H.C.C. Unit for New Brunswick. This was accordingly done, and the transfer of men and documents was completed in July, 1917.

In the early spring of 1917 construction work was begun on a Convalescent Hospital at Camp Hill, Halifax, and by October 1. 1917, the building was completed sufficiently to receive patients. This hospital was fitted up with all modern medical appliances and proved a Godsend to the people of Halifax, when on December 6, 1917, the city was shocked by the terrific explosion.

At the opening of Camp Hill Hospital, Lieutenant Blackwood was placed in charge by the M.H.C.C. and Major (now Lieut.-Col.) C. Morris was Senior Medical Officer. An efficient Staff was soon organized which carried on until the Hospital was transferred to the A.M.C. on December 6, 1917. Immediately after the explosion all patients able to walk were given home leave and the Hospital and Staff complete was turned over to the Medical Relief Commission for the purpose of, dealing with the sufferers of the explosion.

The writer of this article has visited Casualty Clearing Hospitals in Flanders on " Clearing Day " but never has he seen such human suffering as he saw at Camp Hill Hospital when he walked into the Hospital at 4 p.m. on December 6. 1917. The Hospital at Pier 2, also the offices of the M.H.C.C. were destroyed by the explosion. The Hospital was quickly rebuilt. but the offices were removed to Leith House, Hollis Street, Halifax, and these offices were retained until the Unit was disbanded.

On March 31, 1918, the Military Hospitals Commission Command was disbanded by an Order-in-Council. The military end of the work was taken over by No. 6 District Depot, and the civilian end by the D.S.C.R. Final transfer of all equipment and records, etc., of the M.H.C.C. to No. 6 District Depot was effected on April 18, 1918.

CHAPTER XL.

ACADIA UNIVERSITY AND THE WAR.

IN common with other universities in the Empire, Acadia emptied her halls when the call to duty came. Her ideals had always been those directly opposed to war, but to carry out these ideals, it was necessary to participate in it. Between six and seven hundred Acadia men and women enlisted. There was no definite Unit formed by the Acadia men, but they were found in all departments of the service. Sixty were in the Nova Scotia Highland Brigade, mostly in " D " Company, 219th Battalion; and their Platoon, number 13, won the Brigade trophy for efficiency. Ten students left Acadia at one time with the 4th Universities Company Reinforcements, Princess Patricia Canadian Light Infantry. The attendance at the University was cut down to about one half, notwithstanding the fact that the number of young women remained constant. The Freshman class was unusually large, but as soon as the age of eighteen was reached, practically no fit man remained. Of the Acadia students, sixty-three lost their lives in service, sixty-two young men and one young woman.

We have no definite figures concerning honors, but about eighty were conferred on Acadia men, one of which was the coveted Victoria Cross, the only one awarded to a college man in the Maritime Provinces, and, in fact, the only one awarded to a Maritime Province Unit. One of our Acadia men had the distinction of being the youngest Lieutenant-Colonel in the British Army, commanding the 10th Alberta when twenty-six years of age. He received the D.S.O. and two Bars, the Military Cross, was five times mentioned in dispatches, and was recommended for the Victoria Cross. The only colored chaplain in the British Army was an Acadia man. In addition to those who enlisted in the Canadian Expeditionary Force, we had a number who enlisted with the Americans, and still others who enlisted with the British, all of whom gave splendid account of themselves.

When the War broke out, there was a branch of the C.O.T.C. at Acadia, but it went out of business early because practically every member enlisted. The officer in charge of the C.O.T.C. for Military District No. 6 told me that a larger number of C.O.T.C. men went from Acadia than from any other Maritime University. Since the War, many students have returned to the University to complete their work, and, without exception, they are making excellent records. Acadia has offered one year's free tuition to returned men, being the only university in Canada to do that.

In 1919, the returned men at Acadia met, and, after consultation, decided that something should be done in the way of a Memorial for those who had given their lives in the War. The suggestion was made that this memorial should take the form of a Gymnasium, typifying the splendid physical condition, the manly vigor, and sporting spirit of the boys who went Overseas.

In 1914 our Gymnasium had been destroyed by fire, and a committee of eight young men had been appointed to raise funds for a new Gymnasium. Of these eight, six had dropped the burden of responsibility of the Gymnasium and had gone to war, one of whom was killed at Passchendaele. It seemed most fitting that their work should be carried out by those who were left, and the next of kin of all those who had given their lives were consulted, and agreed to the proposal.

As a result, this Gymnasium is now in process of construction, and will be a building in every way suitable as a Memorial for those boys who have fallen. On May 26, 1920, General Sir Arthur W. Currie, G.C.M.G., K.C.B., D.S.O., formerly Commander of the Canadian Corps in France, laid the corner stone of the new Gymnasium and delivered an address on that occasion.

While we feel that Acadia's part in the War was no more than it should have been, we are justly proud of the willing sacrifice, the ready response, and the splendid record made by our Acadia men.

CHAPTER XLI.

DALHOUSIE UNIVERSITY AND THE WAR.

THE activities of Dalhousie University in connection with the Great War may be considered under the following headings. (1) The Activities of the C.O.T.C.; (2) The Dalhousie University Stationary Hospital No. 7, C.E.F.; (3) Activities of the Staff; (4) Independent Undergraduate Enlistment.

THE OFFICERS' TRAINING CORPS.—Great Britain was forced to declare war on Germany on August 4, 1914; so that when the University session of 1914 opened, it was under war conditions. The earliest corporate war effort of Dalhousie University was a mass meeting in the Law Library, held on October 16, 1914, for the purpose of taking steps to form an O.T.C. The chair was taken by Earle C. Phinney, at that time President of the Council of Students. The meeting, which was most enthusiastic, was addressed by President Mackenzie, G. S. Campbell, Chairman of the Board of Governors, and by Major W. E. Thompson, Secretary of the Board. It was ultimately agreed to ask Major Thompson to organize an O.T.C.; and all those willing to co-operate were invited to sign the roll. Ninety-two names were given in at once on the conclusion of the meeting; of these, five were whole-time Professors. Drill began at once in the South End Rink, Sergeant-Major Graham of the Permanent Staff being instructor.

Some of the original officers were:

> Major W. E. Thompson, O.C.
> Capt. D. Fraser Harris, Adjutant.
> Capt. Murray MacNeill.
> Capt. D. A. MacRae.
> Capt. George Henderson.
> Capt. A. W. Cogswell.

Each was in command of a Platoon.

Alumni and business men interested were permitted to join, and there was so much activity in the autumn of 1914 that by the middle of December the Corps was ready to be inspected by General Sir Sam Hughes, Minister of Militia. The inspection took place on December 18th in the South End Skating Rink. The maximum strength during the first winter session was close on 200. On May 4, 1915, the Corps was inspected by General Rutherford, commanding the Garrison. Lectures continued well on into the summer of 1915.

By the session of 1916 Professor John Cameron, of London, had been appointed to the Campbell Memorial Chair of Anatomy in Dalhousie University, and having had a considerable amount of military experience both with the Volunteer Artillery in Scotland and with Infantry Volunteers in England, was well qualified to take command of the O.T.C., Major Thompson, as Lieutenant-Colonel, having been appointed to the Headquarters Staff as A.A.G. of Military District No. 6. This Professor Cameron did with the rank of Major, and retained the command and gave most of the systematic instruction during the remainder of the existence of the Corps. By arrangement with Colonel Papineau, commanding the R.S.I., candidates for commissions were examined at Wellington Barracks. In this way a considerable number of members of the O.T.C. obtained commissions and were enabled to proceed Overseas with the various Units which were being formed as the War progressed. No less than seven officers who had passed through the D.U.C.O.T.C. went Overseas with the 219th Battalion of the Nova Scotia Highland Brigade. Practically every able-bodied male student was a member of the O.T.C. during the first winter session; and no less than twenty-five members of it were students from the affiliated Presbyterian College at Pine Hill.

The session of 1916-17 was a very strenuous one. Drill took place in the evenings at the newly-erected Market Building at the head of Duke Street, Major Cameron superintending the drill and also giving lectures either there or in the rooms of the Board of Trade. During each winter firing practice was systematically carried out at the miniature ranges erected in the Engineering Laboratory of the Technical College. In March, 1917, the Corps was inspected in the Market Building by Major Cooper of the R.S.I. The O.T.C.

is still in existence ready to become active again as soon as the University is in possession of a drill hall.

STATIONARY HOSPITAL UNIT.—The origin of No. 7 Stationary Hospital was the desire of the Medical Faculty of the University to serve their country in the Great War. Early in September, 1914, an offer was made to provide the personnel of a Casualty Clearing Station; this offer was renewed in the spring of 1915, but the Federal Government was not at that time in a position to accept it.

It was very generally felt that the only School of Medicine in the Maritime Provinces ought to have a representation on the Canadian Expeditionary Force. Those who were the most active in renewing the offer were Major George M. Campbell, Major C. V. Hogan, and Capts. J. R. Corston, M. A. MacAulay, L. M. Murray and F. V. Woodbury. The Government accepted the offer on September 27, 1915. On November 1st, the old Medical College building was occupied as rooms for headquarters, and enlistment and training began. On December 16th the Unit was inspected by General Benson, G.O.C., and by Col. J. A. Grant, A.D.M.S., Military District No. 6. On December 31st the Hospital sailed from St. John, N.B., on *H.M.S. Metagama*, arriving at Plymouth on January 10, 1916. On February 5th the Unit took over Shorncliffe Military Hospital, and on June 18, 1916, embarked for France.

The personnel of the Dalhousie Hospital Unit was made up as follows: O.C., Lieut.-Colonel John Stewart, Majors E. V. Hogan and L. M. Murray, Capts. M. A. MacAulay, V. N. MacKay, K. A. MacKenzie, E. K. MacLellan, S. J. MacLennan, D. A. MacLeod, J. A. Murray, John Rankine, Frank V. Woodbury, Karl F. Woodbury, Lieut. S. R. Halcom, Lieut. and Quartermaster Walter Taylor. The Matron was Miss L. M. Hubley, and there were twenty-six nursing sisters. Of all other ranks there were one hundred and twenty-three men. Sixteen additional men were taken on at Shorncliffe, England.

The Unit arrived home from active service early in the morning of St. George's Day, 1919, on the *S.S. Belgic;* in the evening they were entertained at dinner at the Green Lantern in Halifax. Col. John Stewart who returned a little later was entertained at a dinner given in his honor on June 20, 1919.

DALHOUSIE UNIVERSITY AND THE WAR

ACTIVITIES OF THE STAFF: I. *The Faculty of Arts and Science.*
—The only full-time Professor in the Senate to go Overseas on active service was Professor James Eadie Todd, M.A., who saw service with the B.E.F. in India and in Mesopotamia. Professor Todd, who remained with the troops until the end of the War, did not return to Dalhousie University. Professor Howard Murray, LL.D., during the first year of the War, was a member of the O.T.C. Professor MacNeill during the first year of the War had command of a Platoon in the O.T.C. Professor J. N. Finlayson, M.Sc., entered the O.T.C. at its formation and qualified for a commission in the infantry. Mr. J. W. Logan, M.A., went Overseas as Captain in the 25th Canadian Infantry Battalion, attained his majority in June, 1916, and saw service in France until the end of the War. The Rev. H. A. Kent, M.A., D.D., having passed through the O.T.C. obtained his Captain's commission on March 1, 1916, and went Overseas as a combatant in the 219th Battalion of the Nova Scotia Highlanders. Captain Kent saw service until September, 1917, when he was transferred to the Chaplain Service, in which he acted as Adjutant. He was also engaged in educational work in London until he returned to Canada in May, 1919. Mr. Harry Dean, Examiner in Music, had command of a Platoon in the O.T.C., and qualified for a commission in the infantry.

II. *The Faculty of Law.*—The Dean of the Faculty of Law, Professor D. A. MacRae, Ph.D., joined the O.T.C. and had command of a Platoon during the first session. Mr. John E. Read, B.C.L. (Oxon.), B.A. (Dal.), Rhodes Scholar, Lecturer on Real Property, enlisted in the 25th Battalion in November, 1914, but was immediately transferred to the Canadian Field Artillery, and took an officer's training course at the Royal School of Artillery, Kingston. In February, 1915, Mr. Read joined the 23rd Battery of the C.F.A. at Fredericton and immediately proceeded Overseas. In July he was transferred to the Divisional Artillery (1st Canadian Division) and served in the 4th, 8th and 26th Batteries as Lieutenant, being promoted to the rank of Captain in July, 1916, on his transference to the 27th Battery. While Captain Read was Acting-Major he was wounded in January, 1917. From May, 1917, to March, 1918, he was Senior Gunnery Instructor at the Canadian School of Gunnery, being invalided to Canada in April, 1918.

Captain Read was mentioned in Sir Douglas Haig's dispatches in June, 1917.

III. *Faculty of Medicine.*—After Professor Cameron relinquished the command of the O.T.C. he reverted to the rank of Captain, and entering the C.A.M.C. became Resident Physician of the Military Hospital which had been installed in the Presbyterian College at Pine Hill, Halifax.

Professor A. G. Nicholls, who attained the rank of Major, entered the C.A.M.C. as Captain and discharged the duties of Chief Bacteriologist, Serologist and Sanitary Officer for the Halifax Garrison. Dr. W. H. Hattie, with rank of Captain, saw service with the C.A.M.C. in Halifax. Professor Fraser Harris, with rank of Captain, acted as Adjutant to the O.T.C. as long as that Corps remained in activity. The governors could not see their way to granting his request for leave of absence for Overseas service. Besides addressing recruiting meetings, Professor Harris gave courses of instruction in First Aid, under the auspices of the St. John Ambulance Association, to large classes of men, both in the service and to civilians, to women students and to cadets.

The following members of the Staff gave their services in the C.A.M.C. in connection with the Halifax Garrison: Colonels George M. Campbell and M. A. Curry; Capts. W. Bruce Almon, M. J. Carney, J. S. Corston, J. F. Lawlor, G. A. Macintosh, Philip Weatherbe and Hugh Schwartz.

IV. *The Faculty of Dentistry.*—Although the health of the Dean of this Faculty, Dr. Frank Woodbury, precluded him from entering military service, both his sons were able to go Overseas. The elder, Frank Valentine, who at the outbreak of the War was already acting D.A.D.M.S. in Military District No. 6, with the rank of Captain, was immediately mobilized. This appointment he resigned to become Adjutant in the No. 7 Stationary Hospital, C.E.F., in 1915.

In August, 1916, Captain Woodbury was appointed to No. 3 Canadian Intrenching Battalion, and in August, 1916, proceeded to the Front at Ypres with that Unit. Later he was posted to the 9th Canadian Field Ambulance, and saw service at Ypres, on the Somme, at Vimy and at Loos. Having been promoted, Major Woodbury was recalled to headquarters at London for Staff duty.

He was ultimately appointed A.D.M.S. with the rank of Lieutenant-Colonel, returning to Ottawa for duty in November, 1919.

Dr. A. W. Cogswell, Professor of Dental Pathology and Therapeutics, joined the O.T.C. in November, 1914, and as Captain had command of a Platoon.

Dr. George Kerr Thomson, Professor of Crown and Bridgework and Ceramics and Oral Hygiene, at the outbreak of the War, held the rank of Captain in the 63rd Halifax Rifles. Later he was transferred to the C.A.D.C. and appointed Assistant Director of Dental Services in Military District No. 6. When, early in 1915, Sir Sam Hughes ordered the organization of the C.A.D.C. Major Thomson was made First Director of Dental Services. In 1916 the Dental Services at Valcartier Camp were organized by Major Thomson with the assistance of Captain F. H. Bradley of Military District No. 4. Dr. W. W. Woodbury, Professor of Orthodontia, who had been appointed Captain in the C.A.D.C. in May, 1918, proceeded to Aldershot Camp, where as A.D.D.S. for the Camp he had charge of all the Dental Services there. In October, 1918, Dr. Woodbury was posted for special duty at McNab's Island, where he remained until January, 1919, when he was appointed to Camp Hill Hospital, to superintend the dental treatment of returned soldiers. He remained at this centre until general demobilization on November 15, 1919.

Undergraduate Enlistment.—From the very first hour of the War, the attention of the undergraduates had been directed to joining the Canadian Expeditionary Force. Up to the date of the Armistice five hundred and eighty members of the University had enlisted for military or naval service, either Overseas or in Canada. Of these, sixty-seven are known to have lost their lives, and forty-four to have received decorations for distinguished service. Of those who were decorated, five lost their lives. The decorations are as follows:

```
D.S.O............................... 3
D.C.M............................... 3, 1 with Bar
O.B.E............................... 2
M.M................................. 4
M.C................................. 32, 2 with Bar
Croix de Guerre..................... 1
```

These do not include decorations awarded to members of the Staff.

NOVA SCOTIA'S PART IN THE GREAT WAR

The names of those winning the D.S.O. are: John Keeller MacKay of Pictou (Law '13-'15), Colonel and O.C. 22nd Battalion 6th Howitzer Brigade, B.E.F. J. Layton Ralston (Law '02-'03) Amherst, Colonel and O.C. of the 85th Battalion, C.E.F. Barry Wentworth Roscoe, of Kentville (LL.B. '04), Major 5th C.M.R., C.E.F.

At the outbreak of the War the University had on its books 398 students, of whom 90 were women. Of the 308 male students of the session 1914-15 by the end of the session practically every third man had enlisted for military service.

So many students left the Presbyterian Theological College, Pine Hill, Halifax, as to make it only the shadow of its former self. In the session of 1914-15 as many as twenty-five students from Pine Hill were drilling with the O.T.C.; thirteen men from this College ultimately saw service Overseas.

Of students of Engineering in the session of 1914-15, twenty-one were enrolled in the O.T.C.

Of Law students twenty-two were on the roll of the O.T.C. during the first session.

One cannot write of what Dalhousie University did in the War without a few words as to what she suffered. The only son of the Chairman of the Board of Governors, Mr. G. S. Campbell, LL.D., Lieut. George Henderson Campbell, was killed near Ypres in May, 1916. He had graduated B.A. in the previous May, and was within only two days of his 21st birthday. Two Rhodes Scholars lost their lives in the Great War, namely: Walter Melville Billman (B.A. '13), Lieut. 1st Middlesex Regiment, B.E.F.; and Harry Austin MacCleave (B.A. '16), Lieut. 13th Montreal Highlanders, C.E.F. While the accidental death of the young, the healthy and the brave is always a poignant sorrow, the passing of those who are also the finest products of the academic culture of their day is a catastrophe of the first magnitude.

CHAPTER XLII.

KING'S COLLEGE AND KING'S COLLEGE SCHOOL IN THE WAR.

THE University of King's College at Windsor, N.S., has always been small in numbers, but always big in the spirit it has displayed and in the type of men it has fostered.

It was founded in 1789—the oldest University in the British Dominions beyond the Seas—by United Empire Loyalists, by men who readily gave up all they possessed in a material sense rather than forsake their allegiance to an ideal. It is not surprising then that at all times there have been King's men ready to answer the King's call and that the names of men such as Inglis and Welsford are held in special reverence by their *Alma Mater*.

The spirit of loyal service and sacrifice that has actuated King's men was at once evident in her sons when the Great Call came in 1914, and King's has every reason to be proud of her record of loyalty and devotion in the Great War. More than four hundred of her sons were at the King's side during that fierce struggle for freedom.

In 1914 there were at least twelve King's men, including seven Generals, holding commissions in the Imperial Army and the Canadian Permanent Forces.

Fourteen volunteers sailed with the First Contingent of the Canadian Expeditionary Force, four of whom were killed in action. The first King's man to make the Great Sacrifice was Capt. G. L. B. Concanon, who was killed in the Dardanelles Campaign while serving with the 2nd Battalion of Australian Infantry.

In the Second Contingent were some thirty-five students and graduates of the College and a number of "Old Boys" of the School.

Amongst the notable enlistments from College during the War were the nine who volunteered for service in the Cycle Corps of the 2nd Contingent, and some twenty, mostly students, who enlisted together in the 193rd Battalion, Nova Scotia Highland Brigade. This latter represented an enlistment of about 50 per cent. of the student body then in residence at King's College and included one of her Professors.

During the period of the War the largest number of male students in attendance at King's College was forty-eight, and this number was reduced to a few physically unfit men in 1917, and yet sixty-seven students actually enlisted from the College, and ten of them made the supreme sacrifice. In all twenty-three King's men fell in action on the Field of Honor.

So reduced was the student body that when the Military Service Act came into effect there was not one physically fit student left to come under the provisions of that Act.

Early in 1915 a contingent of the Canadian Officers' Training Corps was organized at King's College under Professor Sturley as Officer Commanding, and did very useful work not only amongst the students at College, but also amongst the young men of Windsor, the seat of King's College. Its active life, however was short, for within about twelve months of its organization practically the whole of the personnel of the Corps had enlisted for Overseas Service.

Amongst the honors gained by King's men during the War were:

O. B. Jones....................D.S.O.
J. P. Silver....................D.S.O., C.B.E.
C. Hill........................D.S.O.
C. R. E. Willets...............D.S.O.
H. A. Kaulback.................O.B.E.
A. E. Andrew...................M.C.
G. D. Campbell.................M.C.
R. H. Morris...................M.C.
C. V. Strong...................M.C.
C. Campbell....................M.C.
W. G. Ernst....................M.C. and Bar.
G. B. Murray...................M.C.
R. H. Tait.....................M.C.
D. L. Teed.....................M.C.
P. L. Parlee...................D.C.M.
W. E. Warburton................D.C.M.
G. L. Jones....................D.C.M.
C. Blanchard...................M.M.
T. W. Maynard..................M.M.
H. R. Poole....................Legion of Honor.
R. H. Stewart..................Order of St. George of Russia.
G. F. Mason....................Croix de Guerre.

KING'S COLLEGE AND KING'S COLLEGE SCHOOL

Of the many who distinguished themselves by gallant service, whether officially recognized or not, the record of a few of the younger generation must suffice as typical of all.

Two of the first students to enlist were Edward Jeffery and George Mason. They enlisted together in the ranks of the First Contingent, 17th Battalion, and went over to France together with the 14th Battalion, 1st Canadian Division. For sixteen months they fought side by side—all through the terrible winter of 1914-1915 in the Ypres Salient—and came through that fiery ordeal unscathed. They returned to England together for their commissions, training together at Crowborough. Mason returned to France almost immediately after the course, but Jeffery was taken ill and was operated on for appendicitis; and it was not till April, 1918, that he was again sent to France. In June, 1918, he joined his new Battalion, 16th Canadian Scottish, and found himself posted to a Company commanded by Mason, now a Captain. So they were together again in France. On the night of the 26th September Jeffery received his first wound, but it proved fatal, and the next day he was laid to rest at Ligny St. Frochel, near St. Pol. Only four days later, on October 1st, his great chum followed, and so these two, who for four long years had borne the burden and strife of the Great War with what seemed charmed lives, were reunited once more in that land where there is no more parting and no more strife.

Arthur Leigh Collett, B.A., had left King's for Oxford as a Rhodes Scholar, but at once forsook his work at Oxford and enlisted in the Imperial Army. He served in France as a Lieutenant with the 8th Gloucesters, and in the autumn of 1915, in the Battle of Messines Ridge he was reported missing and later believed killed. Others from his Battalion reported missing at the same time were later reported as prisoners of war in Germany. There is little doubt that Collett fought gallantly facing the odds and choosing to meet death rather than to cease for a moment, while life lasted, from striving for the ideals of justice and righteousness.

A. B. C. Hilbert was one of the most popular students and one of the best athletes at King's. Enlisting with the Cycle Corps he transferred to the Royal Naval Air Service on reaching England.

In July, 1917, he wrote: "I am at present resting after a twenty-two weeks' illness due to a little ducking I got in the North Sea. I am flying again in August." In October came the news that he had fallen a second time in the North Sea, and now there he rests with many other gallant sons of Britain.

Of the others who enlisted with him in the Cycle Corps, Turnbull and McCormick rest in soldiers' graves in Flanders; Crawford died in hospital ere he saw the foe; Foster and Parlee are back with us at King's, and though Parlee has lost a leg, his breast is adorned with that proud emblem of bravery, the Distinguished Conduct Medal; Brittain has recovered from his serious wounds and is serving the King of Peace; Harley, Hallett and the rest are giving the same good account of themselves that they always gave as loyal sons of King's.

George Stewart Burchell was one of that little band who enlisted together with the 193rd Battalion, Nova Scotia Highland Brigade, and joined the 85th Battalion in France. He was one of the most promising of the younger sons of King's, a clever, manly, gentlemanly young fellow. He fought for the cause of liberty and right and now rests in a soldier's grave in France.

In the records of the King's College Advance Movement is the entry, "George Stewart Burchell, killed at the Front, his pay at his request, $100." May King's never cease to honor the memory of this loyal and gallant son.

W. B. Ernst enlisted as a private in the 193rd Battalion, rose to the rank of Captain in the 85th Battalion, and was awarded the Military Cross and Bar. Ernst has not rested on his laurels, and since his return here has shown that in the field of scholarship, too, he will take no second place, and has captured the Rhodes Scholarship from the Province of Nova Scotia. King's will ever have reason to be proud of the records of Ernst, so affectionately known as "Bill."

Of others whom King's will always delight to honor may be mentioned Capt. D. L. Teed, M.C., and Gunner L. Wilkinson, who fell gallantly serving their guns, Lieut. W. E. Warburton, D.C.M., rewarded for his bravery in the Dardanelles, Lieut.-Col. C. R. E. Willets, D.S.O., the gallant and popular Commanding Officer of the R.C.R. in France, and now commanding the famous "Princess

Pats," Cecil Blanchard, M.M., who was too young to enlist except as a bugler, but not too young to show that he came of loyal fighting stock; and the Campbell brothers, six of whom saw active service, and two of whom, Colin and Kenneth, lie "out there," somewhere in France.

Though these records are brief and unworthy may they suffice to show that the true spirit of King's still lives in her sons, and that they, as of old, have upheld nobly her best traditions and realized in some measure her ideals of service,

"DEO, LEGI, REGI, GREGI."

CHAPTER XLIII.

ST. FRANCIS XAVIER UNIVERSITY AND THE WAR.

IN the Great War students, past and present, of St. Francis Xavier University served in every branch of the Forces of Canada, and in the armies and navies of Great Britain, France and America. But it is the especial pride of St. Francis Xavier to have furnished a complete Unit, if a small one, of the Canadian Expeditionary Forces. The Unit was officially known as No. 9 Stationary Hospital, C.A.M.C.

This Unit was organized in November, 1915, and was for some time quartered in the University itself. It left Canada for the United Kingdom in June, 1916, and proceeded to France in November of the following year. Till April, 1918, it was stationed at St. Omer, but the great German offensive of that spring made necessary its withdrawal to Etaples, where it became part of the hospital system of the main British base.

In the notorious bombardment of May 18, 1918, No. 9 was the first hospital to be attacked, and suffered severely. Its premises were completely destroyed, and more than forty per cent. of its personnel became casualties. Towards the end of 1918, the status of the St. Francis Xavier Unit was raised to that of a General Hospital. It returned to Canada in July, 1919, and upon the reorganization of the Military Forces of Canada, was preserved as an integral part of the Active Militia.

More than three hundred and fifty Xavierians joined the colors. Thirty-three were killed, or died on active service. The following decorations were won by students or alumni of the University:

C.M.G.	1
D.S.O.	4
M.C.	11
First Bar, M.C.	1
Second Bar, M.C.	1
O.B.E.	1
D.C.M.	3
M.M.	5
M.S.M.	1

ST. FRANCIS XAVIER UNIVERSITY AND THE WAR

Three professors of the Faculty of the University saw active service in the Canadian, Imperial and American Forces respectively; two were severely wounded and one received the Military Cross.

In Canada during the War St. Francis Xavier took a becoming part in the forefront of every patriotic activity. A contingent of the Canadian Officers' Training Corps was gazetted in April, 1915. Training had hardly been begun when the Corps lost the majority of its officers by enlistment and with the numbers of students continually dwindling—at one commencement a single .individual presented himself for graduation—it became impossible to continue parades.

In every branch of war work pursued in the neighborhood of Antigonish, the locale of the University, the lead was taken by members of the Staff of St. Francis Xavier. The chairman of the local committee for the Patriotic Fund, the Antigonish County Organizer of the Victory Loan Campaign, and the Director of the re-establishment activities of the Knights of Columbus over a wide area of Eastern Nova Scotia, were professors of the University. In connection with the patriotic work of the Knights of Columbus, it may be mentioned St. Francis Xavier did its full share in the launching of the Dominion-wide campaign, which made it possible for this body to perform its splendid services to our troops at the scene of war. In brief in St. Francis Xavier, as in all the universities of the land, it was the aim of all compelled to "carry on" at home to become, by patriotic endeavor and sacrifice, not unworthy of those who went from it to fight their country's and the Empire's battles.

Editor's Note.—No. 9 Stationary Hospital Unit is more fully dealt with in Chapter xxvi.

CHAPTER XLIV.

THE PRESBYTERIAN COLLEGE AND THE GREAT WAR.

MINISTERS of the Gospel are the avowed ambassadors of the Prince of Peace; and it is so constantly their task to allay the passions of the human heart and to preach universal love, particularly in their appeals for foreign missions, that many people felt that their ideal was at variance with the spirit of war and were prepared to find students for the ministry offering for other forms of patriotic service than fighting in the line. The extraordinary response of theological colleges and of sons of the manse all over the Empire showed how mistaken this idea had been. The message of the Cross and the call to self-sacrifice had quite the opposite effect. Young men who were going to be preachers experienced a new sense of responsibility; they knew that they could not consistently call others to a life of service and suffering, if they were not prepared themselves to lead the way. This is the attitude that prevailed among the students at Pine Hill, which is the oldest Presbyterian Theological College in Canada, and which will celebrate in 1920 its centenary.

The intensity of this conviction surprised every one on the parade ground of the South End Rink, Halifax, when Col. W. E. Thompson organized the O.T.C. of Dalhousie University. The large majority of the students in residence at Pine Hill were there. The Divinity classes open late, and thus many had been in the city only a few days when this call came in the beginning of November, 1914. Colonel Thompson has on several public occasions paid a fine tribute to these theological men; and they in return frankly acknowledge how much they were moved by the frank and earnest appeal of the Colonel himself.

The O.T.C. was but a voluntary and preliminary phase of the grave decision; but it had a most stimulating effect, and nearly all the students who joined its ranks found themselves ultimately in active service. Right on the heels of the O.T.C. came the formation of a small Cycle Corps Unit, to which three from Pine Hill were admitted, the first to enlist for Overseas. This Unit was almost entirely made up of students, and its advent in Halifax was celebrated by a dinner given in the residence at Pine Hill. The dining hall was crowded. Colonel Thompson and Colonel Grant, A.D.M.S., spoke; the impression made was very deep; and probably at that hour a large number made up their minds to join the colors. The impression was intensified by the dramatic announcement in the course of the dinner of the splendid sea victory at Falkland Islands, the news of which had just come over the wire.

Before the year was out there came an urgent appeal for an Ambulance Corps, and fifteen responded. Few of them stayed long in the Army Medical Corps after they got across, but asked for transfers to fighting units, in which they played their part nobly, and where some of them laid down their lives.

Early in 1915 the 6th Mounted Rifles were formed and eight more joined, going to England in July. In the summer four others enlisted in the No. 7 Overseas Hospital (The Dalhousie) Unit; and in the winter, 1915-16, five enlisted in the Nova Scotia Highland Brigade and five in the artillery. By the second anniversary of the War the great bulk of the Divinity students had entered the army, and most of these were already Overseas.

Below is given a list of the names and of the Units to which they were eventually attached, and henceforward their history becomes identified with their Units and is told elsewhere. There were forty-eight in all, including the Principal and Professor H. A. Kent, who were ultimately on the strength of the Chaplain Service. Two received the Military Cross and one the Military Medal; seven paid the supreme sacrifice; and many were wounded or gassed. All but seven of those who survived continued their studies for the ministry on their return.

Following is the roll of honor:

John Ross, a Scotch lad, who, in the beginning of the War, joined the fleet, and went down with the *Indefatigable* in the Battle of Jutland.

Arthur P. MacIvor, from Cape Breton, joined the C.M.R., and was killed at Mount Sorel, on June 2, 1916.

NOVA SCOTIA'S PART IN THE GREAT WAR

Earl Lockerby, from P.E.I., in the 42nd R.H.C. Killed at Courcellette, September, 1916.

Ralph B. Clarke, B.A., from New Brunswick, joined the 26th, and was killed at Courcellette, on September 17, 1916.

Stephen Dick, from New Brunswick, joined C.F.A., and survived until the final offensive in 1918.

Lieut. Harold A. Smith, B.A., M.C., from Cape Breton; served in 5th C.M.R.; wounded first on the Somme, and killed in May, 1918.

Cyril Hyde, Lieutenant in the Royal Air Service; killed over the German lines.

PINE HILL STUDENTS WHO SERVED OVERSEAS.

(Those marked with an asterisk were killed.)

FACULTY.

Capt. Principal C. Mackinnon, D.D., LL.D...Chaplain Service, O.M.P.C.
Capt. H. A. Kent, D.D......................Chaplain Service, O.M.P.C.

STUDENTS FOR THE MINISTRY.

Lieut. B. C. Salter, B.A..................42nd R.H.C.
Lieut. D. A. Guildford, M.A..............C.D.A.
*Earl Lockerby............................42nd R.H.C.
*Lieut. R. B. Clarke, B.A.................26th Can. Infantry.
L. B. Campbell, B.A......................3rd Can. Field Ambulance.
Lieut. J. K. Murchison, B.A..............R.F.A.
R. A. Patterson, B.A.....................C.A.M.C.
G. D. MacLeod, B.A.......................C.H.A.
D. J. Morrison...........................C.A.M.C.
P. B. Fox, B.A...........................C.A.M.G.C.
Capt. A. D. Archibald, B.A., M.C.........85th N.S. Highlanders.
Lieut. J. G. Paterson, B.A...............R.F.A.
*Lieut. Cyril Hyde.......................R.A.F.
Neil Macdonald...........................85th N.S. Highlanders.
Capt. Geo. Murray, M.C...................85th N.S. Highlanders.
Victor B. Walls..........................C.A.M.C.
J. S. Nickerson, B.A.....................C.A.M.C.
Colin U. McNiven.........................25th Can. Infantry.
*J. S. Ross..............................H.M.S. *Indefatigable.*
*A. P. McIvor, B.A.......................5th C.M.R.
*Lieut. H. A. Smith, B.A., M.C...........5th C.M.R.
Lieut. McI. McLeod.......................5th C.M.R.
Norman A. MacKenzie......................85th N.S. Highlanders.
D. P. MacLeod............................4th C.M.R.
W. J. V. Tweedie.........................4th C.M.R.
Lieut. John Craigie......................B.E.F.
Capt. R. E. G. Roome.....................R.F.A.
Cadet P. C. Lewis........................R.A.F.
Wm. Matheson.............................85th N.S. Highlanders.
J. D. MacLeod............................13th R.H.C.
H. H. Blanchard, B.A., M.M...............85th N.S. Highlanders.
R. H. Scott..............................85th N.S. Highlanders.

Lieut. E. S. Smith, M.A.................R.A.F.
Lieut. McLaren Keswick................25th Can. Infantry.
Neil M. Rattee, B.A.....................7th Overseas Hospital.
John A. Nicholson, B.A................. C.F.A.
Lieut. T. H. Whelpley..................87th Can. Inf. G.G.
*Stephen J. Dick........................ C.F.A.
A. M. Gillis........................... 10th Siege Battery.
Lieut. A. E. Kerr.......................R.A.F.
John Mackay...........................10th Can. Siege Battery.
A. B. Simpson..........................19th C.F.A.
D. F. Marshall, B.A....................15th R.H.C.
F. Yates...............................10th Can. Infantry.
J. S. Bonnell, B.A.....................8th Siege Battery.

CHAPTER XLV.

RECRUITING IN NOVA SCOTIA.

THE number of men of military age in Canada at the outbreak of the War was approximately 1,720,000, and of this Nova Scotia's quota was 53,500. As the War progressed it was decided that Canada's contribution would be 500,000 and Nova Scotia's proportion 30,000, which was attained.

At first no particular effort was made by the public to raise the various Units, the matter being left entirely in the hands of the Military. The 1st Field Ambulance and the 17th Field Battery proceeded to Valcartier as Units, and thence Overseas with the First Division. The 17th, Nova Scotia's first Battalion, to our lasting disgrace, was left to paddle its own canoe to the rocks in Salisbury Plains, where it eventually became the 17th Reserve Battalion, supplying reinforcements to the Nova Scotia Units in the Field.

The 25th was the first Battalion in which the public evinced any interest. This was mainly recruited from Militia Units, a large proportion coming from the Island of Cape Breton and from Halifax. The 40th Battalion and the 6th Canadian Mounted Rifles, authorized in February, 1915, were recruited with comparative ease, the 40th entirely from Nova Scotia and the 6th C.M.R. from the three Maritime Provinces. At this time the 25th had not proceeded Overseas, and it was not until May that this Battalion, which in France earned for itself the title of the "Fighting 25th," sailed from Halifax, taking as its final complement part of the 40th Battalion.

The 40th was then sent to Aldershot, N.S., for training, and was almost immediately called upon to supply a draft of 5 officers and 250 men. About this time recruiting slackened. The strength of the 40th dwindled, due to casualties from sickness and other causes, and it seemed that unless a special effort were made by the public this Unit would share the fate of the 17th, or worse. Mr. G. S. Campbell, whose son was among the officers of this Unit,

RECRUITING IN NOVA SCOTIA

brought back from Valcartier the news that unless the Battalion was quickly brought up to strength it would be absorbed into a Battalion of another Province, and Nova Scotia would lose it. A strong Committee of prominent citizens was immediately formed. Money for advertising was subscribed, and a campaign launched, the effect of which never ceased during the period of the War. The 40th was brought up to full strength, and in October proceeded Overseas.

As a result of the efforts of this Committee it was thought by Headquarters M.D. No. 6 that the work of recruiting throughout the Province should be inspected and reported on. Lieut.-Col. H. Flowers was selected to undertake this duty. Every important town in the Province was visited except in Cape Breton, which was supplying many men through the energetic work of the Rev. E. Watering Florence. The prominent people in each town were induced to lend their assistance, forming such organizations as they in their wisdom deemed best. All the assistance that headquarters and the Halifax Committee could give was supplied at the request of the other centres.

This proved most successful and when the 64th was authorized in August, 1915, to be recruited from the three Maritime Provinces, so great was the enthusiasm in Nova Scotia that in three weeks the full complement was supplied by that Province alone, and later the men from New Brunswick and Prince Edward Island became the nucleus for the 104th New Brunswick Battalion. Lieut.-Colonel Flowers went to the 64th as Second in Command, and Major W. B. A. Ritchie was appointed Officer in Charge of Recruiting. He was followed in December, 1916, by Major G. B. Cutten, of the Nova Scotia Highland Brigade. These officers were assisted by Capt. F. W. Micklewright and Capt. F. T. DeWolfe. Apart from Capt. E. W. Florence, Captain Micklewright probably recruited more men personally than any other officer.

The 64th Battalion being over strength, the 85th Battalion, Nova Scotia Highlanders, authorized some time previously, was ordered to proceed with recruiting. Numbers flocked to join its ranks. Men of responsible positions and lucrative salaries offered their services. In less than a month the Battalion was over strength and a large number of applicants were turned away.

NOVA SCOTIA'S PART IN THE GREAT WAR

In the gloomy closing days of 1915, when the withdrawal of the Gallipoli Expedition was announced, and many cherished expectations were again doomed to disappointment, the whole British Empire was profoundly stirred, and began to take its grip with characteristic bulldog tenacity. All its resources were demanded, every available man must go. Consequently in January of 1916 the question was mooted, why should not Nova Scotia give a whole Highland Brigade, and those who applied too late for admission to the 85th be afforded another and more liberal opportunity of going to the Front? Perhaps no idea ever suggested in the Province was taken up with more hearty enthusiasm.

During the first few weeks of 1916 organization was developed with great assiduity. It was decided to make use of the popular 85th in the work of recruiting. Every soldier who believed he could recruit another man was given six days' leave to do so; and if he succeeded in recruiting more than one he was granted an additional six days. Officers who volunteered to raise a Platoon were given charge of the territory in which it could be recruited. The results were in some instances amazing. Lads who seemed unlikely enough brought in recruits by the score.

In preparation for this great "drive" a publicity campaign was organized on an extensive scale. Pulpit, press and schoolroom were commandeered, and gave themselves up generously to the work. Religious services were arranged at which moral issues of the War were brought home forcibly to the people. Military uniforms appeared in the pulpits and unwonted martial strains, even from the bagpipes, were heard in sacred precincts.

Perhaps the most unique feature of the campaign was the use made of the public schools. The Union Jack was widely displayed. The children were drilled in patriotic songs. Books were laid aside and mass meetings held at which prominent citizens delivered addresses until to the impressionable mind of the little children it was incredible that anyone should stay at home. A letter was addressed by Lieut.-Colonel Borden to the boys and girls of Nova Scotia. In simple language he explained the meaning of the War, and converted every child into an irrepressible recruiting agent among his big brothers at home, or in the circle of his friends.

RECRUITING IN NOVA SCOTIA

When the country had thus been duly prepared, and public feeling was running high, the master-stroke was given, which resulted in the raising of "three Battalions in three weeks," a feat unsurpassed in the recruiting efforts of Canada. This was a series of meetings, held in every town, village and country hall, crowded to the doors, and characterized by the intense fervor of a religious revival. Notable among those who took part in the campaign for the 193rd and 219th Battalions were Lieut.-Colonel Borden, Lieut.-Colonel Guthrie (invalided home from the Front), President Cutten of Acadia University, Dr. Clarence McKinnon, and a score of other public men, who gladly gave time and talent to the task. The band of the 85th Battalion accompanied the speakers in their tour through the counties of Lunenburg, Queens, Shelburne, Yarmouth, Annapolis, Digby, Kings, Pictou and Antigonish.

Cape Breton had already contributed the 17th and 36th Batteries (the latter Unit was raised in a single day), a large proportion of the 25th and 40th Battalions, six hundred men to the 64th, three hundred men to the 85th, three hundred men to the 106th, besides keeping at full strength its Militia Regiment, the 94th Argyll Highlanders, which had been on active service from the outbreak of the War. Not satisfied with this the Island asked for and received authority to recruit a purely Cape Breton Infantry Battalion, to be included in the Nova Scotia Highland Brigade. Under the supervision of Major Gordon S. Harrington (later appointed Deputy Overseas Minister and promoted to the rank of Colonel) Cape Breton officers and men of the 85th Battalion returned to their former homes and engaged in active recruiting. Meetings were held in every town and village, and addresses made by Mayor Richardson, F. A. Crowell, A. D. Gunn, D. A. Cameron, Dr. C. E. McMillan, Stuart McCawley, the late D. A. Hearn, and many other prominent people. As a result of their work, and in spite of the restrictions placed upon them by the G.O.C. M.D. No. 6, who forbade the enlistment of employees of the Dominion Coal Company and the Dominion Iron and Steel Company, the 185th Battalion, Cape Breton Highlanders was recruited to full strength within three weeks.

In April, 1916, Mr. F. A. Crowell was requested to act as Chief Recruiting Officer for the County of Cape Breton. In a civilian capacity and without remuneration he accepted the position, and, assisted by Lieutenant Chirgwin and Sergt. A. Johnstone of the 94th Regiment, carried on the work until January, 1917. Up to the time the Military Service Act came into force the Island of Cape Breton contributed over seven thousand volunteers, including, in addition to the Units already named, 100 men to the 246th Battalion, 200 men to the Composite Battalion, besides a large number to the several Artillery Units mobilized at Halifax, to the 165th, 169th and 239th Battalions, the Army Service Corps, Forestry Units, Railway Troops and Army Medical Services, with a lower record of rejection than in any other district in Canada—in the case of the 185th only three per cent.

It would have been impossible for the Chief Recruiting Officer and his Staff of paid officers and men to have made the success they did had it not been for the valuable services rendered by the voluntary recruiting officers all over the Province. These men worked faithfully throughout the War without remuneration, and not infrequently labored under misrepresentation.

CHAPTER XLVI.

OCEAN TRANSPORT.

THE importance of the work done in Military District No. 6 during the period of the Great War is doubtless not realized by the public, other than those who were directly interested in the work. Aside from Halifax being a fortified port, and the Naval Base of the Atlantic Fleet during the War, it was the point of embarkation of the Canadian troops for Overseas, with the exception of the First Contingent, which was sent Overseas from Quebec. Therefore the work, devolving on District No. 6, in handling the enormous number of Canadian, American, Australian and New Zealand troops that passed through here was a matter of considerable responsibility and care, not only in checking the men going on board ship, but also in providing accommodations, rations, etc., while they were held ashore at Halifax from a day to three or four weeks, awaiting the arrival of their transports. In addition it was necessary to make preparations for emergencies, of which there were several, including such things as the stranding of a troopship near the mouth of Halifax Harbor, which necessitated the safe removal, landing and caring for the troops by other than the regular methods.

The detail work in connection with these duties was great and varied. For instance, the Department at Ottawa would arrange the date for the sailing of transports and the allotment of troops for each. The Department would then notify this district accordingly. The troops allotted to each ship would arrive by special trains, often before their transport reached port. During this period of waiting many casualties would occur, either through absentees, sickness, or from other causes, necessitating extra accommodation at the local quarters or in hospital. On the arrival of the ship these men would have to be checked on board individually, all casualties accounted for, complete returns made out, such as marching out state, lists of officers, inspection of all documents, and many other details. After that particular ship was loaded she would pull away from the pier and remain in harbor awaiting the loading of the other transports. Very often these transports would lie in the harbor for some days before sailing, awaiting the completion of the convoy, a result being that additional casualties would occur daily on each ship during that period. These had to be taken off the ship, in turn, all documents corrected to date so that when the ship sailed from the harbor an accurate record of every man on board was complete and thus enabled the Government to check the proper charges of the Steamship Companies for transportation. In the early stages of the War transports to the number of forty would sail from Halifax in one convoy, but towards the latter end of the War the Naval Authorities provided for convoys not exceeding seventeen ships at one time.

In all there were 284,455 Canadian troops embarked from Halifax. Some 50,000 Chinamen, and a large number of American troops also embarked from this port. In addition, ships with New Zealanders and Australians on board called at this port to join the convoys, and often were allowed to land for route marches and given shore leave. This also entailed much work on this district, due to the necessity of looking after casualties, absentees, etc.

Of all the casualties occurring during these embarkations a careful record had to be kept, and in due course, that is, as soon as possible after they became fit or were apprehended, they were sent Overseas on later transports.

Many complicated questions arose during this period, as, for instance, men arriving on troop trains under arrest for misdemeanors of various kinds, and thus necessitating this district dealing with such cases.

Following is a summary of the Canadian troops that embarked at Halifax during the war period:—

Date. 1915.	Ship.	Embarked Halifax.	Monthly Total.
Jan. 8	Zeeland	346	
			346
Feb. 23	Megantic	40	
23	Missinabie	13	
28	Scandinavian	23	
			76

OCEAN TRANSPORT

Date. 1915.	Ship.	Embarked Halifax.	Monthly Total.
Mar. 6	Grampian	8	
15	Northland	130	
21	Corsican	40	
22	Orduna		
26	Hesperian	15	
26	Chaleur	68	
28	Missinabie	321	582
Apr. 4	Scandinavian	12	
6	Georgia	76	
9	Chignecto	48	
10	Metagama	641	
12	Manchester Corporation	73	
17	St. George	414	
18	Northland	1,711	
18	Grampian	1,660	
24	Missinabie	440	5,075
May 2	Hesperian	154	
20	Saxonia	2,282	
20	Halifax	37	2,473
June 14	Herschell	523	
15	Caledonia	1,833	2,356
Aug. 8	Italia	1,211	
8	Caledonia	994	
9	Metagama	1,615	
26	Caledonia	1,087	4,907
Oct. 23	Lapland	2,319	
27	Orduna	1,095	3,414
Nov. 19	Chignecto	88	
22	Saxonia	2,494	
23	California	1,909	
27	Lapland	2,281	6,772
Dec. 3	Chaudiere	98	
6	Orduna	1,121	
8	Italia	430	1,649
1916.			
Jan. 22	Missinabie	1,591	1,591
Feb. 10	Caraquet	24	24
Mar. 13	Lapland	2,127	
13	Baltic	2,606	
30	Empress of Britain	3,542	
31	Adriatic	2,440	10,715

NOVA SCOTIA'S PART IN THE GREAT WAR

Date. 1916.	Ship.	Embarked Halifax.	Monthly Total.
Apr. 1	Olympic	5,787	
18	Missinabie	1,717	
21	Chaleur	20	
23	Empress of Britain	4,020	
24	Lapland	2,201	
29	Olympic	5,583	
			19,328
May 6	Chignecto	61	
12	Baltic	2,612	
19	Adriatic	2,325	
20	Empress of Britain	3,788	
26	Grampian	692	
31	Olympic	5,794	
			15,272
June 18	Empress of Britain	3,420	
19	Missinabie	1,663	
28	Olympic	5,755	
			10,838
July 8	Lapland	2,208	
15	Empress of Britain	3,778	
23	Olympic	5,290	
28	Caraquet	162	
			11,438
Aug. 6	Scandinavian	1,351	
7	Cameronia	1,430	
8	Metagama	1,581	
8	Scotian	1,235	
14	Empress of Britain	3,704	
15	Grampian	1,471	
21	Olympic	5,109	
			15,881
Sept. 11	Scandinavian	1,396	
11	Cameronia	1,412	
12	Metagama	1,491	
12	Northland	1,473	
18	Olympic	5,486	
23	Lapland	2,042	
25	Southland	1,379	
25	Corsican	1,426	
26	Laconia	2,230	
26	Tusconia	2,360	
			20,695
Oct. 2	California	1,161	
3	Missinabie	1,708	
3	Saxonia	2,417	
11, 12 & 13	Olympic	5,988	
17	Cameronia	1,401	
17	Metagama	1,721	
17	Northland	1,662	
24	Grampian	1,673	
25	Mauretania	3,089	
25 & 26	Corsican	1,351	
30	Lapland	2,196	

OCEAN TRANSPORT

Date. 1916.		Ship.	Embarked Halifax.	Monthly Total.
Oct.	31	Caronia	4,251	
	31	Empress of Britain	3,796	
				32,414
Nov.	1	Southland	1,700	
	13	Olympic	5,909	
	23 & 24	Mauretania	3,123	
	27	Metagama	1,609	
				12,341
Dec.	16	Olympic	5,999	
	27	Northland	36	
				6,035
1917.				
Jan.	23	Scandinavian	1,350	
	24	Canada	1,244	
	26	Grampian	1,525	
				4,119
Feb.	16	Southland	1,749	
	16	Missinabie	1,727	
				3,476
Mar.	4	Canada	1,241	
	4	Ansonia	1,049	
	25	Metagama	1,641	
	25	Lapland	1,637	
	25	Southland	892	
	26	Missinabie	1,595	
	26	Saxonia	2,357	
				10,412
Apr.	9	Carpathia	2,341	
	9	Canada	1,282	
	17	Scandinavian	1,194	
	18	Ansonia	1,102	
	18	Northland	1,572	
	18	Grampian	1,654	
	27	Olympic	5,605	
	30	Megantic	1,141	
				15,891
May	1	Metagama	1,696	
	3	Justicia	4,445	
	28	Olympic	5,823	
				11,964
June	22	Justicia	4,160	
				4,160
Aug.	6	Olympic	100	
	10	Grampian	1,500	
	11	Missinabie	1,402	
				3,002
Sept.	5	Megantic	1,854	
				1,854
Oct.	4	Metagama	1,276	
	20	Scandinavian	925	
				2,201
Nov.	20	Scotian	1,352	
	24	Megantic	1,637	
	27	Metagama	1,182	
				4,171

Date. 1917.	Ship.	Embarked Halifax.	Monthly Total.
Dec. 21	Missinabie	1,700	
21	Grampian	1,638	
28	Canada	11	
			3,349
1918.			
Jan. 19	Kursk	50	
27	Orita	320	
28	Scandinavian	1,290	
			1,660
Feb. 5	Grampian	1,607	
5	Missinabie	1,678	
5	Canada	826	
13	Lapland	1,815	
21	Megantic	1,822	
21	Meletia	1,830	
21	Saxonia	2,138	
28	Metagama	1,692	
28	Kasmala	111	
			13,519
Mar. 1	Justicia	155	
8	Scotian	23	
8	Toloa	819	
13	Chaleur	29	
17	Saturnia	100	
25	Missinabie	1,656	
25	Scandinavian	1,293	
25	Grampian	1,591	
			5,666
Apr. 9	Metagama	1,672	
9	Tunisian	1,318	
9	Ulua	949	
17	Scotian	1,324	
17	Toloa	1,108	
17	Melita	1,906	
			8,277
May 11	Tierisias	1,252	
11	Runic	394	
16	Ajana	1,435	
16	Valacia	1,020	
23	C. of Marseilles	55	
			4,156
June 17	Pannonia	853	
24	Wiamana	389	
24	Gloucestershire	512	
24	Ionic	27	
			1,781
July 2	Oxfordshire	390	
3	Valacia	185	
			575
Total		284,455	

CHAPTER XLVII.

MUNITIONS.

A BRIEF history of the work of the Shell Committee, its organization, and the part played by the Nova Scotia Steel and Coal Company in producing munitions during the first two and a half years of the War.

On September 8, 1915, Col. Alex Bertram, Thomas Cantley, and George W. Watts were summoned by the Federal Minister of Militia, Sir Sam Hughes, to Valcartier. On meeting the Minister he stated that the British Secretary of State for War had advised the Canadian Government that the War Office were desirous of having shrapnel shells made in Canada, that the Canadian Government had decided to entrust the matter to a Committee of Manufacturers, and had so advised the War Office. It was understood that the advice of the Minister had been accepted, and that the names of the three gentlemen above referred to had been approved by the War Office as a Committee to carry on the work on their behalf. The men above named were then asked to serve as such Committee, without remuneration, which they agreed to do, and were requested to select one of their number as Chairman. On the suggestion of Thos. Cantley, Colonel Bertram was appointed Chairman, the Minister confirming the appointment of the Committee by a memorandum initialed " For Action."

Later, Mr. E. Carnegie, of Welland, was added to the Committee, and at their request the Minister agreed that Colonel Benson, Master General of Ordnance; Colonel Lafferty, Superintendent of the Dominion Arsenal; and Colonel Greville Harston, Inspector of Arms and Ammunition, should be added as Technical Members.

The first meeting was held the same evening (September 8th) at the Chateau Frontenac, Quebec. The second meeting was held the following day at the office of the Superintendent of the Dominion Arsenal. The Committee were accorded the privilege of dissecting the manufacturing costs of the various operations involved in making shells of this type at the Dominion Arsenal, which at that time had an out-turn of about 200 per day.

From the data there available and their experience as manufacturers the Committee advised the War Office that 200,000 shrapnel shells could be produced by the Committee and supplied to the War Office at a price of $8.30 for the 15-pounder, and $8.55 each for

COL. THOMAS CANTLEY.

the 18-pounder. On this information being cabled to London the Committee were at once instructed to proceed with the order.

After the order was in process of execution a contract was presented by a representative of the War Office to the four civilian members, viz., Messrs. Bertram, Cantley, Watt and Carnegie, under which contract they were obligated to supply the War Office with these shells at the prices stated. This contract was duly executed,

MUNITIONS

the Honorable Minister of Militia signing on behalf of and representing, the War Office, the civilian members signing on their own behalf.

While the first order was for 200,000 shells, additional orders were placed by the War Office with the Committee at various times between September, 1914, and November, 1915, aggregating in all $345,222,870.24. The contract prices were in most cases named by the War Office. In some cases the prices were the result of compromise arranged by cable between the Committee and the War Office. In other cases the prices were those suggested by the Committee and were accepted by the War Office.

As already stated, every order was covered by a contract between the War Office on the one hand and the four civilian members of the Committee on the other, for the carrying out of which the civilian members were collectively and individually responsible. When they resigned office a statement, which was prepared and duly audited showing the total cost, together with the surplus based on prices agreed upon and covered by contracts between the War Office and the four civilian members, showed that the contracts entered into amounted in all to $345,222,874.34. Approximately 87½ per cent. of these orders were then completed, and the surplus—the difference between the contract price and the cost of production—was $42,097,584.57, less overhead charges, cost of inspection, guages, etc., of $737,400.31. If 12½ per cent. be added to this overhead charge to meet similar expenses incidental to the completion of the contracts, $92,175.03 would require to be added, making the total overhead expenditure $829,575.34, or a total net surplus to the credit of the Committee on November 30, 1915, of $41,268,009.23. The total overhead cost, covering inspection, cost of guages, accounting, and office expense of the Committee, worked out at .17, or less than one-fifth of one per cent. of contract prices.

In this connection it may be stated that the prices paid by the War Office to American makers in many cases were considerably higher than those paid in Canada for shells and other material. In other cases, where the prices were approximately the same, the volume of orders entrusted to the United States makers were very much greater than the corresponding orders placed with the Canadian Shell Committee, and the American prices should have been considerably lower. Further, the orders placed in the United States were entrusted to an agent, who is reported to have received a handsome commission, whereas the services of the Canadian Shell Committee were freely given.

In the early stages the executive work of the Committee was carried on by General Bertram, whose time was largely taken up in co-ordinating the machining of parts, and the placing of orders for components among Canadian manufacturers, while Thomas Cantley undertook to carry out experiments, both chemical and physical, looking to the production of open hearth basic steel to meet the specifications and tests called for by the War Office. Experiments were also carried out later in regard to steel discs, base plates, nose plugs, alloy steel armor plating, etc. Later Colonel Bertram, Thos. Cantley and G. W. Watts collaborated in fixing prices for component parts and machining and assembling of the different size shells. Later they devised a complete system of records, inspection sheets, transfer and shipping forms, store and stock forms, and a complete system of accounting was worked out and inaugurated by them.

Late in September the Minister of Militia, on the suggestion of the Committee, approved the appointment of David Carnegie as Ordnance Adviser to the Committee, in view of the fact that he had had considerable experience in munition work at Woolwich Arsenal.

When the War Office first appealed to Canada for assistance in supplying munitions, little was known of shell manufacturing in Canada. This being the case the Canadian Government decided that a Committee of Manufacturers could better serve the War Office than could the Government through any of the Departments; and then followed the formation of the Shell Committee as originally outlined. The Committee had before them three problems: First, that of securing steel of the requisite character; secondly, the forging of the steel into shell bodies, together with the supply of other component parts, comprising brass, copper, tin, zinc and antimony; and thirdly, the machining and assembling of these various component parts.

MUNITIONS

Up to the time that the request came from the War Office practically no men in Canada, with the exception of those employed at the Dominion Arsenal, knew anything about the manufacture of shells, or the material required for same. The steel hitherto used at the Dominion Arsenal had been supplied by the Crucible Steel Co. of America, and the War Office had stipulated that only Acid Open Hearth Siemens-Martin steel could be employed in shell forgings. As no Siemens-Martin steel was produced in Canada, and if the War Office adhered to their stipulation in that respect the entire steel supply would have to be obtained in the United States, the American makers, feeling sure that this would be done, promptly advanced their prices approximately forty per cent.

At this juncture the Minister of Militia appealed to Thomas Cantley, then President and General Manager of the Nova Scotia Steel and Coal Co., as to whether the Scotia plant could not produce steel which would meet not only the chemical but physical requirements of the War Office shell specifications. He at once expressed the belief that they could do so, and immediately proceeded to carry out exhaustive experiments, both chemical and physical, which proved conclusively that the Scotia Company could produce steel as called for by the War Office, and offered to supply it at a price as low as the original price asked by the American works, and indeed below the American price. Within a few days of receipt of the first order by the Shell Committee from the War Office, the Scotia Company supplied the Committee with steel for 200,000 shrapnel shells. The difference in price paid to the Scotia Company and the price asked by the American Co. for the steel supplied on this small order amounted to over $40,000.

As regards forging of shells, the cost of producing the various component parts, the labor involved in finishing and assembling these —the Committee were supplied with the cost of these various operations as carried on at the Dominion Arsenal, but the difficulty involved was that the work, having been done there by a class of machine not in general use in Canada, and with the comparatively small order in hand, manufacturers could not be found who would purchase and install plant for this work and turn out shells within a reasonable time and price.

Manufacturers throughout the country were invited to visit the Dominion Arsenal at Quebec, where they would be shown the various operations involved, and given all information *re* cost, methods employed, etc. Quite a number responded to this invitation. Some offered to undertake the work; others declined to undertake it on any basis whatever.

Colonel Bertram volunteered that the John Bertram & Sons Co. would do a certain amount of machining and assembling, and Thos. Cantley, through his Company, the Nova Scotia Steel and Coal Co., undertook to supply the steel and forgings, while Mr. Watt, of the Canadian General Electric Company, agreed to make some of the component parts. Sir Thomas Shaughnessy, on being appealed to by the Committee for assistance, instructed the Superintendent of the Angus Shops to take on some of the work, and generously promised that the Angus Shops would take up their share of the enterprise.

With the start made by these firms to encourage them, a few other manufacturers were induced to take up a share of the work, and thus the supply of components parts and machining of same for the first 200,000 shells was finally placed, and this initial order was shipped complete and to the entire satisfaction of the War Office some considerable time before the contract date.

So soon as the work involved in the first trial order had been accepted by the manufacturers referred to, the Committee took up the organization necessary for the co-ordinating of the work on a larger scale; and as large orders were received in rapid succession from the War Office, contracts were made with different manufacturers for component parts, which were bought outright by the Committee. A full set of component parts for each shell was supplied by the assembly contractors, by whom these were finished and returned as completed shells, they being paid a fixed price on the shells which were completed, and which passed all the tests demanded by the War Office, and were certified as such by the Government Inspection Bureau. The component parts before being accepted by the Committee and delivered to the finishing contractors were inspected and certified by the Committee's inspectors. Any component parts spoiled by the assembly manufacturers had to be paid for by them at the actual cost of same.

The first experiences of the forging and finishing contractors alike were disappointing. It was an entirely new business to everybody engaged in the work, and the usual initial difficulties were met and overcome with varying success.

It is safe to say that as far as the first order of 200,000 shells was concerned, the companies engaged, either as makers of component parts or as assembly contractors, received little, if any, profit for their work. They had only the usual reward that comes to pioneers in any new work.

When the new and larger orders came in, both the material and the work were thrown open to competition. The Dominion Steel Corporation, the Steel Company of Canada, and other smaller steel producers were asked to supply steel and forgings. The same thing applied to manufacturing establishments, which were in a position to supply other component parts or to take on the work of machining and assembling. By the early part of 1915 the work was distributed throughout the entire Dominion.

Those who had done the pioneering work, and who won their position through dearly-bought experience, and by venturing in where others lacked courage to do so, came under criticism from others who had not hitherto undertaken any of the work. To overcome this difficulty and to assure hearty co-operation in the production of the largest amount of munitions possible, the Committee adopted the principle of naming a flat price for each component part, as well as for the machining and assembling of each size shell.

All the orders placed thereafter, from time to time, were placed at a uniform price, both for the component parts and for the finishing of the shells. The instant effect of this was that the accumulated experience of the pioneering firms was placed at the disposal of the other manufacturers. Both forging and finishing shops were thrown open, their methods of working and costs were fully explained, and shown to other manufacturers. The newcomers thus saved the heavy cost of experimental work.

New methods, improvements of great value in connection with the execution of the work, the outcome of the initiative adaptability of Canadians, wrought a revolution in the methods of production. All these improvements were in every case put within the reach of other manufacturers. Many of these have been adopted, not only by Canadian shell makers, but by shell makers in the United States and Great Britain.

During the organization period from September, 1914, to April, 1915, more than one member of the Committee worked from ten to seventeen hours per day, Sundays and holidays not excepted, and none of the members then appointed received one dollar by way of remuneration.

The part played by the New Glasgow works of the Nova Scotia Steel and Coal Company in the Great War is an interesting one. At the beginning of hostilities in August, 1914, there were only two Steel Companies in the United States who had either the plant or experience to produce either shells or armor plates, while none of the Canadian steel plants had any experience whatever.

The first production of munition material, by way of shells and shell steel, was undertaken in Canada by the Shell Committee, and the story of the experiments carried on in the early days of September, 1914, which resulted in convincing the British War Office that basic steel, as made in Canada, would meet all the requirements of both shrapnel and high explosive shells, and which resulted in very large orders for munitions coming to Canada, is well known to all Nova Scotians, and has become a matter of history.

Between October, 1914, when the Scotia plants produced 22,000 shell forgings, and the signing of the Armistice, November 11, 1918, the New Glasgow plant had made more than 15,000,000 shells—these ranging in size from the 15-pounder shrapnel to 12-inch high explosive, the local plant being the only one in Canada which made the latter size. The total tonnage of forged shells produced at New Glasgow amounted in round figures to 180,000 tons. In addition to this a very considerable tonnage of shell and other munition steel was shipped to be worked up in other shell forging establishments in Canada and Great Britain. A further considerable tonnage was worked up into marine forgings. British shipyards about this time experienced great difficulty in obtaining heavy marine forgings to meet Lloyd's specification and tests. The Scotia forges had long been on Lloyd's list as approved makers of Marine Forgings. The British shipbuilders' difficulty was now met by Scotia, which supplied to various yards on the Clyde, the East Coast, and other yards complete sets of marine forgings of all classes for both mercantile and other vessels of large tonnage. The total quantity of marine forgings supplied Great Britain since the outbreak of war amounted to 9,000 tons.

Most Nova Scotians are probably entirely ignorant of the considerable amount of what might be called "research" and experimental work carried out at the New Glasgow plant for the Government, and while this did not produce the tangible results brought about in connection with the manufacture of shells, not a little of the data and knowledge accumulated, contributed in a very considerable degree to the successful development of both the offensive and the defensive equipment of the Allied forces.

While this work was being done secrecy was essential, nothing was said and but little known of the work carried on along these lines. Now that the War is over the necessity for secrecy appears to be past.

In February, 1919, the firm of William Beardmore and Co., of Glasgow, Scotland, in their works magazine, told the story of the evolution and development by them of bullet-proof material for the protection of armored cars, trench shields, armor-plate for the celebrated "tanks," and other work of a like character. The story, as told by the Beardmore people, in many important particulars runs on all fours with the experiments and results obtained at New Glasgow during the latter weeks of 1914 and the early part of 1915, when a series of exhaustive experiments were carried out at New Glasgow, first in connection with the production and testing of bullet-resisting steel plate.

This matter was first brought to the attention of the writer by General Sir Sam Hughes in connection with the shield shovel, of which a good deal was heard during 1915 and 1916. This spade, as supplied by the American makers, was formed with a sharp cutting edge, and a loophole for a rifle, but had no handle. When deliveries began to be made by the American manufacturers, a certain quantity was collected at random and turned over to the writer for testing. This was carried out at the rifle range of the Fifth Royal Highlanders in the basement of the Bleury Street Armory, Montreal. It was then found that while practically all would stand Mark Six British Service Ammunition, they failed to withstand the much greater impact of Mark Seven Ammunition. Mark Six had a muzzle velocity of about 1,800 feet per second. Further investigation showed that the difference in bullet resisting power in the plates submitted was due to lack of uniformity.

No handles had been supplied with the shovels, and no apparent effort had been made by the manufacturers to supply one which was suitable. Scotia's engineers were asked to meet the difficulty, which they did, and finally offered one which was adopted, weighed eight ounces, and was secured by a single rivet passing through a square slotted hole in the body of the shovel below the base of the tang.

At this time the question of supplying our army with armored machine-gun automobile trucks had become a pressing matter. The question had been turned over to a Toronto Committee. Great delay was experienced in securing sufficient suitable bullet-resisting plate, and serious confusion resulted. The experiments in connection with the shovel had thrown great doubt on the efficiency of the steel being supplied by the Americans, and again the Scotia Company were asked to carry out tests and advise as to the matter.

From hints which had filtered through from the army in France and Flanders it was known that the German Spitzer bullet was much more effective than the British new Mark Seven, and while the armor-plating contracted to be supplied by the Americans for these cars was guaranteed to withstand Mark Seven British Ammunition at 300 yards, the rumors in regard to the penetrating powers of the German Spitzer ammunition were most disquieting, and could not be ignored.

At that time the United States were neutral, but were making ammunition for the Allies and others. By methods, which it is not necessary here to refer to, or explain, the General Manager of the Scotia Company was able to obtain a German Mauser Service Rifle, and by an expenditure out of all proportion to the real value, 1,000 rounds of German Mauser Spitzer service ammunition was

MUNITIONS

also secured. An improvised range was set up on the ice on the East River, Nova Scotia, at a point where, protected by steep banks, firing tests could be carried out, when it was demonstrated that .311 Spitzer German ammunition, which, carefully chronographed, gave a muzzle velocity of 2,915 feet per second, easily penetrated the armor plate which resisted Mark Seven British Ammunition fired from either the Lee-Enfield or Ross Rifle.

The effect, of course, was to call a halt to the manufacture of these plates, and at the same time to push forward experiments then under way in the production by the Scotia Company of bullet-resisting alloy armor plates. Within a short time New Glasgow was able to offer the Department of Militia alloy steel, heat-treated plates, not exceeding 3-16th of an inch thick, which successfully withstood point-blank impact at one yard from Mark 7 ammunition fired from the latest model Ross rifle. In one case two shots had struck the plate within less than one-half inch of each other, and they neither penetrated nor cracked the plate.

Plates somewhat thicker were later supplied which withstood German Mauser ammunition at point blank range, and the result given by these plates when tested at the Proving Station in Toronto were so satisfactory that the Artillery Proving Officers, after the tests, placed them on exhibition outside the Camp, and later reported that the men felt the utmost confidence with the protection afforded them by this plating, which later was supplied and fitted to a proportion of the machine-gun trucks then being equipped. Later the British Government asked the Scotia Company to tender for similar protective plating for armored trucks.

CHAPTER XLVIII.

DEMOBILIZATION.

DEMOBILIZATION, following a war of such length and intensity as that of the Four Years' War from August, 1914, to November, 1918, is not a mere problem of repatriation, it is a problem of reconstruction—a gigantic one at that—desiderating the undivided efforts of every organization in the nation and the assistance of every citizen.

Consider for a moment what had happened in the industrial world. During the four years of war, Governments were the chief employers of men, the chief purchasers of raw materials, and the chief sources of revenue for an overwhelmingly large portion of the population. To retain the ideals of democracy Governments were given unlimited power—power which was utilized in organizing practically the entire life of the belligerent nations into a vast machine for turning out implements of war. Not only was this war-time industry mobilized under unified control, but the market for which its product was turned out could not be flooded. Indeed, it continually called for greater and greater production regardless of cost. The expansion of business, and the building up of a huge army of war workers, the scarcity of labor and raw materials, the shifting of markets, the meteoric rise of prices, the less rapid rise of wages, Government control of prices, raw materials and exports, the inflation of currency, the huge increase in national debts—these were some of the phenomena which characterized the period. They justify the assertion that a revolution in the economic and industrial life of the nations had occurred. Even in Canada, remote from the scene of actual strife, a generation's changes were compressed into four short years.

Then suddenly, on November the eleventh, the object for which the vast war machine had been built up was attained. The necessity for its existence vanished over-night, and the world found itself

DEMOBILIZATION

face to face with the task of scrapping the industrial machine which had so effectively served the requirements of war, and of rebuilding one which would serve just as effectively the entirely different requirements of peace. The new task was more difficult than the old, and had to be accomplished in a much shorter period—a few months, instead of four years. Again, the problems themselves were more delicate and intricate; largely problems of human psychology, not of mechanics, requiring for their solution not compulsion, but education, persuasion and co-operation. The world has learned that it is much easier to make war than to make peace.

The early days of 1914 and 1915 were days of mobilization problems, and they were problems indeed. The provision of arms, equipment and food had to be undertaken on a scale unheard of before. It was necessary to provide transportation for vast bodies of troops and great quantities of stores, to say nothing of the construction of training camps, rifle ranges, and all the paraphernalia of war. The human element, fresh and easily responsive to patriotic appeal, presented few difficulties at that time.

There are, however, certain conditions inherent in military life which go far towards unfitting the soldier for civilian occupation. Without entering into a discussion of the reasons for these conditions, two of them at least may be enumerated. In military life individual liberty is impossible, but it is of supreme importance in civil life. Further, in military life ambition or self-interest, which may be considered a fundamental motive in human action, becomes of secondary importance. Self-interest is, in fact, disciplined into complete abeyance. The moment the soldier becomes a civilian the restraints upon his individual liberty are more or less removed, and it is entirely in keeping with the impulses of human nature if he should, for a time, go to the opposite extreme. Then again, he finds it no easy task to awaken the ambition lying dormant within him, and it frequently happens that it is only from bitter experience that he learns it is necessary to rely, in the first instance, upon himself. These two conditions alone emphasize how different are the various problems of demobilization and mobilization. The success or failure of the work of reconstruction depends, not so much on the highly-developed organization as on the amount of personal service, whole-hearted sympathy and understanding brought to the work by those who, together with the soldier, must face the many obstacles confronting him in the first stages of his return to citizenship.

Without the active co-operation of the soldiers themselves the work of reconstruction could not be a success. Undoubtedly our present stability, in comparison with many other parts of Canada is, in a large measure, due to the initiative and strength of purpose with which our soldiers have met, and are meeting, the tasks of a humdrum every-day life. It would, no doubt, be surprising to the average citizen were he to know how many men in Nova Scotia have re-established themselves without assistance from the Government.

It was not until the closing days of 1915 and the return of casualties gassed and wounded from Ypres, Festubert, and Givenchy, that the problems of demobilization began to press for attention. The country was sadly lacking in proper hospital accommodation and equipment, especially for the treatment of surgical cases. The disabled man was finding it no easy matter to re-establish himself and the provision of industrial training or suitable employment for him was an urgent need. In many other ways the necessity for a radical change made itself apparent.

The actual work of getting the soldiers home and out of khaki was in the hands of the Department of Militia and Defence; but the methods of peace and war are as far removed as day and night, and it was soon recognized that the re-absorption of returned soldiers into civil life, with the least disturbance of economic conditions, could not be best performed by an organization of the military type. The first step in the direction of providing a suitable organization was taken when the Military Hospitals Commission was formed in the same year. The duties of this Commission eventually embraced almost every phase of the problem of demobilization, from the provision of hospitals, convalescent homes and treatment, to vocational re-education for those who, through a disability were unable to return to their former occupation.

Not all the emergencies were, of course, foreseen; and from time to time changes for the better were made in the regulations. Shortly after the formation of the Commission a conference of representatives from the various Provincial Governments was called

DEMOBILIZATION

at Ottawa, and the suggestions there adopted involved an extension of the work by the appointment of a sub-committee of the Federal Commission in each Province, to assume the responsibility of finding employment for discharged soldiers.

Immediately following this conference the Returned Soldiers' Employment Committee of Nova Scotia, or, as it was afterwards known, the Nova Scotia Returned Soldiers' Commission, was appointed. The importance of this work, at the time could not be overestimated, for is not reconstruction fundamentally a problem of employment and employment conditions? This function, however, by no means exhausted the activities of the Provincial Commission. On executive questions of a local nature it was the advisory body of the Federal Commission at Ottawa, and its scope was extended as the need arose, until it embraced practically all matters dealing with returned men. On certain occasions the Commission maintained an early and aggressive stand on problems which were not merely of a local character, but which affected the economic life of the Dominion.

When the Military Hospitals Commission was formed, it was found necessary to operate Interviewing Departments in conjunction with the Clearing or Discharge Depots at Halifax, St. John and Quebec, in order to secure information from which to compile records. Each returning soldier on the ship's nominal roll was questioned regarding his pre-war occupation, his future prospects and intentions, as well as other general information required. In the case of casualties the proceedings of the last medical board were also secured. At Halifax a Staff of returned men were engaged in this work under the supervision of W. B. MacCoy, Secretary of the Provincial Commission. As the interviewing for the whole of Canada was performed at the ports, it can be appreciated what a vast amount of work this entailed, particularly when handling hospital ships. The severely disabled men were, of course, unable to visit the Interviewing Department. Consequently it was not possible to proceed as rapidly as in the case of ordinary transports.

Another detail of the disembarkation which involved a great deal of work on the part of the Commission was that of notifying the next-of-kin of returning soldiers. A copy of the Nominal Roll, prepared on the voyage across, was secured immediately after the ship had docked and the Secretaries of the Returned Soldiers' Commissions in the various other Provinces were telegraphed a complete list of the men going forward with the names and addresses of their relatives or friends.

The Nova Scotia men were, of course, dealt with first, as in many cases they would arrive home within a few hours. Their names were either telegraphed or telephoned to the Secretaries of the Town Reception Committees who, in turn, notified the relatives and aided in providing a suitable reception.

During the War, Nova Scotia was exceedingly fortunate in the matter of employment. The number of unemployed soldiers seldom averaged more than ten per cent., and was usually between two and seven per cent. However, the abnormal conditions prevailing after the signing of the Armistice rendered the number of placements by the Commission, for a time at least, almost negligible. Numbers of men were suddenly thrown on the labor market by the closing of war-time industries, while at the same time our soldiers were being returned in thousands. This was by no means the critical period. Many of the men returning after years of service Overseas felt the need of a well-earned vacation more than they did of a job, while those who had dependants and who were anxious, but unable, to secure immediate employment, were temporarily provided for by the war service gratuity. For the majority, the most anxious time arrived during the succeeding fall and winter months. It is not the intention, however, to deal with the employment activities of the Commission. Attention must be confined to work of a more general nature.

As previously stated, the country, particularly Nova Scotia, was sadly lacking in hospital accommodation. In the spring and early summer of 1915, nearly all returned soldiers either came through the Port of Quebec, or, if disembarked at Halifax, were forwarded to the Discharge Depot there. Save in a few instances, such as severe casualties, these men as soon as medically examined were given transportation to their homes. Discharge Certificates were usually not issued for months after their return, and a great deal of confusion resulted. Indeed, few of the men were aware of their status, and it not infrequently happened that, instead of the longed-for piece of parchment, they received a letter from their Military District instructing them to report for duty,—this after having perhaps accepted civilian employment. The uncertainty of their future added to the difficulties of obtaining a satisfactory position, for after a few experiences, employers generally hesitated to engage a man who was not in possession of a certificate releasing him to civilian duties. As time went on, too, pay complaints began to pour in by the score, due no doubt to an antiquated system of handling documents, and the poor working facilities afforded the District Pay Staffs.

About the end of the following year the Provincial Commission advised the erection of a hospital, but although the officials of the Military Hospitals Commission apparently concurred in the Provincial Commission's views, the conditions remained unchanged. Repeated reports were made by the Secretary and concrete cases submitted, showing the necessity in certain instances for providing treatment. The situation became so acute that at a meeting of the local Commission, held on February 21, 1917, certain members, feeling that the existing state of affairs might be construed as reflecting upon them, tendered their resignations to the Chairman. These resignations were, however, held in abeyance for a few days, and a strongly-worded resolution was passed and forwarded to Sir James Lougheed. Several days later a special meeting was called at the request of the Director of the Military Hospitals Commission, at which were present two officials of that body with full authority to take what steps were deemed necessary in order to relieve the situation. The writer, who has had access to the correspondence and records, can state without fear of contradiction, that it was wholly due to the efforts of the Provincial Commission that Camp Hill Hospital was erected in 1917. Readers who are familiar with conditions both then and during the period following the Halifax disaster must realize what a boon it was to have had this splendid institution awaiting any and all emergencies.

The subject of Vocational Training was one in which the Commission took a deep interest from the very first. One of its early steps was to institute a careful survey of all existing educational facilities throughout Nova Scotia, which could be used for the re-education of disabled men. The re-training of this class was of the utmost importance, and the Commission successfully fought for the enactment of several regulations tending to broaden the scope of the Vocational Department.

One of the most persistent efforts was made in the interest of the physically fit "boy soldier." Aside from the minor who had been disabled, no provision existed whereby these young boys could be afforded the opportunities of re-education or re-training. The need for this was foreseen by the Provincial Office some two years before the close of the War and no opportunity was lost in the furtherance of their proposal to place them on the same footing as the disabled man. It was most desirable to provide facilities for the education of these young soldiers who enlisted in the Forces at an immature age. Their decision was made at a time when they could not probably measure the consequences of their act, and for this reason the public was responsible for any disadvantages accruing to them. The years spent in the army were just those during which they should have been fitting themselves to win a position of self-support and independence; and it is not only an advantage to themselves, but to the country, that they have been assisted in preparing for the earning of a livelihood rather than having been forced into the ranks of unskilled labor. The step taken by the Government in the early part of last year was indeed satisfactory in consideration of the initial and continuous efforts of the Provincial Commission.

The Soldier Settlement Act, passed in 1917, has proved to be one of the most satisfactory measures of re-establishment provided by the Government. As originally framed, however, it was of very little value to a man who desired to go on the land in the Maritime Provinces. The free grants provided by the Act were restricted to Dominion Lands, while here any land of value for agricultural purposes is privately owned. This was clearly placing under a handicap the Nova Scotian soldier who wished to stay in his native Province, inasmuch as the maximum amount which could be borrowed under the Act was only $2,500. The Provincial Commission urged very strongly that the benefits to be derived should be equally distributed and enjoyed by soldiers wishing to go on

DEMOBILIZATION

the land in any Province. At the 1918 yearly meeting of Provincial Secretaries, held at Ottawa, the other Provinces were unanimous in supporting the Maritime representatives, and a resolution was passed petitioning the Federal Government to extend the provisions of the Act. This was done some time afterwards, and to-day we have in Nova Scotia some three hundred and fifty farms producing, and as many soldiers re-established in this way.

The months which followed the erection of Camp Hill Hospital brought many changes. The Military Hospitals Commission ceased and was succeeded by the Department of Soldiers' Civil Re-Establishment. New organizations arose, and new methods were inaugurated in old ones to meet the constantly increasing needs and changing problems. But space will not permit to deal with all the phases of this many-sided and deeply interesting work. At best details can only be touched upon, and the three instances quoted of the Commission's connection with the larger problems of reconstruction by no means exhausts an interesting store of past events. The part taken by W. B. MacCoy, K.C., Secretary of the Commission, is deserving of the fullest public recognition. No man has been more sincere or more zealous in safeguarding the interests of the Nova Scotian soldiers. His work was not undertaken without a sacrifice, but the appreciation of thousands of soldiers and dependants expressed in the letters of thanks contained on the fyles of the Commission, and in many other ways, has doubtless repaid him in full.

W. B. MACCOY, K.C.

Victory was the reward of loyalty and co-operation and the willingness of each and every soldier to subjugate self in the welfare of the whole, and play the game as best he could. Demobilization has required no less devotion, energy, and co-operation than did the War itself and the measure of success attained through the sympathy, tact, and ability displayed by however humble a servant in the great work of reconstruction will be reflected in the national life of Canada for the next generation.

CHAPTER XLIX.

VOCATIONAL TRAINING.

THE aftermath of the Great War, which virtually ended with the Armistice on November 11, 1918, should be historically different from the social and economic muddles and messes which have succeeded other prolonged struggles. Human nature has not changed, but society is more enlightened, more highly organized, and more averse to waste.

The soldiers who returned to Canada from the Boer War were paid small Imperial pensions for disabilities incurred and were rewarded by grants of land in the great Canadian West, which almost all of them realized on immediately, selling them to "land sharks" for ridiculously small cash sums. It has been stated that most of the British veterans of the Crimea died in the workhouses.

Just as the last War was fought with more highly developed death-dealing machines and apparatus, and consequently evolved entirely new means of counter-offensive and protection, so the Allied nations employed entirely new methods to compensate the disabled fighting men for the incapacities they suffered through service. The aim was to develop all of the remaining abilities and aptitudes of the crippled soldier so that he might be able to retain his place in civilian life as an active, independent, self-supporting citizen.

Nova Scotia can justly claim the credit for starting the plan of vocational re-training developed in Canada. In July, 1915, Miss I. Matthews, who was assisting her sister, Mrs. J. K. L. Ross, in preparing the residence of the latter in Sydney for use as a convalescent home for soldiers, secured a pamphlet describing the early efforts of France in rehabilitating war cripples. She brought it to the attention of Hon. G. H. Murray, who asked Principal F. H.

VOCATIONAL TRAINING

Sexton, of the Technical College, for some concrete practical suggestions. The latter prepared a careful report on the methods which the Dominion might use to organize this work, and this was submitted to the Premier of Canada, Sir Robert Borden.

Just before this there had been created the Military Hospitals Commission to control the treatment in Canada of wounded and

DR. F. H. SEXTON,
Principal Nova Scotia Technical College.

disabled men returning from Europe. The report on vocational re-training was submitted to the Commission for consideration and action. The subject was regarded of such importance that a conference of Provincial Premiers and other representatives was called to consider this and some other questions affecting returned men.

Principal Sexton was sent as a Nova Scotian delegate to this conference and explained his ideas. He asserted that nearly all maimed and crippled men could be put on their feet again as wage-earners by a short, practical, intensive course in vocational training. The men were adults who had already had some industrial experience and consequently would not need as much or as long training as youths being apprenticed in trades. During the last twenty-five years industry had been sub-divided into many specialized occupations, in many of which little physical effort was required. Advantage could be taken of the vocational experience of the soldier previous to enlistment and, in most cases, he could be trained for some occupation in the same industry where his disability would not be a handicap. That is, the crippled men could be moved sidewise in industry to some parallel occupation or, by means of a little education, could be lifted up higher and fitted for some supervisory position as boss, foreman, or superintendent. Thus, a structural steel worker, with some physical deficiency, would be trained for a position of draftsman. The coal miner, who was disabled, so that he could no longer dig coal at the face could, in a comparatively short time, be trained for the position of shot-firer, fire boss, mine examiner, overman, underground foreman, or mine manager.

There were endless opportunities for fitting men for occupations that required more technical knowledge, more skill, and more mental capacity. Most of the Canadian soldiers had not much opportunity for vocational education in their youth, and the great majority could be prepared for better jobs with their disability than they had been able to qualify for before they enlisted. It was pointed out that technical schools could offer some courses for disabled men, and that the rest of them could be given intensive short apprenticeships in industry. The disabled men and their families should be supported in respectability during the course of training. It was emphasized that the soldier in the hospital should begin to do some work as soon as possible, so that he would not lose his habits of industry by too prolonged an idleness during treatment. This method of technical education would be expensive, but it would more than repay the country by making almost all the disabled men competent to maintain themselves as wage-earners for the remainder of their lives, and eliminate the great proportion of indigent, idle pensioners that had succeeded other great wars.

VOCATIONAL TRAINING

The conference in September, 1915, enthusiastically recommended that the Military Hospitals Commission proceed to develop vocational training of disabled soldiers along the lines proposed. Soon after this steps were taken to put the suggestions into actual practice. Principal Sexton was appointed, under the Commission, as Vocational Officer for Quebec and the Maritime Provinces, which office he has held for four and one-half years.

When the convalescent hospitals were first opened in Canada, it was thought at first that all the men needed was the necessary medical treatment and a rest and then most of them would naturally return to work. People who had not had army training, and who had not endured the terrible experiences in the front line trenches, did not understand the psychological reversal most of the soldiers had suffered. The ordinary Canadian was noted for his power of initiative. In times of peace he had developed resourcefulness and individuality. From thousands of occupations our men donned the khaki uniform. The first great lesson for the new soldier was that of implicit obedience to his superior officers. He was instructed that others would do his thinking for him. The responsibility of providing food, shelter, and raiment for himself and his dependants, which had been his constant effort in waking hours, was lifted from his shoulders. His habits were regularized to conform to a single standard,—that of the well-disciplined soldier. In action he was forced into a condition of personal dirtiness that would have been absolutely repellent to him in ordinary life. He was subjected to the nerve-racking, soul-splitting ordeal of continuous fire of high explosives. Death lurked at his elbow continuously in a thousand hideous forms. He lived like a worm, and the taking and giving of human life became an hourly experience. He forgot what a normal mode of living was like, and his tours back and forth to the trenches seemed the whole of existence, with only a ghastly way out of it. Then came his "blighty," and the long, painful period of hospital experience where willing and loving hands ministered to every need. He was doctored, nursed and entertained lavishly. Is it any wonder that he found himself in an abnormal mental state, and that ordinary civilian life seemed petty and cold and humdrum? Is it surprising that he found himself slow to rouse himself and prepare to take up again some civilian task in the treadmill of industry which would reward him with only food, clothing and lodging? After the glorious comradeship with his fellows in facing death, the competitive system in a life of routine duties seemed dull and deadly.

It seemed evident from the first experience that work was the only panacea. Definite, interesting occupation alone offered the means of making the man forget himself, and of wrenching him around into the footpath of peace. Self-imposed routine duties of an absorbing nature provided the necessary attraction and distraction to enable the man to prepare himself again for a useful life in industry. Therefore interesting work of all kinds was provided to suit different abilities and disabilities.

Three divisions of the work of re-training the disabled soldier developed as progress was made with this task, viz.: (1) Ward Occupations; (2) Curative Workshops; (3) Industrial Re-training. These will be taken up in the order named.

1. WARD OCCUPATIONS. Basketry, weaving, leather work and other handicrafts were taught to the men in hospital right in the wards, as recreational activity, during the time of convalescence when the soldiers, as patients, are not advanced far enough in their recovery to leave their beds or to take up serious education.

2. CURATIVE WORKSHOPS. Every hospital had either a separate vocational building or a portion of its space set aside for curative workshops. Here were held a variety of classes for men taking treatment who were able to leave their wards and who wished to study some subjects which would be of advantage to them when they were discharged from hospital and would re-enter civilian life or take up training for a new occupation.

3. INDUSTRIAL RE-TRAINING. This was the most important division of the work and, in fact, constituted the main activity of the Vocational Branch of the Department of Soldiers' Civil Re-establishment. All soldiers who received a disability in military service through disease, accident or wounds which prevented them from returning to their old occupations, were entitled to industrial re-training. Any man who enlisted under the age of eighteen, and whose apprenticeship or training for some useful occupation was seriously interrupted by the War, was also entitled

VOCATIONAL TRAINING

to an industrial re-training course. Thousands of men had to be intensively trained for hundreds of different occupations in the shortest possible time. During their courses they and their dependants received pay and allowances to support themselves. Every kind of institution which offered definite vocational training was utilized, but a great proportion of the men were placed in industry itself to learn their new occupations. Special trade classes and schools had to be organized and equipped by the Department of Soldiers' Civil Re-establishment to meet the new need. The main aim was to train the disabled soldiers and minors in six to ten months, so that they could earn the prevailing wage in suitable vocations. This aim was realized with results that have amply justified the predictions of experts in industrial education and the enormous expenditure of money necessary. The development of the three main divisions of the vocational work in Nova Scotia is interesting and illuminating, and promises much for the future in pointing the way to further developments in our hospital treatment and the reclaiming of the productive power of our men who have been or will be crippled by accident or disease.

It was very evident from the first experience with returned disabled soldiers in Canadian convalescent hospitals, that they needed some definite work to engage their attention just as soon as they were able to do it. After a prolonged illness their morale was very low, and many were convinced that they were so badly disabled that they would never be good for anything again. Nerves, muscles, and tendons which had been seriously damaged by wounds, could be healed and brought back to part of their former power by operative treatment, massage, electric therapy, etc., but at a certain stage further improvement could take place only through the action of the *will* of the patient. At this point the soldier will try to make his damaged body function properly if he is absorbed in some interesting task.

Consequently, handicraft work was introduced into the hospitals under the title of ward occupations. In the summer of 1917 volunteers from the V.A.D. of the St. John Ambulance Association were trained in different handicrafts at the Nova Scotia Technical College, and gave their services to the patients at Camp

Hill and Pine Hill Hospitals. The value of the work soon became apparent, and a central training school for ward aides, as the handicraft teachers were called, was opened in Toronto. Young women of education, character, and aptitude were carefully selected for this work, and as soon as they had been given training, they were placed in every military hospital and sanitarium. They co-operated with the medical officers and nursing sisters in every particular, and a combined effort was made to get every patient busy at some kind of work just as soon as he was able to do anything. Basketry, weaving, embroidery, leather tooling, raffia work, toy-making, wood carving, art craft, metal work, and other forms of occupation were provided. The chief difficulty was in first getting the individual interested; and this task took an immense amount of tact and persuasion in some instances.

The underlying motive was to divert the man's mind from its morbid state and to give him a mental stimulus back toward civilian life. In the majority of cases, the patient would make artistic objects for his relatives and friends. If he wished to keep the articles he merely paid for the cost of the material, but if he did not want them the Vocational Branch offered them for sale at a fair commercial value, deducted the cost of raw materials and gave the balance to the patient. There was no idea of instructing the men in gainful trades which they could follow after their discharge.

Too high a tribute cannot be paid to the high character and ability and the unflagging devotion of the Nova Scotia Ward Aides. They gave the same high form of unselfish, patriotic service that was characteristic of the best groups of women workers. The ward occupations were of enormous benefit in making the weary hours of the days pass quickly, in improving the discipline in the institutions, and in materially shortening the time of treatment in many cases. The handicraft work has been specially developed for insane patients, and helps to fill the pathetic lives of the soldiers confined in the Nova Scotia Hospital for the Insane.

A large proportion of the men in the institutions were not confined to their wards. Their disabilities were such, or they had reached such an advanced stage in their treatment, that they were

VOCATIONAL TRAINING

able to move about and to perform light work. For these cases there was only a half-hour a day of treatment, and the rest of the time might be spent in playing cards, in reading magazines, or in sheer idleness. There was great danger that the men might become "hospitalized" and unfitted for the stern tasks of industrial life. Therefore, curative workshops were provided, where a wide range of classes was held for six or seven hours a day. Practical and accomplished instructors were in charge of the various branches, and nearly every soldier, physically fit to pursue such studies, could find something of interest and value. Many of the patients had never had a fair chance to get a good education, and a goodly number who had had such an opportunity had not availed themselves of it. A few of the soldiers did not even know how to read and write. As mechanics, most of the soldiers had acquired such skill as they possessed in a careless and haphazard manner and were not thoroughly competent. To suit the general needs and tastes of the patients, instruction was offered in business English, practical arithmetic, practical algebra, geometry and trigonometry, bookkeeping, stenography and typewriting, telegraphy, mechanical and architectural drafting, gardening, woodworking, shoe repairing, automobile driving and repair, etc.

These adult students made amazing progress in their studies. Those who had forgotten all their mathematics, except the first four rules, covered years of school work in a few months, and in going over it the second time would never again forget it. Foreigners and men who were illiterate learned the rudiments of arithmetic and the English language in a surprisingly short time. Others were absorbed in the work of the different classes, and gained valuable knowledge according to their ability and the length of time they stayed in the hospital. For some of them, who were not entitled to industrial re-training after discharge, it was their only opportunity to get general or vocational education. For those who were so disabled that they could not return to their old occupations, the curative workshops offered a trying-out ground where they could test their aptitudes and often lay a solid basis for further training. It was a pathetic as well as an inspiring sight to see some grizzled hero bringing back muscular power to a scarred and withered arm in planing a piece of wood to make some piece of furniture for his home. The workshop offered practically the only method of treatment to the neurasthenic or "shell-shocked" patient. No medicine or massage or operation could help him, and only the stimulation of his self-interest in class work could get him to forget himself and thus gradually bring him back to normal.

The first curative workshop classes to be opened in the Dominion started at the Ross Convalescent Hospital in Sydney, on April 4, 1916. They were rapidly developed in every hospital and sanatorium throughout Canada, and proved of immense benefit in helping to re-establish our disabled soldiers who received treatment in Canada.

By far the most important division of the vocational work of civil re-establishment, however, was the industrial re-training. France and Belgium showed the way in which crippled men could be trained for future usefulness in suitable trades; and practically every belligerent country evolved a system of human rehabilitation for maimed soldiers. Canada had the advantage of time to plan and develop her methods of dealing with this problem before she was swamped with numbers, and consequently was able to establish a uniform system with centralized authority. The basis of the whole work was to give suitable training for every soldier who, through some disability incurred in military service, could not efficiently resume the occupation which he followed prior to enlistment. In addition to this class, all men classed as minors, who had enlisted under the age of eighteen, were later given training if their war service had seriously interfered with their preparation for their chosen occupation, whether they were disabled or not.

Every effort was made to place the disabled man in the right position. He was interviewed by a sympathetic and competent official and counselled intelligently about the important choice of a new trade. The soldier already had industrial experience and, in the majority of cases, had some definite idea of what he wished to do. If his conceptions of the duties, remuneration, conditions of work, chances for promotion, stability, etc., in the new occupation,

VOCATIONAL TRAINING

were wrong, he was reasonably and patiently advised to make another choice. The disabled man, however, always made the decision about his own future. His own wishes were followed as far as possible, because he would make a failure of his training and of his new occupation if he himself was not satisfied and enthusiastic.

The queer trait of human nature that considers "distant fields as ever green" was much in evidence. During his former experience, the disabled soldier had always had a conviction that some other job completely outside of his own vocation was easier and better paid, or that some new development of industry was holding out its arms and screaming for workers. Consequently, there was a common tendency to enter some vocation wholly outside of his former experience. Most of the men were extremely reasonable and when all the facts were put before them they made wise decisions. Every definite effort was made to keep the man as close as possible to the industry in which he was employed before enlistment. If they had all tried to crowd into a few of the highly skilled occupations, there would not have been vacancies enough to give them all employment. So the training was made as wide as business and industry. Schools and classes were organized and equipped for those vocations which needed preliminary education under skilled instructors, and for which comparatively large groups of men were preparing. In cases where men were deficient in general education, and needed some fundamental knowledge of English and arithmetic in order to succeed, they were given intensive preliminary instruction for one, two or three months before starting specialized vocational training. Every educational institution which offered intensive practical courses leading to wage-earning power, was made use of to the fullest extent. Industry itself, however, offered the widest opportunities, and a great proportion of the students were placed directly in industry to learn there how to fill the job acceptably under working conditions, so that at the end of their period of training they could slip over on the pay roll of the employer without any break. Other men, who had preliminary training in the special trade classes established by the Department of Soldiers' Civil Re-establishment, were placed in industry for the latter part of their period of education so that they would get accustomed to workshop conditions, and in order that there would be no appreciable hiatus between training and employment.

In order to provide ample means for the training and employment of the thousands of men the War produced, it was necessary to secure the closest co-operation of the employers, trade unions, and the general public. It is a pleasure to chronicle the fact that everybody gave active help without stint. The Dominion Steel Corporation and the Nova Scotia Steel and Coal Company, the largest single employers of labor in Nova Scotia, announced publicly that they would find a suitable place for every one of their former employees who had gone into military service and who desired work after his discharge. They carried out their promise, and also provided every possible facility for re-training disabled men. Trade unions also gave generous assistance, and waived all restrictions regarding apprenticeship where these might be detrimental to maimed and crippled soldiers who were learning new trades. Without all this splendid co-operation, the results achieved in Canada in re-training the disabled soldiers for future usefulness would have been impossible.

The usual period of time that was found necessary to put the discharged soldiers on their feet so that they could earn the prevailing wage in a new occupation, was seven or eight months. During the War, when all labor was very scarce, employers would accept men and give them full wages after about six months' training, but when competition became keener and more workers became available in 1919, eight months was found to be necessary in most cases, and sometimes even a whole year. During the period of learning a new vocation, the soldier's pension was suspended, and he and his dependants received a uniform scale of pay and allowances as follows:—

Single man	$60 00	per month.
Married man and wife	85 00	" "
Married man with wife and one child	95 00	" "
Married man with wife and two children	103 00	" "
Married man with wife and three children	110 00	" "
For each additional child above three	6 00	" "

VOCATIONAL TRAINING

If training caused the man to live apart from his dependants, an extra allowance of $16.00 per month was granted. Owing to the increased cost of living, these rates were advanced on September 1, 1920.

All classes carried on by the Department of Civil Re-establishment in Nova Scotia were conducted for eight hours per day in order to get the men accustomed to the conditions prevailing in industry. Where men were sent to educational institutions, or were apprenticed in industry, they were subject to the rules and regulations in force at the place where they were learning.

The scope of the work widened rapidly as it progressed until men were being re-trained for more than 300 different occupations. It is not necessary to give a list of these occupations, but the comprehensive field covered may be imagined if only those classified under the letter " A " were mentioned:—

Accountant.
Adding Machine Operator.
Adding Machine Repairer.
Advertising Agent.
Aeroplane Manufacturing Worker.
Agriculture—Bee Keeping.
    Dairying.
    Farm Tractor Operating.
    Farm Mechanics.
    Floriculture.
    Fruit Raising.
    General Farming.
    Horticulture.
    Market Gardening.
    Poultry Raising.
    Seed Testing.
    University Course.
Air Brake Mechanic.
Architectural Draftsman.
Armature Winder.
Artificial Limb Maker.
Art Lead Glazer.
Art Metal Worker.
Assayer.
Auctioneer.
Automobile Mechanic.
Automobile Painter.
Automobile Salesman.
Automobile Storage Battery Repairer.
Automobile Tire Vulcanizer.
Automobile Truck Driver.
Automobile Upholsterer.

The man who was placed in industry for training or employment was kept under constant supervision and visited every two or three weeks to ascertain his progress. If he was not securing proper treatment or opportunity to learn, he was moved to some other position. If his choice of occupation had not been wise, he was tried out in some other line of work. After he had finished his course, he was visited at least once a month for four months to see that his re-establishment was complete and his progress satisfactory.

The first group to receive industrial re-training in Canada consisted of a number of unfortunate members of a British West India Regiment. A large number were landed in Halifax in February, 1917, from a transport and were sent to hospital to be treated for severe frost bite. Nine of them had to have both legs amputated and eight of them lost one leg or a portion of a leg. Previous to enlistment these Jamaicans had been "cultivators" or agricultural laborers, and had very little education. When their hospital treatment was completed they were re-trained by the Vocational Branch in Halifax. Mr. W. J. Clayton gave over his whole residence and the Provincial Branch of the Red Cross Society fitted it up completely for a convalescent hospital and re-training centre. The men were given instruction in three trades suitable to their disability, viz., tailoring, shoe repairing, and tin-smithing. At the end of five and one-half months they were sent back to Jamaica able to earn at least fifty per cent. more in their new occupations than they had received before as laborers.

The work of re-training disabled Nova Scotian soldiers began seriously in the spring of 1917. A centre was established at the Technical College in Halifax. It was fortunate, indeed, that the Province had embarked on its scheme of technical education before the War, and that this splendid institution stood ready with all its equipment and trained Staff to render service to the men disabled in war. The Provincial Government turned practically the whole establishment over to the Dominion Government for this work. Classes in garage mechanics, automobile tire vulcanizing, electricity, mechanical, architectural and ship drafting, land surveying, machine tool operation, stationary engineering, oxyacetylene welding, shoe repairing, etc., were organized. The institution became a busy hive of industry. The numbers grew until larger quarters had to be secured for part of the classes. In the summer of 1919 a large group of demobilization barracks on Cunard St., Halifax, was taken over and specially fitted and equipped for educational purposes. This was called the Borden Re-training Centre, and the main portion of the work has been done there since that time. A number of the classes are still maintained at the Technical

VOCATIONAL TRAINING

College, and this service will be rendered by the College until the whole task is completed.

The number of re-training students in Nova Scotia increased rapidly in 1919 until it reached its peak with a strength of about 2,300 in March, 1920. From this number it has rapidly declined. Altogether, in the Province, about 4,000 returned men have been granted courses to this date. When one considers that they were training for nearly 300 trades, and that they were being admitted to and discharged from courses every day, that they and their dependants must be paid twice a month, that employment must be found for them, that they must be followed up for four months after completing their training, and thousands of their difficulties smoothed out, the magnitude of the task can be appreciated.

A centre for re-training men in agriculture was established at the Nova Scotia Agricultural College at Truro. Here again this advantage of having a fully equipped institution, with a Staff of highly-trained specialists ready to render service to the discharged soldiers, cannot be overestimated. All the re-training students from the three Maritime Provinces were sent here, because it was the only place in this area competent to meet their needs. Special courses adapted for the purpose were provided, and the regular Staff of the College gave unstintingly of their time and knowledge. Like the Technical College, the Agricultural College allowed discharged soldiers to attend all regular courses without any tuition fees. The number of men applying for re-training in agricultural branches was small because most forms of farming demand physical fitness, and the army experience of the soldiers tended to make them wish to stick to industries in the towns.

Contrary to the expectations of the public, very few men were blinded in the army. Wounds that would deprive a man of his sight usually killed him. Out of our forces of about a half million men, only 130 have had their vision impaired to such an extent that they require re-training. The Canadian authorities arranged with Sir Arthur Pearson that the blind men should all be trained in that splendid institution, St. Dunstan's Hostel, in London. In the early days of the War, however, a few blinded men drifted back to Canada without training. These were collected and about a dozen sent to Halifax, where they were given special instruction under the Military Hospitals Commission at the School for the Blind. They were taught Braille reading and writing, typewriting, Braille stenography, massage, and shoe repairing. Most of the men made remarkable progress, and are successfully earning their own livings to-day.

Altogether Canada has granted about 53,000 courses of re-training. From the very first she has followed a sane, practical policy, and has enjoyed the advantages of uniformity and centralized control throughout all the Provinces.

The results speak for themselves. In Nova Scotia 65 per cent. of the men who have completed their courses are successfully re-established in the occupation for which they were trained. Another 20 per cent. are earning satisfactory wages in other lines of work than those for which they were specifically prepared. These men have changed because they saw better opportunities for themselves, individually, in another vocation, or they may have felt fit enough, after their course, to return to their old occupation. Their training will not be lost, because they are so much more competent because of having it. Ten per cent. of the men have gone out of the Province and cannot be traced. It is safe to conclude that most of these are successfully re-established. Two per cent. of the men are reported as unemployed, but it is not known to what extent this is due to lack of temporary opportunity or disinclination on the part of the man. Three per cent. of the men are reported as still ill and temporarily under treatment.

This high salvage among war-wrecked men can be accepted with great satisfaction by every patriotic Canadian. Without the loyal co-operation of every section of society and the unflagging devotion to duty on the part of the large Staff of returned men who were engaged in administration and instruction, these results would have been impossible. Canada's record of reconstruction and her efforts to rehabilitate the brave soldiers who gave of their youth and strength in the service of the country, stand on a par with her military achievements.

CHAPTER L.

THE PATRIOTIC FUND.

THE Nova Scotia Branch of the Canadian Patriotic Fund was organized in Halifax, September 2, 1914, with the late Lieutenant-Governor Hon. James D. MacGregor as Chairman of the Provincial Executive. On completion of his term of office as Governor, he was succeeded by Hon. David McKeen as Chairman, who acted to the time of his death, November 13, 1916. On appointment to the office of Lieutenant-Governor, His Honor MacCallum Grant became Chairman of the Executive. Other members of the Executive who have continued in office from September, 1914, to date, are:—Hon. G. H. Murray, M.P.P., Premier and Provincial Secretary; Hon. Chief Justice Harris, Hon. E. N. Rhodes, M.P., the Chairman of County Branches; H. A. Flemming, Treasurer; and Arthur S. Barnstead, B.A., LL.B., Secretary.

The total amount raised and remitted to the Honorary Treasurer to March 31, 1919, was $1,847,883.31, and to March 31, 1920, was $1,862,431.80. The total amount disbursed was to March 31, 1919, $1,628,177.04, and to March 31, 1920, $1,726,520.30.

The Central Executive arranged for the collection of the amounts allotted to the Province in connection with the various campaigns, and county committees co-operating. With but one exception, every county municipality contributed to the Fund, and practically every town of the Province made grants. In two or three towns, private individuals made collections for the Fund where no grant was made by the Town Council.

The distribution of relief was supervised by the Provincial Executive, requisitions being drawn by the treasurer of every county for the money required, the list of beneficiaries being carefully checked before the money was placed to the credit of the local treasurer. The result of co-operation between the Provincial Executive and the various relief committees was so beneficial that very little difficulty arose and the rules and regulations of the Fund were very carefully observed. Complaints by the families of soldiers themselves were very few, and all complaints were readily adjusted. The expense of both collections and disbursements was kept at a low figure, there being only one or two paid officials in the larger counties, and these but part time. In addition to that, some small grants were made for stenographic and clerical assistance.

CHAPTER LI.

VICTORY LOAN, 1919.

Provincial Executive Committee.
G. S. Campbell............................... Chairman.
S. A. Heward................................... Secretary.
R. H. Metzler. R. W. Elliott.
P. R. Jack. B. G. Burrill.
W. B. Milner. W. F. Mahon.
A. F. Mackintosh. W. I. MacDougall.
H. M. Bradford. H. C. Coughtry.

Bankers' Committee.
D. Macgillivray .... Chairman.
H. A. Flemming. F. St. C. Harris.
A. E. Nash. F. O. Robertson.

Publicity Committee.
Chairman..................... J. R. McLeod.

Special Names Committee.
Chairman..................... B. G. Burrill.

Provincial Press Committee.
Chairman..................... Dr. J. D. Logan.

Chairmen.

County.	1917-18.	1919.
Annapolis	Hon. S. W. W. Pickup.	Hon. S. W. W. Pickup.
Antigonish	Rev. J. T. Tompkins.	Rev. R. S. Macgillivray.
Cape Breton	John E. Burchell.	Walter Crowe, K.C.
Colchester	A. J. Campbell, K.C.	A. J. Campbell, K.C.
Cumberland	J. R. Douglas.	Percy C. Black.
Clare	E. L. Comeau.	E. L. Comeau.
Digby	H. B. Short.	H. B. Short.
Guysboro	E. C. Whitman.	E. C. Whitman.
Hants	Rev. Dr. T. S. Boyle.	Rev. Dr. T. S. Boyle.
Inverness	Rev. A. L. McDonald.	Rev. A. L. McDonald.
Kings	W. H. Chase.	George E. Graham.
Lunenburg	J. J. Kinley, M.P.P.	J. J. Kinley, M.P.P.
Pictou East	R. M. McGregor.	John D. McDonald.
Pictou West	R. M. McGregor.	J. Ed. McDonald.
Queens	A. W. Hendry.	George S. McClearn.
Richmond	D. H. Campbell.	D. H. Campbell.
Shelburne	R. Irwin, M.P.P.	R. Irwin, M.P.P.
Victoria	Hon. W. F. McCurdy.	Hon. W. F. McCurdy.
Yarmouth	E. K. Spinney, M.P.	E. K. Spinney, M.P.
Halifax County	Hon. G. E. Faulkner.	Hon. G. E Faulkner.
Halifax City	W. A. Black.	W. A. Black.

GEORGE S. CAMPBELL.

WILLIAM BLACK.

VICTORY LOAN, 1919

1917 and 1918 Victory Loans—Final Returns.

County.	No. Sub. 1917.	No. Sub. 1918.	Volume 1917.	Volume 1918.	Objective 1918.
Halifax City	7,656	9,918	$4,592,500	$9,314,050	$5,000,000
Halifax County	1,472	2,402	533,200	1,003,950	615,000
City and County	9,128	12,320	5,125,700	10,318,000	5,615,000
Annapolis	1,418	1,357	497,950	623,750	500,000
Antigonish	1,218	1,369	430,000	554,050	430,000
Cape Breton	11,251	17,551	4,208,100	6,631,900	4,000,000
Colchester	2,294	2,693	1,003,500	1,374,130	1,000,000
Cumberland	3,605	3,388	2,137,800	3,080,350	1,500,000
Digby Municipality	844	927	292,850	463,100	500,000
Clare Municipality		152		124,250	
Guysboro	1,079	1,258	377,900	425,850	375,000
Hants	1,460	1,873	527,300	793,100	650,000
Inverness	920	922	324,900	399,700	325,000
Kings	1,817	2,305	586,150	847,060	650,000
Lunenburg	1,236	2,880	570,250	1,462,600	1,000,000
Pictou	5,679	7,661	2,073,750	4,044,500	2,000,000
Queens	628	634	258,150	343,400	300,000
Richmond	638	564	164,500	200,650	175,000
Shelburne	679	896	317,400	411,150	350,000
Victoria	429	504	161,600	178,400	160,000
Yarmouth	1,115	1,505	457,450	767,760	600,000
Total	45,438	60,759	$19,515,250	$33,043,700	$20,130,000

Unofficial objective, $25,000,000, being Nova Scotia's proportion of $500,000,000.

Nova Scotia Victory Loan Campaign, 1919.

County.	Objective.	Subscribed.	No. of Subs.
Halifax City	$4,750,000	$6,896,900	6,781
Halifax County	475,000	1,521,000	2,421
City and County	5,225,000	8,417,900	9,202
Annapolis	350,000	628,250	1,008
Antigonish	300,000	453,200	786
Cape Breton	3,500,000	4,936,200	8,801
Colchester	700,000	1,182,000	1,843
Cumberland	1,250,000	3,199,650	2,266
Digby (Clare Municipality)	175,000	180,350	144
Digby (Digby Municipality)	175,000	339,350	458
Guysboro	275,000	490,000	893
Hants	500,000	618,000	1,147
Inverness	225,000	399,100	711
Kings	550,000	932,800	1,523
Lunenburg	750,000	1,247,750	1,789
Pictou	2,000,000	3,174,700	2,812
Queens	245,000	335,000	453
Richmond	100,000	201,850	295
Shelburne	275,000	376,100	628
Victoria	100,000	229,700	358
Yarmouth	450,000	1,180,000	1,281
Total	$17,145,000	$28,521,900	36,398

CHAPTER LII.

RED CROSS SOCIETY, WILLING WAR WORKERS, GREEN FEATHER SOCIETY, AND CATHOLIC LADIES SOCIETY.

THE Red Cross has been the Angel of Mercy to the soldier lying on his fevered couch in hospital, for it brought to him succor and a message of hope and cheer. But coming in contact with it at a time when he was least able to apprehend the efforts which brought the help so sorely needed, he is apt to regard the Red Cross as a field institution and fails to appreciate the labor and sacrifice of the women at home who made its work of mercy possible.

The work of the Nova Scotia Branch of the Canadian Red Cross Society has been the raising of money, manufacturing and distribution of goods, visiting and supplying the needs of hospital ships, trains, military and convalescent hospitals, and arranging concerts, drives and entertainments at private homes for returned men. Its work did not terminate with the declaration of peace but still goes on in almost as great a measure as in time of war, and will continue to do so as long as one returned soldier remains in our hospitals.

Many Nova Scotians, as well as returned men, do not appreciate the magnitude of the task accomplished by the Nova Scotia Branch of the Canadian Red Cross, and it is only possible here to give a brief outline of its activities. The women of every city, town and village in the Province gave the best of their thought, substance and action in order that the citizen soldier of Nova Scotia, whether in the fighting line or in hospital convalescing from wounds might have every possible comfort. At the end of 1915 the Province had thirty-one chartered and two hundred and sixty-eight auxiliary branches of the Red Cross. Every village and hamlet had its workers who contributed a steady stream of supplies and an enormous amount of labor devolved upon the Provincial Branch at

RED CROSS SOCIETY

Halifax, which acted as a Clearing House for all branches throughout the Province.

The officers of the Provincial Branch during the War, with slight changes of office but not of personnel, were as follows:

Patrons.
His Honor Lieutenant-Governor and Mrs. Grant.

President.
Mrs. William Dennis.

MRS. DENNIS.

MRS. CHARLES ARCHIBALD.

Vice-Presidents.

Mrs. F. H. Sexton.
Mrs. Chas. Archibald.
Mrs. F. B. McCurdy.
Mrs. Hector McInnis.
Mrs. M. A. Curry (Hon.)

Hon. Secretary.
Miss Margaret Brown.

Hon. Treasurer.
H. E. Mahon, Ess.

Executive Committee.

Mrs. T. Benson.
Mrs. A. W. Jamieson.
Mrs. G. S. Campbell.
Mrs. F. Woodbury.
Mrs. W. J. Armitage.
Mrs. E. A. Kirkpatrick.
Mrs. N. Duffus.
Mrs. A. Costley.

Mrs. W. E. McLellan.
Mrs. F. B. McCurdy.
Mrs. H. W. Cunningham.
Mrs. L. J. Donaldson.
Mrs. G. A. MacIntosh.
Mrs. W. R. Foster, Dartmouth.
Mrs. A. P. Scarfe, Dartmouth.
Mrs. Crathorne, Dartmouth.

NOVA SCOTIA'S PART IN THE GREAT WAR

Mrs. W. S. Munnis.
Miss Jean Forrest.
Miss Constance Bell.
Mrs. Sedley Thompson.
Miss Ella Ritchie.
Mrs. McKay McLeod, Sydney.
Mrs. M. A. Curry.
Mrs. T. S. Rogers.

Mrs. Frank Hope.
Mrs. J. A. Clark.
Mrs. I. B. Schaffner.
Mrs. P. J. McManus.
Mrs. W. T. Allen.
Mrs. J. W. Longley.
Mrs. Geoffrey Morrow.

Also the President of each Chartered Branch.

Provincial Representatives on Central Council at Toronto.

Mrs. William Dennis.
Mrs. Charles Archibald.

J. L. Hetherington.
H. E. Mahon.

Advisory Board.

Mr. J. L. Hetherington, Chairman.
Mr. H. E. Mahon, Treasurer.
Mr. Chas. V. Monoghan.
Mr. R. Corbett.
Mr. W. H. Dennis.

Mr. J. A. Neville.
Mr. C. C. Starr.
Mr. Emil Gaboury.
Mr. H. McF. Hall.
Mr. F. A. Gillis.

The annual report of the Provincial Branch for the year ended October 31, 1916, shows a balance on hand at first of year of $10,961.26 and receipts for the year of $52,667.62. Disbursements amounted to $56,584.89, of which the principal items were:

Remittances to Head Office, Toronto	$29,278 38
Remittances to endow 50 cots in Princess Patricia Hospital....	2,500 00
Material for surgical dressings and garments, and wool for socks	18,163 17
Office maintenance and expenses at Shipping Pier	1,388 12
Clayton Military Convalescent Home	1,993 67
Contributions to Special Objects	1,141 21

The sum of $9,405.25 was collected for Prisoners' Relief Account and $8,800 sent to England for expenditure. In addition to the above amounts the people of Nova Scotia subscribed $1,500 to the Duchess of Connaught Prisoners' Fund and $78,433.03 to the British Red Cross.

Two thousand four hundred and seventy cases of goods were sent Overseas during the year, including 78 cases furnished No. 7 (Dalhousie) Stationary Hospital, 112 cases to No. 9 (St. Francis Xavier) Stationary Hospital, 11 cases to Serbia and 60 to France.

During the year ended October 31, 1917, the following amounts were collected:

For General Purposes	$62,179 80
For Prisoners' Fund	18,790 22
For French Red Cross	21,897 63
British Red Cross Collection	100,000 00
	$202,867 65

RED CROSS SOCIETY

The principal items of expenditure were:

Purchase of materials, hospital supplies, etc.	$39,674 84
Sundry supplies	1,318 60
Marine and Fire Insurance	2,351 50
Contributions to Special Objects	4,706 51
Tobacco, fruits and comforts at Pier 2 and City Military Hospitals	3,963 05
Remittance to Head Office, Toronto	32,020 70
Office Expenses	2,055 66
Forwarded to England for support of prisoners	12,000 00
Forwarded to Toronto	2,000 00
Forwarded to England for books for prisoners	100 00

Two thousand and ninety-nine cases of goods were sent Overseas, and a greatly enlarged demand for goods was made on this side of the water owing to the increasing number of returned men and the opening of the new convalescent hospitals as well as the arrival and departure of hospital ships and trains. The following institutions were supplied with goods on their requisitions:

Clayton Military Convalescent Home.
C.E.D. Corps.
Discharge Depot.
Hospital at Pier 2.
Pine Hill Convalescent Home.
Rockhead Hospital (Soldiers' ward).
Infectious Hospital.
Military Hospital, Cogswell Street.
Hospital Ships.
Hospital Trains.
Kentville Sanitarium.
Dalton, P.E.I.
Camp Hill Hospital.
Truro Military Hospital.
Aldershot Field Hospital.

Visitors were always on hand on the arrival of hospital ships and the departure of hospital trains to welcome the returning men and to see that they had every comfort necessary for the remainder of their journey. A room was given to the Red Cross Society for the storing of supplies at Pier 2. This was found most useful, as boats and trains were despatched as soon as possible—only a few hours' notice being

MRS. F. B. M'CURDY.

given for the filling of requisitions, which work, however, was speedily and ably done by Mrs. Sexton and her committee, Mrs. F. B. McCurdy and Mrs. W. T. Allen, the latter of whom carried on the work to the termination. Many returned men were detained for days at Pier 2 until they went before their medical board. For these, concerts and entertainments were provided every evening by the Y.M.C.A., the Red Cross Society and the Churches. A special Y.M.C.A. Musical Club was formed in this connection which gave entertainments at a few hours' notice.

Two exhibitions of Red Cross work were held during the year, one at the Nova Scotia Provincial Fair, and another at the Exhibit of War Trophies, held in the Armories.

A Committee on Sphagnum Surgical Dressings, under the able supervision of the Secretary, Miss Margaret Brown, was appointed. Dalhousie University very kindly gave the use of a fine laboratory, where boxes of sphagnum, collected from various points along the sea coast of the Province were prepared for use.

Miss Jean Forrest was appointed Superintendent of Supplies at

MISS MARGARET BROWN.

MISS JEAN FORREST.

the Technical College and distributed parcels of yarn and cut-out work at wholesale prices, to some one hundred and thirty branches who found it difficult to obtain supplies locally.

The cost of maintaining a prisoner of war at this time was $15 per month. The Nova Scotia Red Cross assumed the burden of two-thirds, or $10 per month for 270 men, the Canadian Red Cross paying the additional $5. The monthly sum required from Nova Scotia for the support of prisoners was therefore $2,700.

Receipts for the year ended October 31, 1918, amounted to $408,482.66, of which $334,176.40 was raised by a Provincial Red Cross drive for funds during the second week in July.

RED CROSS SOCIETY

The Canadian Red Cross Society at their Annual Meeting, held in Toronto in 1917, decided to ask the different Provinces to raise certain sums of money during the year. Two hundred thousand dollars was named for Nova Scotia, but the Finance Committee knowing full well that the people of the Province would gladly contribute to the Red Cross War Fund raised the objective to $250,000, and then started to work under the able direction of Mr. J. L. Hetherington and Mr. H. E. Mahon. Committees of citizens were formed in all the counties, and a complete organization arranged, with the result that every county "went over the top," and the total amount contributed was $343,701.77. From this was deducted $9,525.37 for expenses in connection with the campaign, leaving the net amount of $334,176.40 to the Red Cross Society. Never did men and women from one end of the Province to the other work more enthusiastically, and never did our people contribute more liberally than to this appeal from "the Greatest Mother in the World."

The following amounts were raised in the several counties:

Counties—
Annapolis	$9,713 54
Antigonish	5,598 33
Cape Breton	42,150 29
Colchester	20,444 29
Cumberland	20,196 46
Digby	4,464 04
Guysboro	5,521 24
Halifax (City)	110,416 87
Halifax (County)	15,425 31
Hants	10,340 00
Inverness	2,903 67
Kings	10,650 00
Lunenburg	14,446 47
Pictou	40,235 27
Queens	6,341 61
Richmond	2,332 47
Shelburne	7,500 00
Victoria	2,463 38
Yarmouth	11,510 36
Special	1,048 17
Total	$343,701 77
Expenses	9,525 37
Final Total	$334,176 40

NOVA SCOTIA'S PART IN THE GREAT WAR

The expenditure for the year 1918 included:

Purchase of materials, hospital supplies, etc.	$38,700 04
Sundry Supplies	1,218 32
Comforts to City Military Hospitals and Hospital Ships	9,331 67
Special objects designated by remitters	4,158 53
Remittances to Head Office, Toronto	325,931 70
Office Expenses and wages at Pier 2	2,746 49

During the year 1918 the public maintained their interest in the Prisoners of War Department of the Red Cross. The amount collected was $20,943.01, of which $19,013.00 was forwarded to headquarters in London, England, for the support of prisoners. The food rations of each prisoner of war were despatched regularly three times every fortnight, which, considering there were 270 men on the list, was no light undertaking. In addition to the food supply the prisoners received two complete outfits of clothing, including everything from shoes and socks to overcoats.

After the signing of the Armistice the work of repatriating prisoners went steadily on, and each steamer brought men who had spent many weary months in the prison camps, and they all testified to the value of the work done by this Society and declared that it was solely due to this that they were enabled to return to their homes. This department of Red Cross work has been most ably conducted by Mrs. Charles Archibald, nobly assisted by Miss Ritchie and Mrs. Longley.

The beginning of this year was marked by the terrible Halifax explosion, by which 1,635 persons lost their lives and 10,000 people were rendered homeless. Much generous help was received by the stricken city. Everyone knows the splendid aid sent by the American Red Cross, and the people and Government of the United States in despatching to Halifax train loads and boat loads of supplies, together with surgeons and nurses. Their neighborly kindness will never be forgotten.

But the help rendered by our own Canadian Red Cross is perhaps not so widely known. The Chairman of the Executive in Toronto wired to the shipping agent in St. John to render every assistance possible in money and goods. The agent, Mr. Milburne, immediately requisitioned a special train, and brought with him all the Red Cross goods he had ready for shipment Overseas, making

RED CROSS SOCIETY

two car loads in all. This train was the first assistance from outside the Province to reach Halifax. Hearing that some of the injured had been conveyed to Truro, Mr. Milburne put off cases of hospital necessaries for their use at that station. A medical supply committee of the Canadian Red Cross Society was immediately formed with the sanction of the Halifax Relief Committee, Mr. Milburne being appointed Chairman, and Mrs. Sexton, Vice-Chairman, with a Staff of forty-four voluntary workers. Twice daily all the emergency hospitals were visited and their wants noted and supplied the same day. The number of these hospitals, dressing stations, etc., amounted to sixty-two.

At the same time, gifts of clothing, food and money poured in from Red Cross Branches all over Canada. Ottawa Branch shipped in one day eight carloads of clothing. The Nova Scotia Branch, under its President, Mrs. Dennis, co-operated heartily, practically every Branch and Auxiliary in the Province sending substantial and generous aid.

Special mention must be made of the work of the President of the Windsor Red Cross, Mrs. P. M. Fielding, who organized a special train which arrived the evening of December 6th, bringing doctors and nurses from Kentville, Windsor, Truro and neighboring towns. The Windsor Red Cross alone spent $422.74 on Red Cross supplies and provisions for this trip, Hantsport and other Branches also providing hampers of food, so that the doctors and nurses had their meals en route and arrived in Halifax ready to go to work without an instant's delay, thereby saving many lives. Mrs. Fielding remained in the city, established and equipped three dormitories, which accommodated in all seventy-five nurses. What this meant to the stricken city will never be computed, and the Red Cross feels that all who helped can never be sufficiently thanked.

It was not until the end of March that the Red Cross was able to resume its work for returned invalided soldiers. By that time the hospital on Pier 2, wrecked by the explosion, had been repaired. The hospital ships once more made their trips, and the Red Cross storeroom on the pier was re-stocked. Large requisitions were filled each month; sometimes only a few hours' notice was given to get the supplies on board—sometimes only a few minutes' notice in the case of a hospital train. On one trip the ship docked in the morning, landed her men and went out again with her new supplies in the afternoon. At another time 1,400 shipwrecked men from S.S. *City of Vienna* were visited and supplied with filled kit bags, containing toilet necessaries, pipes and tobacco. Directly after, the Committee were called upon to minister to 300 influenza contact cases. This necessitated the workers going into quarantine for two days, very busy days, too, the telegrams alone requiring upwards of 300 telephone calls. The Y.M.C.A. and the Knights of Columbus Musical Club were always at hand to cheer up men who were detained by the Medical Board, arranging for their benefit concerts, entertainments, motor drives and teas at private houses.

One thousand seven hundred and sixty-eight cases of goods were sent Overseas, and the distribution of supplies on this side grew very greatly during the year owing to the increasing number of returned men and the opening of new convalescent homes.

The financial statement for the year ended October 31, 1918, shows receipts of $36,848.65. Expenditures amounted to $41,804.01, including the following items:

Purchase of materials, City and Provincial Hospitals	$12,172 04
Kentville Sanitarium	1,014 42
Soldiers' Reception Committee	9,000 00
Cigarettes	2,456 51
Soldiers' Comforts	2,260 23
Libraries	319 79
Nurses	378 10
Furnishings	2,201 36
Clayton Hospital	175 00
Rental and Expenses at Headquarters, 314 Barrington St.	3,858 89
Office Expenses	1,789 85
X-Ray Machines, Kentville	2,396 43
Hospital Ships	823 63

No salaries whatever were paid to officers of the Red Cross Society. The only persons connected with the work who received anything for their services were the shipper at Red Cross warehouse at Pier 2, who was responsible for the receiving and sending forward of our boxes, and the Office Secretary who took charge of the correspondence, kept the books, etc. She was assisted by a large corps of voluntary workers.

RED CROSS SOCIETY

With the signing of the Armistice great changes naturally took place in the daily work of the Nova Scotia Red Cross. Workers decreased in number, and those who remained faithful had to work extremely hard, as, although it was considered that the stores already sent would be sufficient for all Overseas demands, the reserve stock of stores for use in the hospitals in our own Province had to be kept up.

At the time of the Armistice the surgical sphagnum dressings were still very greatly needed. Special efforts were put into this work, which continued till free transportation ceased on March 31st. Forty-five boxes of the dressings were sent Overseas. An eminent Surgeon-Colonel in one of the Overseas hospitals gave it as his opinion that sphagnum dressings had saved the situation.

Work for refugees of the devastated area of France was then taken up, sanctioned by the Head Office in Toronto, who provided samples and gave permission to use Red Cross materials for this good work. The patterns were duplicated in our office and distributed to Branches throughout the Province. The work was carried on for two months and 217 boxes of garments were sent over.

Change of quarters for the Red Cross became imperative. The Technical College, which had sheltered Red Cross workers during the four years of the War, and had so generously allowed them the use of valuable equipment of every kind, was now overcrowded with its own work for returned soldiers. It was therefore decided to take over the lease of No. 314 Barrington Street from the American Red Cross, which had occupied it for the last year.

It was thought best to continue the Canteen which the American Red Cross had established until such time as the Y.M.C.A. should take up this work. This Canteen, under the management of Mrs. Sexton, had a wonderful success, becoming a happy and home-like centre for returned men and greatly appreciated—especially the hot Sunday dinners served by devoted workers. Much regret was expressed when, at the end of three months, it was closed and the work handed over to the newly-opened Red Triangle Hut next door.

The principal work throughout the year was supplying the needs of the hospitals. Mrs. Munnis, who worked so faithfully as the Convener of the Hospital Committee resigned and was replaced by

Mrs. Sexton. An enlarged committee was formed and a large staff of visitors began their duties, each having a special ward assigned to them.

Twelve sun parlors at Camp Hill Hospital were furnished for the use of convalescents and made as comfortable and home-like as possible. The estimated cost was $500 each, subscribed for by the following Red Cross Branches: Amherst, Windsor, Wolfville, Westville, Trenton, Glace Bay, Halifax, Truro, Hazel Hill, Joggins Mines, New Glasgow and North Sydney. A brass plate, bearing the name of the donor, was affixed to the wall of each parlor. The cost exceeded the estimate by $240 each, which excess was paid from the central treasury.

From November 11, 1918, until September 30, 1919, 220,000 men passed through the Port of Halifax, and 92 ships were met and as far as possible these men had the use of the Red Cross rooms at the pier. The Port Committee was on hand day and night to help make their landing on Canadian soil (many of them after years of service) a great home-coming.

In the first days of disembarkation all men for Canada were held at Halifax for documentation. Later the military authorities changed their plan and it became their ambition to disembark and entrain these men in the shortest possible time so that only Maritime men waiting for local trains or men held for hospital treatment came under the care of the Committee.

Later on the Repatriation Department of the Canadian Government requested the Red Cross to undertake the care of the returning soldiers' families. About 5,000 soldiers' dependants passed through Halifax and a fully trained nurse was placed on each train containing soldiers' wives and children.

Hospital equipment was provided at Pier No. 2 for any women and children who were unfit to travel after landing from boat, or whose husbands were military patients and could not proceed. Often their luggage was not obtainable, and the Red Cross was called upon to supply such necessaries as infants' outfits, women's pyjamas and bath robes, towels, soap, combs, hot water bottles, medicines, etc.

In March when the Canadian Government decided to send the hospital ships to Portland, Maine, instead of Halifax, Col. Noel

RED CROSS SOCIETY

Marshall requested that a Committee of our Port Workers should inaugurate the work at the new port. Mrs. W. T. Allen, Mrs. J. L. Hetherington and Mrs. F. B. McCurdy accordingly proceeded to Portland and very satisfactory arrangements were made whereby the Canadian Red Cross continued to fit ships with hospital stores, while the American Red Cross very courteously and generously provided canteen facilities and served refreshments to all the wounded.

Perhaps no department of the Red Cross has developed more enthusiasm or been more splendidly supported than the work of Prisoners' Relief. From a very small beginning it grew to be work of great importance, and one in which the people of Nova Scotia have abundantly shown their practical interest. It did not draw upon the general Red Cross Funds but appealed for a special offering from the public or from friends of men who were prisoners of war and found a most gratifying response, no less than $41,448 having been contributed for this special purpose.

Approximately 270 Canadian prisoners of war in forty-one different internment camps in Germany were maintained wholly or in part through the kindness of the people of Nova Scotia, at a cost per head of $10 per month. Almost all these men were " adopted " by friends or societies; that is, such persons or societies agreed to pay a certain sum per month towards their maintenance, two dollars and fifty cents having been fixed as the minimum amount. The name and address of the adopted was given to the man, and his name, number and prison address to the adopter, and letters and cards were exchanged between them, often arousing a deep personal interest on the one hand and a sense of gratitude and appreciation on the other.

Mrs. Archibald and Miss Ritchie were brought in close contact with the homes and families of prisoners of war. The amount of correspondence was very considerable, and the system used entailed a lot of book-keeping. The name and number of each man, date of capture, prison camp and any details that could be gathered were registered on a card index. The name of the " adopter " was also registered both here and with the Prisoners of War Department in London.

NOVA SCOTIA'S PART IN THE GREAT WAR

Close touch was kept with the Department of "Missing Men," conducted in London and in a few instances it was possible to convey reassuring news to sorrow-stricken friends of the "missing men," although, too often, it became necessary to deprive them of the hope they so touchingly clung to. Yet even the bad news was softened somewhat by details of the death or capture of a man, obtained under the system inaugurated by Lady Drummond of "Searchers" in hospitals who sought out wounded men of the same Platoon or Battalion of the person enquired for. These men, if able to write, would themselves send a few words telling when and where they had seen their less fortunate comrades. Even these meagre details were of some comfort to the mourning ones.

MRS. W. M'K. M'LEOD.

MISS CLARA DENNIS.

Some of the heart-broken letters received were very hard to reply to, but when news was good and food parcels arrived safely showers of "acknowledgment cards" flowed in; and when, as often happened, the mail brought a personal letter from some grateful mother or a few words from some of the poor boys behind barbed wire "somewhere in Germany," or when a rapturous letter came from some poor fellow transferred from his prison as "totally unfit" and sent to the free air of Switzerland, the ladies conducting this Department felt more than happy in being permitted to participate in such a work of mercy. Mrs. Archibald, Miss Ritchie, and their co-workers possessed in no small degree the confidence of the prisoners' friends throughout the Province and deeply appreciated

RED CROSS SOCIETY

their attitude toward them and their loyalty and patience with the many unavoidable delays and mistakes.

During the last two years of the War, as the work became heavier, this Department had associated with it Mrs. W. McK. McLeod, who acted as Secretary for Cape Breton, and Miss Almon. Special mention must also be made of the work of Miss Clara Dennis in meeting and welcoming home repatriated men who had been prisoners of war. During 1918-19 one thousand and eight of these men were met and greeted by Miss Dennis. To each man was handed a card of welcome from the Red Cross and a box of confectionery. He was asked to record his name, regimental number, German prison camp, and his home address in a book specially prepared for the purpose. That the men appreciated this informal but hearty welcome home is abundantly proved by the fact that Miss Dennis has since received from them hundreds of letters of thanks.

It is impossible to give in detail the names of the many thousands of devoted and faithful voluntary workers throughout the Province of Nova Scotia who sought no reward for their labors but the joy of knowing that the Society achieved its aim—the alleviation of the sufferings of our fighting men.

Red Cross Chartered Branches.

Place.	President.
Amherst	Mrs. W. R. Fishleigh.
Arichat	Mrs. C. D. Terrio.
Antigonish	Mrs. D. G. Kirk.
Baddeck	Mrs. F. W. McCurdy.
Barrington	Mrs. Wilson Crowell.
Berwick	Mrs. Alex. Anderson.
Bishop's Mountain	Mrs. C. O. Downie.
Brass Hill	Mrs. F. Nickerson.
Brule	Mrs. A. C. Cook.
Barney's River	Mrs. Wm. McDonald.
Boulardarie	Mrs. J. Fraser.
Canso	Mrs. C. O'Donoghue.
Cape North	Miss Grace Gwynn.
Chester	Dr. C. O. Hebb.
Dartmouth	Mrs. W. R. Foster.
Dominion No. 6	Mrs. Anna B. Wight.
Goldboro	Mrs. Edgar Silver.
Glace Bay	Mrs. P. E. Ogilvy.
Halifax	Mrs. Wm. Dennis.
Hazel Hill	Mrs. Dunning.

NOVA SCOTIA'S PART IN THE GREAT WAR

Place.	President.
Hantsport	Miss Marcia Braine.
Lawrencetown	Mrs. D. M. Balcom.
Lawrencetown S.S.	Mrs. J. F. Brown.
Moser's River	Mrs. Walter Smith.
Mulgrave	Mrs. L. C. Dixon.
New Glasgow	Mrs. P. A. MacGregor.
North Sydney	Mrs. J. J. Pallen.
Pictou	Mrs. A. S. Stalker.
Port Morien	Miss C. Macaulay.
Port Bickerton	Mrs. George Taylor.
Point Tupper	Mrs. James Swaine.
St. Peters	Mrs. J. Kemp.
Sydney	Mrs. H. A. Nicholson.
Sydney Mines	Mrs. B. Archibald.
South Berwick	Mrs. G. R. Nichols.
Tancook Island	Miss Beulah Wilson.
Trenton	Mrs. C. W. Stromberg.
Truro	Mrs. Harold Putnam.
West Quoddy	Mrs. Alex. Gamnon.
Westville	Mrs. R. Fraser.
Windsor	Mrs. P. M. Fielding.
Wolfville	Mrs. Harold Barss.
Woodlawn	Mrs. Jane Nauffts.
Westchester Station	Mrs. W. O. Webb.
Yarmouth	Mrs. W. D. Ross.

Red Cross Auxiliaries.

Avondale	Miss Bertha Crossley.
Advocate Harbor	Mrs. L. L. Hill.
Athol	Mrs. J. W. Boss.
Aylesford	Mrs. C. N. McIntyre.
Apple River	Mrs. E. Slocum.
Billtown	Mrs. C. R. Bill.
Bayhead	Mrs. James Johnson.
Baxter's Harbor	Mrs. Fred Ells.
Bayfield	Mrs. F. C. Gass.
Bedford	Mrs. E. Butler.
Blandford	Mrs. C. Woods.
Bear River	Mrs. L. J. Lovitt.
Bridgetown	Mrs. O. T. Daniels.
Baccaro	Mrs. G. L. Crowell.
Barney's River	Mrs. (Rev.) McDonald.
Barronsfield	Miss Nettie Baker.
Beacon Hill	Mrs. E. H. Langille.
Big Baddeck	Mrs. Alex. Anderson.
Birch Grove	Mrs. D. B. McDonald.
Brooklynn (Queens)	Mrs. W. P. Godfrey.
Brandford	Mrs. C. Woods.
Broughton	Miss Ida McLeod.
Centre Burlington	Mrs. F. G. Brown.
Clarke's Harbor	Mrs. George Phillips.
Central New Annan	Miss A. McIntosh.
Cherry Brook	Mrs. Mary Grosse.

RED CROSS SOCIETY

Place.	President.
Chignecto Mines	Mrs. F. M. Blenkhorn.
Clam Harbor	Mrs. J. B. Homans.
Collingwood	Mrs. Davies.
Cook's Brook	Mrs. Warren Cook.
Caledonia	Mrs. B. Lempton.
Canaan	Miss Bessie Shipley.
Central Grove	Mrs. Byron Melaney.
Centre Gore	Mrs. N. Grant.
Centre Rawdon	Mrs. J. E. Wood.
Centreville	Rev. H. M. Manzer.
Clementsport	Miss L. Hicks.
Cleveland	Mrs. D. A. McLeod.
Conquerall Bank	Mrs. Angus Weagle.
Dalhousie East (Kings)	Mrs. M. Oickle.
Dalhousie East (Annapolis)	Mrs. John Long.
Dean	Mrs. Campbell Brown
Deep Brook	Mrs. G. Marsters.
Diligent River	Mrs. W. W. Lamb.
Digby	Mrs. Eber Turnbull.
Durham	Miss Janet Blaikie.
Ellershouse	Mrs. H. D. Archibald
Elmsdale	Mrs. Chas. Thompson
East Walton	Mrs. Levi Lake.
Economy	Mrs. P. Huntley.
Five Islands	Mrs. Calvin Corbett.
Fenwick	Mrs. F. B. Dickinson
Freeport	Mrs. Egar Ring.
Five Mile River	Mrs. H. Hennigar.
Fraserville	Mrs. Gaius Fraser.
Glenville and Claremont	Mrs. C. A. McCabe.
Grand River	Mrs. McDonald.
Guysboro	Mrs. G. E. Buckley.
Glengarry	Miss Christine Fraser.
Granville Ferry	Mrs. W. Patterson.
Giant's Lake	Miss K. A. McLean.
Goldenville	Mrs. L. Fraser.
Goshen and Argyle	Mrs. J. A. Sinclair.
Great Village	Mrs. C. B. Spencer.
Greenwood	Mrs. Chas. Neilly.
Hammond's Plains	Miss S. Schmidt.
Hubbards	Mrs. Bessie McLean.
Harmony (Kings)	Mrs. C. S. Spinney.
Hemsford	Mrs. James Falconer.
Inverness	Mrs. E. Brassett.
Joggins Mines	Mrs. R. J. Bell.
Kingston Station	Mrs. G. G. Power.
Karsdale	Mrs. G. W. Chisholm.
Lake Ainslie	Mrs. M. A. McKay.
Louisburg	Mrs. A. L. Bates.
Liverpool	Mrs. John More.
Lunenburg	Mrs. Emily Smith.
Lower Selmah and Sterling Brook	Miss Lena Spicer.
Lochaber	Mrs. John Brown.
Latties Brook	Mrs. W. J. Macdonald.
Liverpool	Mrs. John More.

NOVA SCOTIA'S PART IN THE GREAT WAR

Place.	President.
Lockhartville	Miss F. McInnes.
Londonderry	Mrs. J. G. R. Smith.
Lower Granville	Mrs. George Anthony.
Lyons Brook	Mrs. A. Hogg.
Lockeport	Mrs. Churchill Locke.
Mosherville, Stanley and Clarkeville.	Mrs. H. B. Smith.
Milford Station	Mrs. Pooley.
McPhee's Corner	Mrs. James McPhee.
Margaretsville	Mrs. A. B. Coulstan.
Marriott's Cove	Mrs. Rupert Millett.
Middle River	Mrs. Mary MacDonald.
Mabou	Mrs. E. S. Bayne.
Maccan	Mrs. (Dr.) Forbes.
Mahone	Miss Nettie Zwicker.
Malagash	Mrs. Jacob Treen.
Malagawatch	Mrs. Hudson.
Manchester and Port Shoreham	Mrs. W. Bruce.
Mapleton	Mrs. G. E. Fletcher.
Margaree Harbor	Mrs. A. R. MacDougall.
Melvern Square	Mrs. E. F. McNeil.
Merigomish and Piedmont	Mrs. T. B. Olding.
Middleton	Mrs. W. Gwillim.
Mill Village (Hants)	Mrs. Hattie Wallace.
Mira Gut	Mrs. J. J. Philips.
Moose Brook and Tennycape	Mrs. W. F. Stevens.
Millsville	Mrs. R. MacKay.
Mount Uniacke	Miss Sadie Robinson.
Nappan	Mrs. Robert Donaldson.
Neil's Harbor	Mrs. Ed. Dowling.
New Annan	Miss Agnes McIntosh.
New Port	Mrs. J. F. Rathburn.
North Dartmouth	Mrs. C. V. Vernon.
New Campbellton	Mrs. W. McKinnon.
New Germany	Mrs. H. P. Chesley.
N.E. Margaree	Mrs. J. H. Tulston.
Noel Shore	Mrs. E. S. Main.
North Kingston	Mrs. H. J. Neily.
Oxford	Mrs. J. R. Gilroy.
Owl's Head	Mrs. J. E. Parker.
Oxford Junction	Mrs. S. Colburne.
Port Maitland	Mrs. E. H. Porter.
Port Greville	Mrs. R. S. Kerr.
Pleasantfield	Mrs. Charles Arnburg.
Paradise	Mrs. H. P. Layte.
Port Medway	Mrs. Grace Andrews.
Parrsboro	Mrs. F. A. Rand.
Pentz	Miss Alberta Smith.
Port Dufferin	Mrs. E. W. Dunlop.
Port Hawkesbury	Mrs. D. Gillis.
Port Hood	Mrs. Daniel McLennan.
Port La Tour	Mrs. D. Snow.
Port Hilford	Miss Isabella Reid.
Parker's Cove	Mrs. H. Anderson.
Plainfield	Mrs. W. A. Graham.
Princedale	Mrs. Forman Wright.

RED CROSS SOCIETY

Place.	President.
Ragged Island, East Side	Mrs. Chas. Matthews.
Richmond	Mrs. A. G. McIntosh.
River Herbert	Mrs. T. Shipley.
Rockingham	Mrs. W. J. Clayton.
Rodney and Windham	Mrs. M. Y. Boss.
River John	Mrs. C. W. MacKintosh.
River Philip	Mrs. G. L. King.
Rossway	Mrs. Bessie Crowell.
Sandy Point	Mrs. Anzo Long.
Sandy Cove	Mrs. E. D. Morehouse.
Shag Harbor.	Mrs. N. C. Nickerson.
Shelburne	Mrs. Martha C. Morton.
Ship Harbor Lake	Mrs. Alvin Webber.
Shubenacadie	Mrs. A. E. Culton.
Smith's Cove	Mrs. Edward Winchester.
Southampton	Mrs. Victor Brown.
Spencer's Island	Mrs. Edmund Spicer.
Sackville.	Mrs. Robinson.
South Athol	Mrs. L. D. MacKeen.
Seal Island	Mrs. John Smith.
St. Croix and Sweet's Corner.	Mrs. J. F. Rathburn.
Stake Road	Dr. Barbara McKinnon.
Sutherland's River	Mrs. Dwight Burns.
South Side Cape Sable Island	Mrs. E. C. Nickerson.
South Farmington	Mrs. Wilkins.
Springhill	Mrs. David Stewart.
Stellarton	Mrs. George Gray.
Stewiacke	Mrs. Rachel Pollock.
Stony Island	Mrs. S. L. Brannen.
Sydney River	Miss Sarah McDougall.
Selmah	Mrs. Cyrus Weldon.
South Rawdon	Mrs. W. H. Lawson.
South Bay	Mrs. T. A. Young.
Torbrook	Mrs. A. B. Payson.
Tupperville	Mrs. L. H. Chipman.
Tatamagouche	Mrs. D. A. Cunningham.
Upper Burlington	Mrs. Harry B. Sandford.
Upper Lakeville	Mrs. Margaret Webber.
Upper Musquodoboit	Mrs. W. B. Hutchinson.
Upper Economy	Mrs. C. F. Lewis.
Upper Rawdon	Mrs. J. E. Weatherhead.
Upper Port La Tour	Miss Rosa Snow.
Wallace	Mrs. A. S. Murphy.
Wilmot	Mrs. J. B. Kilton.
West New Annan	Mrs. W. Wilson.
Westport	Mrs. E. C. Bowser.
Wallace River	Mrs. Chas. Fisher.
Waterville	Mrs. D. R. Pineo.
Waverley	Mrs. E. Fauchea.
West La Have	Mrs. Clarence Wambolt.
Welton's Corner	Mrs. P. A. Smith.
West Apple River	Mrs. Robert McWhirter.
West Berlin and Eagle Head.	Mrs. B. Conrod.

NOVA SCOTIA'S PART IN THE GREAT WAR

THE WILLING WAR WORKERS, GLACE BAY.

AN organization that blazed a new and unique track in the War, and accomplished great results, especially in the colliery districts of Cape Breton, was the Willing War Workers of Glace Bay.

A number of the mothers, sisters, wives and sweethearts of the boys " over there," finding that other Societies lacked the personal touch, banded themselves together to send parcels every week to their own home boys in France, and kept up the good work enthusiastically until Armistice Day, when they disbanded.

MRS. G. S. HARRINGTON.

Mrs. Gordon S. Harrington, wife of Colonel Harrington, Deputy Overseas Minister, was the first President, and Mrs. Stuart McCawley, of Glace Bay, the Secretary-Treasurer.

Mrs. Harrington went to England in November, 1916, and became actively interested in war work for Canadian soldiers in that country, particularly at the Beaver Hut, Strand, London, and St. Dunstan's Hostel for blinded soldiers.

THE GREEN FEATHER SOCIETY LADIES' AUXILIARY OF THE 185TH BATTALION.

THE Society was organized on March 9, 1916. The aim of the Society was, first, to aid recruiting; second, to look after the comfort of the men while quartered at Broughton, and as far as possible after they had gone Overseas; third, to assist in every possible way the wives and families of the men enlisting.

OFFICERS ELECTED:

Mrs. E. J. Johnstone, *President.* Mrs. O. Leiers, *Treasurer.*
Mrs. J. A. McLellan, *Vice-President.* Miss Daniels, *Secretary.*

From the time of the Society's organization until the 185th Battalion was disbanded, the Society raised the sum of $2,075.36,

WAR WORKERS' SOCIETIES

which was devoted entirely to the use and comfort of the Battalion. In addition to this, Mr. Walshaw, of the D.T.S. Co., collected the sum of $70.00, and the North Sydney Branch of the Green Feather Society also donated the sum of $43.00. These amounts were sent to England for the purpose of procuring Christmas dinners for the men.

The visiting committee of the Society did very good work in looking after the wives and children of the men who had gone Overseas.

At the close of the War there was the sum of $12.00 in funds, which was presented to the G.W.V.A. after their organization.

THE CATHOLIC LADIES' PATRIOTIC SOCIETY, SYDNEY.

THIS Society was organized the second year of the War by the ladies of the Sacred Heart Parish, Sydney, and was intended to supply the religious needs of the Cape Breton soldiers and Chaplains, and to send comforts direct to the soldiers in the trenches. However, as the War went on, the Society enlarged its scope and embraced all kinds of patriotic work. The work of the Society was carried on by packing tin boxes with fruit cake, candy, cigarettes, socks, khaki shirts, and other things too numerous to mention. These were addressed to each soldier and acknowledged in due time.

The success of the Society was in no small measure due to the activity of the President, Mrs. V. F. Cunningham, who held that office during the four years of the Society's existence.

The following short statement will give some idea of the work of the Society:

RECEIPTS.

Total amount received from general city collections	$2,058 89
Amount from other sources	975 80
	$3,034 69

EXPENDITURE.

Paid supplies for boxes sent Overseas	$2,153 79
" Chaplain's supplies	250 00
" Catholic Hut Fund	200 00
" Hospital supplies	305 90
" Local Hospital, Khaki Club, etc., etc.	125 00
	$3,034 69

CHAPTER LIII.

THE KNIGHTS OF COLUMBUS.

UNTIL the spring of 1918, the war work of the Knights of Columbus in Nova Scotia consisted in aiding the work carried on at St. Mary's Army and Navy Club at Halifax, and in sending money Overseas to aid the Catholic Army Huts in England and at the Front. The work done by these Huts became more and more extensive as the War went on, and the amount of money that each council could send from its own funds became wholly inadequate to enable these Huts to give efficient service.

In May, 1918, His Lordship the Right Reverend James Morrison, Bishop of Antigonish, addressed a letter to the Knights of Columbus of the Maritime Provinces, setting out the needs of the Catholic Army Huts and the slender financial resources at their disposal. "Accordingly," he says, "I feel it a pressing duty to ask the Knights of Columbus to organize a general public campaign for funds to provide our Catholic soldiers Overseas, or wherever they may be assembled, with Catholic Huts, Club Rooms and accessories thereto, in which the Army Chaplains may be enabled more efficiently and more conveniently to minister to their religious welfare, and where the soldiers themselves, irrespective of denominational affiliations, may have at their disposal such accommodations in social life as may be a proper safeguard for their moral welfare."

On the receipt of this letter the Knights began the work of organizing a campaign which extended throughout the whole of Canada. More than one million dollars were raised in the

THE KNIGHTS OF COLUMBUS

Dominion, to which sum the various counties of Nova Scotia contributed as follows:—

Halifax	$56,621 95
Cape Breton	28,562 80
Pictou	9,509 63
Antigonish	6,635 49
Cumberland	5,337 73
Inverness	4,802 46
Guysboro	3,330 05
Yarmouth	2,877 97
Colchester	2,475 29
Kings	2,405 57
Hants	1,961 66
Richmond	1,723 25
Digby	1,542 67
Victoria	1,144 25
Queens	1,102 20
Lunenburg	669 50
Annapolis	444 55
Shelburne	68 50
Total for the Province	$131,215 52

The "Drive" by which this money was raised took place during the week of August 19-24, 1918. The whole of the amount raised was intended for work in England and France but, with the signing of the Armistice, the returned soldier problem demanded the attention of the Knights, and Huts were opened in Halifax and the other dispersal areas in Canada. The work in Canada and Overseas was under the supervision of Lieut.-Col. Clarence F. Smith, of Montreal, Comptroller. Large sums of the money were sent Overseas and the balance was devoted to the work of serving the returned men.

Following are the names on the Executive Committee of the Knights of Columbus War Activities:—Messrs. John A. Neville, John F. O'Connell, Jas. D. O'Connor, Walter M. Godsoe, Thos. W. Murphy, Frank A. Gillis, Dan. T. Lynagh, Wm. A. Hallisey, Jno. P. Quinn, Hon. Judge Chisholm, and Mr. William R. Wakely.

The Knights of Columbus Catholic Army Hut, at No. 372 Barrington Street, was opened December 1, 1918, and Halifax may be regarded as the birth-place of the work of the Knights of Columbus Catholic Army Huts in Canada. All men of the Allied

NOVA SCOTIA'S PART IN THE GREAT WAR

Armies and Navies were welcome, irrespective of race, creed or color. The Knights of Columbus' slogan, "Everybody Welcome, Everything Free," was carried out to the letter, with the exception that a charge of 25c. was made for beds, although of the total number of beds used about half were donated, inasmuch as many of the guests were in need of funds. Men arriving in transports were also given a bed free of charge. Mr. J. D. O'Connor was Chairman of the Hut Committee, and associated with him were Mr. John F. O'Connell, Mr. D. T. Lynagh, the late W. A. Monoghan, Mr. W. J. Williams, Mr. E. J. Scanlon, Mr. W. A. Hallisey, Mr. W. T. Murphy, Mr. W. E. Donovan, Mr. J. K. Kelleher, and Mr. W. R. Wakely. There was an average daily attendance at the Hut during December, 1918, January, February and March, 1919, of 1,300 to 1,500, and a total attendance of 177,060 from December 1, 1918, until the Hut closed on September 13, 1919.

Mr. W. E. Donovan, Chairman of the Entertainment Committee, arranged for weekly entertainments. The men in uniform were always most appreciative of the class of entertainment given at the Hut under the direction of the Chairman. He had the happy faculty of selecting the very best artists, and had the Columbus Musical Club to draw from as well as other local clubs.

Refreshments were always served. Mr. W. E. Donovan never failed to have a number of young ladies in attendance, and they saw that every guest was generously supplied. The Hut was open daily from 10 a.m. to 11 p.m., and on Sundays from 1 p.m. to 11 p.m., and the men had free use of the reading, writing and billiard rooms. Canadian and American newspapers and magazines were supplied; writing paper and envelopes and all billiard and pool games were free. 12,983 games of billiards and pool were played from December, 1918, to September 13, 1919. May 10, 1919, a dormitory of fifty beds was opened, and from that date to September 13, 1919, 2,725 beds were used. Of that number 1,279 were supplied free of charge.

Space in the building would not permit of the Knights of Columbus War Activities having a cafeteria, but there was a canteen from which the following supplies were given away free, from December 1, 1918, to September 13, 1919:—

Soft Drinks (bottles)	6,684
Apples (barrels)	32
Cigarettes (packages)	27,872
Cigars	2,000
Tobacco (pounds)	830
Gum (packages)	1,605
Coffee (cups)	55,175
Oxo (cubes)	3,783
Biscuits (pounds)	2,389
Chocolate Bars	7,668
Matches (boxes)	8,304

LETTERS MAILED.

Canadian	27,121
British and Foreign	6,042
American	8,067

It was not until after the Armistice was signed that a Pier Committee was organized under the able leadership of Mr. John P. Quinn as Chairman. His associates were Messrs. John Neville, Henry T. Kline, Harry C. Murphy, John D. Campbell, E. J. Murphy, John Fry, J. J. Penny, P. J. Hanifen, R. J. Flinn, Geo. A. Gauvin, and W. E. Donovan.

The Returned Soldiers' Reception Committee, made up of twenty-five men selected from the various clubs and organizations of Halifax City, with an Auxiliary Committee of five ladies, was organized in November, 1916. From that date the Committee received troop and hospital ships, and raised by voluntary subscription $9,178.96. It also received $3,000.00 from the Halifax Victory Loan canvassers. Mr. John P. Quinn waited upon Mr. W. S. Davidson, Chairman of the Returned Soldiers' Reception Committee, and informed Mr. Davidson that the Knights of Columbus were prepared to spend an amount of their funds toward the reception of the troops returning from Overseas, either in conjunction with the Returned Soldiers' Reception Committee, or alone. This brought in the Red Cross and the Y.M.C.A., and an agreement was made by each of the three organizations to contribute to the funds of the Returned Soldiers' Reception Committee to the extent of one-third each of the amount required by the Returned Soldiers' Committee. From January 1, 1919, until the last troopship arrived, $9,000.00 was contributed from each of the three organizations—a total of $27,000.00. These funds were used for the purpose of purchasing cigarettes, fruit, chocolate bars, matches, flowers, newspapers, welcome cards, and for postage and telegrams.

From the time the work began, one hundred and thirty-eight troopships disembarked about 305,655 men. In the distribution of supplies at the pier, the work was divided among seven teams of twelve each, each team having a captain and an equal number of representatives from the Knights of Columbus, the Red Cross, Y.M.C.A., and the Returned Soldiers' Reception Committee. Mr. Felix P. Quinn, of the Knights of Columbus, was a captain of one of the teams.

WORK AT THE VARIOUS MILITARY HOSPITALS.

There existed what was known as the Knights of Columbus Hospital Comfort Bureau. The following are the names of those serving on that Committee: Rev. John Quinan, Capt. M. Ryan, Jas. J. Bates, T. J. Burke, E. J. Griffen, Geo. J. Lynch, Jas. P. Mulcahy, Frank A. Gillis, and O. G. Burke.

MRS. JOHANNA M. TERNAN.

Mrs. Johanna Mary Ternan was appointed Secretary.

Daily supplies were sent to Camp Hill Military Hospital and Cogswell Street Station Hospital and weekly visits were made. On these visits fruit, candy and cigarettes were distributed by the following committee of ladies: Mrs. Geo. Metzler, Miss Nita Gauvin, Miss Fannie Clark, Miss Metzler, Mrs. M. Foley, Miss Mary Neville, and Miss Frances Chisholm.

In addition to the above Hospitals, supplies were sent to Pine Hill Convalescent Home, Rock Head Military Hospital, Kentville Sanitarium, Naval Hospital, County Jail, Victoria General Hospital, Lawlor's Island, Quarantine Station, Air Station, U.S. Flying Corps and H.M.S. Hospital Ship *Essequibo*.

THE KNIGHTS OF COLUMBUS

Weekly visits were made to the Kentville Sanitarium by Mrs. W. S. Rothburn, of Kentville, and a committee of ladies, Miss McCormack, Miss Farrell, and Miss Kearney, under the supervision of Mrs. Johanna M. Ternan, of Halifax.

At Christmas, 1918, there were:

	Patients.
Camp Hill Hospital	440
Naval Hospital	38
Cogswell St. Hospital	300
Kentville Sanitarium	200
Nova Scotia Hospital, Dartmouth	70
Pine Hill Convalescent Home	125
Rock Head Military Hospital	60
Total	1,233

It was decided by the Hospitals Committee on Thursday, December 19, 1918, that candy and smokes should be sent to Kentville for the 200 patients. Four hundred boxes were prepared containing three packages of cigarettes and a half-pound of candy for each patient. This work was done by a voluntary committee of three little girls and one little boy (the Misses O'Connor and Master O'Connor, daughters and son of Mr. J. D. O'Connor), and by little Miss Elliott. Provision was made for Rock Head and Cogswell Hospitals.

December 18, 1918, 328 stockings were made and filled by a committee of ladies at the Knights of Columbus Club Rooms, Hollis Street. The stockings were all of different shades, and each contained fourteen articles, consisting of the following: One box of notepaper, one lead pencil, one cube of tooth paste, one tooth brush, three packages cigarettes, two boxes of matches, one small comb, one pocket handkerchief, one ash-tray, two chocolate bars, collar buttons, one pipe, one package tobacco and one tobacco pouch.

Two hundred and three of these were sent to Camp Hill and one hundred and twenty-five to Pine Hill. As there were a number of very sick patients at Cogswell Street Station Hospital, it was requested that fruit be sent, and three cases of oranges, four cases of grape fruit and one keg of grapes were supplied. To the Nova Scotia Hospital, Dartmouth, one hundred and forty parcels were sent containing three packages of cigarettes and a half-pound of candy. Stockings were sent to four soldiers in the County Jail, and nine stockings to soldiers in the Victoria General Hospital. To the N.S. Naval Air Station were sent two cases of oranges, two hundred packages cigarettes, two hundred cigars and two hundred chocolate bars.

CHRISTMAS, 1919.

Christmas boxes were sent from the Head Office in Montreal, specially made for the Knights of Columbus Catholic Army Huts for distribution on this day to all Military Hospitals in the Dominion. Each box contained one package gum, one Durham Duplex Safety Razor, one package razor blades, one shaving stick, one shaving brush, one package cigarettes, one box matches, one chocolate bar, one tooth brush, one tube tooth paste, one handkerchief, and short stories. In addition twenty-six quarts of ice cream were distributed, also five hundred apples, fifty pounds of assorted kisses and fifty pounds of frosted cake.

Many picnics were given patients who were convalescing during the summer of 1919, and entertainments given to special wards in Camp Hill and Cogswell Street Hospitals.

From January 1, 1919, to April 30, 1919, no fewer than 125,466 personal requests for comforts were granted by the Knights of Columbus Hospital Comfort Bureau.

CHAPTER LIV.

THE YOUNG MEN'S CHRISTIAN ASSOCIATION.

FOR years previous to the Declaration of War, the Y.M.C.A. carried on its work in the summer Militia Camps; consequently the War did not find the Association without some idea of the requirements of troops, and from the early days of the first big concentration at Valcartier, the "Y" tried hard to measure up to each new phase of war activity.

In 1914 about 5,000 men were served in the camps of the Maritime Provinces. During the succeeding winter Y.M.C.A. work was established in the various barracks, and in 1915 the work on the piers at the points of embarkation was started. All this work was carried on continually from this time with increasing efficiency, not only in camps, barracks, and hospitals, but also on board transports and on troop trains carrying returning men. It consisted of the erection of large recreation buildings, giving assistance with the equipping of recreation rooms in barracks; the provision of free writing and reading materials, games, athletic goods, music, pianos, gramophones and records, moving picture machines and films; the organizing of concerts on land and on board ships; social evenings in homes, churches, barracks, hospitals and otherwise; athletics, religious services; supplying free hot drinks and doughnuts or biscuits at the disembarkation points and demobilization centres.

The first large financial appeal was made to the people of the Maritime Provinces in the spring of 1916, when approximately $34,500 were raised for home and Overseas' military work. During that year Association service was rendered to troops in eighteen different places in these Provinces. Each succeeding year saw most successful campaigns for larger sums of money, until 1918, when requirements began to decrease. Altogether about $679,600 were raised in the Maritime area and spent on military work at home and Overseas.

Large recreation buildings, which were much needed, were erected at Aldershot and Sussex Camps, each capable of accommodating close to 1,000 men. These were used to capacity, and were practically the only adequate recreation centres. A large hut was erected in the Naval Dockyard, Halifax, for the men of the navy and the merchant marine. It was destroyed by the explosion, but was replaced by a larger structure, and was the great social centre for the men of the navy and the merchant marine.

The large Red Triangle Hut, on Barrington Street, Halifax, was erected as a demobilization service to offset the inadequate housing facilities in Halifax, to provide meals and beds for returning men who had to remain in the city while waiting for trains or demobilization, to assist returned men to become re-established in civil life by providing them with wholesome meals and beds at prices within their means, to help men taking Government re-training courses and drawing barely enough money to live on, and to provide them with a clean, attractive recreation centre.

Other recreation huts were built and equipped at St. John, New Brunswick, and Cogswell Hospital, Halifax. A large building was leased and equipped as a Red Triangle Club at St. John, N.B. Clubs on a smaller scale were operated in Sydney, Windsor, Kentville, Nova Scotia, and Fredericton and Sussex, New Brunswick.

Work was carried on among the German prisoners of war at Amherst in return for which the German Government permitted the Y.M.C.A. to carry on work in certain camps in Germany where Canadians were confined. Only the work in the Internment Camps in Canada made this concession possible.

Co-operating with the Sailors' Comforts' Committee, Halifax, the Y.M.C.A. workers visited many ships of the merchant service and supplied the men with reading and writing materials, games, mufflers, sweaters, socks, gloves, mitts, underwear, etc. Concerts were frequently arranged for the crews on shore.

Uniform reports of activities and the attendance were not kept in the early days of the War, and it is impossible to arrive at anything like accurate estimates of the extent of some of the services

THE YOUNG MEN'S CHRISTIAN ASSOCIATION

rendered. The report of a few activities for the *two years of maximum efficiency* may serve to indicate, however, the great extent to which the men patronized the Y.M.C.A. military services.

Activity.	Number.	Attendance.
Concerts	694	84,550
Social evenings	815	112,800
Moving Picture Shows (free)	1,365	210,800
Religious Services	1,108	88,100
Theatre parties arranged and conducted through courtesy of theatre managers, without charge to patients	356	12,619
Illustrated Lectures	98	18,050

	Supplies Used.
Magazines	162,685
Sheets of writing paper	1,511,000
Sex and health education booklets	39,000
Athletic goods	large quantities
Pianos in continual use	22
Billiard tables in continual use	31
Gramaphones and records supplied continually	50
Moving picture machines in continual use	9
Reels of picture films per week provided, no charge made	40

At the disembarkation piers, in co-operation with various women's organizations, the Creche in Halifax, and the combined organizations in St. John, free hot or cold drinks and mixed biscuits were provided. At the Demobilization Centre, Halifax, co-operating with the G.W.V.A. Ladies' Auxiliary, drinks and doughnuts or mixed biscuits were supplied free, and a six months' membership ticket in any Y.M.C.A. was given to each man.

A "Y" representative accompanied each troop train to its destination and carried a standard stock of equipment, gramophones, portable organs, music, song sheets, games, fruits, chocolate, and cigarettes. He rendered personal services in every way possible, such as wiring ahead, mailing letters, and carrying on a programme of concerts and games. These representatives were principally business men, and all gave their services voluntarily. In all 449 representatives accompanied troop trains.

Further assistance was given returned men to re-establish themselves by Red Triangle Clubs at Halifax and St. John, where bed and board could be had at reduced rates. During the first year of the Halifax Club, 147,713 meals were served, and 38,855 beds occupied for one night or more. This work is still going on. The rate for bed and board was $1 per day. The food was far above the average meal at similar prices. A programme of entertainments, athletics, moving pictures, religious services, and educational lectures and discussions was carried on. The Association's hospital service will be continued as long as necessary, and funds are available.

CHAPTER LV.

THE HALIFAX CITIZENS' RECEPTION COMMITTEE.

THE splendid service performed by the Halifax Citizens' Returned Soldiers' Reception Committee had its inception in the fall of 1916, when Mr. P. F. Martin, at that time Mayor of the city, called a number of representative citizens together at the city hall for the purpose of forming a committee to extend a welcome to the men returning home. The matter did not take definite form, however, until a little later on, when a score of energetic citizens selected by the various National Societies, the Board of Trade and other organizations of the city, met at the Board of Trade Rooms in November, 1916, at the call of Mr. W. S. Davidson, Vice-President of the Board. At this meeting the Committee was organized, as also an Auxiliary Committee of the following ladies:—Mrs. G. McGregor Mitchell, Mrs. Geoffery Morrow, Mrs. T. Sherman Rogers, Mrs. Norwood Duffus, and Mrs. (Dr.) Ryan. Mr. W. S. Davidson was elected Chairman, Mr. Arthur B. Mitchell, Secretary, Mr. A. M. Smith, Assistant-Secretary, and Mr. W. A. Major, Treasurer. The excellence of the choice of this Executive was amply proven by the fact that the personnel remained unchanged from the night the Committee was formed until the last transport docked, and the work was finished.

W. S. DAVIDSON.

The following gentlemen composed the original Committee: Messrs. W. S. Davidson, W. A. Major, H. H. Marshall, C. H. Mitchell, J. McL. Fraser, Felix P. Quinn, C. E. Creighton, W. A.

Hart, A. M. Smith, Paul Creighton, W. E. Hebb, C. H. Climo, W. L. Kane, J. P. Quinn, P. T. Strong, and R. B. Colwell, representing the North British Society, St. George's Society, the Charitable Irish Society, the Canadian Club, and the Citizens of Halifax in general.

These gentlemen, who became known as "the originals," carried or through fair weather and foul, night or day as occasion required from start to finish. The only exception was Mr. H. H. Marshall, who, to the great regret of his friends and fellow-workers, was ordered by his physician to seek a change of climate, his health having broken down, but nevertheless, he was with the work in spirit, always keeping in touch, sending greetings and material aid from time to time.

In addition to those above-mentioned, the following gentlemen joined the movement later, entering into the spirit of the work with energy and enthusiasm: Messrs. E. J. Murphy, G. J. Allen, Cyril Gorham, A. W. Robb, W. R. Morton, H. C. Murphy, Hugh Fraser, Chas. Waterfield, R. A. Wood, W. S. Munnis, John D. Campbell, P. J. Hannifen, Geo. M. Wood, F. M. Guildford, R. K. Elliott, George Ritchie, G. W. Perry, J. A. Neville, H. T. Kline, J. A. Reid, V. B. Faulkner, J. L. Wilson, E. M. McLeod, Geo. T. McNutt, John Fry, J. J. Penny, J. M. Davison, George Robinson, W. R. Scriven, Wm. Wilson, Capt. W. F. Mitchell, W. E. Donavon, G. A. Smith, J. F. Roue, Walter Black, R. J. Flinn, G. A. Gauvin, George Winters, Howard Lawrence, W. Cyril Smith, Cyril Stairs, Sedley E. Thompson, J. L. Hetherington, H. E. Mahon, C. H. Wright, the late Professor Eben McKay, F. A. Marr, Allen Patrick, and H. R. Price.

A number of ladies, Mrs. W. T. Allen, Mrs. M. R. Morrow and others, joined the original Auxiliary Committee of five above-mentioned, doing splendid work in connection with the cot cases, etc., but unfortunately a complete list is not available. Two young ladies deserving of special mention who became associated with the General Committee are Miss Edna Davison and Miss Helen Creighton. Their work was admirable, being here, there, and everywhere when required, untiring in their efforts, having the capacity to perform, as well as zeal to undertake. It is safe to say that the soldier

THE HALIFAX CITIZENS' RECEPTION COMMITTEE

boys who landed at Halifax will never forget the ladies connected with this Committee; for their bright kindly faces, apart from their work, gave them a welcome home which is hard to express in words; and it was not only on fine days when the sun was shining that they were to be seen on the pier when transports were expected, but in all kinds of weather, night as well as day, and only those who worked there know how cold it sometimes was at Pier 2 on a winter night. However, the welcome given the boys was warm enough to take away the chill of the weather.

During the period in which this Committee carried on its work, 138 transports disembarked some 200,000 Overseas men at Pier 2, and of this number very few indeed missed the kindly attentions of the Committee.

The amount expended was as follows:—

Paid for	Cigarettes, Tobacco, etc.	$14,473 51
"	Fruit	7,931 82
"	Postage, telegrams, telephones, etc.	462 42
"	Welcome Cards, badges, printing, etc.	1,294 49
"	Newspapers	1,813 62
"	Taxi service conveying local returned men to their homes	118 80
"	Music	15 00
"	Baskets, equipment and sundries	278 66
"	Matches	4,782 25
"	Chocolate bars, cakes, etc.	7,157 21
"	Deficit exchanging money	9 50
"	Flowers (for cot cases)	34 50
	Money refunded Provincial Recruiting Committee	9 00
	Total	$38,380 78

A word or two in connection with these figures which are from the Treasurer's report. The item for postage, etc., would have been much larger but through the representations of the Committee, after the work had been carried on for a considerable time, the Government was induced to allow letters from returned men, on arrival, to be posted free, thus conserving the funds for other purposes. The item $15 for music does not mean that this was the extent of the music by any means; for the Commanding Officers of local military units very cheerfully permitted their bands to play on the pier on arrival of transports.

NOVA SCOTIA'S PART IN THE GREAT WAR

Of the above total amount, the sum of $9,178.96 was received in voluntary subscriptions, and $3,000 from Halifax Victory Loan canvassers, which came in spontaneously and entirely unsolicited.

As the end of the War approached and the number of returning men became greater, it became apparent that the funds would require to be largely augmented, and in order to cope with the good work, the Y.M.C.A., the Red Cross Society, and the Knights of Columbus very generously contributed equal amounts of $9,000, less a refund to each of these organizations of $266.06, being the balance or surplus left over at the close of the work.

It was not long after the work began until a splendid system was evolved which worked with almost clock-like precision. The usual procedure was as follows: Immediately a transport was docked a certain number of the Committee were told off to go on board with the latest newspapers, collect telegrams and letters which were, as mentioned above, sent off free of charge, thus doing away with the inconvenience of hunting up stamps, etc. Whenever it happened that a ship had to drop anchor in the stream while waiting for a berth to dock at the pier—and as these were busy days in shipping circles in Halifax, this very frequently happened—a tug-boat was promptly secured by the energetic Chairman, and a contingent landed on board with newspapers, cigarettes, matches, fruit, etc.; and, in most cases, if the ship was to remain at anchor overnight, a concert party was always ready to join their efforts with those of the Committee in extending a hearty welcome to the boys, many excellent entertainments being given on board transports waiting to dock. The very best musical talent in Halifax was always ready and willing to respond at a moment's notice to calls of this nature. Mr. Davidson being one of the principal members of the large shipping firm of Messrs. G. S. Campbell and Co., of course always knew where to locate one of these tug-boats, as they own and operate a number of them, and although in the forefront as business men, and blessed with good memories, they must have forgotten to render any bills or charge for this excellent service.

When the men left the ship and were entrained, a sufficient number of Committee-men having in the meantime been told off and sub-divided, allowing an equal number to look after each car.

THE HALIFAX CITIZENS' RECEPTION COMMITTEE

the cars being designated by letters "A," "B," "C," and so on, beginning with the car nearest the engine, and each party knowing the particular car it had to look after, confusion or oversight was practically nil. The first Committee-man went through the car with baskets of apples and oranges, being followed by another with cigarettes and matches, a third and fourth bringing up the rear with chocolate bars, welcome cards, newspapers, and collecting any letters or postal cards the boys had scribbled while waiting for their train to back in. Oftentimes when large steamships like the *Olympic, Mauretania,* or *Aquitania* arrived, fifteen or twenty trains would be dispatched with an average time between of twenty or twenty-five minutes; so that the necessity for system was evident, or otherwise only a portion of the boys would be looked after; but in the way in which the work was handled every man received attention; and usually a few minutes were left over, before the conductor called "All aboard," in which to chat with them, give them a hearty handshake and wish them "Bon voyage" and a safe journey to their destination.

This sketch of the work of the Halifax Citizens' Returned Soldiers' Reception Committee is necessarily short. It does not begin to express the scope or extent of the work carried on by this Committee, but the boys who returned home no doubt still remember the way they were received and treated.

Letters of appreciation were received from all parts of Canada and points in the United States. Such evidence of appreciation amply rewarded the Committee for any efforts they had made to ensure a hearty, and pleasant welcome home to those splendid men, who made the name of Canada for ever respected and glorious.

CHAPTER LVI.

ST. JOHN AMBULANCE BRIGADE OVERSEAS
and
THE CRECHE AT PIER 2, HALIFAX.

THE first branch of the St. John Ambulance Brigade Overseas established in Nova Scotia was organized in June, 1916, as the Halifax Central Nursing Division No. 17, with Mrs. Bowman, Superintendent of the Victoria General Hospital, Halifax, as Lady Divisional Superintendent. This division, besides being the first in the Maritime Provinces, was the largest in Canada. Most of the officers were graduate nurses, and all of the members had received their instruction in First Aid and Home Nursing through classes held in Halifax by the sister organization, the St. John Ambulance Association.

On Mrs. Bowman's removal from Halifax, Mrs. G. A. MacIntosh was appointed Superintendent (April, 1917). Owing to greatly increased membership, and for the purposes of more efficient administration, the division was divided in July, 1918, into two Units, A. No. 17 and B. No. 47, Mrs. MacIntosh being promoted at the same time to be Lady District Superintendent in charge of the Women's Aid Department (Military District No. 6). In January, 1920, a reorganization of the two divisions was made effective by which all active officers and members were assigned to Division A. 17, and the inactive members, or those in reserve for emergencies, to B. 47. The active division continues as one of the most efficient and effective in Canada under the able superintendence of Miss E. M. Pemberton, of the Victoria General Hospital.

The war work in Nova Scotia of this organization falls under four heads:

(a) Its work in Military Hospitals as auxiliary to the Army Medical and Nursing Service.
(b) Its work in Nova Scotia in connection with the Red Cross Society, Y.M.C.A. Canteens, and other voluntary patriotic organizations.
(c) Its work of ministration to women and children returning from England.

(d) Its emergency work on the day of the Halifax Disaster and in the relief work and hospital service for the weeks and months following the disaster.

(a) HOSPITAL SERVICE.

Hospital duties performed by the members of the Halifax Divisions during the War include:—

(a) Eleven members who went Overseas, serving with great credit in hospitals in England.

(b) Local hospitals.

We believe Pine Hill was the first Military Hospital in Canada to recognize or use the services of the Brigade members. Three pioneers served for two years and were followed by others.

In the latter part of 1918 the Women's Aid Department was formed in Canada in co-operation with the military authorities, the Lady District Superintendent furnishing to the A.D.M.S. of each Military District the following personnel, the number given below being that of those who served in M.D. No. 6:—

1. *Volunteer Section*:—
    (a) Nursing service of Brigade members, eight of whom served at Pine Hill Military Hospital.
    (b) Function Trainers, also Brigade members trained at Hart House, Toronto, two of whom served at Camp Hill.
2. *Special Service Section*:—
    Masseuses, trained at Hart House, Toronto, members of St. John Ambulance Brigade, and serving at Camp Hill, Moxham Ross, Prince Edward Island Military Hospitals.

Section 3:—
    General Service Section consisting of a General Service Superintendent Assistant Superintendent, bookkeepers, domestics and many there not Brigade members, but for a short time recommended by the Women's Aid Department of the Brigade.
    (c) Before the Women's Aid Department came into effect five members had served at the Nova Scotia Sanatorium in the tent Colony for tubercular soldiers.
    (d) During the Influenza epidemic of 1918 six members assisted the depleted staffs in the Victoria General, the Dartmouth Emergency for two months, two members at Infants Home for two months, also for two months in the homes of the sick, at the Emergency Hospital, Hazelwood Hospital, St. Mary's Emergency Hospital, and for three weeks at Brocton Field Hospital, Mass. During the epidemic in the spring of 1919 a diet kitchen was organized and conducted and proper nourishment prepared and delivered to all asking for it, in the majority of cases no charge being made. The Brigade responded to requests for diet from the Victorian Order of Nurses, City Board of Health, Social Welfare Bureau, etc.
    (e) The hospital work performed after the explosion is mentioned separately.
    (f) Miscellaneous duties performed in hospitals include mending each week at the Station Hospital, emergency bedmaking at Camp Hill and hospital train service.

NOVA SCOTIA'S PART IN THE GREAT WAR

(b) MISCELLANEOUS WORK

At the Clearing Depot, Pier 2, a splendid work was accomplished. Over 13,000 beds were made for soldiers disembarking at this port. At very short notice members in sufficient numbers quickly responded to a call from the C.O. to prepare the beds required (at times as many as 800 beds were needed) in readiness for the men.

An important work carried on at Pier 2 was the serving of meals three times daily for over a week to 150 men.

Boats were met by the Lady District Superintendent, who, assisted by the members, welcomed and assisted when necessary any V.A.D.'s returning to Canada from Overseas duty.

A very interesting and important service rendered by the organization was in connection with the vocational re-education of the soldiers. For eight months two members read daily to blinded soldiers, assisting them in this way with their study. Four other members also performed like service for five and a half months. Ten members took a special two months' course in weaving and basketry, nine of whom were able to instruct patients at Camp Hill Hospital for from one to seven months.

Truly patriotic work has been performed under the Y.M.C.A. At their Red Triangle Hut a team of eight members have given one day each week and every sixth Sunday for one and a half years to serve meals to returned soldiers taking vocational courses in the city. Members have also served refreshments on trains to soldiers recently discharged and entraining for their homes. At the Armories members have responded at all hours, sometimes working all night to serve refreshments to soldiers just disembarked and awaiting their discharge.

The Red Cross has been ably assisted by the making of numerous garments, surgical supplies, sphagnum moss dressings, and the raising of funds during campaigns.

The following "drives" have been given willing and able support:—

Navy League, Patriotic Fund, Knights of Columbus, Children's Hospital, Victorian Order, Salvation Army, Maternity Hospital, and the Canadian Red Cross.

ST. JOHN AMBULANCE BRIGADE OVERSEAS

For two years a rest and refreshment room has been conducted at the city market and has been of great benefit to the market people who often drive long distances.

For two years the Halifax Dispensary has had the assistance daily of a member for clerical work.

The Halifax Welfare, Victorian Order of Nurses, and many other organizations have had assistance, and many kindnesses have been performed, such as assistance given at orphans' picnics.

First aid booths have been conducted at exhibitions, Wanderers Athletic Grounds, and first aid rendered during public processions and individually in the every-day life of the members.

All service rendered except that required in the last two sections of the Women's Aid Department has been voluntary and performed quietly and systematically in times of emergencies, and in war as in times of peace for the public good.

THE DISASTER WORK

It is unnecessary here to refer to the causes and disastrous results of the great explosion on the morning of December 6, 1917. As nearly as can be ascertained more than 1,500 people lost their lives, approximately 5,000 people were injured, of whom about 1,000 received more or less serious injuries. With hundreds of other citizens the members of the Halifax Divisions of the Brigade responded at once to the calls for assistance, and within an hour more than 140 members were on duty in the devastated area; on the Common, in improvised aid stations, and in the various emergency hospitals rendering first aid to the injured, the very object for which they had all been trained.

Later in the afternoon and through the two or three days following they added to their duties those of material relief, and until a few days later the citizens' organization was established when the Brigade workers were fitted in under their Lady Superintendent as part of the medical relief work.

About sixty of the members remained on duty as V.A.D.'s in Camp Hill Hospital, the Y.M.C.A., Morris Street, and the various other hospitals for from one to five months following the explosion. For a short period following the disaster eight members of the St.

John (N.B.) Division assisted the local division in providing personnel for the various hospitals.

The total of the services rendered during the period December 6th to 31st shows 1,098 days of hospital work, 217 cases of district relief followed up, 140 missing children located, as well as other missing persons traced, food distributed, and first aid service rendered.

An official report forwarded through regular channels to the headquarters of the Brigade in England was referred by headquarters to the parent organization, the Ancient Order of the Hospital of St. John of Jerusalem in England, and in the spring of 1920 selected members of the Halifax Division and various citizens who co-operated with the Brigade in its invaluable work, were presented by the Lieutenant-Governor with the beautifully engraved certificates of thanks of the Order for their services rendered on the occasion of the disaster.

THE CRECHE AT PIER NO. 2, HALIFAX.

IN the spring of 1917, when the German submarines were trying to starve Britain into surrender, the Canadian Government thought it wise to bring home the dependants of our soldiers who were not actualy engaged in war work in the United Kingdom. The *Olympic* arrived in Halifax Port one morning with 1,000 women and children aboard, as well as her usual number of invalided soldiers. Many hours passed before the last travellers entrained for their homes, and one may imagine the scene at Pier 2 where these tired women waited for long hours with no shelter or food and no comforts for their little ones.

It was felt that something must be done to welcome those soldiers' dependants who had left their loved ones in England or France, and who could not surmise what the future held in store for those from whom they were separated. A committee of ladies was formed to look after all soldiers' dependants on their arrival in Canada. Spacious rooms, with kitchen, dining-room, rest-room, nursery and bath-rooms were provided by the Government at Pier 2, together with a sum of money sufficient to furnish necessaries.

THE CRECHE AT PIER NO. 2, HALIFAX

For three years a band of ladies under the presidency—first of Mrs. Benson, wife of General Benson, and later of Mrs. J. G. McDougall—met all boats and cared for all travellers with the most wonderful devotion. As soon as the gangway was secured their work began. It mattered not whether the ship was docked at 7 a.m., or at midnight, on a summer morning, or on a cold winter evening, the workers were always there. Two of the Committee went on board to see if there were any special cases to be looked after and to notify those aboard of the Creche Committee's willingness to help them in every possible way.

Some stood at the gangway to welcome tired mothers and relieve them of their tiny but very heavy burdens. Others led them to the warm and comfortable quarters provided for them. In the kitchen busy hands had been at work, and sandwiches and fragrant hot coffee were not wanting; while in the nursery many young girls were preparing beds with cool white sheets in which to lay Canada's young and welcome immigrants.

Although the railway authorities were wonderfully expeditious in getting the trains despatched, still many hours had to be spent at the Creche—days sometimes—and, once or twice, even nights. The scenes when a boat arrived with many hundreds of women and children defy description. Parties were constantly being brought to the rooms by willing and helpful guides. If husband or father was there, he saw his dear ones safely housed, and he himself returned to look after the tickets and baggage. If the mother was in charge, she accompanied her little ones to the Creche, and after seeing them safe and happy, was assisted in collecting her baggage and procuring transportation. Kind hands undressed the babies, washed, warmed and fed them and laid them to sleep in comfort. The older children were also fed and then amused by toys and picture books. Older travellers, completely tired out by the long and often rough voyage, found indeed a warm and steady bed a source of joy. Times and movements of trains were called in the waiting rooms, and to the outgoing trains the travellers were finally escorted, as comfortable and as happy as it was possible to make them.

The Red Cross placed a most efficient trained nurse at the disposal of the Committee, and it is not possible to tell how much her services were appreciated by those who, though not fit for hospital and anxious to complete their journey, were still much in need of care. In a general way, as well as in her professional capacity, the trained nurse rendered services of a very high order. Space does not permit to tell of all the various activities carried on at the Creche—money was exchanged, hotel accommodation secured for those remaining over in Halifax for a few days, telegrams were sent, meal tickets given to those who needed them on the trains, babies were supplied with necessaries for travelling, and money was many times given to those who through stress of circumstances had not the wherewithal to complete their journey.

The returned men were always eager to assist in any way they could, and the bands of the Canadian Battalions gave all great pleasure by their delightful music.

Arrangements were made for any needing hospital care; and they were continually visited by members of the Committee while in Halifax City. The military authorities placed an ambulance at the disposal of the Committee for such cases. The Committee had the fullest support and co-operation of the military authorities. They also had the assistance of a hundred workers who gave up all engagements and pleasures when it was known that a boat was expected.

The Creche Committee deeply regretted the departure from Halifax of Mrs. Benson and Mrs. McKelvey Bell, under whom they began their work. The ladies who carried on to the close of operation were:—

Mrs. McCallum Grant .... *Hon Chairman.*
Mrs. J. G. McDougall .... *Chairman.*
Mrs. Hector McInnes .... *Vice-Chairman.*
Mrs. W. A. Henry .... *Secretary.*
Mrs. W. E. Thompson .... *Treasurer.*

    Mrs. David McKeen.   Miss Jessie MacKenzie.
    Mrs. G. S. Campbell.   Lady Townshend.
    Mrs. Clarence MacKinnon.   Mrs. M. A. Curry.

The Creche closed on 31st December, 1919. Since the 18th November, 1918, the Committee and its helpers met 120 ships laden with returning Canadian soldiers, their wives and families. On one steamship alone, the *Megantic,* were 600 women and children, 180 of the children being under twelve months of age. On several occasions there have been as many as 900 women and children on a steamer, and, in one instance, the *Olympic* brought 1,000. All were

THE CRECHE AT PIER NO. 2, HALIFAX

sent on their homeward journey rested, refreshed, and cheered; and the kindly welcome they received has made the name of the Atlantic Gateway dear to the hearts of thousands of people the Dominion over. Countless letters bear testimony to unfeigned appreciation and gratitude. One newspaper extract may be permitted.

The *Ottawa Journal* of December 28, 1918, says: " While this work, and, to a large extent, its financial obligations have been borne almost entirely by the citizens of Halifax, as the benefits accrue to the country as a whole the gratitude of the people of Canada is due to the small band of workers who for the past eighteen months have generously and patriotically assumed the burden for the whole Dominion."

Those were busy days at Pier 2; and although much sacrifice was demanded of the Halifax Creche Committee, it is not too much to say that it was willingly and joyfully given by those who wished to have some small share in the work of the Great War.

FROM LEFT TO RIGHT—MRS. J. G. M'DOUGALL, MRS. HECTOR M'INNES, MRS. W. A. HENRY, MRS. M'CALLUM GRANT.

CHAPTER LVII.

ST. MATTHEW'S CHURCH AND THE WAR.

[A description of the work done by each of the churches in Nova Scotia would require a book in itself. The following article on the activities of St. Matthew's Church, Halifax, is typical of the manner in which the churches of all denominations throughout the Province watched over the spiritual and material welfare of men of the Overseas' Units.—EDITOR.]

EARLY in the War, as soon as it became evident to the citizens of Halifax that the struggle against "Might" would endure for some time, and that this station would become again and remain an important rendezvous for the army and navy while hostilities lasted, the question of showing some tangible appreciation to the volunteers who were rallying to the colors became paramount in many minds. Noticing the presence of many of these men at the regular church services in St. Matthew's the minister (Rev. J. W. Macmillan, D.D.) conceived the idea of having special receptions so that they, while in Halifax, should find a real church home and get sociably acquainted with members of the congregation.

Such receptions were held at the close of the usual Sunday evening services. Many of the men were met thus and later welcomed at various homes during the week. It was later found expedient for these hosts to join forces so as to be able to entertain larger numbers than could be accommodated at the houses, and it was thus that the Thursday evening entertainments originated in the schoolroom of St. Matthew's Church during October, 1914. These gained immediately in popularity until crowded houses with S.R.O. signs continued for five winters without intermittence, except for a few weeks following the great explosion of December, 1917.

The ladies of the congregation were from first to last the chief motive power at all these meetings, and the secret of their success.

ST. MATTHEW'S CHURCH AND THE WAR

Some were not publicly in evidence but worked "behind the scenes" in supplying and providing the refreshments that formed a most important part of these functions and did yeoman service. The work was quickly organized into a perfect system, everybody being assigned to a task that suited the particular attitude of the worker, with plenty of eager helpers always on hand as reserves.

This organization was not any premeditated system nor was it arranged on the basis of any other movement, but being almost impromptu formed itself with a naturalness according to the needs as they developed until it appeared to become as perfect as is humanly possible and so it continued with an earnest patriotic zeal on the part of the people anxious to help but unable to go to the field of war because of their sex or their age limit. Some distinguished themselves as caterers, cooks, coffee makers, waiters or waitresses and even as dishwashers. Others at the doors as welcoming committees or indoors as cartoon makers, lantern manipulators, contest managers, leaders of choruses and accompanists or "masters of ceremonies" and chairmen. Others again found work in advertising the meetings at the various ships and barracks until it became the rule that every new Regiment or warship arriving at Halifax was promptly advised of these Thursday evening meetings.

The entertainment itself evolved into a systematic method by natural causes too, rather than by design. Noting the crowds of soldiers and sailors on the streets at an early hour the doors were opened at 6.30 p.m. and immediately the hall began filling. To entertain the early arrivals a magic lantern displayed reproductions of recent war cartoons and cheery messages, while various popular songs and choruses thrown on the screen by the same method with a good accompanist at the piano got every one settled down for a hearty sing-song. Each week the cartoons were supplemented with additions and new songs added, along with items of current interest and latest news, more pictures of local topics and jokes that were fully appreciated. These opening features proved attractive and were followed with some contest varying weekly in their style and nature, for which prizes were awarded—always two at the least and sometimes as many as twelve, most of them being made and given by the ladies of the congregation—that were keenly contested for by the men in uniform. This first portion of the meeting soon became, an essential part of the entertainment and was usually controlled by a "master of ceremonies," who between 7.45 to 8 o'clock would surrender his position to the chairman of the evening, and he in turn would call the meeting to order with the singing of the National Anthem, and after a few words of welcome the concert proper was conducted.

In this respect all the best and cleverest artists, without distinction of class or creed, responded willingly and enthusiastically to the committees having charge of the programmes. These committees rotated in their work and there arose a healthy competition between them in acquiring special performers and singers to assure successful concerts.

At nine o'clock an adjournment for refreshments took place. This half-hour provided an opportunity for conversation as well as for eating; the lantern threw cartoons and pictures, jokes and songs on the screen so that good humor continued to prevail. During this interval some committee members moved among the audience seeking for impromptu items for a programme that was continued along with choruses from 9.30 to 10 o'clock and even later for the benefit of such as had special "late leave."

The interest in these entertainments did not wane. It never flagged at any period of the five winters. The workers never tired of their tasks, nor was there ever any difficulty noticed in obtaining a bountiful supply of musical talent or refreshments to ensure success.

The secret of any extra degree of popularity for these Thursday evenings cannot be attributed to any one cause but rather to a combination of circumstances. To a great degree the down-town position of St. Matthew's made a strong appeal. The early start of these concerts caused them to be better known perhaps, and the fact of their regularity and continuity helped matters greatly, and yet, perhaps more than all, the ladies of St. Matthew's were a greater factor than all these. This can be stated without in any degree disparaging the great work done by other churches and institutions or of ladies who were equally active in other places, and yet these ladies as a body were able to greet all the men in uniform with a heartiness that was promptly felt and without at any time the semblance of that familiarity that breeds contempt or of a

ST. MATTHEW'S CHURCH AND THE WAR

patronizing air to which soldiers and sailors especially are most sensitive, and at no time was there anything but the most respectful and kindly feeling shown on either side.

No smoking was indulged in at these gatherings, and none appeared to wish the privilege. The men refrained out of their natural respect to the ladies in the audience. Later on some " No Smoking Allowed" signs were placed in the ante-rooms, where some were wont to indulge in a few puffs during the intervals, but this was done on account of the fire risks in the older part of the structure and did not occasion much if any comment.

To the credit of the men themselves it can be recorded now that though between 125 and 150 of these meetings were held and the average attendance was well over 400 men in uniform at each, only two men were noticed to be the worse for liquor, and one of these occasioned the only instance of a disagreement over any contest that took place on those evenings, and in his case the offender came back to the following meeting and apologized for his own unseemly behavior. This is a record for our soldiers and sailors of which the people of St. Matthew's feel particularly proud. In itself it repays them fully for any efforts that were undertaken and leaves them ready to entertain such men whenever an opportunity occurs.

The Sunday evening services of song were in some respects even more successful than the Thursday night concerts. A better chance to meet and know the men was afforded, and a better opportunity provided to intermingle and converse. The strangers invariably seemed to meet people from their own home towns or provinces, and the men from Britain found enthusiasts from Scotland, England, Ireland or Wales ready to greet them on mutual racial grounds.

The addresses on these occasions always had a more serious, religious or sentimental strain than was noticeable on week nights, and the Rev. Dr. Clarke, who succeeded Dr. Macmillan in 1916 as minister of the congregation was always ready to tell a good story and point a moral with good effect. The lantern was used for throwing the words of well-known hymn tunes on the screen, and the singing often had the fervor of a revival meeting. As each Unit or Regiment was known to be embarking for the Front, " God Be With You Till We Meet Again " was invariably sung and often that hymn, "Eternal Father Strong to Save" and various wartime versions thereof were prayerfully sung. Besides the hymn singing there were always solos, duets or quartettes rendered by the church choir and other artists. Refreshments were served before dispersing, but were plainer than the fare dispensed on Thursdays, being confined to tea and biscuits so as to lessen the labor in deference to the Sabbath. These however, were greatly appreciated by men who had eaten their suppers at 4 p.m. with no other meal in prospect until the next day.

Some thousands signed their autographs in visitors' books that were frequently passed around for signature, and among them are those of hundreds who now lie in Flanders fields or gave their lives for God and King and Country in other spheres of the War zone. Many appreciatory letters were received from boys and men after they left Halifax, expressng their appreciation of these receptions, some of them comparing the wintry nights in the trenches or on the North Sea with the peaceful hours spent at St. Matthew's. Many wives and mothers in all parts of Canada have heard of St. Matthew's and Halifax and have shown their thankfulness in many ways for the attention given their husbands and sons while here. The work of the Halifax Churches combined with the activities of the Citizens' Reception Committee and the Y.M.C.A. work at Pier 2 throughout the War have made the name of Halifax well and favorably known throughout the land. Even now that the War is over the duty of the churches towards the strangers within their gates should be continued—the need is great though the boys and men may not be in uniform and many of these could enjoy and appreciate as the soldiers and sailors did, a warm and kindly welcome from a Christian community.

SPECIAL SKETCHES

PROMINENT NOVA SCOTIANS

SOME KILLED IN ACTION—OTHERS "CARRYING ON"

To the organizing ability, and more especially the extraordinary genius for administration, of Col. W. E. Thompson must be given the chief credit for the splendid achievement and unsullied record of

COL. W. E. THOMPSON.

Military District No. 6. Second in Command of the 63rd Halifax Rifles at the outbreak of the War, he was, in December, 1914, called in by headquarters to assume the duties of Inspector of Outposts and Detachments throughout the district, with the rank of

NOVA SCOTIA'S PART IN THE GREAT WAR

Lieutenant-Colonel. In March, 1915, he was appointed Assistant Adjutant-General and Officer in Charge of Administration of Military District No. 6. In May, 1916, he was promoted to the rank of Colonel; and during the summer of that year, in addition to his duties as Assistant Adjutant-General, was Commandant of the Camp at Aldershot. In December, 1918, Colonel Thompson succeeded to the command of Military District No. 6.

The effect of his personality and of his genius for organization and, more particularly, administration, on the whole service of Military District No. 6, as well as on its morale, was extraordinary. He was regarded by Headquarters Staff, even by the three General Officers Commanding, before he succeeded to the command, as the authentic administrative " Mind " of the district. No other military district had such varied and great administrative problems and such heavy responsibilities as Military District No. 6, and yet the War was concluded with not a single mark against the administration and not a breath of scandal on its personnel and their conduct of the various Departments. For that splendid achievement Colonel Thompson was chiefly responsible.

In heart, however, he was eminently the soldier. Repeatedly he volunteered for active service Overseas, and even specially appealed to Ottawa for permission to go Oversas with a Unit, but the Canadian Militia Department was obdurate, declaring that his genius for organization and administration was of such a character that he could not be spared from headquarters Military District No. 6. Strict, firm, and soldierly at headquarters, Colonel Thompson, notwithstanding, exemplified democracy in the most undemocratic of institutions, the army. His genuine democracy, his tempering of justice with mercy, and his fine kindliness won for him the high respect and admiration of all ranks.

Col. Gordon S. Harrington, K.C., is a son of the late C. S. Harrington, K.C., of Halifax, N.S. He was admitted to the Bar on October 19, 1904, and practised his profession at Glace Bay, N.S. He was one of the original Company Commanders of the 85th Battalion with the rank of Major, and, on the formation of the Nova Scotia Highland Brigade, returned to Cape Breton and supervised the recruiting of the 185th Battalion. He was transferred to that Unit with his rank of Major and proceeded Overseas with it. When the Brigade was broken up he was sent to the Imperial First Senior Infantry School at Bedford, where he passed the qualifying examination with the highest marks ever attained at that institution. On reporting to the Nova Scotia Regimental Depot at Bramshott he was posted to the 17th Reserve Battalion, of which he was successively Second in Command and O.C. In May, 1917, he was

COL. GORDON S. HARRINGTON.

transferred to the Staff of the Overseas Minister, London, and a short time later was appointed Assistant Deputy Minister. In 1918 he was appointed Deputy Minister and promoted to the rank of Colonel. He served in the field on Corps Headquarters.

Having in mind the fact that at the sudden outbreak of war, August, 1914, the permanent military force of Canada only numbered 3,075, it will be readily understood that the Department of Militia and Defence was at once compelled to grapple with an enormous task for which no one could expect it to be prepared. The situation had to be met. The work had to be done. It had to be done quickly, and it is to the everlasting credit of Canada that we had men of outstanding ability and energy to cope successfully with the urgent situation.

By July, 1916, our military force was 312,844. Of these

HON. F. B. M'CURDY,
Secretary of Department of Militia.

136,185 were in Canada and 176,659 were Overseas. The number was daily increasing; and only those who were in close touch with the tremendous work of organizing, equipping, supplying and despatching such an army can realize what that meant in comparison with the work of administering affairs in regard to about 3,000 men during times of peace.

PROMINENT NOVA SCOTIANS

In these circumstances, and in view of the further fact that the exigencies of affairs frequently called the Minister of Militia away from Ottawa for the purpose of visiting recruiting centres and military camps in Canada, as well as Canadian Headquarters in England, the Government decided that it was necessary to have a Parliamentary Secretary of the Department of Militia and Defence: and, accordingly, on July 16, 1916, by an Order-in-Council the office was created endowing the holder with general authority in regard to administration of the Department, and directing that during the absence from Ottawa of the Minister, the Parliamentary Secretary should also preside at all meetings of the Militia Council and report to the Privy Council through the Prime Minister.

Fortunately, the services of a man of wide experience in business affairs, of well-known executive ability and withal energetic in discharge of duty, in the person of Mr. F. B. McCurdy, M.P., was available, and the Prime Minister wisely asked him to take up this very important work.

Mr. McCurdy willingly agreed; but with one stipulation. The salary affixed to the office was $5,000. Mr. McCurdy was past military age, but he believed that every man should, as far as was in his power, contribute to national duty. He, therefore, stipulated that his services as Parliamentary Secretary of the Militia Department would be a free contribution to the country, and he so served.

Immediately after Mr. McCurdy's appointment, Sir Sam Hughes, Minister of Militia and Defence, went Overseas; and from that time, which, it will be remembered, was a very active and critical period of the War, until the creation of the Ministry of Overseas Military Forces of Canada, Mr. McCurdy played a very important part in the vital work of building up and strengthening Canada's great army.

Naturally Mr. McCurdy while discharging his weighty duties with due and patriotic regard to the national interests of the whole country, had a sympathetic ear for his fellow Nova Scotians; and it is well known that his good judgment and influential voice prevailed in regard to irritating questions as to the representation of Battalions at the Front, with results that afforded great satisfaction

to the people of his native Province. It is sufficient to say that
Mr. McCurdy's eminent record as Parliamentary Secretary proved
the unerring judgment of the Prime Minister in selecting the right
men for responsible positions.

At the election of December, 1917, Mr. McCurdy was returned
by acclamation for Colchester, his native county.

MAJOR-GENERAL G. L. FOSTER, M.D.,
F.R.C.S., LL.D., C.B.

Son of George and Elmira Foster. Born at North Kingston,
Kings County, Nova Scotia, May, 1874. Graduated M.D. 1896,
University of New York, U.S.A. First appointment, Canadian
Militia, August 4, 1897, Lieutenant and Assistant Surgeon, 68th
Regiment, Kings County, Nova Scotia. Served with Yukon Field
Forces as P.M.O., March, 1898, to July, 1900. April, 1913, appointed
Assistant Director of Medical Services, Military District No. 2, with
headquarters at Toronto, Ontario. September, 1914, sailed from
Quebec with First Canadian Contingent and appointed A.D.M.S.
1st Division Canadians, with the rank of Colonel. Served in
France from February, 1915, to September, 1915, as A.D.M.S. 1st
Division Canadians. September, 1915, appointed Deputy Director
of Medical Services, Canadian Corps, on its formation and served
with Canadian Corps in France until February, 1917, when appointed Director-General of Medical Services, Overseas Military
Forces of Canada with the rank of Major-General, headquarters in

London, England. March, 1920, appointed Acting Director-General of Medical Services, Canadian Militia, with headquarters at Ottawa.

Medals and Decorations.
  1914-15 Star.
  General Service Medal.
  Victory Medal with Leaf.

Decorations, Military.
  Companion of the Order of the Bath.
  Knight of Grace, St. John of Jerusalem.
  Officer Legion of Honour.

  Civil Honors received as Head of the Canadian Medical Service during the Great War, 1914-15.
  October, 1919, Edinburgh University conferred the degree of F.R.C.S.
  June, 1920. McGill University, conferred the degree of LL.D.

LIEUT.-COL. CHARLES E. BENT,
C.M.G., D.S.O.

Lieut.-Col. Charles E. Bent was a Captain in the 93rd Cumberland Regiment at the outbreak of the War. He immediately volunteered for active service and, as Adjutant of the 17th Battalion, accompanied the First Division to England. On the breaking up of that Unit he took a draft over to the 13th Battalion, arriving in France April, 1915. He reported for duty with the 15th Battalion and was given command of a Platoon. He became a Company Commander immediately after the fighting of Festubert, 1915; Second in Command December 31, 1915; and Officer Commanding the 15th Battalion in May, 1916. He took part in all fighting with the First Division until wounded August 9, 1918, near Caix, east of Amiens. He rejoined his Battalion on October 1st, and after the Armistice proceeded with the Army of Occupation to Germany. He acted as Brigade Commander on several occasions and was in command of the 3rd Brigade from October 20 to November 24, 1918. He took part in the following battles:

Festubert 1915	Hill 60 1916	Telegraph Hill ...1918
Givenchy 1915	Sanctuary Wood..1916	Amiens 1918
Messines 1915	Somme 1916	Drocourt-
Ypres 1916	Vimy Ridge 1917	Queant Line ...1918
Ploegsteerte 1916	Hill 70 1917	
Ypres 1916	Passchendaele 1917	

and others up to the signing of the Armistice, November 11, 1918.

Decorations.
C.M.G.
D.S.O. and Bar.
1914-15 Star.
Colonial Auxiliary Forces' Long Service Medal.
Seven mentions in despatches.

LIEUT.-COL. J. A. M'DONALD.

Lieut.-Col. J. A. McDonald started his military career by enlisting in the 17th Sydney Field Battery in 1896, receiving first-class certificate from the R.S.A., Quebec, winter of 1897-98, enlisted for service in South Africa 1899, served in " E " Battery and 4th C.M.R., obtained commission in the 17th 1906, qualified and promoted through the various stages until he took command of the Battery in 1913, was still in command at outbreak of the War in August, 1914, when he volunteered the Battery for Overseas service through the then Brigade Commander, Lieut.-Col. H. G. McLeod, August 8, 1914. On arrival at Valcartier he was posted as Captain to the 5th Westmount Battery, 2nd Brigade, C.F.A., promoted in Field to rank of Major May, 1915, and took command of 7th Battery, promoted to rank of Lieutenant-Colonel April, 1917, and

PROMINENT NOVA SCOTIANS

was posted to command the 3rd Brigade, C.F.A., commanded this Brigade until it was demobilized in Canada in May, 1919, except for period of three months, during which time he was attached to the 4th Canadian Division Artillery Headquarters, acting as C.R.A.

During the above period of four years and ten months on active service he went through every engagement in which the Canadian Corps took part from the day the First Canadian Division landed on French soil (February 12, 1915) up to the day of the Armistice, November 11, 1918.

Decorations are as follows:—
Queen's South Africa Medal, Three Clasps.
D.S.O., London Gazette, 1—1—17.
Mentioned in despatches, London Gazette, 4—1—17.
Mentioned in despatches, London Gazette, 28—5—18.
Mentioned in despatches, London Gazette, 31—12—18.
Mentioned in despatches, London Gazette, 11—7—19.
Awarded Bar to D.S.O., London Gazette, 1—2—19.
1914-15 Star, London Gazette, 3—5—19.

Total period of service, twenty-three years, of which six years and four months were spent on active service.

LIEUT.-COL. T. HOWARD MACDONALD, C.A.M.C.

Went Overseas January, 1915, unattached, with the rank of Major. He was first attached to the Canadian Convalescent Hospital at Bearwood Park. From there he went to Bath, thence to Moore Barracks Hospital, and was later appointed Medical Examiner of the Pension Board, London. He went to France as Medical Officer of a Labor Battalion. He was promoted to the rank of Lieutenant-Colonel and received the appointment of Commanding Officer of the medical personnel of the Hospital Ship

NOVA SCOTIA'S PART IN THE GREAT WAR

Llandovery Castle. This ship was torpedoed by an enemy submarine on June 27, 1918, and Lieutenant-Colonel Macdonald was drowned. Out of the entire ship's company there were only twenty-four survivors, and of the hospital personnel of ninety-seven only one officer and five other ranks escaped. In spite of their appalling circumstances the conduct of all on board was in fitting keeping with the proudest traditions of the British Army and the mercantile marine. And throughout nothing was more marked than the coolness and courage of the fourteen Canadian Nursing Sisters, every one of whom was lost. Two of the nursing sisters—Pearl Fraser and Minnie Follette—were Nova Scotians.

MISS MARGARET MACDONALD, L.L.D., R.R.C.,
Matron-in-Chief of Canadian Nursing Sisters.

Miss Macdonald was born at Bailey's Brook, Pictou County, and is a daughter of the late D. D. Macdonald. She is a sister of Col. R. St. John Macdonald, who was in command of the St. Francis Xavier Unit. Miss Macdonald served in the Spanish-American War, in the South African War, and later in the Canal Zone at Panama. In November, 1906, she was appointed a Nursing Sister in the Canadian Army Permanent Medical Corps, and after taking a course in England received the appointment of Matron-in-Chief and was in command of three thousand Canadian Nursing Sisters during the Great War. She has been decorated with the Royal Red Cross and the Florence Nightingale medal.

Lieut. M. F. Gregg, a graduate of Acadia University, Wolfville. won the Victoria Cross while serving with the Royal Canadian Regiment. The following is the official record as published in the *London Gazette:*

"On September the 28th, when the advance of the Brigade was held up by fire on both flanks and by thick, uncut wire, he crawled forward alone and explored the wire until he found a small gap, through which he subsequently led his men and forced

LIEUT. M. F. GREGG, V.C.

an entry into the enemy trench. The enemy counter-attacked in force and through lack of bombs the situation became critical.

"Gregg, although wounded, returned alone under a terrific fire and collected a further supply, then rejoined his party which was now much reduced. Despite a second wound he reorganized his men and led them in the most determined way against the enemy trenches, which he finally cleared. He personally killed or wounded eleven of the enemy and took twenty-five prisoners, besides capturing twelve machine guns in this trench. Remaining with the Company, despite his wounds, he again, on September 30th, led the men in attack until severely wounded. The outstanding valor of this officer saved many casualties and enabled the advance to continue."

PTE. JOHN CROAK, V.C.

Pte. John Croak, V.C., was born in Newfoundland and came to Glace Bay with his parents at four years of age. He attended St. John's School, New Aberdeen, Glace Bay, and afterwards worked as a miner in No. 2 Colliery, Glace Bay (the biggest in the world). He volunteered for Overseas service in the 55th Battalion and was transferred to the 13th Battalion. He died of wounds received in action on August 8, 1918. His father, mother, two sisters and two brothers are living at Glace Bay.

The official notice from the War Office announcing the award of the Victoria Cross was as follows:

"On August 8, 1918, during the attack on Amiens Defence System, after being separated from his section, Private Croak encountered a machine-gun nest in Ring Copse, which he dealt with by first bombing unassisted and then jumping into the post, taking the gun and crew prisoners. Shortly afterwards he was severely wounded in the right arm but refused to desist.

"In a few minutes his Platoon, which this soldier had rejoined, again encountered a very strong point, containing several machine-guns and they were forced to take cover. Private Croak, however, seeing an opportunity, dashed forward alone, and was almost immediately followed by the remainder of the Platoon in a brilliant charge. He was the first to arrive at the trench line, into which he led the men, capturing three machine-guns and bayoneting or capturing the entire garrison.

"The perseverance and courage of this gallant man were undoubtedly responsible for taking the strongest point in the whole day's advance.

"Private Croak was again severely wounded in the knee and died in a few minutes."

On November 23, 1918, Lieutenant-Governor Grant formally presented the Victoria Cross to his mother, Mrs. James Croak, of New Aberdeen, Cape Breton. The Lieutenant-Governor complimented the parents and a sister who accompanied them on the fact that their son and brother had so well demonstrated that he came of good stock and was a good soldier, a brave man, and a hero.

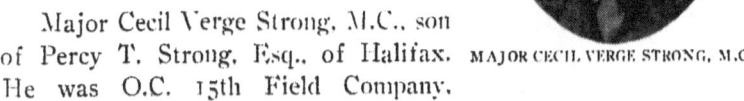

MAJOR CECIL VERGE STRONG, M.C.

Major Cecil Verge Strong, M.C., son of Percy T. Strong, Esq., of Halifax. He was O.C. 15th Field Company, Royal Engineers, and the youngest Commanding Officer in the British Army. He was killed in action March 10, 1917, aged 23 years. Buried Piney Post Cemetery, Maurepas, near Peronne. Mentioned in despatches five times.

MAJOR J ARNOLD DELANCEY, M.C.   MAJOR EDWARD W. JOY.

Major J. Arnold Delancey, M.C., joined the 40th Battalion and transferred to the 25th Battalion as machine gun officer. He was Adjutant of the 25th in France and attained his majority in October, 1916. He was killed at Vimy Ridge, April 9, 1917, while leading his Battalion, of which he was in temporary command. He was decorated with the Military Cross. He had a distinguished career and was rapidly promoted on account of his good work at the Front.

Major Edward W. Joy went Overseas with 106th Battalion. Transferred to 78th Battalion in France. Killed in action at Vimy Ridge, April 9, 1917.

Lieut. Kennet Stairs. Born 1889. Killed in action September 30, 1918, while serving with 60th Battery, C.F.A., near Cambrai.

Lieut. Philip Boyd Stairs, D.S.O. Born 1895. Wounded while serving with 5th Canadian Division, T.M.B. Died of influenza at Valenciennes, November 21, 1918.

Capt. George W. Stairs. Born 1887. Killed at St. Julien, April 24, 1915, while serving with the 14th Battalion.

Capt. John C. Stairs. Born 1891. Killed at Courcellette, September 15, 1916, while serving with the 25th Battalion.

Capt. Gauvin L. Stairs. Born 1896. Killed at Moquet Farm, near Courcellette, September 7, 1916, while serving with the 14th Battalion.

Pte. Graham Stairs. Born 1894. Died of pneumonia at Halifax, December 10, 1915, while serving with the 85th Battalion.

"One by one Death challenged them. One by one they smiled in his grim visage and refused to be dismayed."

THE STAIRS FAMILY.

LIEUT. KENNET STAIRS.   LIEUT. PHILIP R. STAIRS.

Sons of Mrs. Edward Stairs, Halifax.

CAPT. GEORGE W. STAIRS.   CAPT. JOHN C. STAIRS.

Sons of George Stairs, Halifax.

CAPT. GAUVIN L. STAIRS.   PTE. GRAHAM STAIRS.

Sons of Gauvin L. Stairs, Halifax.

CAPT. E. J. DWYER.

CAPT. L. RAY CUTTEN.   CAPT. EDGAR S. SPURR, M.C.   CAPT. GEORGE COLLINS PARISH, YARMOUTH, N.S.

PROMINENT NOVA SCOTIANS

Capt. E. J. Dwyer was Second in Command of " C " Company, 85th Battalion. He left the Battalion shortly after it arrived in England to join the 25th Battalion in France. After serving with the latter Unit for six months he was detailed to proceed to Mesopotamia, and sailed on the *Nyanza*. This ship was torpedoed and Captain Dwyer was drowned.

Capt. L. Ray Cutten, an officer in the 93rd Cumberland Regiment. He volunteered for service Overseas at the outbreak of war and was Assistant Adjutant of the 17th Battalion. He transferred to the 15th Battalion and again to the 2nd Battalion, in which he was a Company Comander and was recommended for the Military Cross. He was killed at Maple Grove, near Hill 60, June 5. 1916. Buried near Poperinghe.

Capt. Edgar S. Spurr, M.C., obtained his commission in 112th Battalion. Promoted to rank of Captain July 24, 1916. Reverted to go to France, where he served with the 25th Battalion. Awarded the Military Cross and regained the rank of Captain, August 15, 1917. Killed in action, June 14, 1918.

Capt. George Collins Parish, Yarmouth, N.S. Immediately after the outbreak of the Great War, was appointed Lieutenant in the 81st Regiment Canadian Infantry.

Commissioned as a Lieutenant in the 40th Battalion, C.E.F. Recruited a Platoon in Yarmouth for that Unit, took them to Valcartier. After a period of training he was sent Overseas in command of a reinforcing draft of 250 men.

He was attached to the 17th Reserve Battalion at Bramshott for a period, when, in 1916, he was posted to the 25th Battalion, and sent to Belgium, was severely wounded and invalided home. On his partial recovery he was posted to the 1st Nova Scotia Regiment, Depot Battalion, as Paymaster, with the rank of Captain. He contracted influenza and died October 28, 1918. Was interred at Mountain Cemetery, Yarmouth.

NOVA SCOTIA'S PART IN THE GREAT WAR

Six sons of G. Douglas and Kate G. Campbell, of Weymouth, were volunteers in August, 1914.

COLIN, the youngest, enlisted first and served at McNab's Island. He joined the 23rd Battery at Fredericton in November. Proceeded Overseas in March, 1915, and arrived in France the following June. Severely wounded at La Bassee, June 19th. On discharge from hospital he joined the Imperial Service and obtained his commission. Returned to the Front during the winter of 1915-16. Received multiple wounds July 19th and was awarded the M.C. After discharge from hospital he was decorated by the King and again returned to the Front. Passed examination for aviation during the summer, but returning to the artillery was killed in action near Passchendaele, October 10, 1917.

TOM, also joined the 23rd Battery and proceeded to England with Colin. He was transferred to the 3rd Battalion and served at the Front from June to December, 1915. Trench life and its filthy conditions undermined his health, and in December he was shell-shocked and sent to hospital. He returned to Canada in 1916.

KENNETH, began his training for active service at Halifax, later going to Valcartier. He was sent to Weymouth to assist in recruiting the 85th and 219th Battalions. He proceeded Overseas in August, 1916, and joined the 42nd Battalion. He became Bombing Officer of that Unit, and was killed at Vimy Ridge, January 18, 1917, and buried at Mount St. Eloi.

JOHN DUNCAN, joined the 106th Battalion at Truro in January, 1916. Arrived in England, July, 1916, and at the Front in December, 1916. Wounded in hand and thigh at Vimy Ridge, April 8, 1917. Returned to the Front and served until shell-shocked at Rochmont. Returned to Halifax, June, 1918.

GLIDDEN, the eldest, was already in the Militia when the War broke out, his commission being dated June, 1914. He was in

THE SIX CAMPBELL BROTHERS.

command of the Digby Detachment of the Garrison Artillery at Barrington, N.S., and joined the 85th Battalion in October, 1915, as Machine Gun Officer. He proceeded Overseas with that Unit, arriving in France in time for the Vimy show. He was appointed to the command of "B" Company in October, 1917. He led his Company at Passchendaele, wiping out over a dozen machine gun nests and capturing a pill-box single-handed. Was blown into the air by a shell and, although wounded, refused to leave the line. He was awarded the M.C. He carried on with the Battalion until June, 1918, when, after an attack of trench fever and suffering from the effects of gas, he was sent to the South of France to recuperate. He later transferred to the Forestry Corps, taking command of the 79th Company and was promoted to the rank of Major.

ALBERT MUNGO, volunteered in 1914, but as his five brothers had left his father's business, it was decided that he should remain at home. He was so anxious to join up, however, that he was reluctantly permitted to do so, and in the early spring of 1916 enlisted in the 58th Battery, C.F.A. He went to the Front with that Unit and remained with it to the finish. He was the last of the four surviving brothers to arrive home.

CAPT. H. A. MURRAY.

Capt. H. A. Murray joined the 24th Battalion as Lieutenant during the winter of 1915 from the McGill C.O.T.C., and served as Transport Officer until May, 1916. Promoted to Captain in July, 1916, and to Acting-Major while in command of a Company in September, 1916. Was Company Comander of "D" Company, 24th Battalion, when killed in fighting for Regina Trench, near Courcellette, on October 1, 1916.

PROMINENT NOVA SCOTIANS

Capt. Edward C. Clayton, M.C., son of W. J. Clayton, Halifax. Appointed Lieutenant 85th Battalion, December 28, 1916. Promoted to rank of Captain, August 9, 1917. Awarded Military Cross, Eleudit Leauvette. Although not his turn to lead his Company in the attack on Passchendaele Ridge he urged his reasons for doing so upon his Commanding Officer so strongly that permission was given him. He was killed by a piece of shell just as his Company advanced in the attack, but he had made his preparation so carefully that they carried on, annihilated the enemy, gained their objectives, dug in, and held their position intact until the Battalion was relieved.

CAPT. EDWARD C. CLAYTON, M.C.

Capt. Harry Elthan Hilton, only child of Mr. and Mrs. A. H. Hilton, of Kingston, Nova Scotia. Born September 16, 1894. When war broke out was on the Staff of the Bank of Nova Scotia. He enlisted in the 63rd Regiment on August 14, 1914, gazetted Lieutenant the following month and sailed for England with a draft of the 63rd on March 1, 1916. Went to France, June 14, 1916, and was attached to the 42nd Battalion. He fought at Courcellette and various other engagements throughout the Somme campaign. Later was transferred to the 7th Trench Mortar Battery and was killed at Vimy Ridge. Gazetted Captain, January 13, 1917.

CAPT. HARRY ELTHAN HILTON.

Capt. A. S. Allen, M.C., son of Mr. Arthur E. Allen, of Yarmouth, N.S. Born at Glenwood, Yarmouth County, July 23, 1895. At the age of sixteen he entered the service of the Bank of Nova Scotia, and in 1913 was transferred to the Barrington Street Branch, Halifax. He qualified as Lieutenant in the 81st Regiment

NOVA SCOTIA'S PART IN THE GREAT WAR

and proceeded Overseas with the 40th Battalion. In March, 1916, he joined the 18th Battalion in France. He was later gazetted Captain and awarded the Military Cross. In November he trans-

CAPT. A. S. ALLEN, M.C.

ferred to the R.F.C. On April 30, 1917, while reconnoitering over Gouzeaucourt his plane was attacked by six enemy machines. Captain Allen was hit by a machine-gun bullet and was dead when his plane crashed. Lieut. D. Mactavish, Inverness, Scotland, who accompanied him on this flight, writes:

"I can never forget him as I saw him at the last, calm and collected to the end, sighting and firing until his strength gave out and he was overcome by exhaustion."

It is given to a few men to live greatly, but to be able to die as he did is a gift of God. Truly he won—*Per ardua ad astra.*"

CAPT. J. E. ALMON.

LIEUT. CYRIL M'LELLAN MOWBRAY.

Capt. J. E. Almon, son of the late Dr. Thomas Almon, of Halifax. Killed in action at Passchendaele, while serving with the P.P.C.L.I.

Lieut. Cyril McLellan Mowbray, only son of Lieut. Col. J. A. C. Mowbray, O.B.E., Senior Pay Officer, Military District No. 6. Killed in action, November 10, 1917, at Passchendaele, aged nineteen years, while serving with the 5th Canadian Battalion.

PROMINENT NOVA SCOTIANS

Second Lieut. John Struan Robertson, son of Lieut.-Col. Struan G. Robertson, of Pictou. Born in Westville, Pictou County, November 17, 1896. Got his commission from the Royal Military College, Kingston, Ont., in 1917. Attached to the R.F.A., B. 46th Brigade, 14th Division, 5th Army. Killed near Benay, in the neighborhood of St. Quentin, March 21, 1918.

SECOND LIEUT. JOHN STRUAN ROBERTSON.

LIEUT. GEORGE MACDONALD SYLVESTER.

Lieut. George Macdonald Sylvester. Went Overseas with 40th Battalion as Assistant Adjutant. Transferred to 14th Battalion and was killed at Regina Trench, September 26, 1916.

Lieut. Walter Melville Billman. At Oxford at outbreak of war. Joined Officers' Training Corps, Oxford. Appointed Second Lieutenant 6th Battalion 1st Middlesex Regiment. Died of wounds received at Battle of Somme, November 5, 1916.

LIEUT. WALTER MELVILLE BILLMAN.

LIEUT. HOWARD CHARLES DAWSON.

LIEUT. JOHN H. FIENDAL.

LIEUT. THOMAS LOUIS BRENNAN.

LIEUT. G. H. CAMPBELL.

LIEUT. F. P. H. LAYTON.

LIEUT. ALFRED S. CHURCHILL.

PROMINENT NOVA SCOTIANS

Lieut. Howard Charles Dawson, son of Mr. and Mrs. C. M. Dawson, of Truro, N.S. He was killed while on scout duty at Ablain, St. Nazaire, on January 12, 1917, at the age of 22 years. He was buried in Sucrerie Cemetery, near Lens. He enlisted in January, 1916, in the 106th Battalion and transferred to the 26th Battalion in October, 1916. He was scout officer of this Battalion when killed.

Lieut. John H. Fiendal went Overseas as a Sergeant in No. 1 Casualty Clearing Hospital. Was given a commission and joined the 25th Battalion in 1916. He was killed at Vimy Ridge, April 9, 1917.

Lieut. Thomas Louis Brennan trained at Aviation School, Toronto, and went to England December, 1915. Completed his training there and went to France early in 1916. Was wounded, and after being discharged from hospital was employed as an Instructor, and returned to Canada early in 1918. Up to the time of his death was attached to the Aviation School in Toronto. He died of influenza October, 1918.

Lieut. G. H. Campbell, son of George H. Campbell, Esq., of Halifax, joined the 40th Battalion with the rank of Lieutenant. He proceeded Overseas with that Unit, and was later transferred to the 1st Canadian Pioneers. He was killed at Battersea Farm, Ypres, May 16, 1916, aged 22 years.

Lieut. F. P. H. Layton, only son of George A. Layton, Esq., of Truro. Born April 13, 1888. Educated at King's College School and Dalhousie University. Admitted to the Bar in 1912. When war broke out was practising in Vancouver. He obtained a commission in the 40th Battalion and transferred to the 4th Canadian Mounted Rifles. He was killed in action July 23, 1916.

Lieut. Alfred S. Churchill. Killed in action April 9, 1917, at Vimy Ridge, while serving with the Royal Canadian Regiment.

LIEUT. ALBERT F. MAJOR.

LIEUT. W. T. BECK.

LIEUT. GORDON M. HEBB.

LIEUT. J. T. PROBERT, M.C.

LIEUT. HAROLD ARCHIBALD SMITH, M.C.

LIEUT. GERALD E. CRAGG.

LIEUT. W. S. FIELDING.

PROMINENT NOVA SCOTIANS

Lieut. W. T. Beck. Served in Egypt with Royal Air Force. Killed November 15, 1918.

Lieut. Harold Archibald Smith, M.C. Born at Londonderry May 13, 1893. Educated at Sydney Academy and Dalhousie University. Graduated B.A. 1913 and went to Labrador as missionary. At Pine Hill College autumn of 1914. Enlisted in 6th C.M.R. January, 1915. Wounded at the Somme, September 15, 1916. After convalescence went to Bexhill and rejoined his Unit as Lieutenant. Awarded Military Cross August 26, 1918. Two days later at Monchy Heights was severely wounded. Died September 14th at Prince of Wales Hospital, London, and buried in Brookwood Cemetery.

Lieut. Albert F. Major, son of F. G. Major, Esq., of Halifax. Went Overseas with 14th Battalion of Montreal. Killed in action at Zillebeke Heights June 3, 1916.

Lieut. Gordon M. Hebb, son of Levi Hebb, Esq., of Bridgewater, N.S. Killed in action near Courcellette while serving with 78th Battalion.

Lieut. W. S. Fielding, son of George H. Fielding, Esq., Stipendiary Magistrate, Halifax, N.S. Called out for service with his Regiment, the 66th Princess Louise Fusiliers, at the outbreak of war. Proceeded with a draft from that Regiment to England in January, 1916. He was transferred to the 7th British Columbia Battalion in France. He was twice wounded. Killed in action at Passchendaele.

Lieut. J. T. Probert, M.C. Before the War Lieut. Probert was an accountant in the service of the Intercolonial Railway at Halifax. He was attached to the Royal Canadian Regiment in France, and was killed in action at Cambrai, September 30, 1918.

Lieut. Gerald E. Cragg, son of C. J. Cragg, Bridgewater, Nova Scotia. Killed in action June 3, 1916, aged 22 years, 4 months, near Ypres, Belgium, while serving with the 3rd Toronto Regiment.

Lieut. Jas. O'Neill Fitzgerald, M.C., enlisted in the 40th Battalion, was transferred to 25th Battalion in France, May, 1916, and served till April, 1917, when he was promoted to commissioned rank. He rejoined his Battalion in October, 1917, and was wounded at the Battle of Amiens, August 9, 1918, and awarded the Military Cross.

Cadet H. S. Simson enlisted in the 2nd Canadian Divisional Cyclist Company on April 19, 1915. He accompanied his Unit to France on September 15, 1915, and was wounded October 8, 1916, during the Somme offensive. He was awarded the Medaille Militaire (French) on July 6, 1917, for work on the Somme. Joining the Royal Air Force in July, 1918, he served until the signing of the Armistice.

Lieut. Walter O. Barnstead joined the 6th Canadian Mounted Rifles at Halifax, February 11, 1915, and proceeded to France with his Unit in October, 1915. He was transferred to the 5th C.M.R., promoted to commissioned rank in April, 1917, and served with his Unit until the Armistice. He was awarded the Croix de Guerre at Amiens, 1918.

Capt. G. M. Drew was called out with his Regiment, the 1st Canadian Garrison Artillery, on August 22, 1914, and left for Valcartier early in September. From Valcartier he proceeded to England, joining the Royal Garrison Artillery. He proceeded to France with the 1st Siege Battery in September, 1915, and served with this Unit and various Trench Mortar Batteries until June, 1916, when he was invalided to England suffering from trench fever. After service in England, Capt. Drew returned to France in May, 1917, with the 259th Siege Battery, and served in the Ypres Salient and Nieuport areas till the signing of the Armistice.

The four boys mentioned above are all in the employ of the Furness Withy Company, Limited.

LIEUT. JAS. BLAIR.

LIEUT.-COL. CHARLES J. T. STEWART, D.S.O.

LIEUT. J. C. SUTHERLAND.

CAPT. N. P. FREEMAN.

LIEUT. J. G. LAURIER FRASER.

LIEUT. IAN C. M'GREGOR.

EMILE GABOURY.

PROMINENT NOVA SCOTIANS

Lieut.-Col. Charles J. T. Stewart, D.S.O., was the son of the late Lieut.-Col. C. J. Stewart, of Halifax. He went Overseas with the P.P.C.L.I. Was awarded the D.S.O. and French Croix de Guerre. He was killed in action September 28, 1918.

Lieut. J. G. Laurier Fraser, son of the late Lieut.-Governor D. C. Fraser. Enlisted at Moose Jaw in the 229th Battalion and sailed for England in September, 1916. Transferred to the 16th Battalion. Killed in action March 6, 1918.

Lieut. Jas. Blair, son of Lieut.-Col. H. C. Blair, of Truro. Killed in action.

Lieut. J. C. Sutherland. Killed in action.

Lieut. Ian C. McGregor. Went Overseas November, 1916. Trained in England with Royal Flying Corps. Went to France as pilot, April, 1917, attached to Squadron 56, and later transferred to Squadron 60. Wounded September 21, 1917, and was eight months in hospital in France. Died at Saranac Lake, N.Y., March 5, 1920. Officially credited with eleven machines.

Capt. Nelson P. Freeman, of Bridgewater, stricken with paralysis while on service in England, was invalided to Canada, and died.

Emile Gaboury, son of Dr. T. C. Gaboury, the late representative of the County of Pontiac, Quebec. Came to Halifax in 1911 as Manager of the Nova Scotia Branch of the Imperial Tobacco Company of Canada, Limited, and after war broke out was appointed French Consul. Notwithstanding his many duties, Mr. Gaboury took an active interest in the Victory Loan, Red Triangle, Knights of Columbus, and the Salvation Army. He was a particularly strong and active member of the Red Cross, and played a large role in the welcoming of returned soldiers at Pier 2. During the War he appealed for the Red Cross in all the theatres of Halifax as well as throughout the Province, and organized Red Cross branches in many of the smaller towns.

COLWELL FAMILY.

Garnet James Colwell, Lieutenant 66th Halifax Regiment. Served in Canada 1915-1918. Sent Overseas May 16, 1918.

Cyril Henry Colwell, Lieutenant 63rd Halifax Regiment. Served in Canada 1915-1917. Sent Overseas September 5, 1917.

MRS. MAY B. SEXTON, B.SC.

Ray John Colwell, Lieutenant 63rd Halifax Regiment. Served in Canada 1916-1918. Sent Overseas August 3, 1918.

Mrs. May B. Sexton, B.Sc., Vice-President, Canadian Red Cross Society. Nova Scotia Branch. Ex-Municipal Regent for Halifax, I.O.D.E. Ex-Chairman Halifax Playgrounds Commission. Ex-Vice-President Local Council of Women.

LIST OF OFFICERS OF THE ROYAL BANK WHO ENLISTED FROM BRANCHES IN NOVA SCOTIA.

Andrewes, F. L.
Annand, C. D.
Anthony, L. F.
Atkinson, C. H.
Aucoin, J. D.
Austen, G. A.
Banks, C. N.
Barry, J. R.
Bezanson, G. A.
Blair, R. G.
Boudreau, L. P.
Bowers, C. C.
Boyd, R. J.
Browne, A. S.
Bryson, W. E.
Buckley, W. A.
Butler, J. K.
Cain, C. L.
Cairns, J. A.
Cameron, J. A.
Cameron, N. P.
Campbell, J. A.
Campbell, J. A.
Campbell, R. B.
Chisholm, A. D.
Chisholm, J. D.
Chapman, P. T.
Cornwall, H. A.
Cosman, E. A.
Cotter, J. G.
Coumans, R. G.
Crowell, A. L.
Crowell, C. L.
Cunningham, H.
Curll, M. H.
Daniel, G. H.
Demers, J. C.
DesBrisay, A. S.
Dexter, R.
Dickie, E. C.
Dickie, K. R.
Dickie, L. W.
Dickson, G. M.
Dodge, C. M.
Doucette, H. H.
Douse, G. A. P.
Durham, E. B.
Dustan, S. B.
Embree, D. T.
Ernst, W. A.
Farnell, A. H.
Flannery, C. G.
Flinn, G.
Forsythe, J. S. G.
Fraser, A. Elmer.
Fraser, A. Ernest.
Fraser, A. M.
Fraser, L. G.
Gage, L. G.
Gass, C.
Gorham, E. R.

Goudrey, K. H.
Grant, B. E.
Gregory, H. S.
Haines, R. S.
Hains, A. P. R.
Hall, H. L.
Hanna, V. M.
Harding, C. E.
Hatfield, A. W.
Hawkins, G. S.
Henderson, H. F.
Herman, R. R.
Johnston, J. L.
Johnstone, G. H.
King, D. A.
King, J. J. W.
Kirk, J. H.
Kierstead, A. L.
Knowles, J. E.
Kyte, S. E.
Kinnie, E. F.
Knowles, J. E.
Langille, L. H.
LeLievre, P.
Lordly, E. F.
Longley, E. G.
Love, H. A.
MacDonald, D. W.
MacDougall, J. I.
MacDougall R.
MacKenzie, W. K.
MacKay, J. W.
MacLean, C. W.
Mann, C. H.
March, J. E. R.
Matthews, C. F.
Melvin, W. D.
Merriam, S. G.
Merritt, F. G.
Milner, C. H.
Millett, J. N. L.
Moore, A. J.
Morrison, W. H.
Morrow, J.
Morash, J. R.
Mosher, A. T.
Mosher, W. A.
Mulcahey, T. J.
Murray, B.
McAlpine, A. F.
McCallum, H. M.
McClafferty, J. K.
McDonald, A. H.
McDonald, D. A.
McIntyre, J. A.
McKenzie, H.
McKenzie, K.
McLaren, A. F.
McLean, M. A.
McLeod, H. H. D.
McRobert, J. A. V.

Neville, E. V.
Newell, A. D.
Newell, E. D.
Nickerson, E. C.
Noonan, P.
O'Connell, J. F.
O'Keefe, T. P.
O'Toole, A. G.
Page, E. H.
Peers, R. H. C.
Peters, W. H.
Pickard, H. J.
Pitman, M. R.
Power, M. L.
Poirier, W. P.
Price, E.
Prince, W. S.
Rafuse, S. A.
Redding, R. E.
Rhind, C. E.
Richardson, R. B.
Ripley, L. W.
Risser, W. A.
Roche, G. E.
Ross, C. S.
Ross, J. K.
Ryan, A. M.
Scriven, J. A.
Shaw, H. J.
Shields, D. D.
Smith, A. R.
Smith, G. J.
Snell, L. L.
Spence, C. M. V.
Spence, R. E.
Stanley, F. A.
Sterns, H. E.
Stephens, A. E.
Stewart, W. I.
Strople, H. G. A.
Stubbs, H. C.
Stewart, D. J.
Tanner, H. R.
Troy, L. T.
Tupper, M. L.
Turnbull, G. A.
Turnbull, G. V.
West, C. F.
Whidden, E. L.
Wicks, W. E.
White, G.
Wickwire, L. H.
Wilmot, A. J.
Wallace, H.
Wilson, J. L.
Wilson, W. M.
Winters, G. W.
Withrow, C. A.
Zinck, A. M.
Zinck, H. A.

MRS. G. S. CAMPBELL.
One of Nova Scotia's Leading Patriotic War Workers.

MISS MARION DOULL, V.A.D., MISS MADELINE SCOTT, V.A.D., MISS EDITH PIKE, V.A.D.
"The Three Shining Lights" of Pine Hill Military Convalescent Hospital.

NURSING SISTER MINNIE FOLLETTE.
Drowned at sea, *Llandovery Castle*, June 27, 1918.

NURSING SISTER PEARL FRASER.
Drowned at sea, *Llandovery Castle*, June 27, 1918.

J. G. M'DOUGALD, M.D., C.M., F.A.C.S.
Especially noted for his Surgical Work following the Great Explosion, December 6, 1917.

SONS OF A. B. WISWELL, HALIFAX.

"Felt Dawn"

By Stuart McCawley

WE were sitting on the beach at Mira. Just a lovely Cape Breton moonlight night. The youngsters were singing and telling yarns. One kid recited McCrae's great poem, "In Flanders Fields," and one of the boys who had been "over there" asked us if we knew what McCrae meant when he wrote the phrase, "Felt Dawn." Nobody seemed to be entirely clear on the question, and we asked our friend, the veteran, to describe it for us. Here are his words:

A cold, drizzly rain that is eating through your khaki into your very heart.

A sea of mud—black, slimy, sticky, stinking mud.

The duck boards floating in ooze.

Your feet wet and heavy, and your toes squichy.

Not a sound of any kind.

The nearest human ten yards away—just around "the bay."

Darkness supreme. Not even an enemy flare.

You strain your eyes over the parapet to the barb-wire.

Your battalion's life depends on your keeping awake.

Oh, the strain! Oh, the funk that is trying to grip your very soul!

Would to God something would happen! This eternal watching is fearful.

Then a rustle in the grass; a wave of movement first like the ripple you hear when a stone is "skipped" on a quiet pond; then an extra chill in the air; then a glow to the east—'Tis Dawn.

You let loose your "clip" and you fire like mad towards the Hun. Other sentries fire, and the salvo to dawn gets the whole line. Thousands of men all along the front start a strafe—a crazy, aimless strafe—which lasts for only minutes. Then, as if some great unseen General had whispered a command, men regain their "morale," and the rifle fire quietens, and dies away.

The sun struggles up.

A bird on a shattered stump whistles, "Coo, Coo."

Your blood warms again. You have "felt dawn." Another day has had its birth. The rations will soon be up. Relief is coming. The war is still on, and the bird has showed you that, after all, it is better to smile than to worry.

God is still in command!

www.ingramcontent.com/pod-product-compliance
Lightning Source LLC
Chambersburg PA
CBHW031248230426
43670CB00005B/86